I do actually have some hobbies, but none worth talking about. Just little things that I dabble in.

In short, *Dragon Ball* is the only thing I can talk to people about.

—Toyotarou, 2020

Toyotarou

Toyotarou created the manga adaptation for the *Dragon Ball Z* anime's 2015 film, *Dragon Ball Z: Resurrection F*. He is also the author of the spin-off series *Dragon Ball Heroes: Victory Mission*, which debuted in *V-Jump* in Japan in November 2012.

Akira Toriyama

Renowned worldwide for his playful, innovative storytelling and humorous, distinctive art style, Akira Toriyama burst onto the manga scene in 1980 with the wildly popular *Dr. Slump*. His hit series *Dragon Ball* (published in the U.S. as *Dragon Ball* and *Dragon Ball Z*) ran from 1984 to 1995 in Shueisha's *Weekly Shonen Jump* magazine. He is also known for his design work on video games such as *Dragon Quest*, *Chrono Trigger*, *Tobal No. 1* and *Blue Dragon*. His recent manga works include *COWA!*, *Kajika*, *Sand Land*, *Neko Majin*, *Jaco the Galactic Patrolman* and a children's book, *Toccio the Angel*. He lives with his family in Japan.

DRAGON BALL SUPER 12

SHONEN JUMP Manga Edition

STORY BY **Akira Toriyama**
ART BY **Toyotarou**

TRANSLATION **Caleb Cook**
LETTERING **Brandon Bovia**
DESIGN **Joy Zhang**
EDITOR **Rae First**

DRAGON BALL SUPER © 2015 BY BIRD STUDIO, Toyotarou
All rights reserved. First published in Japan in 2015 by SHUEISHA Inc., Tokyo.
English translation rights arranged by SHUEISHA Inc.

The stories, characters and incidents mentioned
in this publication are entirely fictional.

No portion of this book may be reproduced or
transmitted in any form or by any means without
written permission from the copyright holders.

Printed in Italy

Published by VIZ Media, LLC
P.O. Box 77010
San Francisco, CA 94107

10 9 8 7 6 5
First printing, March 2021
Fifth printing, February 2024

 viz.com

PARENTAL ADVISORY
DRAGON BALL SUPER is rated T for
Teen and is recommended for ages 13
and up. This volume contains realistic
and fantasy violence.

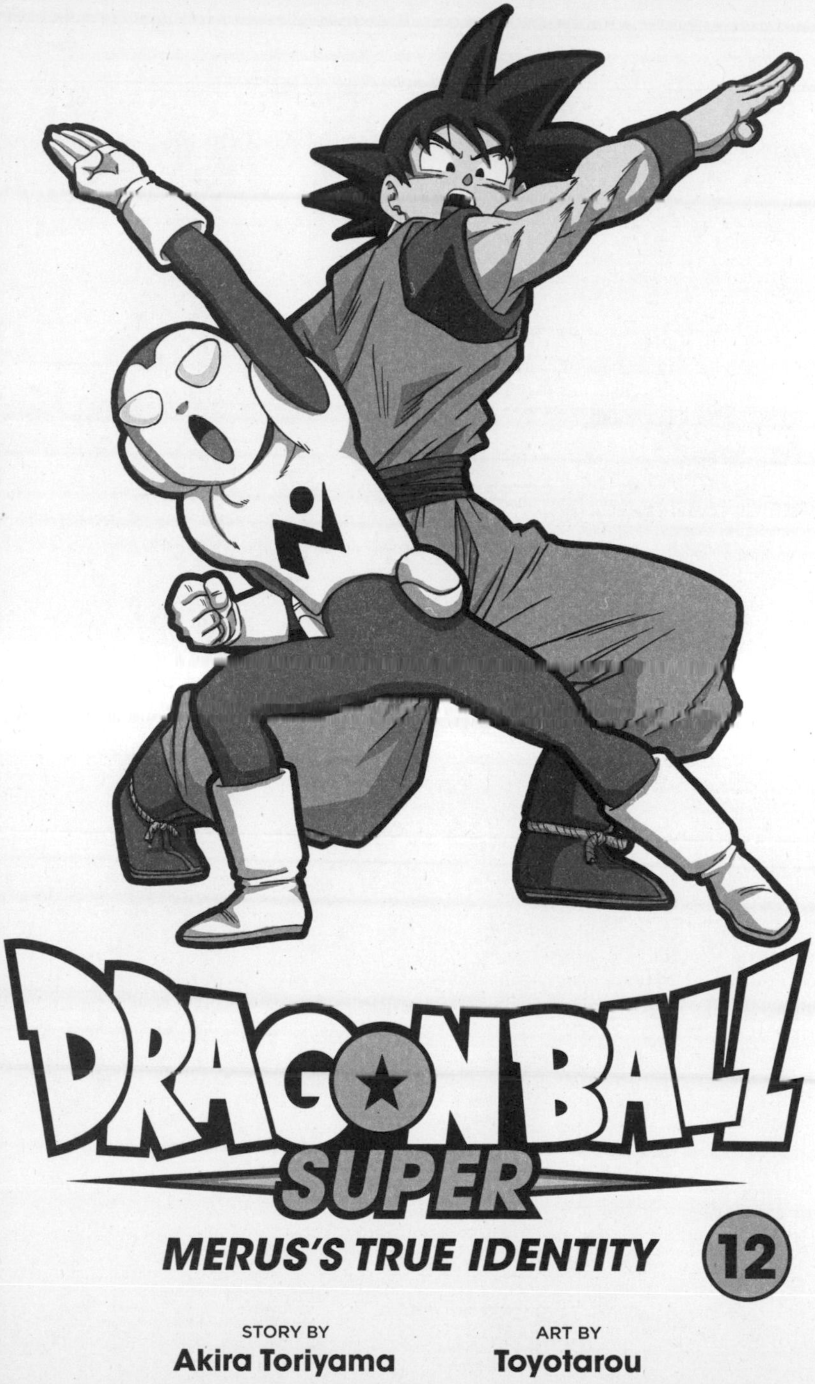

DRAGON BALL SUPER

MERUS'S TRUE IDENTITY

12

STORY BY
Akira Toriyama

ART BY
Toyotarou

CAST OF CHARACTERS

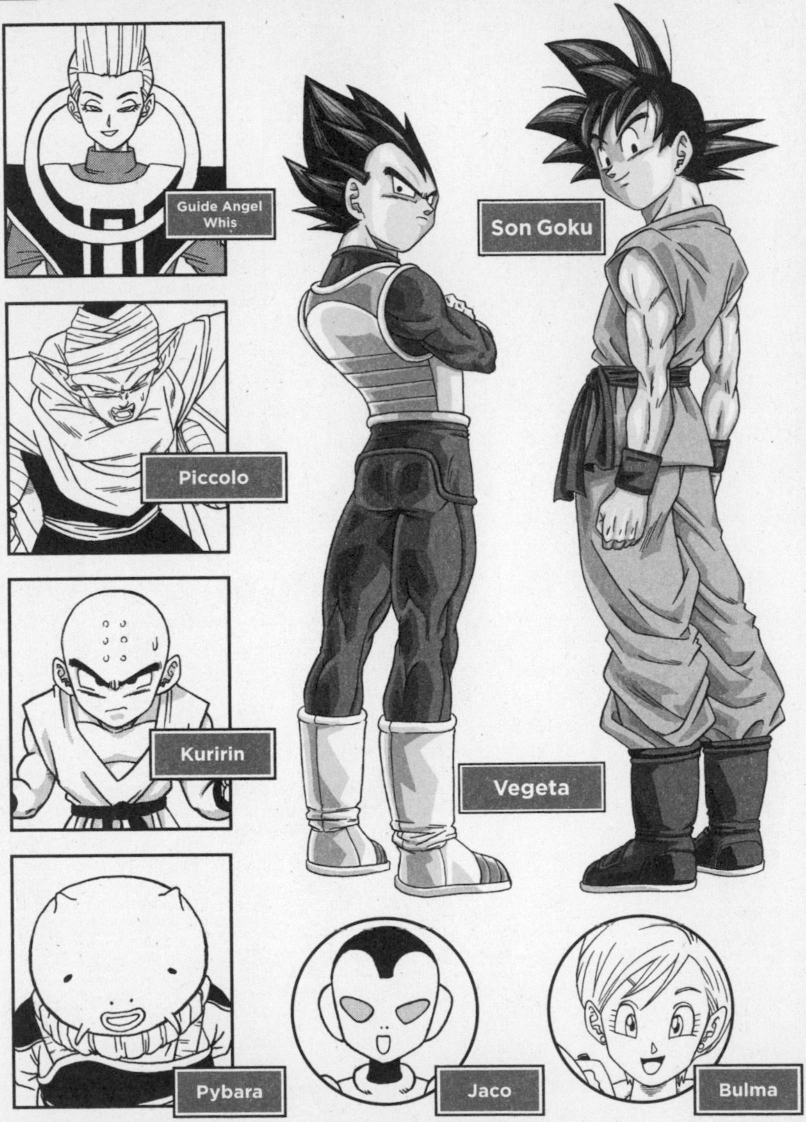
Guide Angel Whis
Son Goku
Piccolo
Kuririn
Vegeta
Pybara
Jaco
Bulma

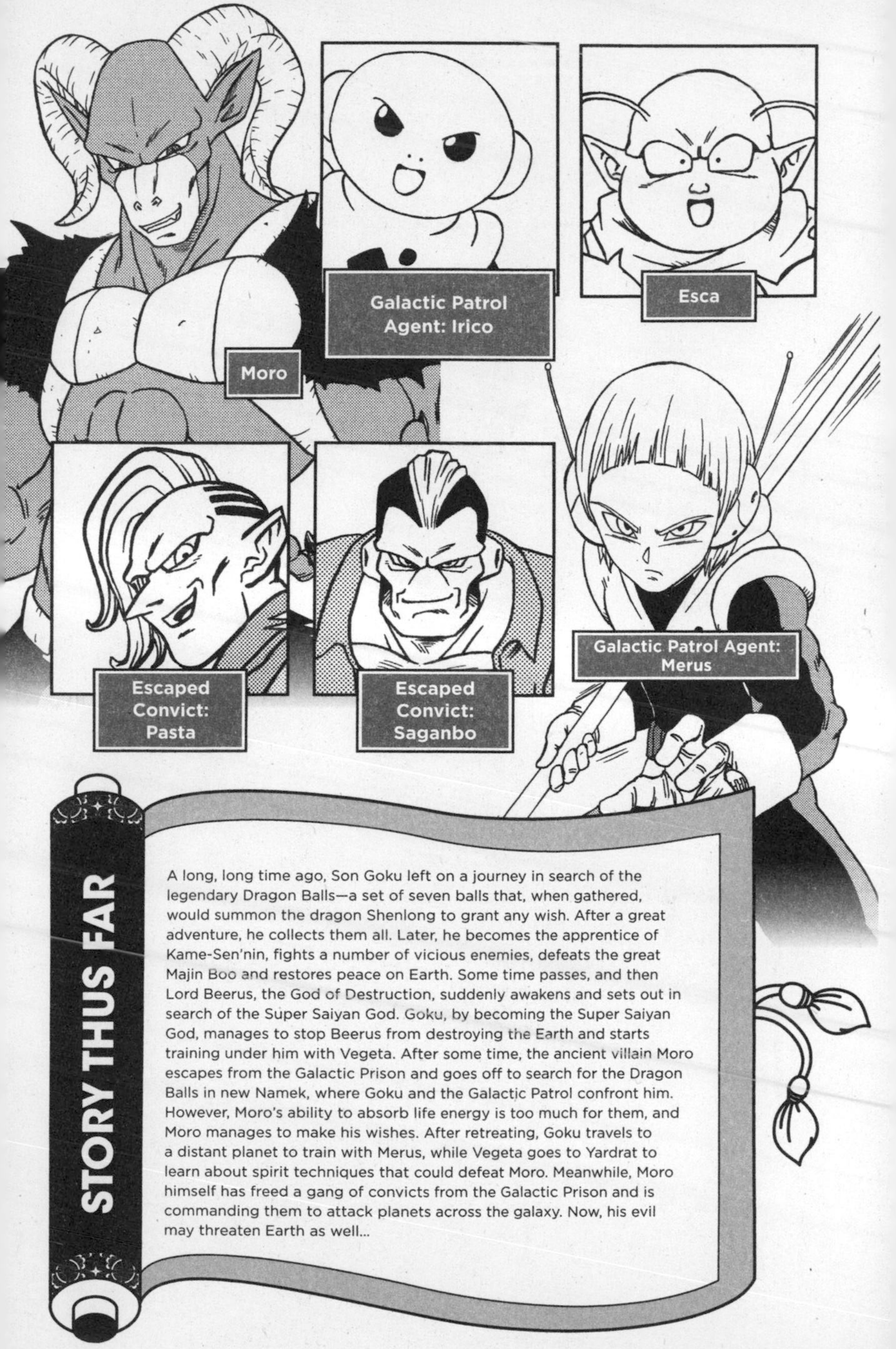
Moro
Galactic Patrol Agent: Irico
Esca
Galactic Patrol Agent: Merus
Escaped Convict: Pasta
Escaped Convict: Saganbo

STORY THUS FAR

A long, long time ago, Son Goku left on a journey in search of the legendary Dragon Balls—a set of seven balls that, when gathered, would summon the dragon Shenlong to grant any wish. After a great adventure, he collects them all. Later, he becomes the apprentice of Kame-Sen'nin, fights a number of vicious enemies, defeats the great Majin Boo and restores peace on Earth. Some time passes, and then Lord Beerus, the God of Destruction, suddenly awakens and sets out in search of the Super Saiyan God. Goku, by becoming the Super Saiyan God, manages to stop Beerus from destroying the Earth and starts training under him with Vegeta. After some time, the ancient villain Moro escapes from the Galactic Prison and goes off to search for the Dragon Balls in new Namek, where Goku and the Galactic Patrol confront him. However, Moro's ability to absorb life energy is too much for them, and Moro manages to make his wishes. After retreating, Goku travels to a distant planet to train with Merus, while Vegeta goes to Yardrat to learn about spirit techniques that could defeat Moro. Meanwhile, Moro himself has freed a gang of convicts from the Galactic Prison and is commanding them to attack planets across the galaxy. Now, his evil may threaten Earth as well...

12

DRAGON★BALL SUPER

TABLE OF CONTENTS

DRAGON BALL SUPER

CHAPTER 53: SAGANBO'S GALACTIC BANDIT BRIGADE

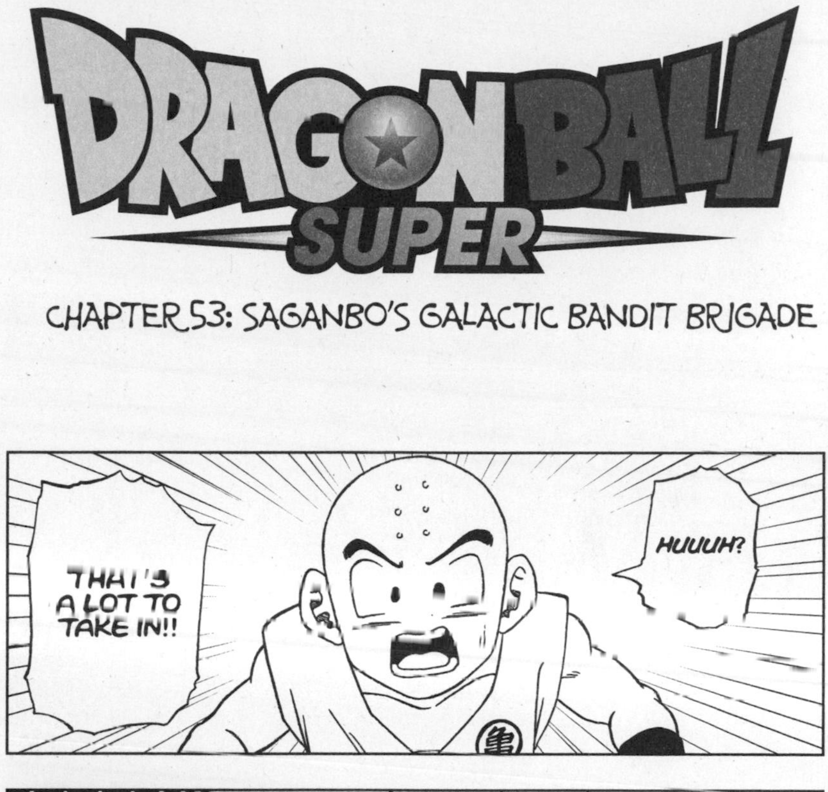
HUUUH?
THAT'S A LOT TO TAKE IN!!

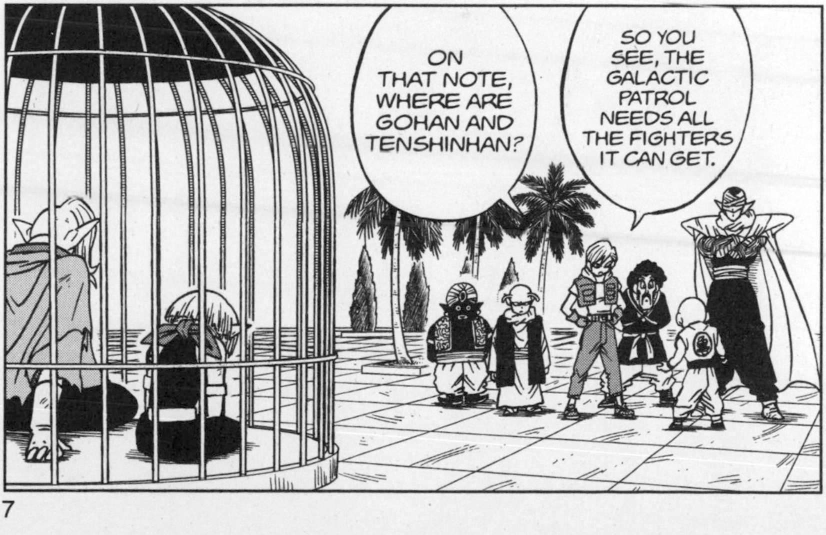
SO YOU SEE, THE GALACTIC PATROL NEEDS ALL THE FIGHTERS IT CAN GET.
ON THAT NOTE, WHERE ARE GOHAN AND TENSHINHAN?

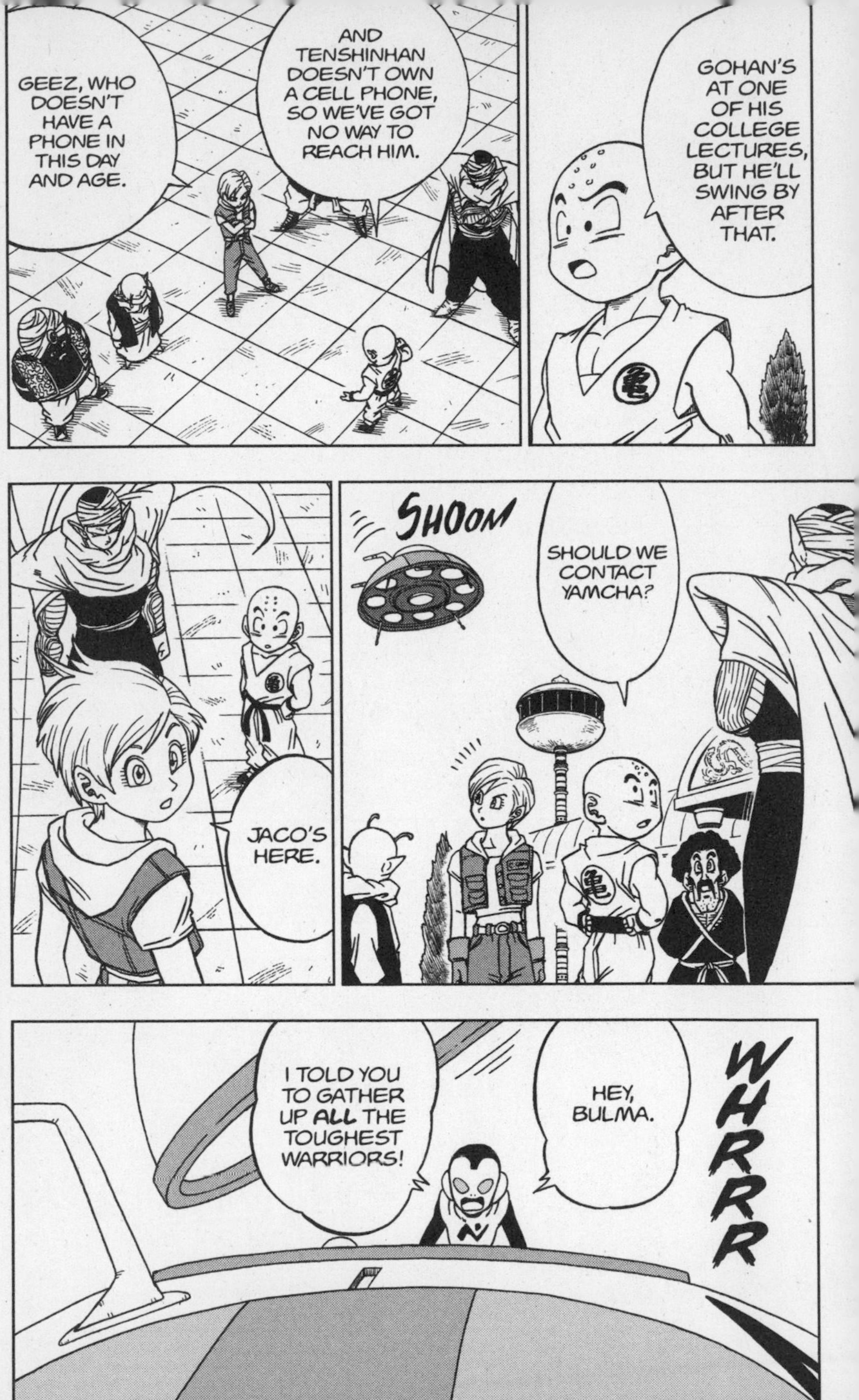
GOHAN'S AT ONE OF HIS COLLEGE LECTURES, BUT HE'LL SWING BY AFTER THAT.
AND TENSHINHAN DOESN'T OWN A CELL PHONE, SO WE'VE GOT NO WAY TO REACH HIM.
GEEZ, WHO DOESN'T HAVE A PHONE IN THIS DAY AND AGE.
SHOOM
SHOULD WE CONTACT YAMCHA?
JACO'S HERE.
WHRRR
HEY, BULMA.
I TOLD YOU TO GATHER UP **ALL** THE TOUGHEST WARRIORS!

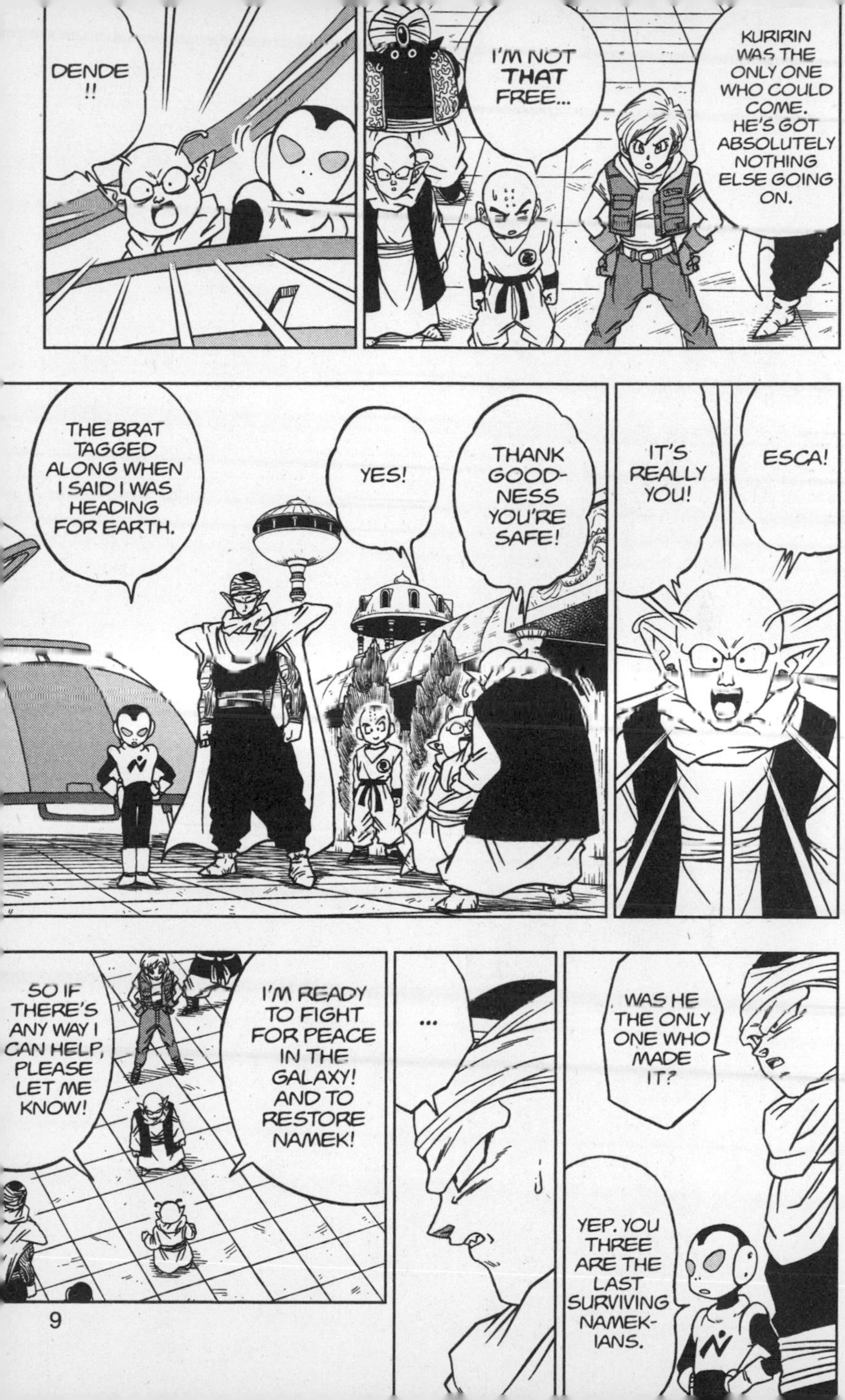
KURIRIN WAS THE ONLY ONE WHO COULD COME. HE'S GOT ABSOLUTELY NOTHING ELSE GOING ON.
I'M NOT THAT FREE...
DENDE !!
ESCA!
IT'S REALLY YOU!
THANK GOODNESS YOU'RE SAFE!
YES!
THE BRAT TAGGED ALONG WHEN I SAID I WAS HEADING FOR EARTH.
WAS HE THE ONLY ONE WHO MADE IT?
YEP. YOU THREE ARE THE LAST SURVIVING NAMEKIANS.
...
I'M READY TO FIGHT FOR PEACE IN THE GALAXY! AND TO RESTORE NAMEK!
SO IF THERE'S ANY WAY I CAN HELP, PLEASE LET ME KNOW!

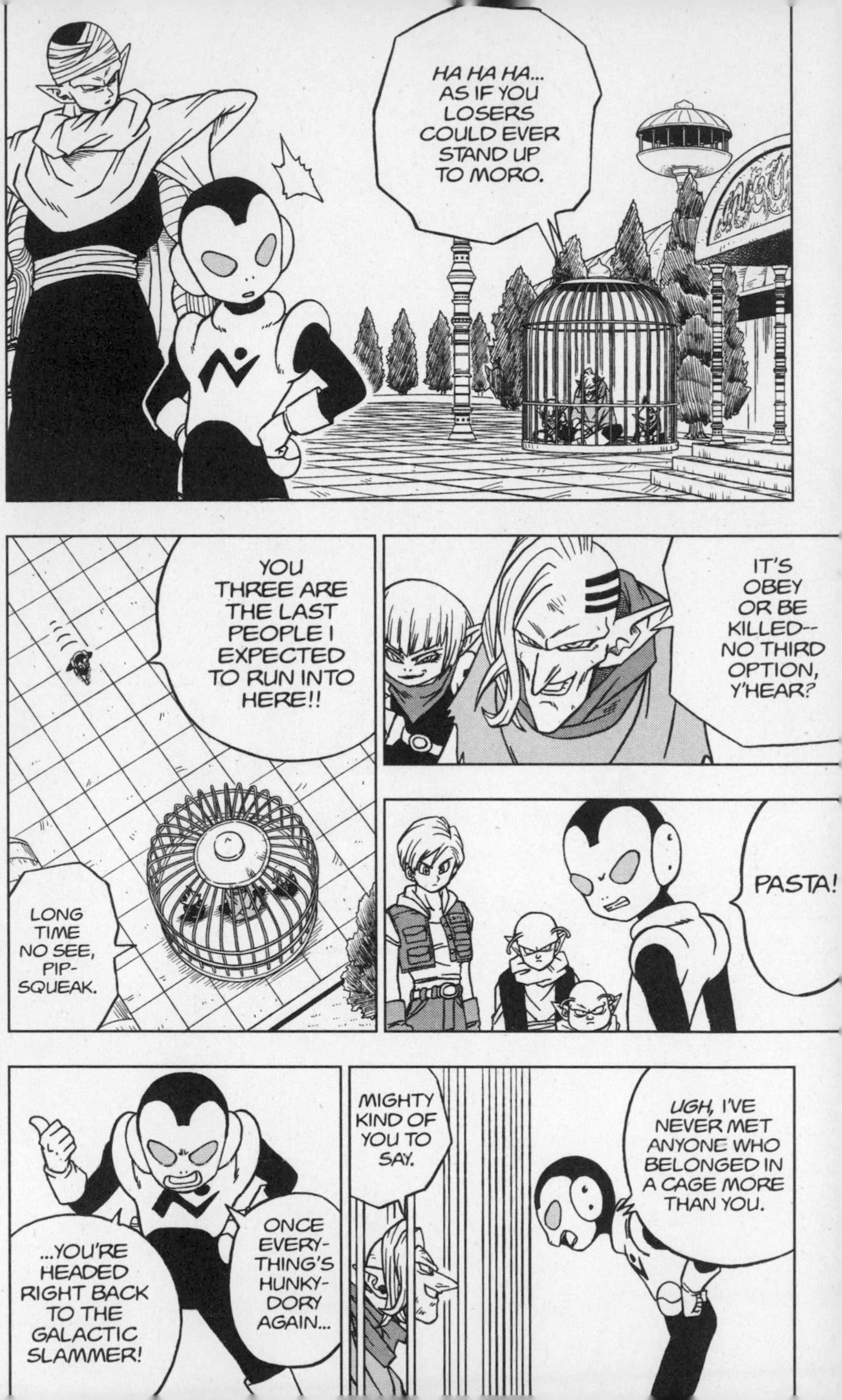
HA HA HA... AS IF YOU LOSERS COULD EVER STAND UP TO MORO.
IT'S OBEY OR BE KILLED-- NO THIRD OPTION, Y'HEAR?
PASTA!
YOU THREE ARE THE LAST PEOPLE I EXPECTED TO RUN INTO HERE!!
LONG TIME NO SEE, PIP-SQUEAK.
UGH, I'VE NEVER MET ANYONE WHO BELONGED IN A CAGE MORE THAN YOU.
MIGHTY KIND OF YOU TO SAY.
ONCE EVERY-THING'S HUNKY-DORY AGAIN...
...YOU'RE HEADED RIGHT BACK TO THE GALACTIC SLAMMER!

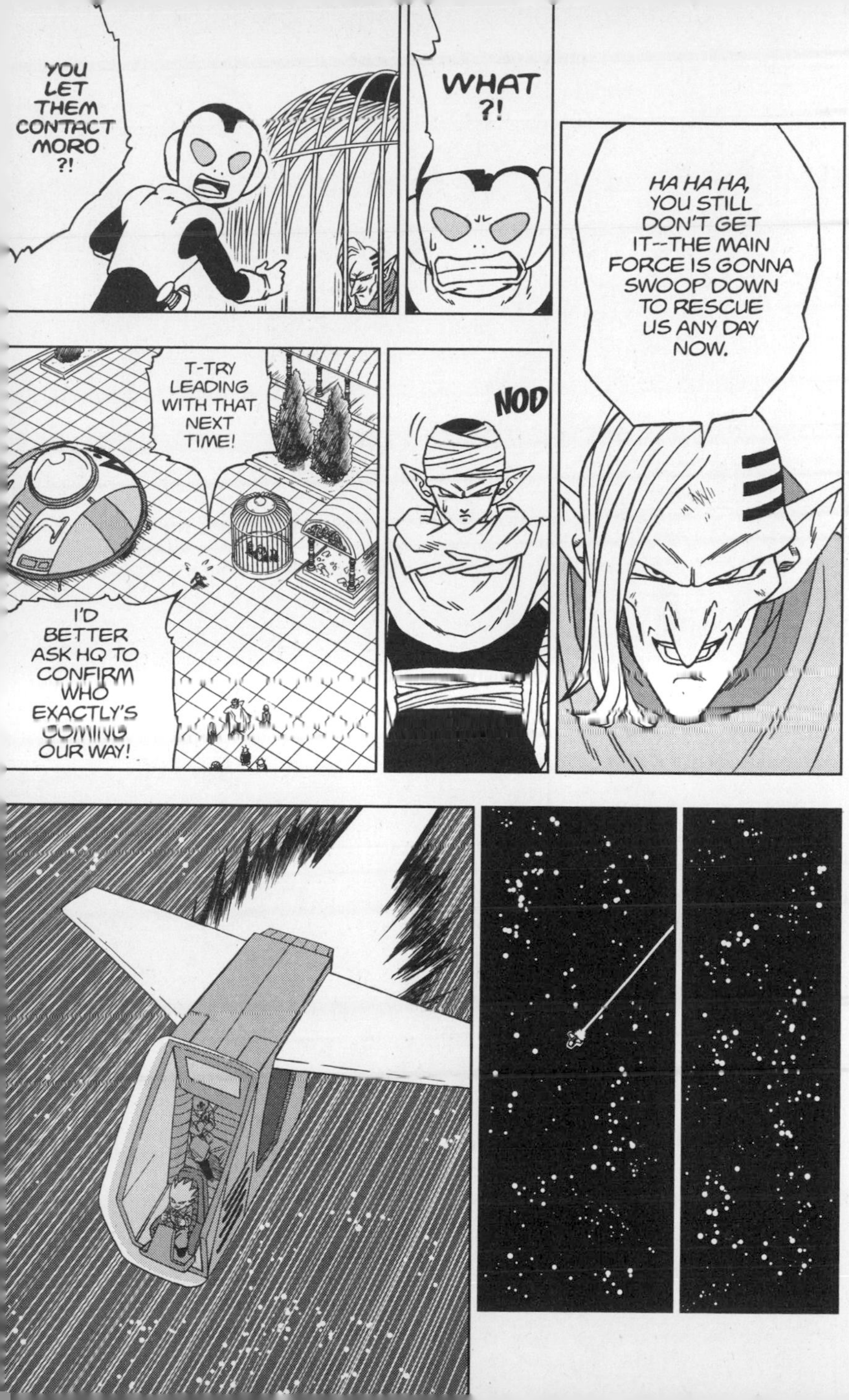
HA HA HA, YOU STILL DON'T GET IT--THE MAIN FORCE IS GONNA SWOOP DOWN TO RESCUE US ANY DAY NOW.
WHAT ?!
YOU LET THEM CONTACT MORO ?!
NOD
T-TRY LEADING WITH THAT NEXT TIME!
I'D BETTER ASK HQ TO CONFIRM WHO EXACTLY'S COMING OUR WAY!

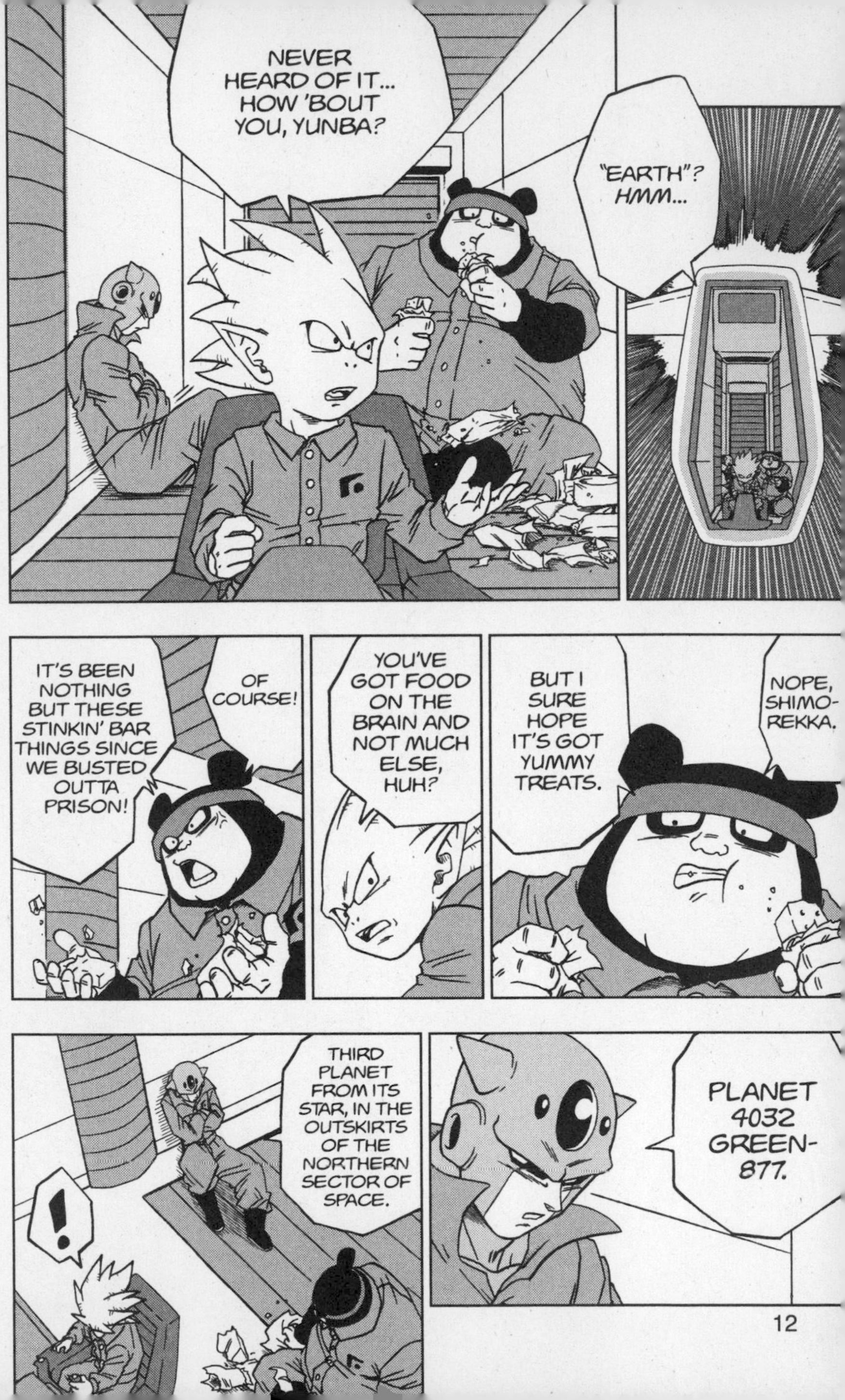
"EARTH"? HMM...
NEVER HEARD OF IT... HOW 'BOUT YOU, YUNBA?
NOPE, SHIMO-REKKA.
BUT I SURE HOPE IT'S GOT YUMMY TREATS.
YOU'VE GOT FOOD ON THE BRAIN AND NOT MUCH ELSE, HUH?
OF COURSE!
IT'S BEEN NOTHING BUT THESE STINKIN' BAR THINGS SINCE WE BUSTED OUTTA PRISON!
PLANET 4032 GREEN-877.
THIRD PLANET FROM ITS STAR, IN THE OUTSKIRTS OF THE NORTHERN SECTOR OF SPACE.
!

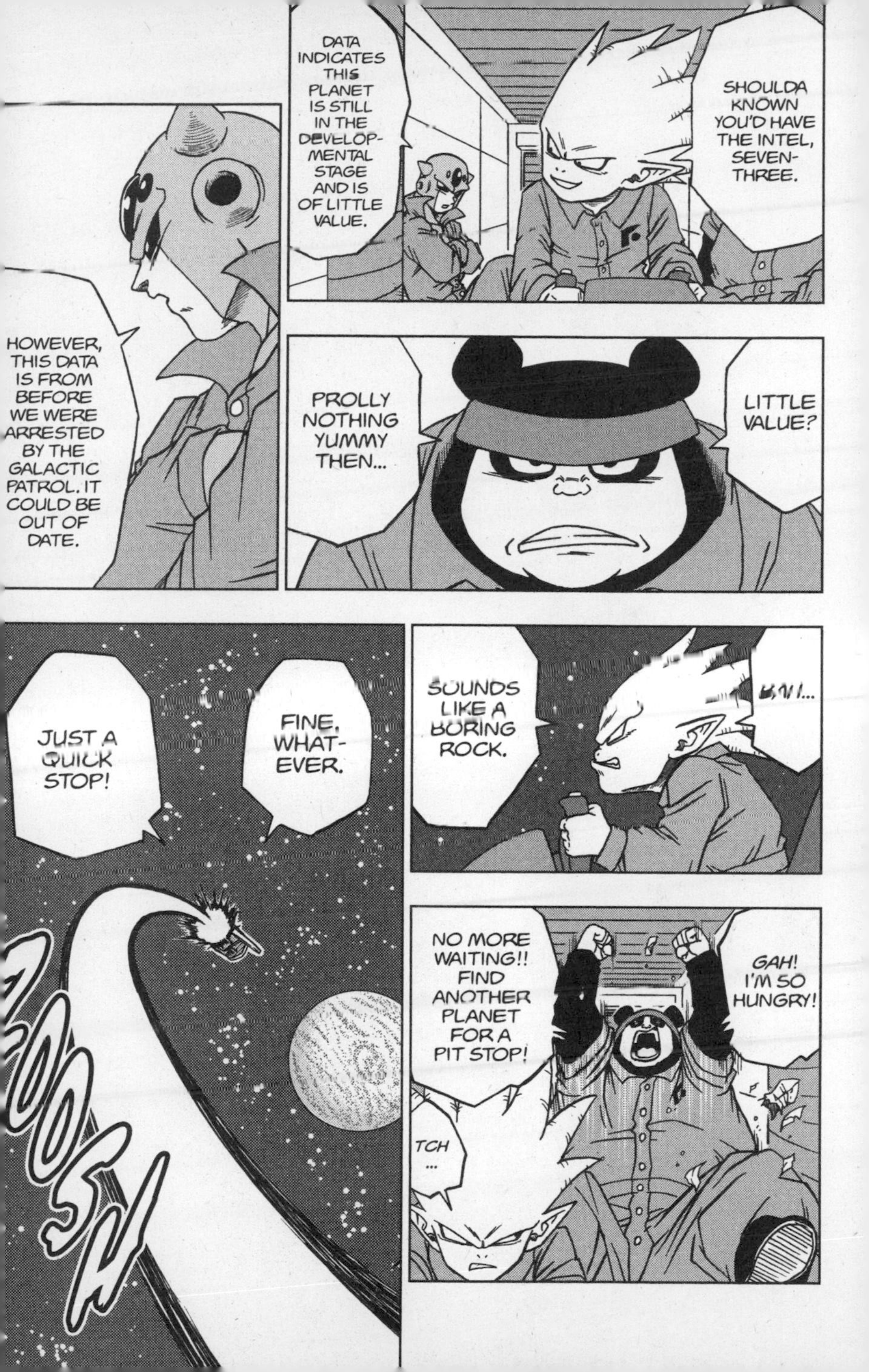
SHOULDA KNOWN YOU'D HAVE THE INTEL, SEVEN-THREE.
DATA INDICATES THIS PLANET IS STILL IN THE DEVELOP-MENTAL STAGE AND IS OF LITTLE VALUE.
LITTLE VALUE?
PROLLY NOTHING YUMMY THEN...
HOWEVER, THIS DATA IS FROM BEFORE WE WERE ARRESTED BY THE GALACTIC PATROL. IT COULD BE OUT OF DATE.
SOUNDS LIKE A BORING ROCK.
GAH! I'M SO HUNGRY!
NO MORE WAITING!! FIND ANOTHER PLANET FOR A PIT STOP!
TCH...
FINE, WHAT-EVER.
JUST A QUICK STOP!
WHOOSH

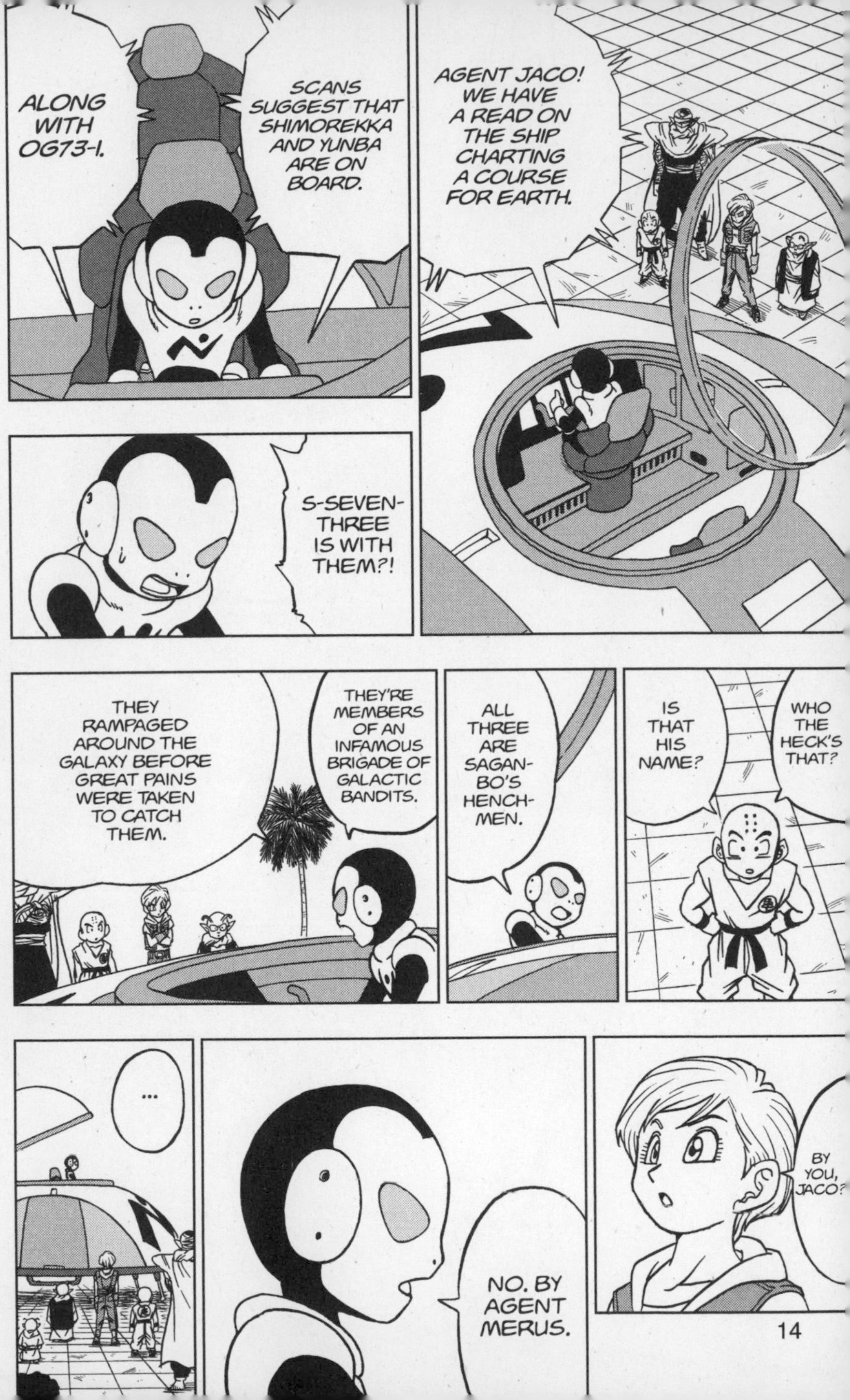
AGENT JACO! WE HAVE A READ ON THE SHIP CHARTING A COURSE FOR EARTH.
SCANS SUGGEST THAT SHIMOREKKA AND YUNBA ARE ON BOARD.
ALONG WITH OG73-1.
S-SEVEN-THREE IS WITH THEM?!
WHO THE HECK'S THAT?
IS THAT HIS NAME?
ALL THREE ARE SAGAN-BO'S HENCH-MEN.
THEY'RE MEMBERS OF AN INFAMOUS BRIGADE OF GALACTIC BANDITS.
THEY RAMPAGED AROUND THE GALAXY BEFORE GREAT PAINS WERE TAKEN TO CATCH THEM.
BY YOU, JACO?
NO. BY AGENT MERUS.
...

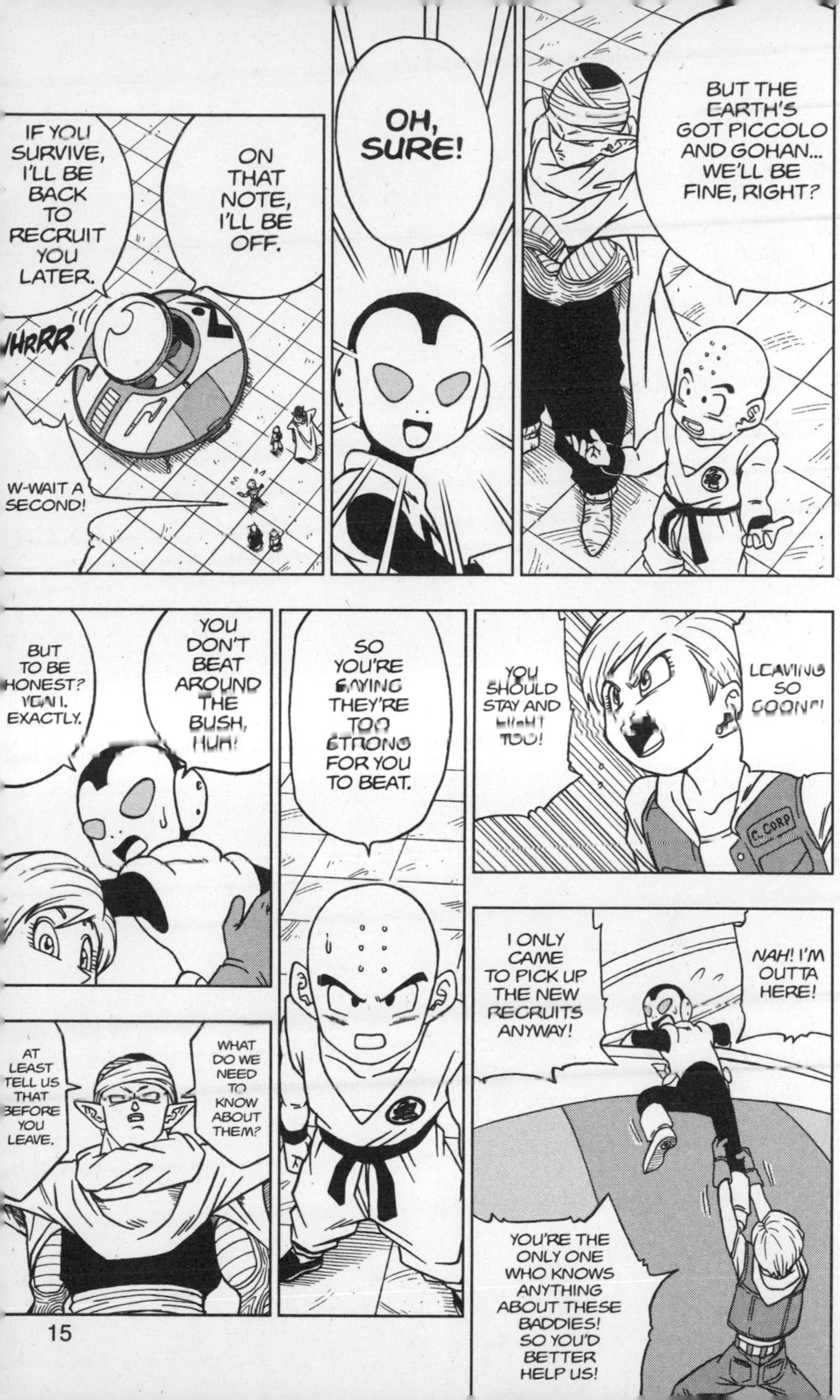
BUT THE EARTH'S GOT PICCOLO AND GOHAN... WE'LL BE FINE, RIGHT?
OH, SURE!
ON THAT NOTE, I'LL BE OFF.
IF YOU SURVIVE, I'LL BE BACK TO RECRUIT YOU LATER.
VHRRR
W-WAIT A SECOND!
LEAVING SO SOON!?
YOU SHOULD STAY AND FIGHT TOO!
NAH! I'M OUTTA HERE!
I ONLY CAME TO PICK UP THE NEW RECRUITS ANYWAY!
YOU'RE THE ONLY ONE WHO KNOWS ANYTHING ABOUT THESE BADDIES! SO YOU'D BETTER HELP US!
SO YOU'RE SAYING THEY'RE TOO STRONG FOR YOU TO BEAT.
YOU DON'T BEAT AROUND THE BUSH, HUH!
BUT TO BE HONEST? YEAH. EXACTLY.
WHAT DO WE NEED TO KNOW ABOUT THEM?
AT LEAST TELL US THAT BEFORE YOU LEAVE.

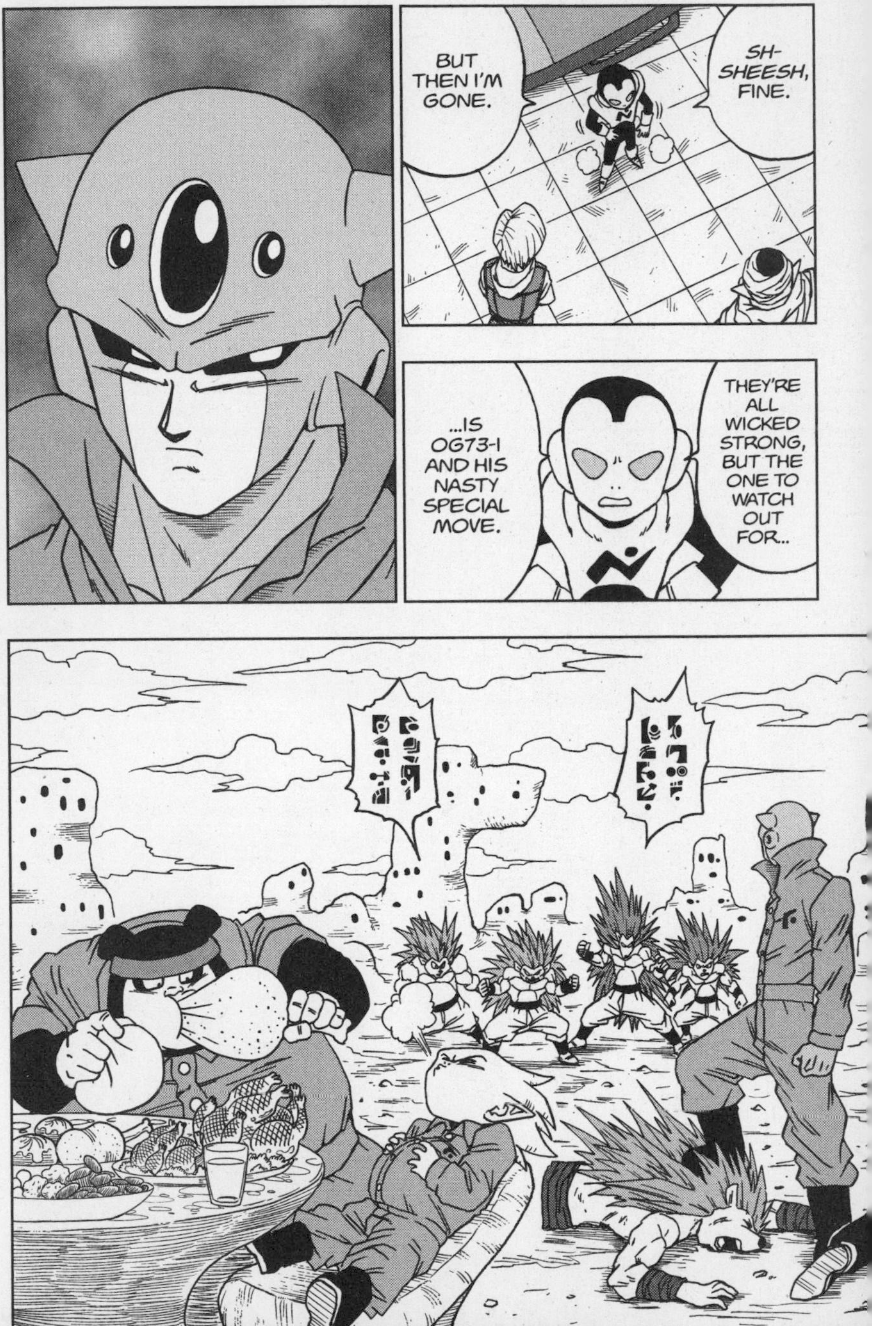
SH-SHEESH, FINE.
BUT THEN I'M GONE.
THEY'RE ALL WICKED STRONG, BUT THE ONE TO WATCH OUT FOR...
...IS OG73-1 AND HIS NASTY SPECIAL MOVE.

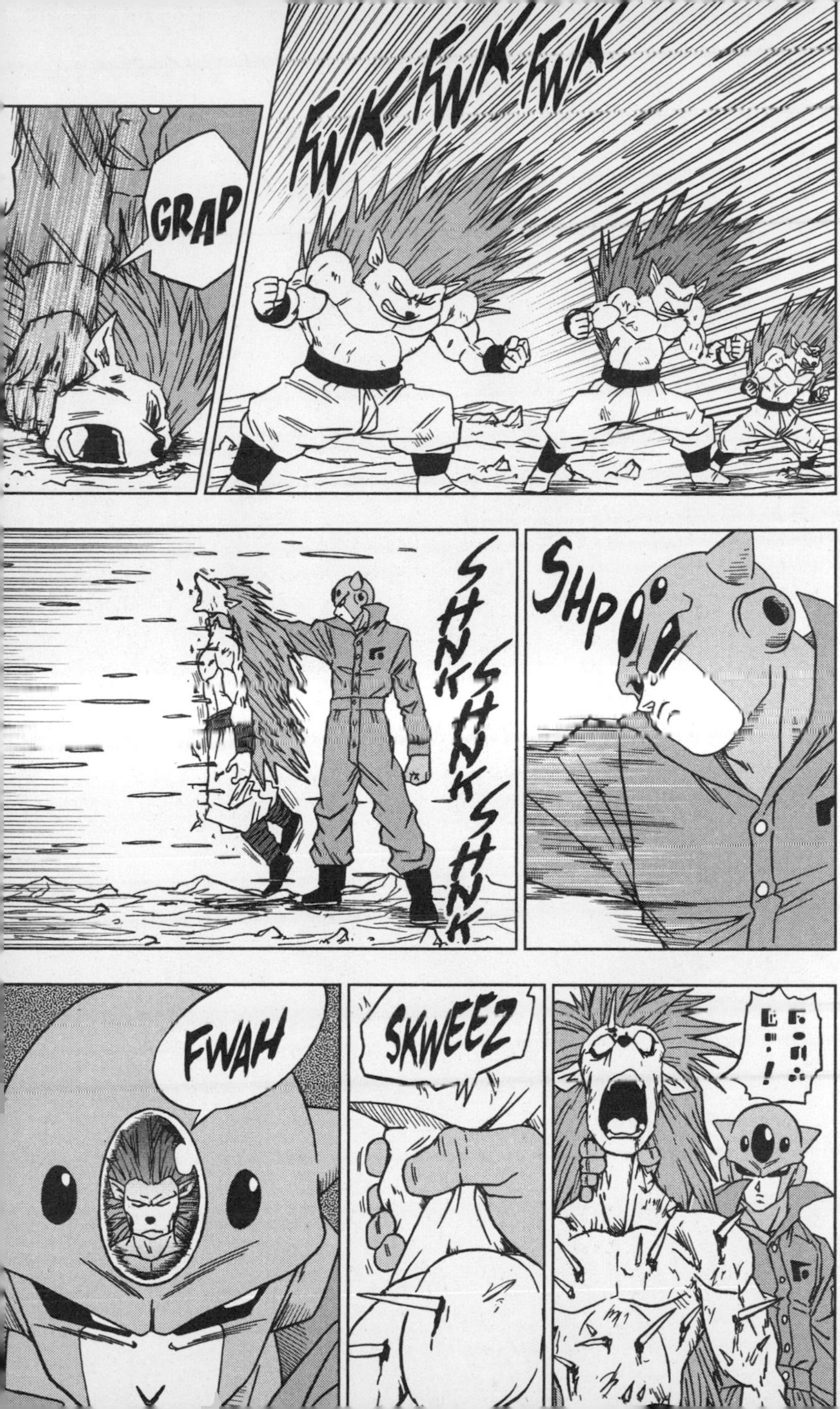
FWK FWK FWK
GRAP
SHP
SHUNK SHUNK SHUNK
SKWEEZ
FWAH

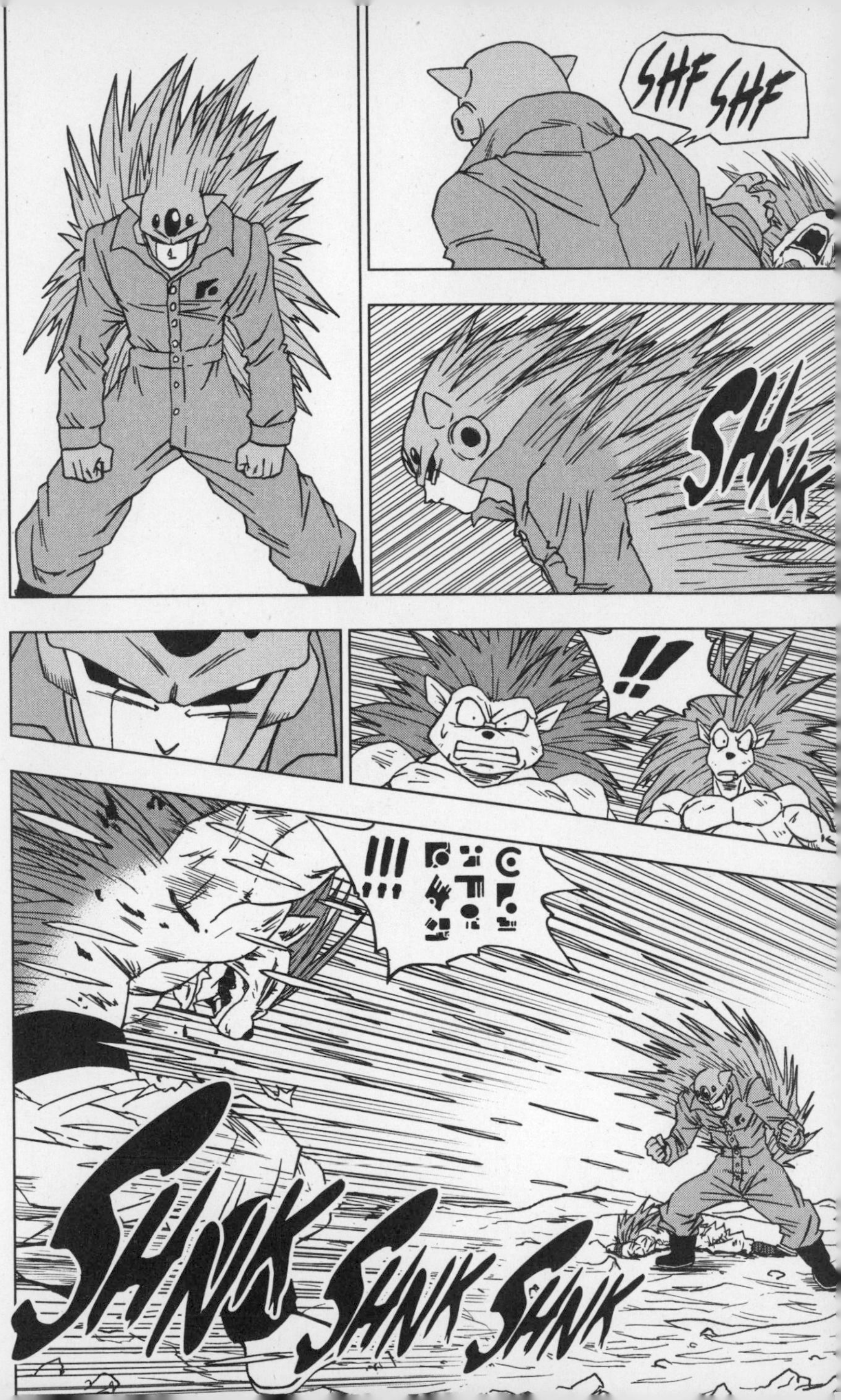
SHF SHF
SHNK
!!
!!!
SHNK SHNK SHNK

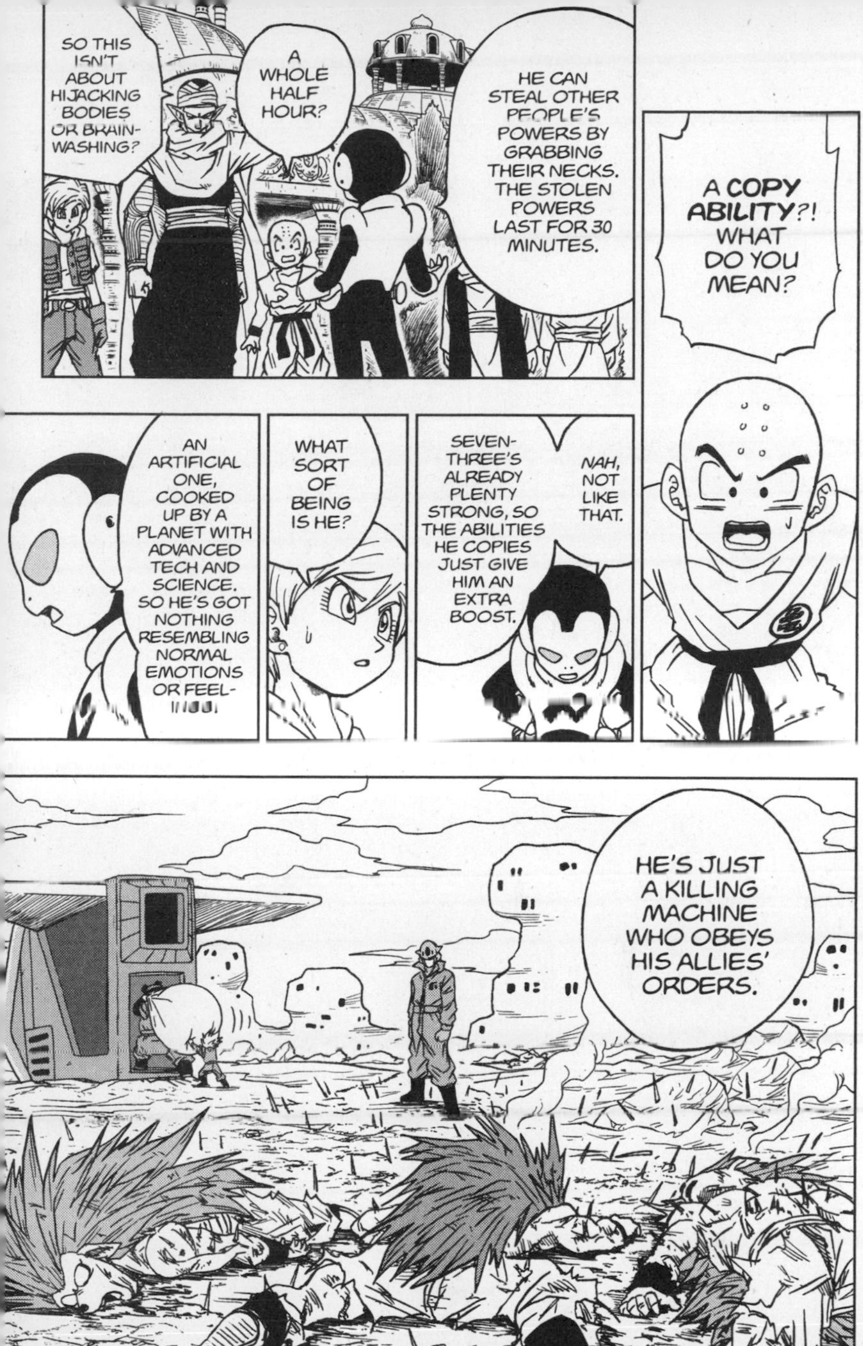

A COPY ABILITY?! WHAT DO YOU MEAN?
HE CAN STEAL OTHER PEOPLE'S POWERS BY GRABBING THEIR NECKS. THE STOLEN POWERS LAST FOR 30 MINUTES.
A WHOLE HALF HOUR?
SO THIS ISN'T ABOUT HIJACKING BODIES OR BRAIN-WASHING?
NAH, NOT LIKE THAT.
SEVEN-THREE'S ALREADY PLENTY STRONG, SO THE ABILITIES HE COPIES JUST GIVE HIM AN EXTRA BOOST.
WHAT SORT OF BEING IS HE?
AN ARTIFICIAL ONE, COOKED UP BY A PLANET WITH ADVANCED TECH AND SCIENCE. SO HE'S GOT NOTHING RESEMBLING NORMAL EMOTIONS OR FEEL-INGS.
HE'S JUST A KILLING MACHINE WHO OBEYS HIS ALLIES' ORDERS.

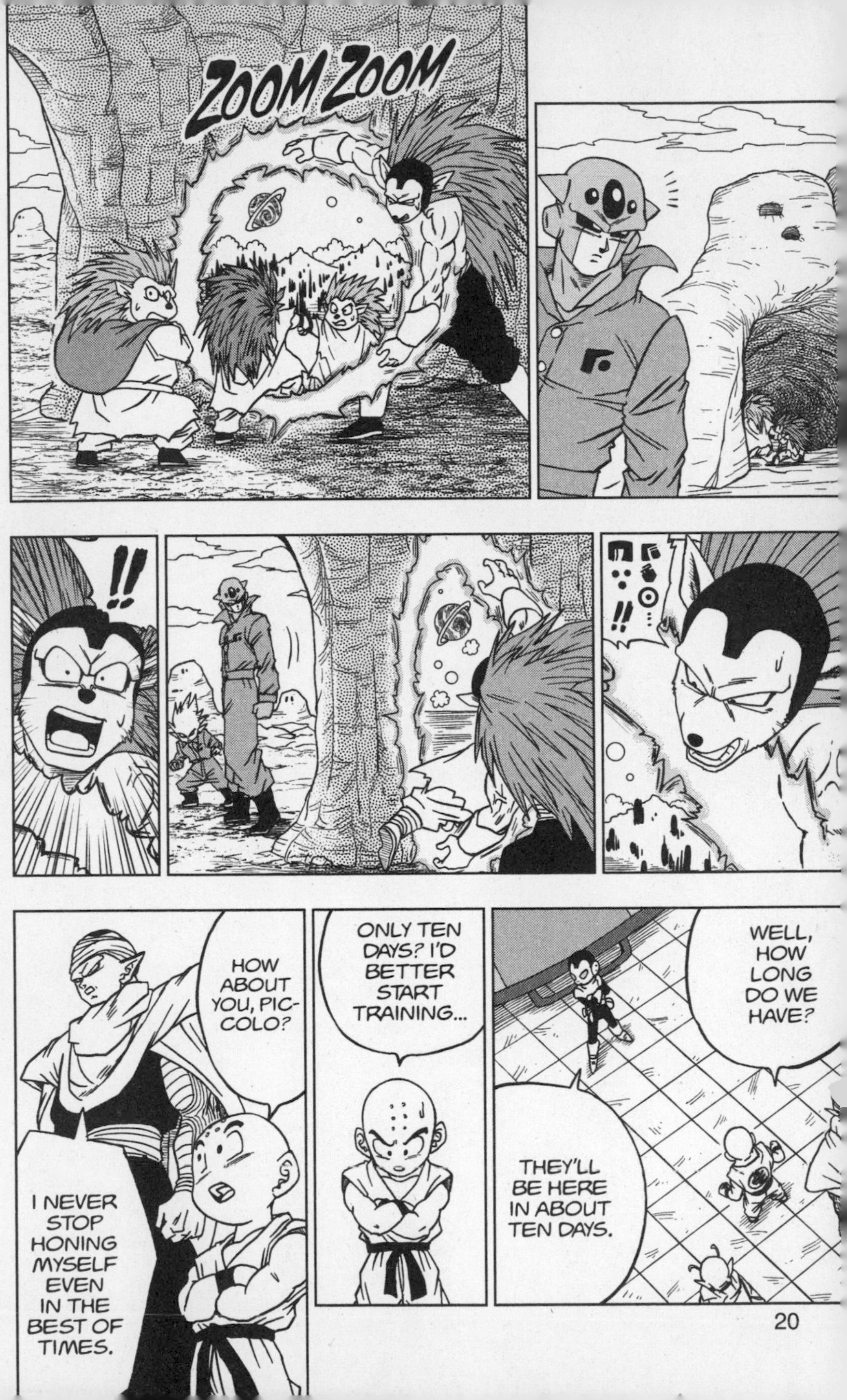
ZOOM ZOOM
!!
!!
WELL, HOW LONG DO WE HAVE?
THEY'LL BE HERE IN ABOUT TEN DAYS.
ONLY TEN DAYS? I'D BETTER START TRAINING...
HOW ABOUT YOU, PIC-COLO?
I NEVER STOP HONING MYSELF EVEN IN THE BEST OF TIMES.

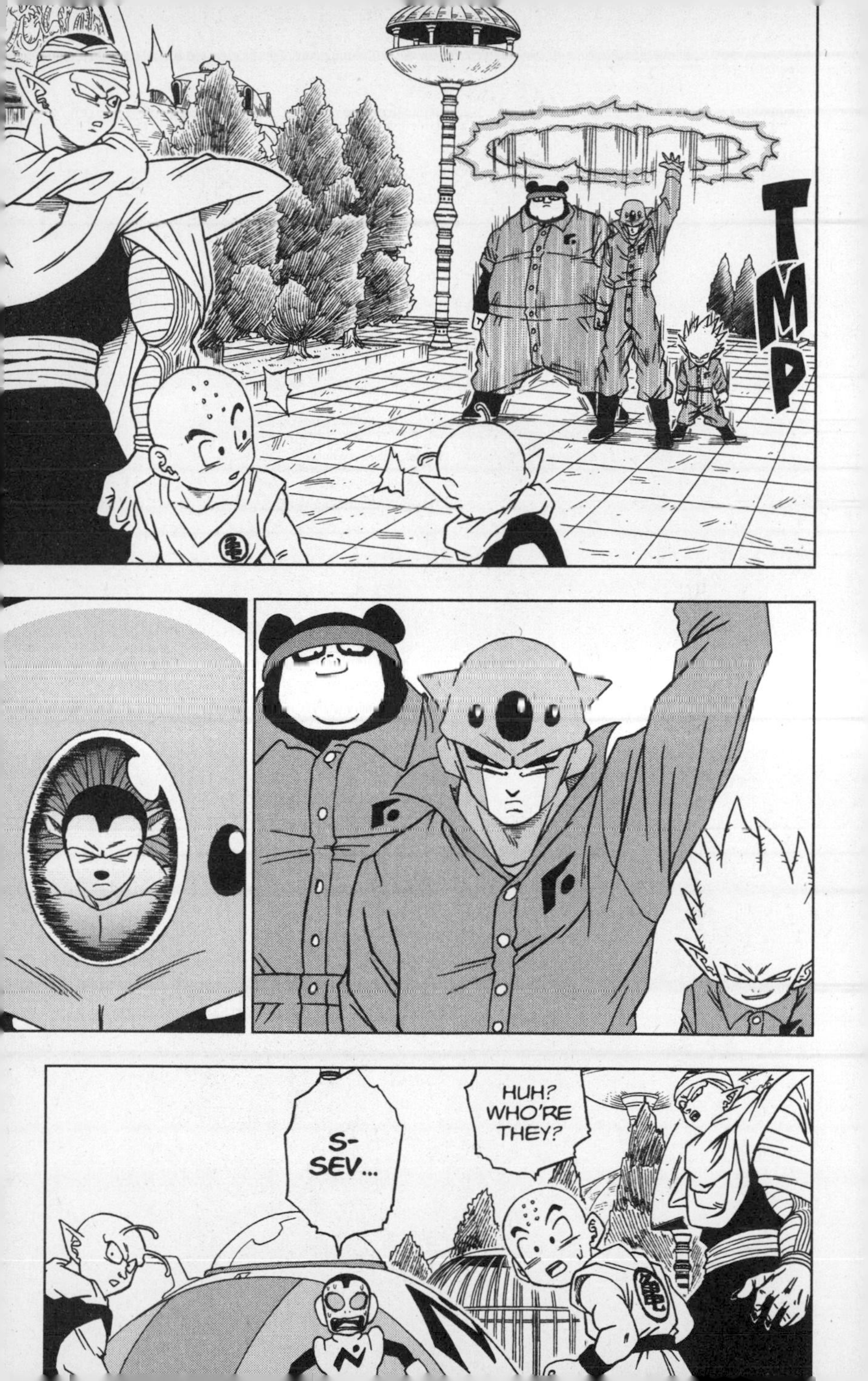
TMP
HUH? WHO'RE THEY?
S-SEV...

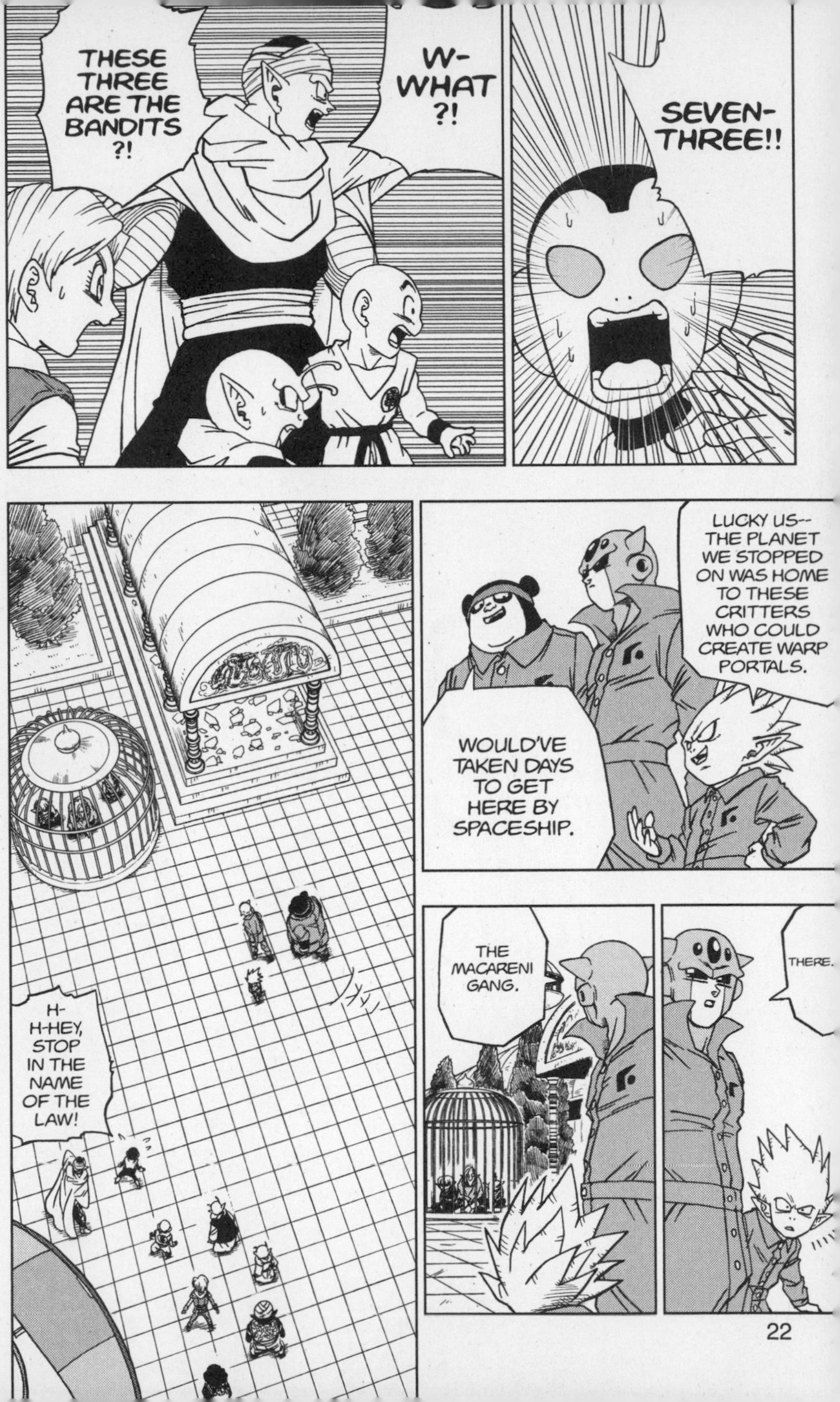
SEVEN-THREE!!
W-WHAT?!
THESE THREE ARE THE BANDITS?!
LUCKY US-- THE PLANET WE STOPPED ON WAS HOME TO THESE CRITTERS WHO COULD CREATE WARP PORTALS.
WOULD'VE TAKEN DAYS TO GET HERE BY SPACESHIP.
THERE.
THE MACARENI GANG.
H-H-HEY, STOP IN THE NAME OF THE LAW!

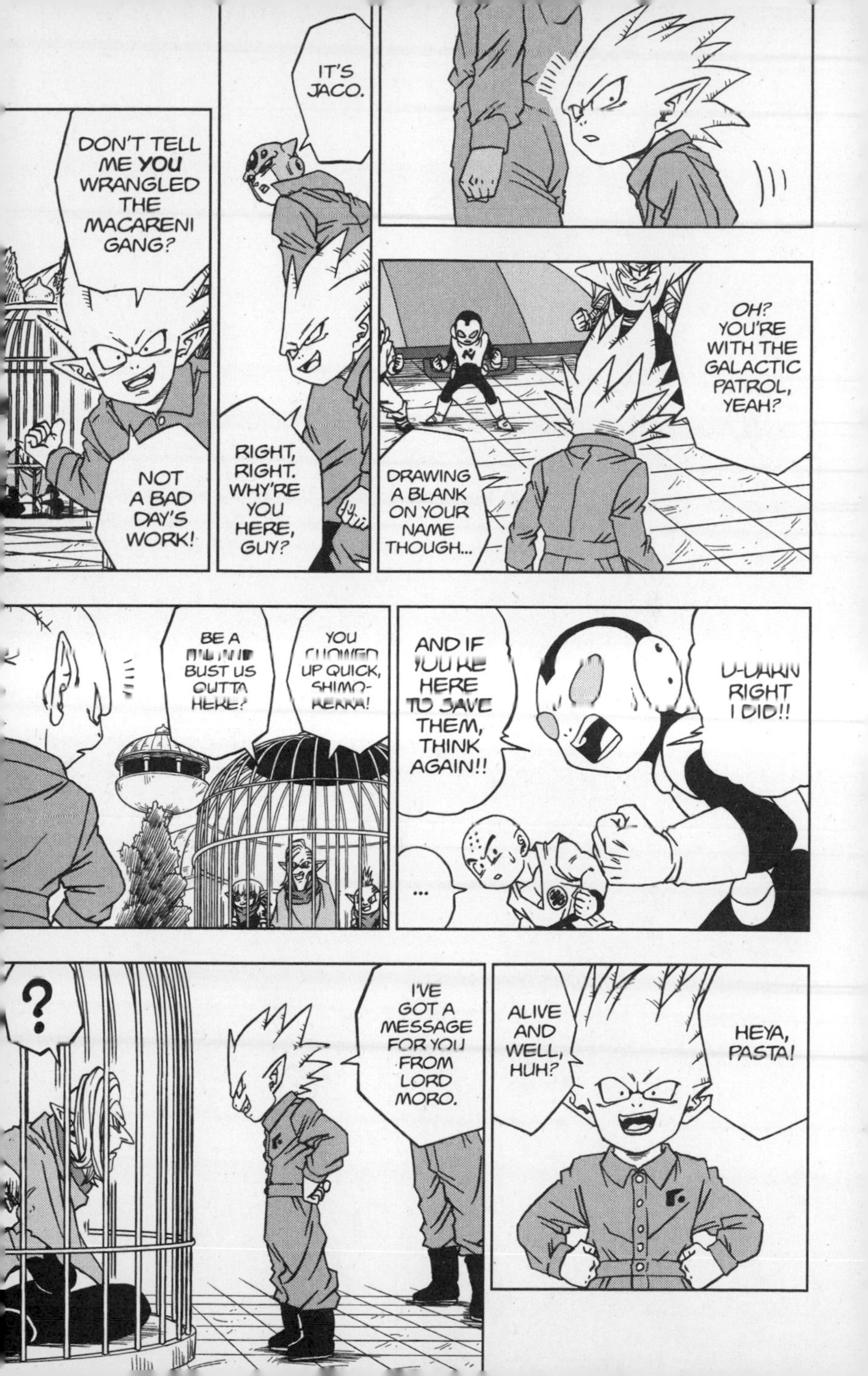
OH? YOU'RE WITH THE GALACTIC PATROL, YEAH?
DRAWING A BLANK ON YOUR NAME THOUGH...
IT'S JACO.
RIGHT, RIGHT. WHY'RE YOU HERE, GUY?
DON'T TELL ME **YOU** WRANGLED THE MACARENI GANG?
NOT A BAD DAY'S WORK!
D-DARN RIGHT I DID!!
AND IF YOU'RE HERE TO SAVE THEM, THINK AGAIN!!
...
YOU SHOWED UP QUICK, SHIMO-KERRA!
BE A
BUST US OUTTA HERE?
HEYA, PASTA!
ALIVE AND WELL, HUH?
I'VE GOT A MESSAGE FOR YOU FROM LORD MORO.
?

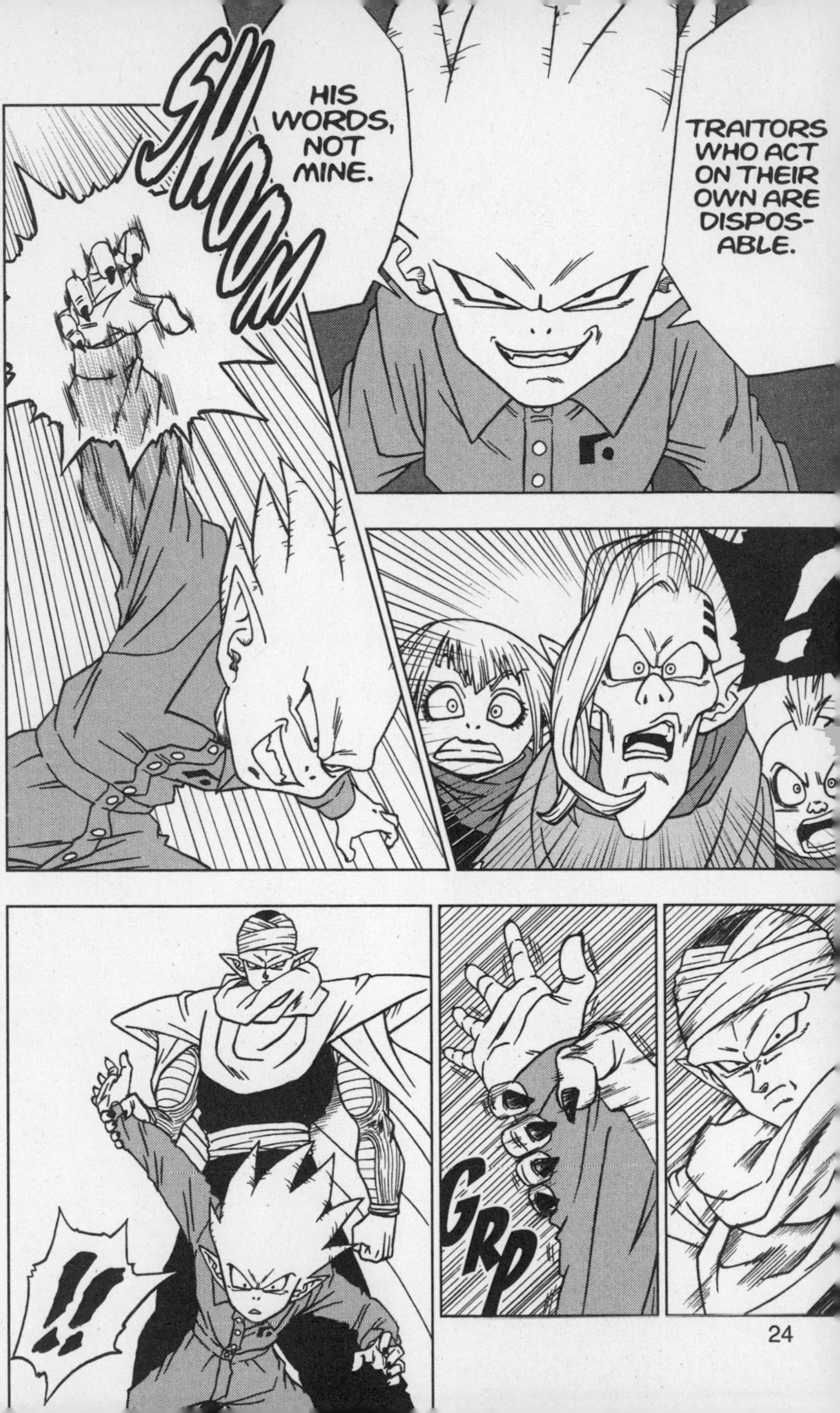
TRAITORS WHO ACT ON THEIR OWN ARE DISPOSABLE.
HIS WORDS, NOT MINE.
SHOOM
GRP
!!

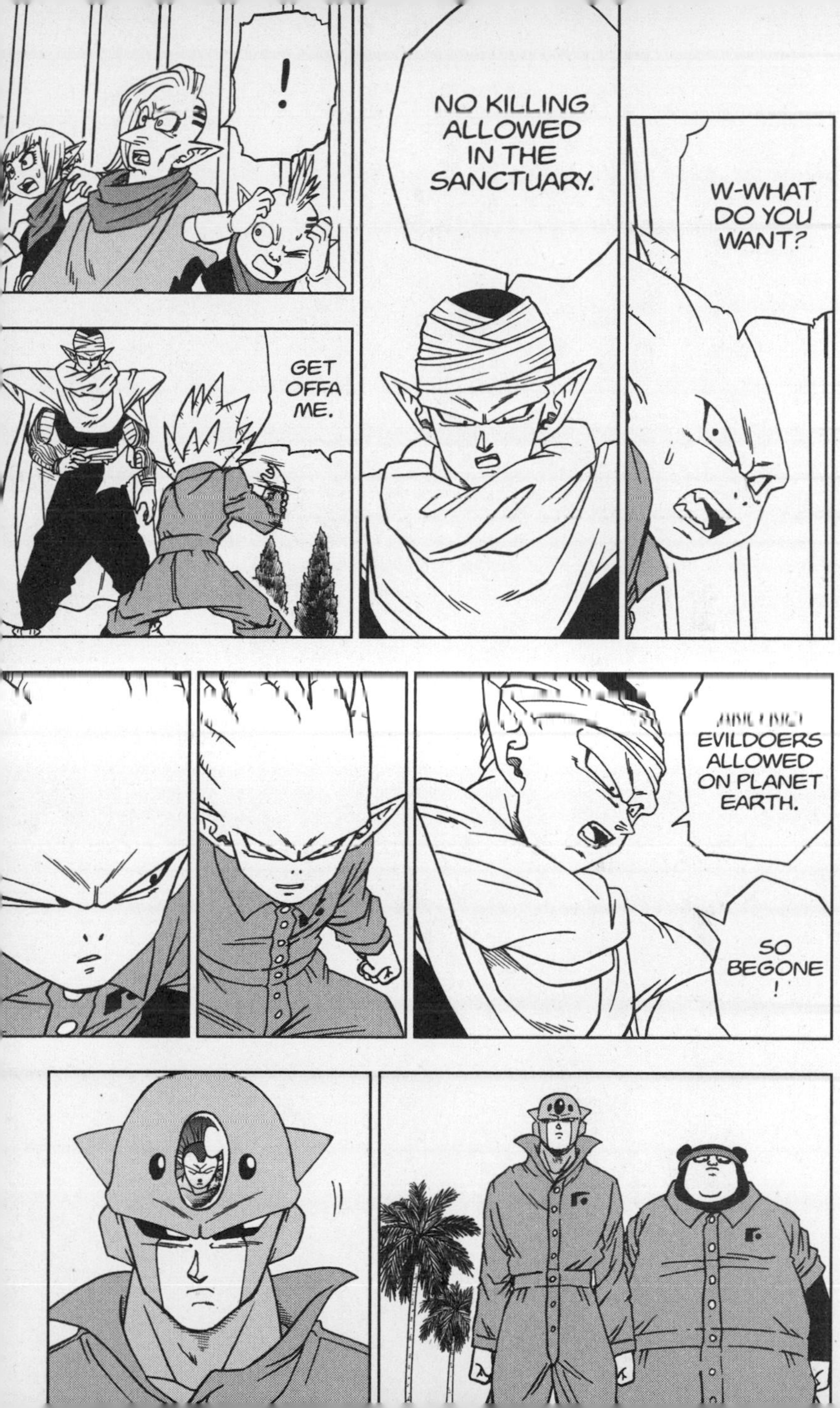
W-WHAT DO YOU WANT?
NO KILLING ALLOWED IN THE SANCTUARY.
!
GET OFFA ME.
EVILDOERS ALLOWED ON PLANET EARTH.
SO BEGONE!

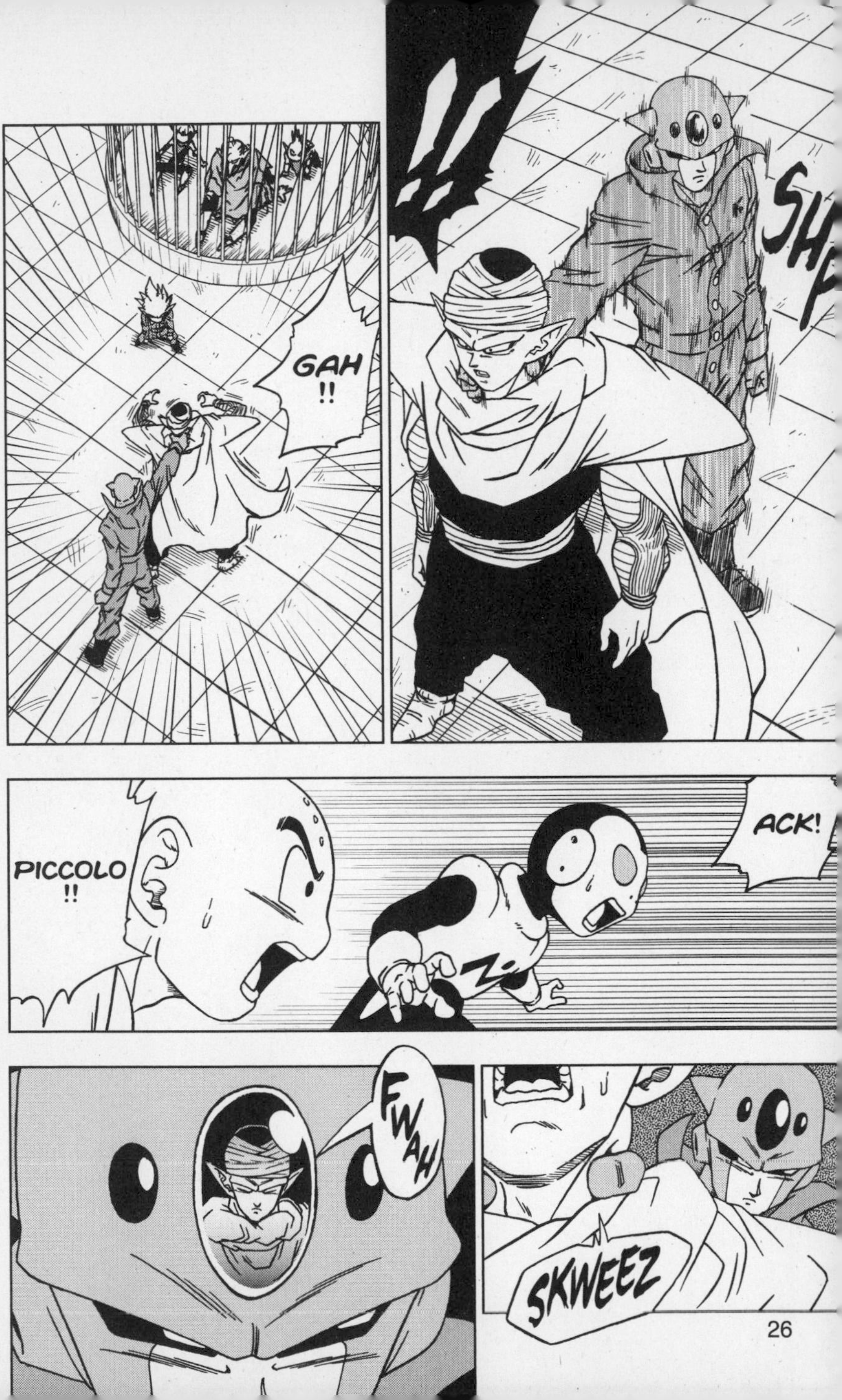
GAH !!
ACK!
PICCOLO !!
SKWEEZ
FWAH

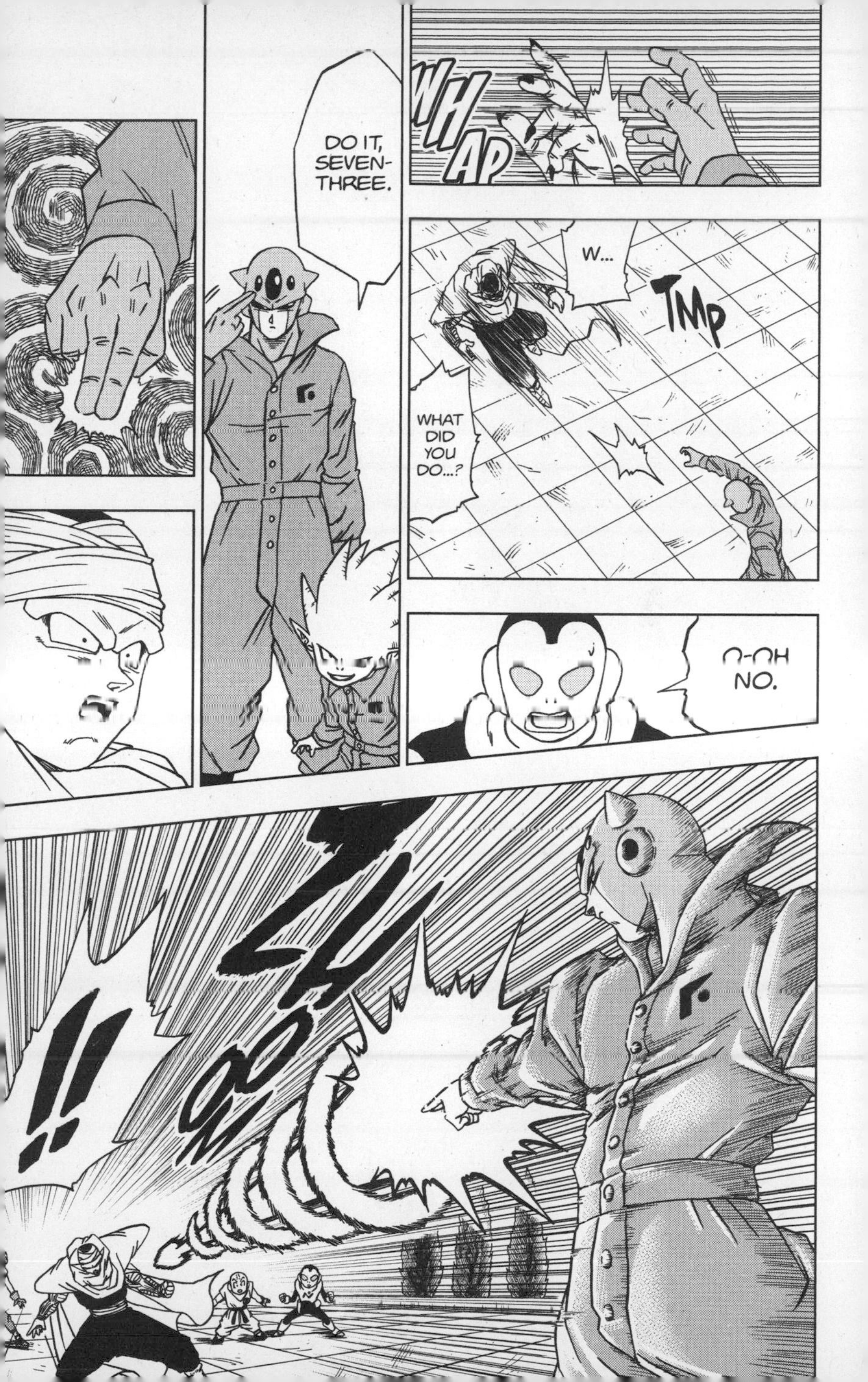
WHAP
W...
TMP
WHAT DID YOU DO...?
U-UH NO.
DO IT, SEVEN-THREE.
!!

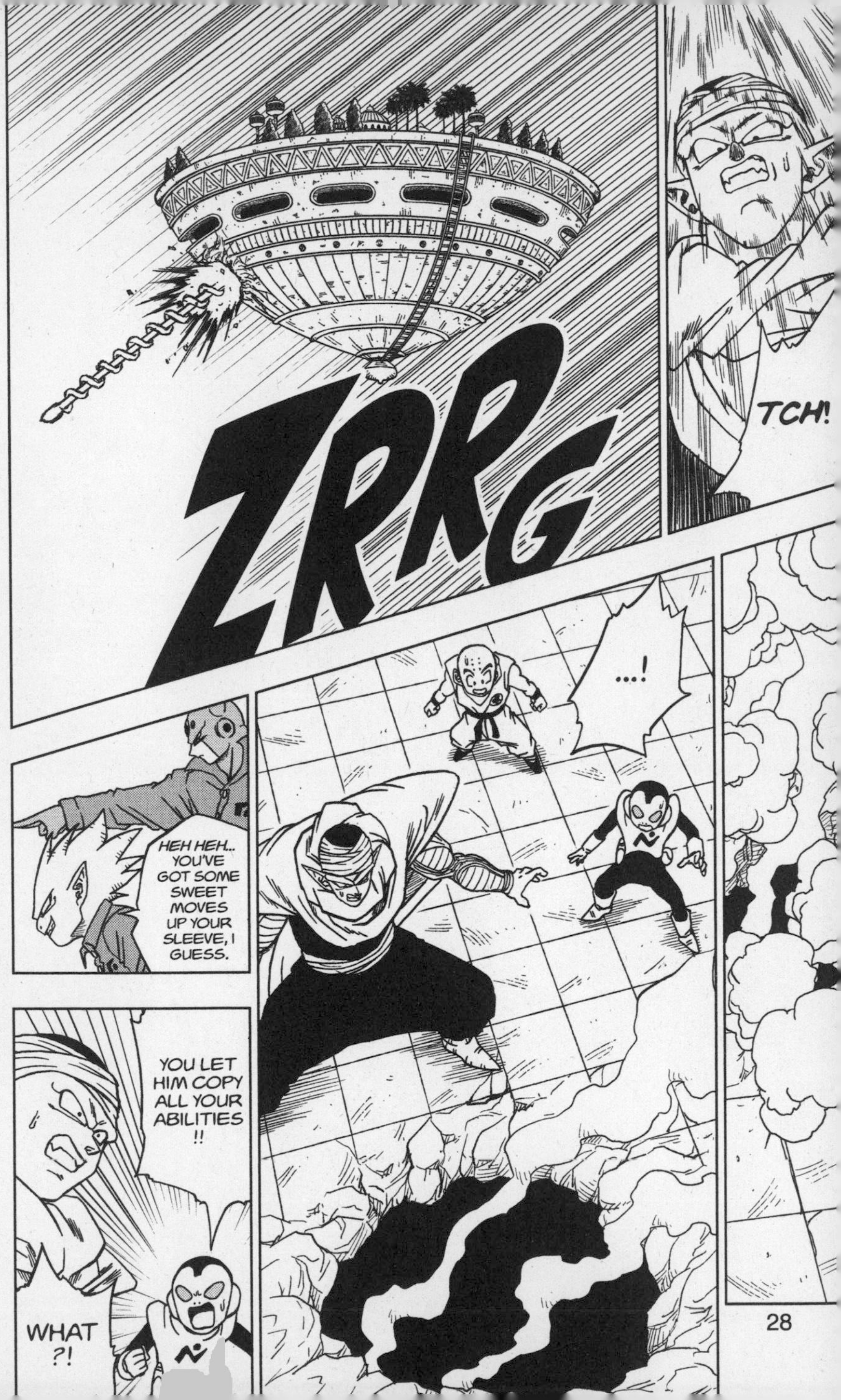
TCH!
ZRRG
...!
HEH HEH... YOU'VE GOT SOME SWEET MOVES UP YOUR SLEEVE, I GUESS.
YOU LET HIM COPY ALL YOUR ABILITIES!!
WHAT?!

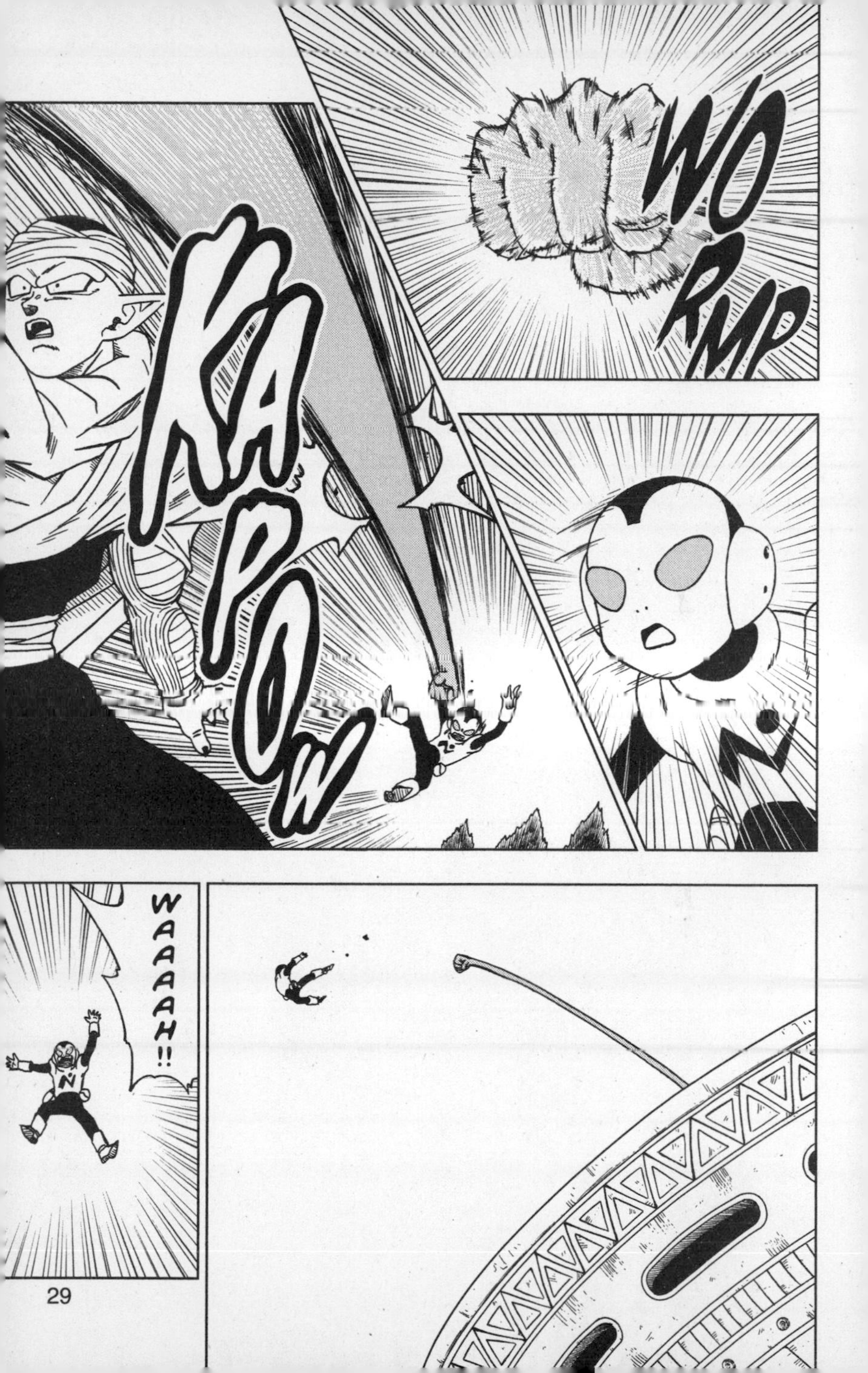
WORMP
KAPOW
WAAAAAH!!

JACO!!

AFTER THEM.

ZOOM

GRp

W-WAIT UP!

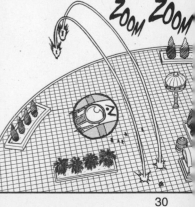

ZOOM ZOOM

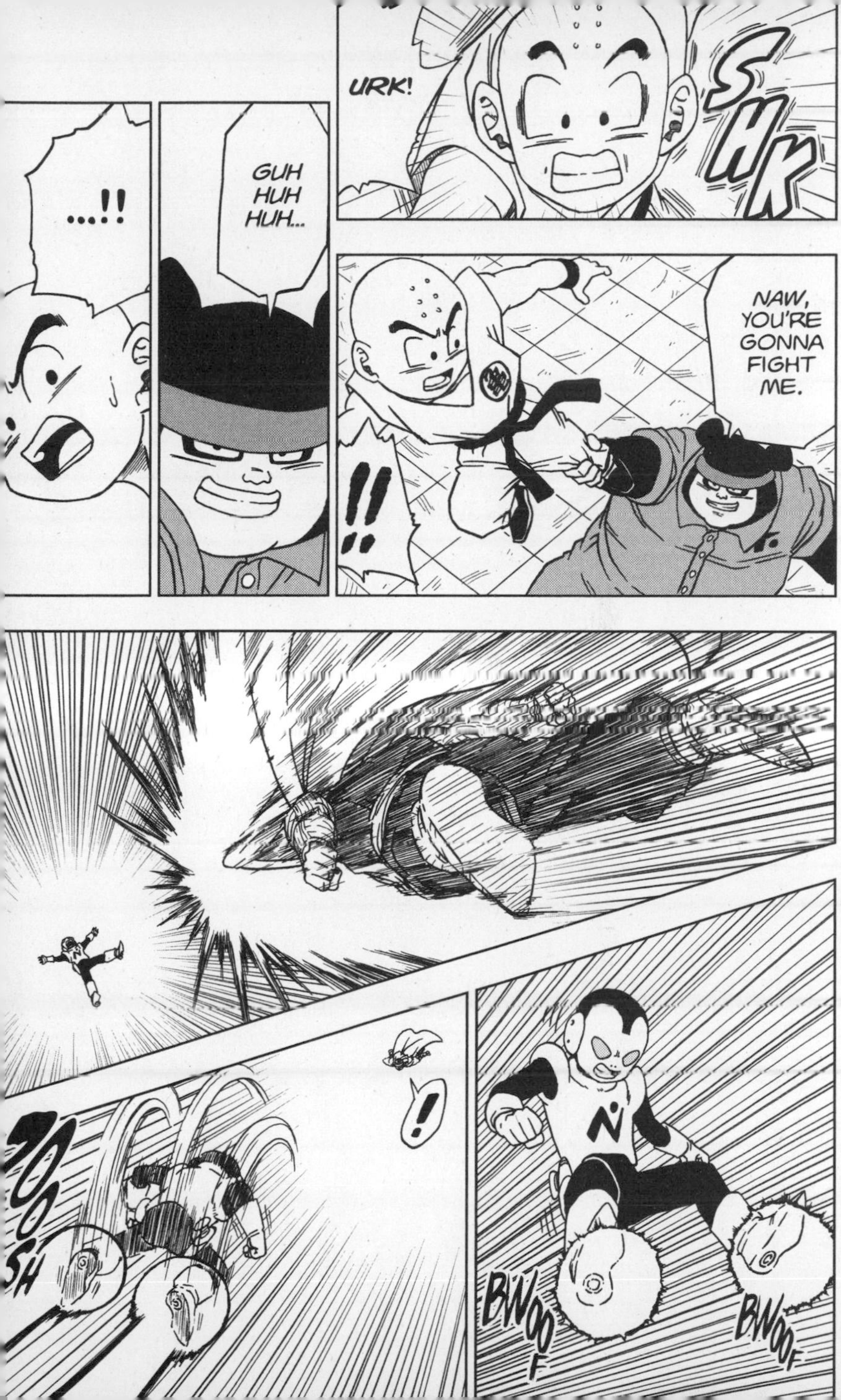
URK!
SHK
NAW, YOU'RE GONNA FIGHT ME.
!!
GUH HUH HUH...
...!!
BWOOF
BWOOF
!
WOOOSH

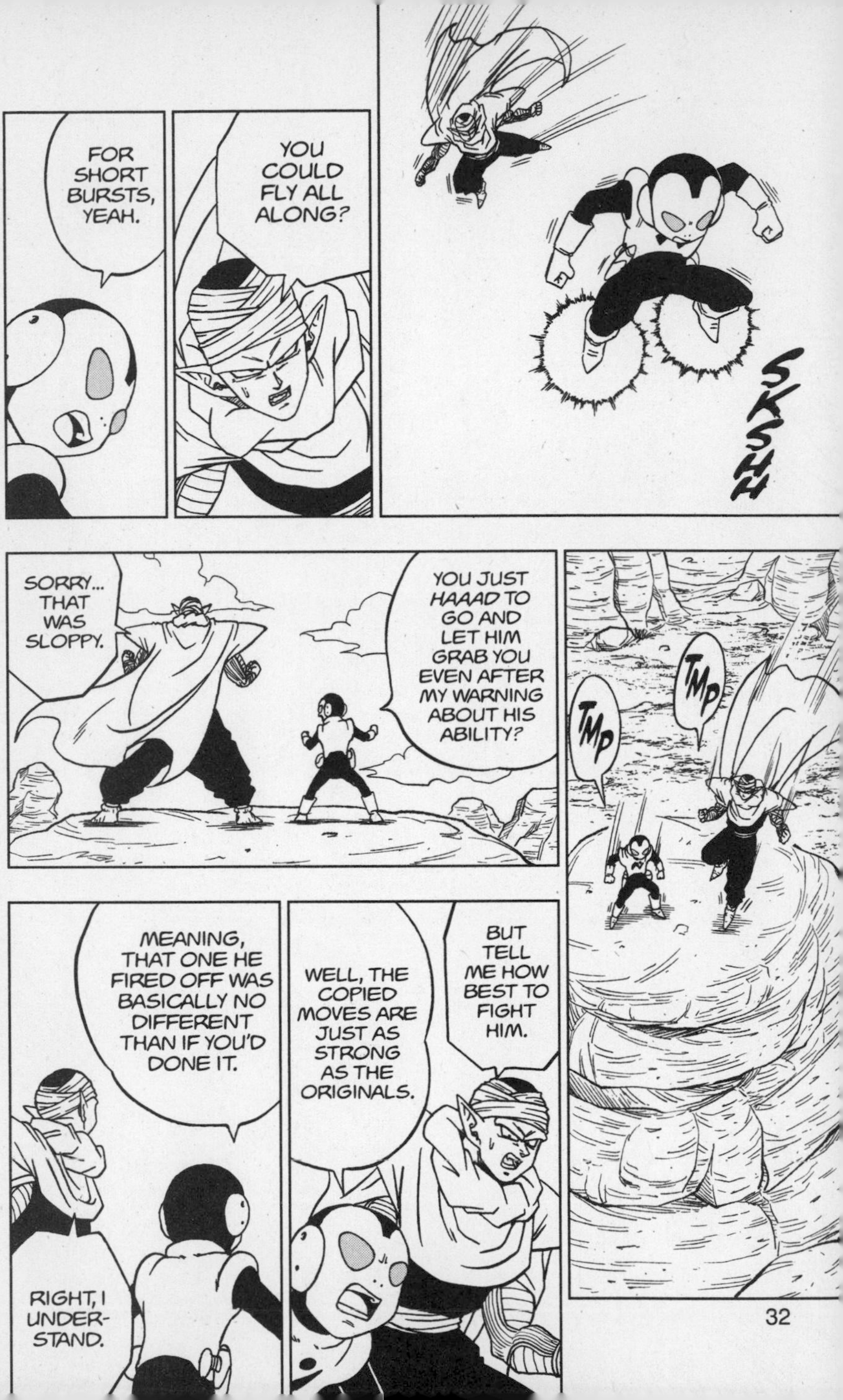

SKSHH
YOU COULD FLY ALL ALONG?
FOR SHORT BURSTS, YEAH.
TMP
TMP
YOU JUST *HAAAD* TO GO AND LET HIM GRAB YOU EVEN AFTER MY WARNING ABOUT HIS ABILITY?
SORRY... THAT WAS SLOPPY.
BUT TELL ME HOW BEST TO FIGHT HIM.
WELL, THE COPIED MOVES ARE JUST AS STRONG AS THE ORIGINALS.
MEANING, THAT ONE HE FIRED OFF WAS BASICALLY NO DIFFERENT THAN IF YOU'D DONE IT.
RIGHT, I UNDER-STAND.

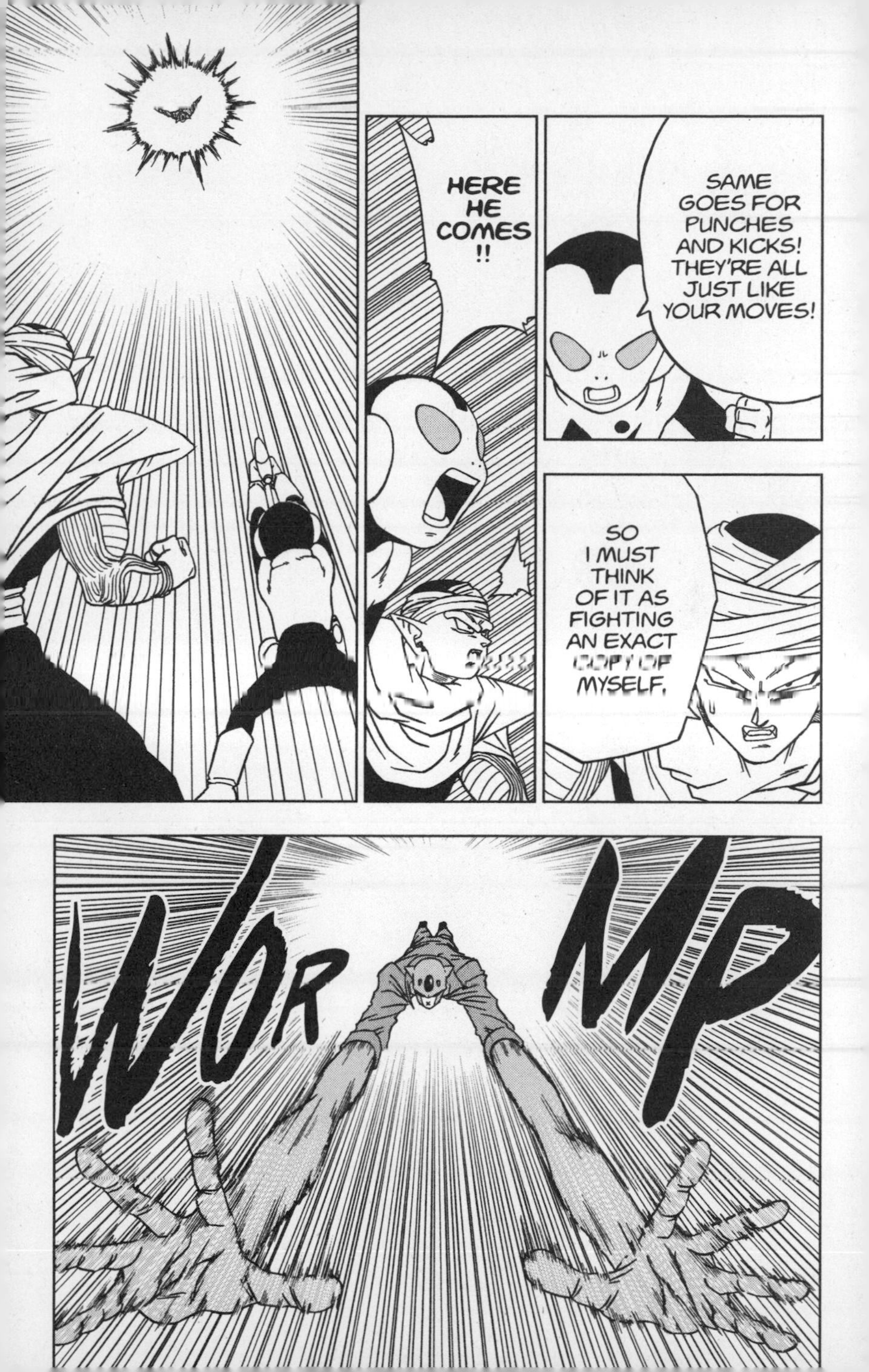
SAME GOES FOR PUNCHES AND KICKS! THEY'RE ALL JUST LIKE YOUR MOVES!
SO I MUST THINK OF IT AS FIGHTING AN EXACT COPY OF MYSELF.
HERE HE COMES!!
WORMP

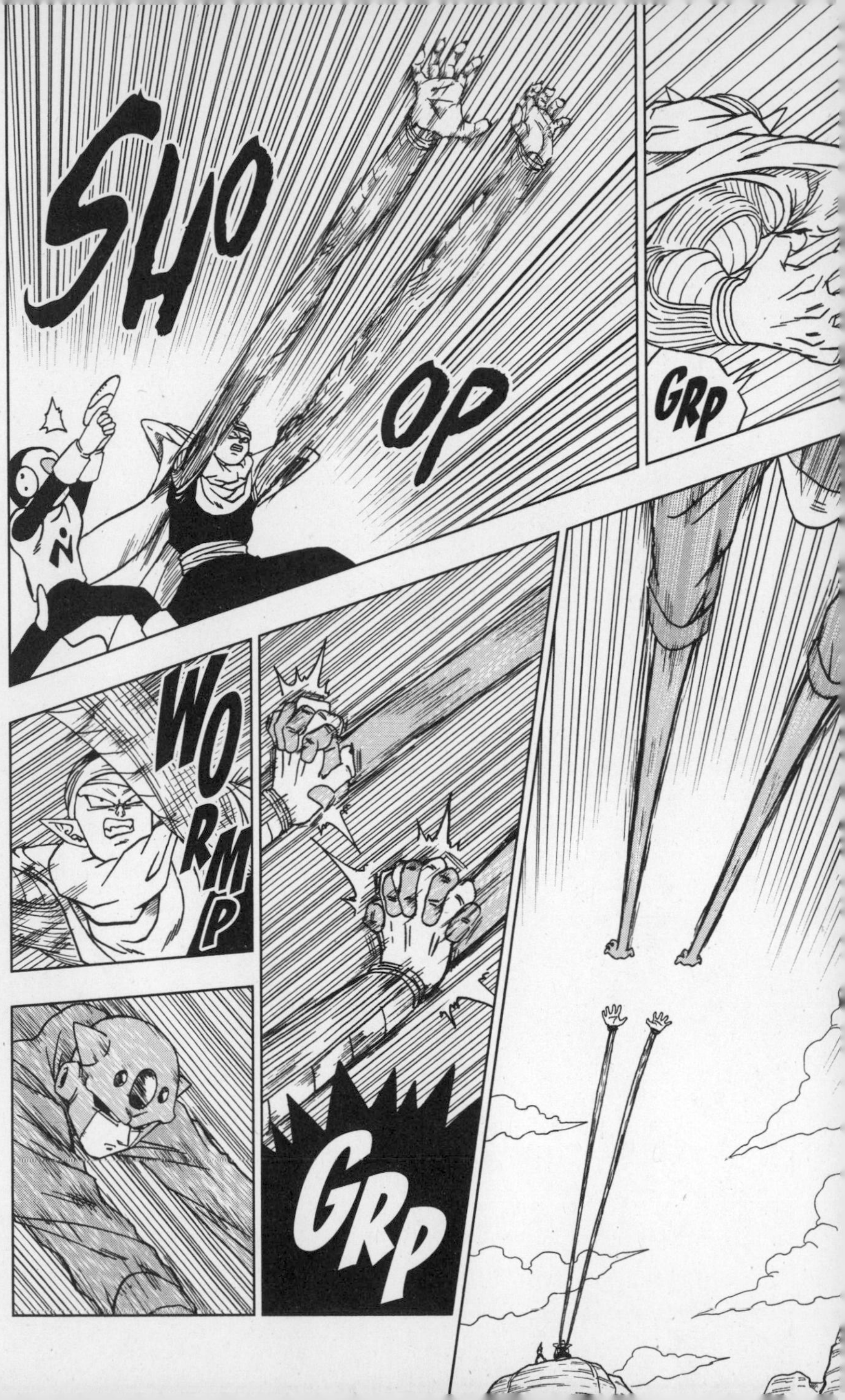
GRP
SHOOP
GRP
WORMP

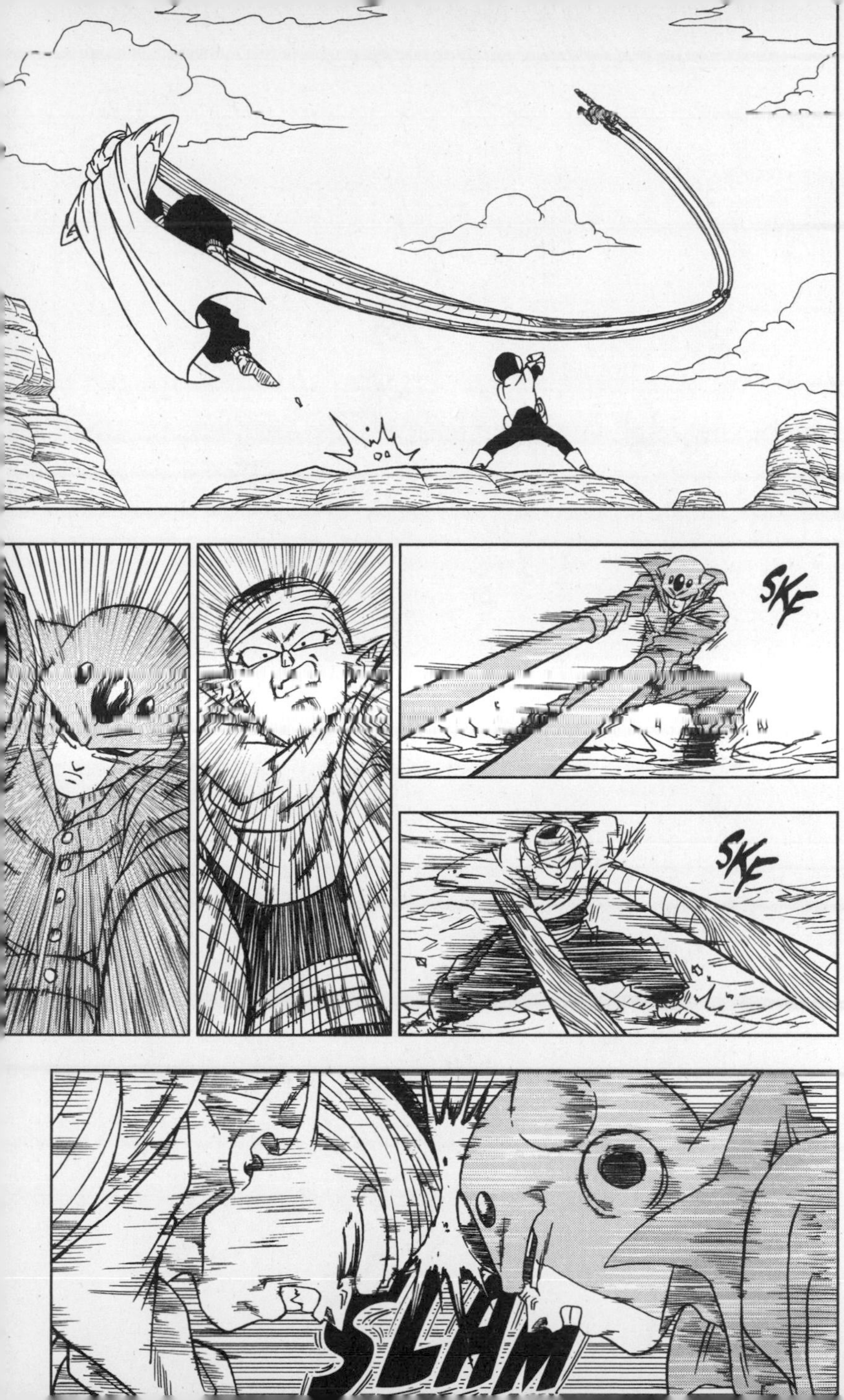

SKF
SKF
SLAM

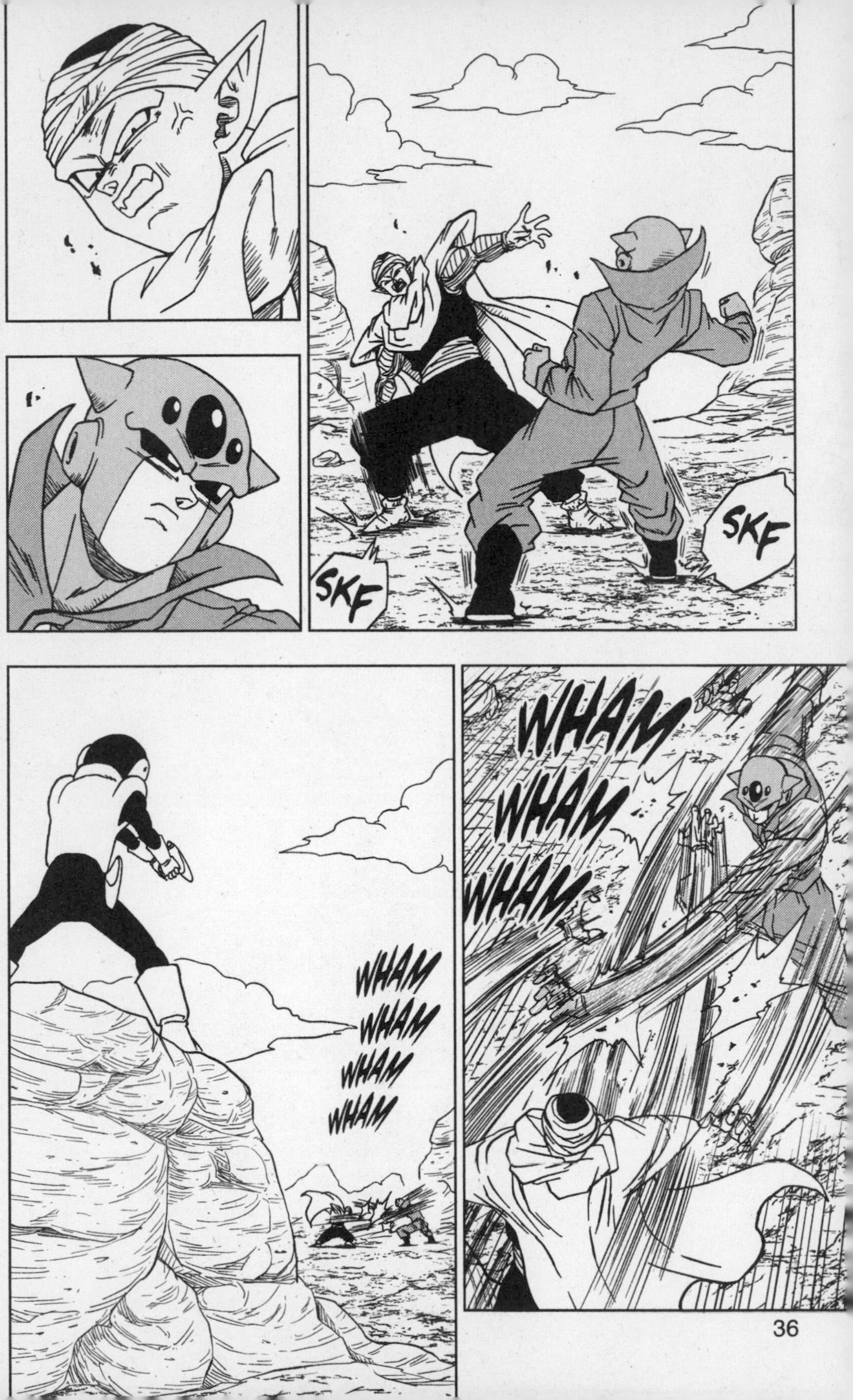
SKF
SKF
WHAM
WHAM
WHAM
WHAM
WHAM
WHAM
WHAM

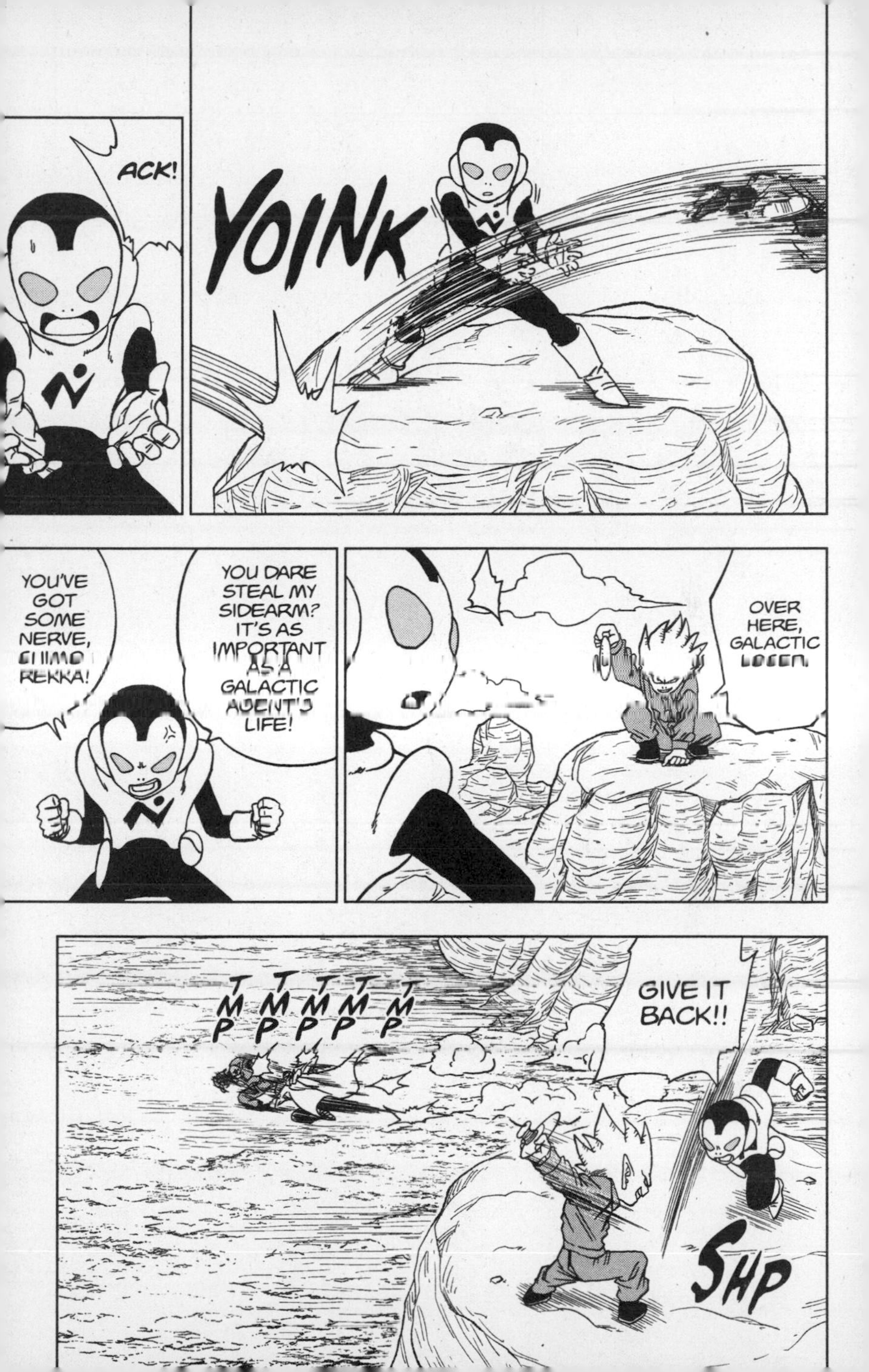
YOINK
ACK!
OVER HERE, GALACTIC LOSER.
YOU DARE STEAL MY SIDEARM? IT'S AS IMPORTANT AS A GALACTIC AGENT'S LIFE!
YOU'VE GOT SOME NERVE, CHIMO REKKA!
GIVE IT BACK!!
TMP TMP TMP TMP TMP
SHP

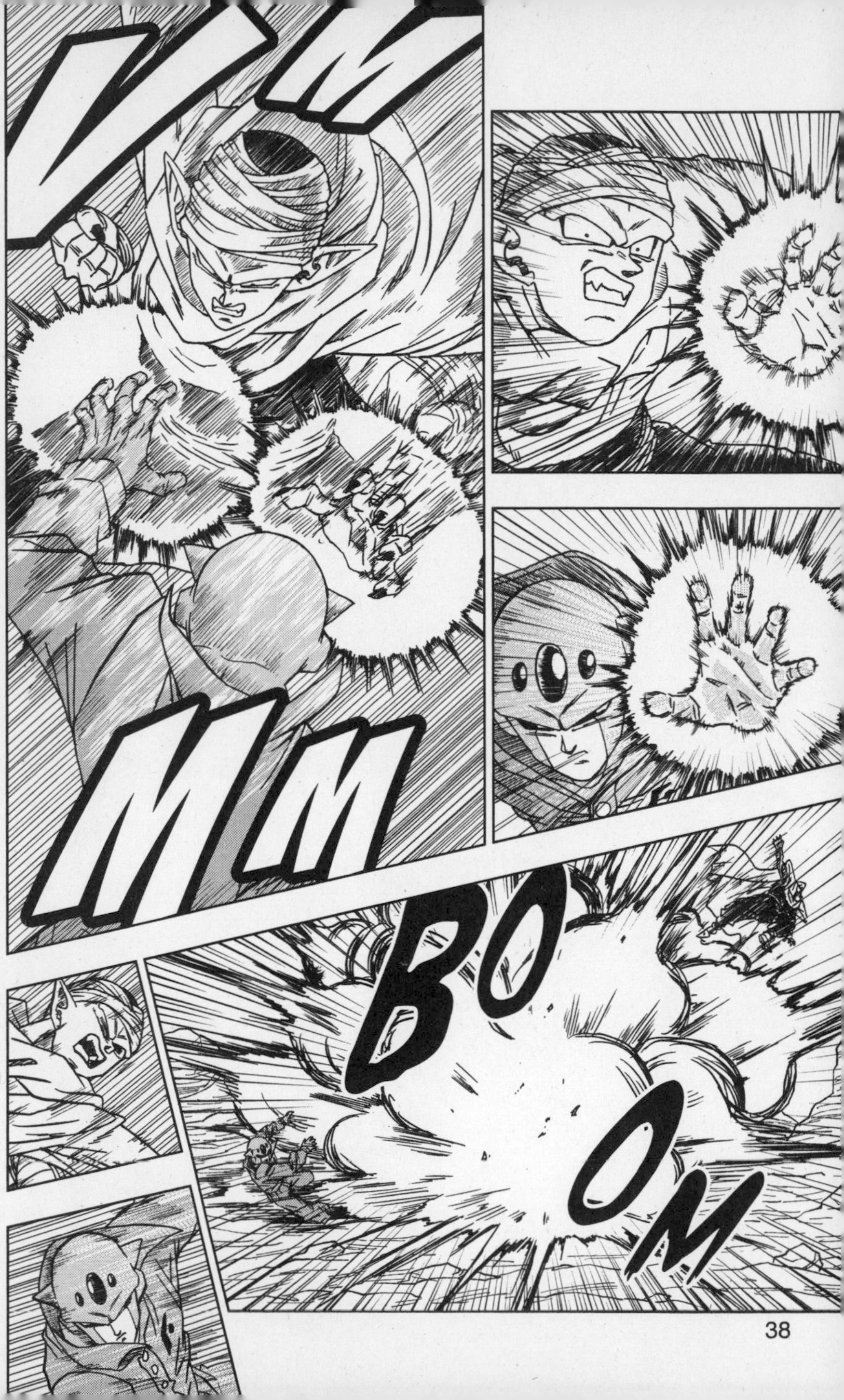
VM
MM
BOOM

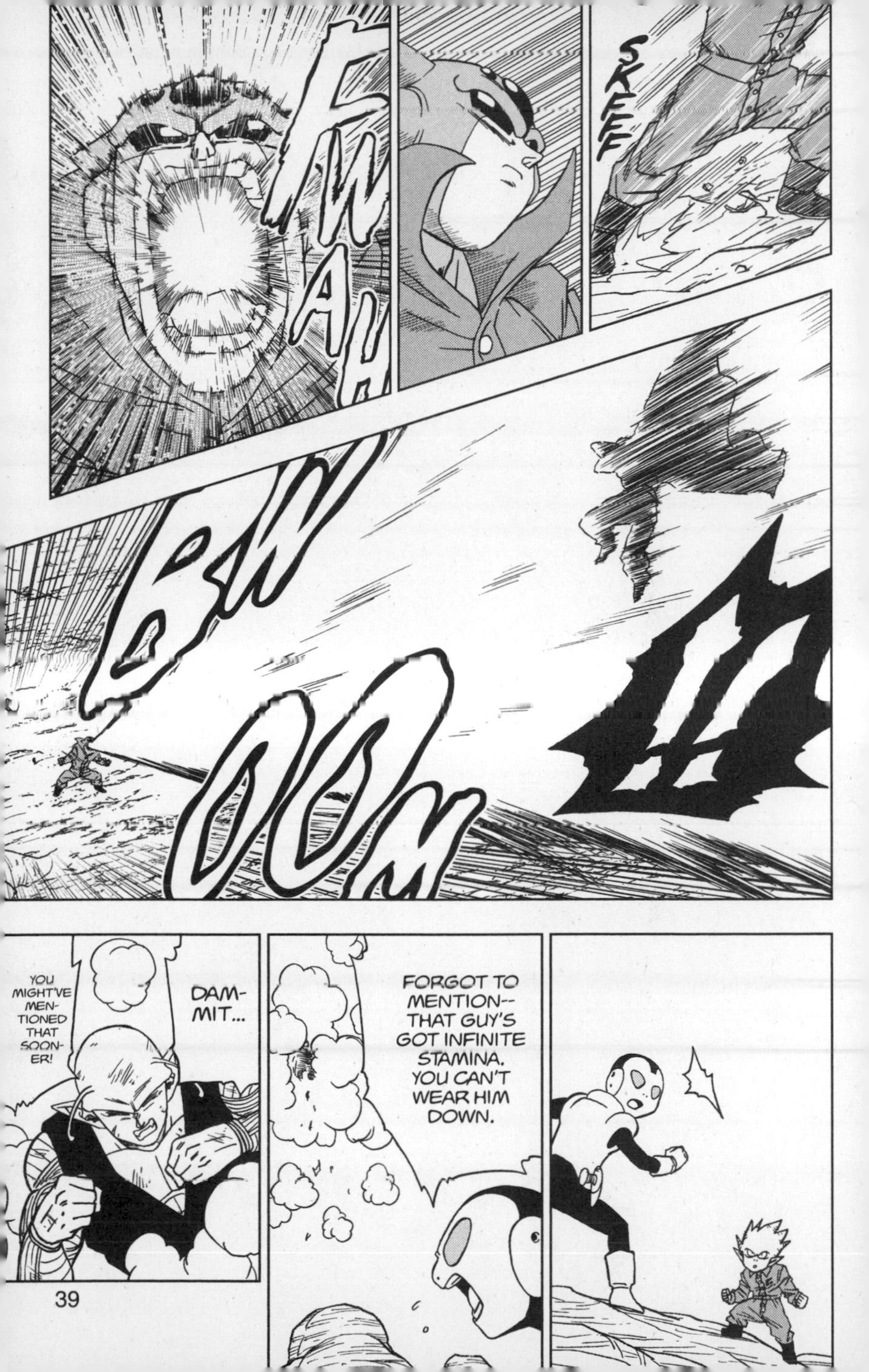
SKEFF
FORGOT TO MENTION-- THAT GUY'S GOT INFINITE STAMINA. YOU CAN'T WEAR HIM DOWN.
DAM-MIT...
YOU MIGHT'VE MEN-TIONED THAT SOON-ER!

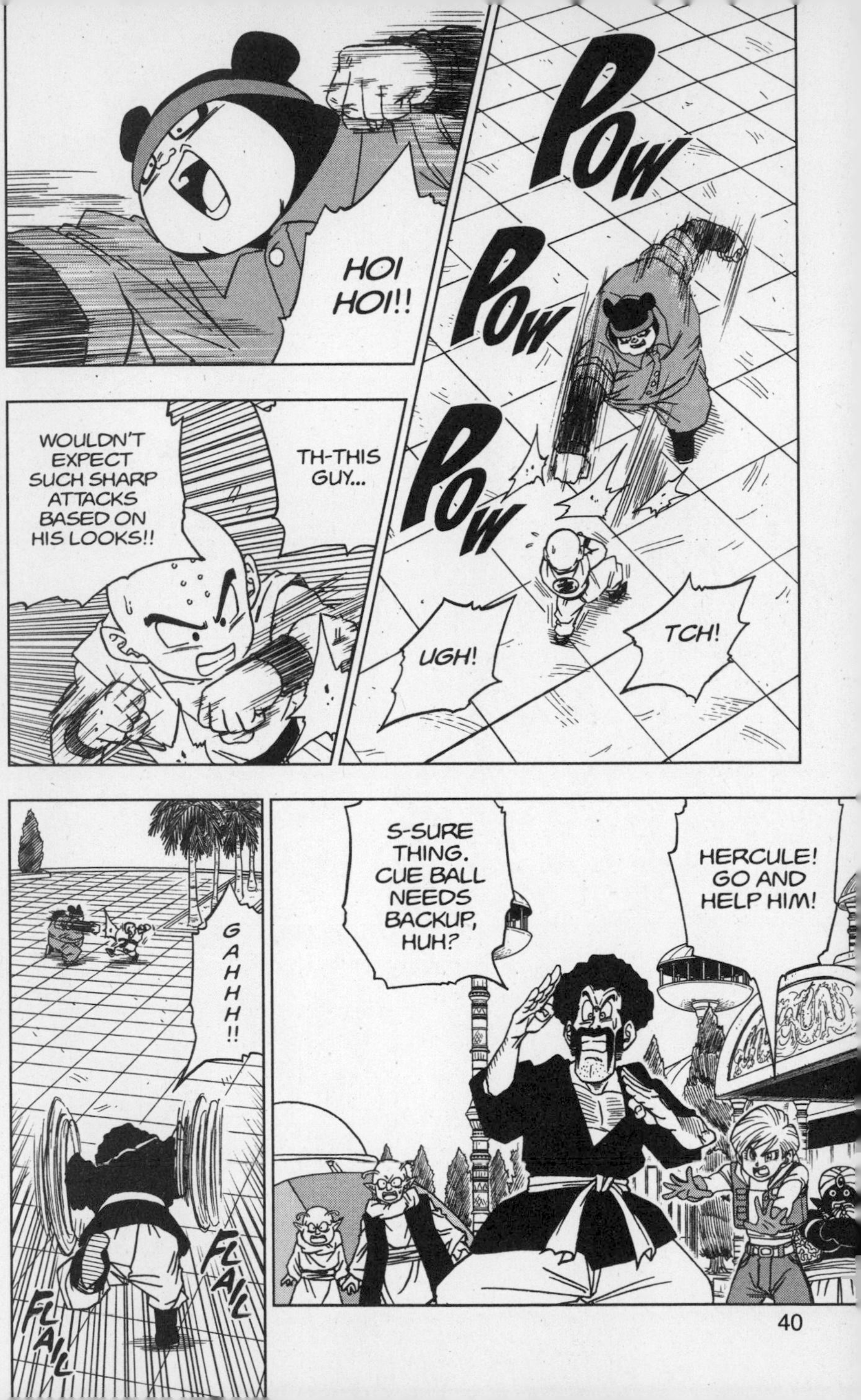
POW
POW
POW
TCH!
UGH!
HOI HOI!!
TH-THIS GUY...
WOULDN'T EXPECT SUCH SHARP ATTACKS BASED ON HIS LOOKS!!
HERCULE! GO AND HELP HIM!
S-SURE THING. CUE BALL NEEDS BACKUP, HUH?
GAHHH!!
FLAIL
FLAIL

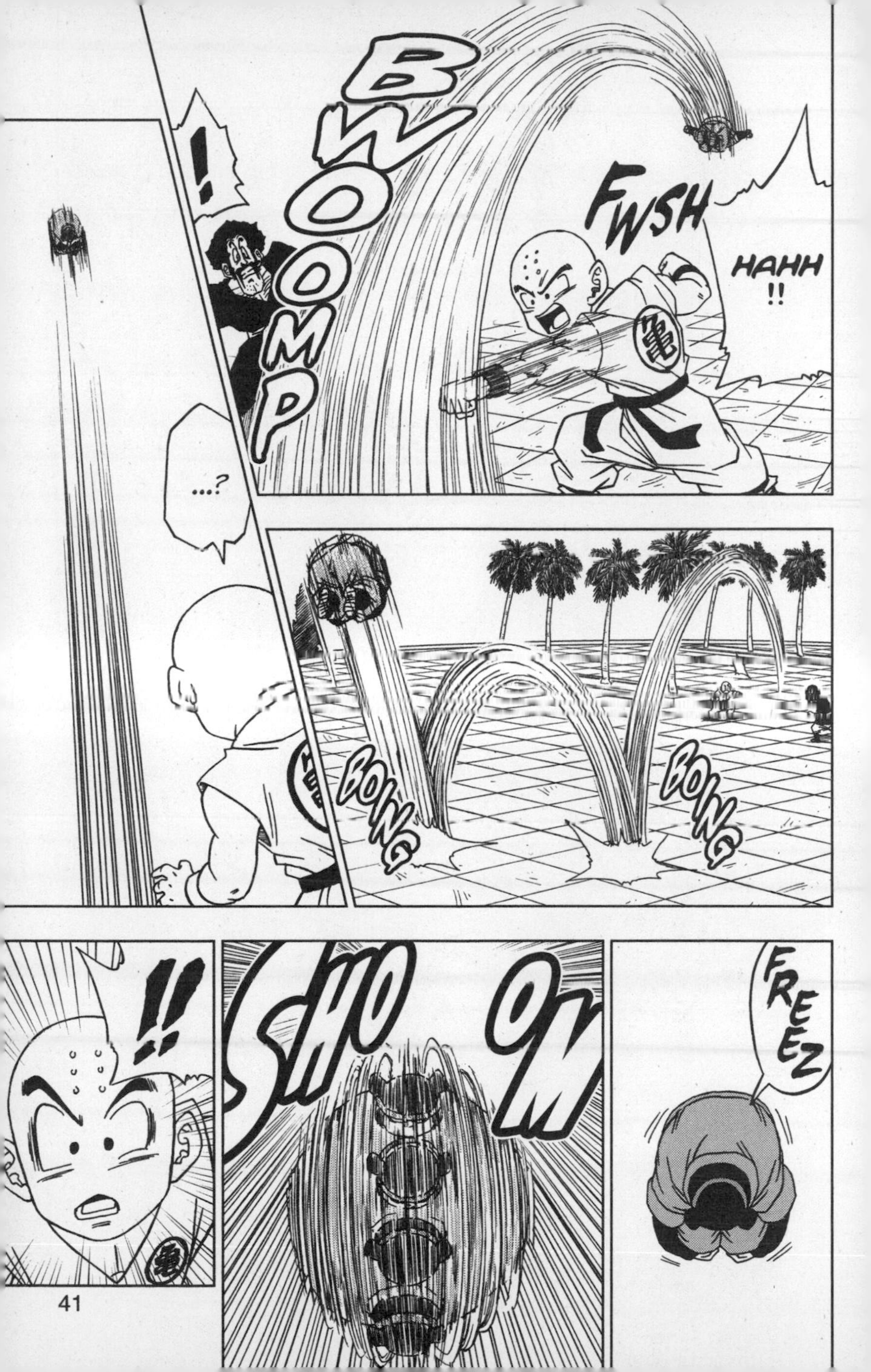
FWSH
HAHH!!
BWOOOMP
BOING
BOING
!
...?
FREEZ
SHOO OM
!!

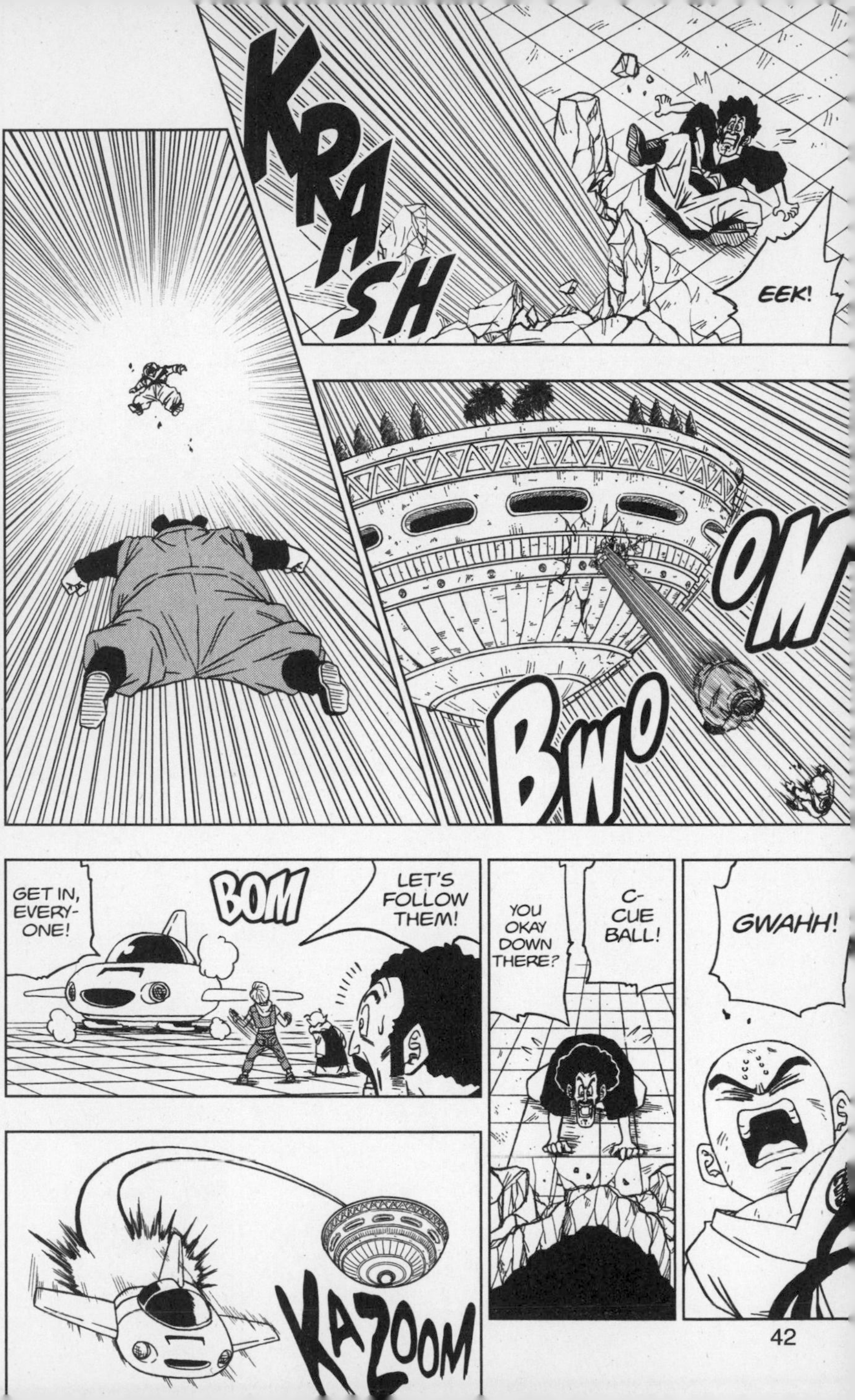
KRASH
EEK!
BWOOM
GWAHH!
C-CUE BALL!
YOU OKAY DOWN THERE?
LET'S FOLLOW THEM!
BOM
GET IN, EVERY-ONE!
KAZOOM

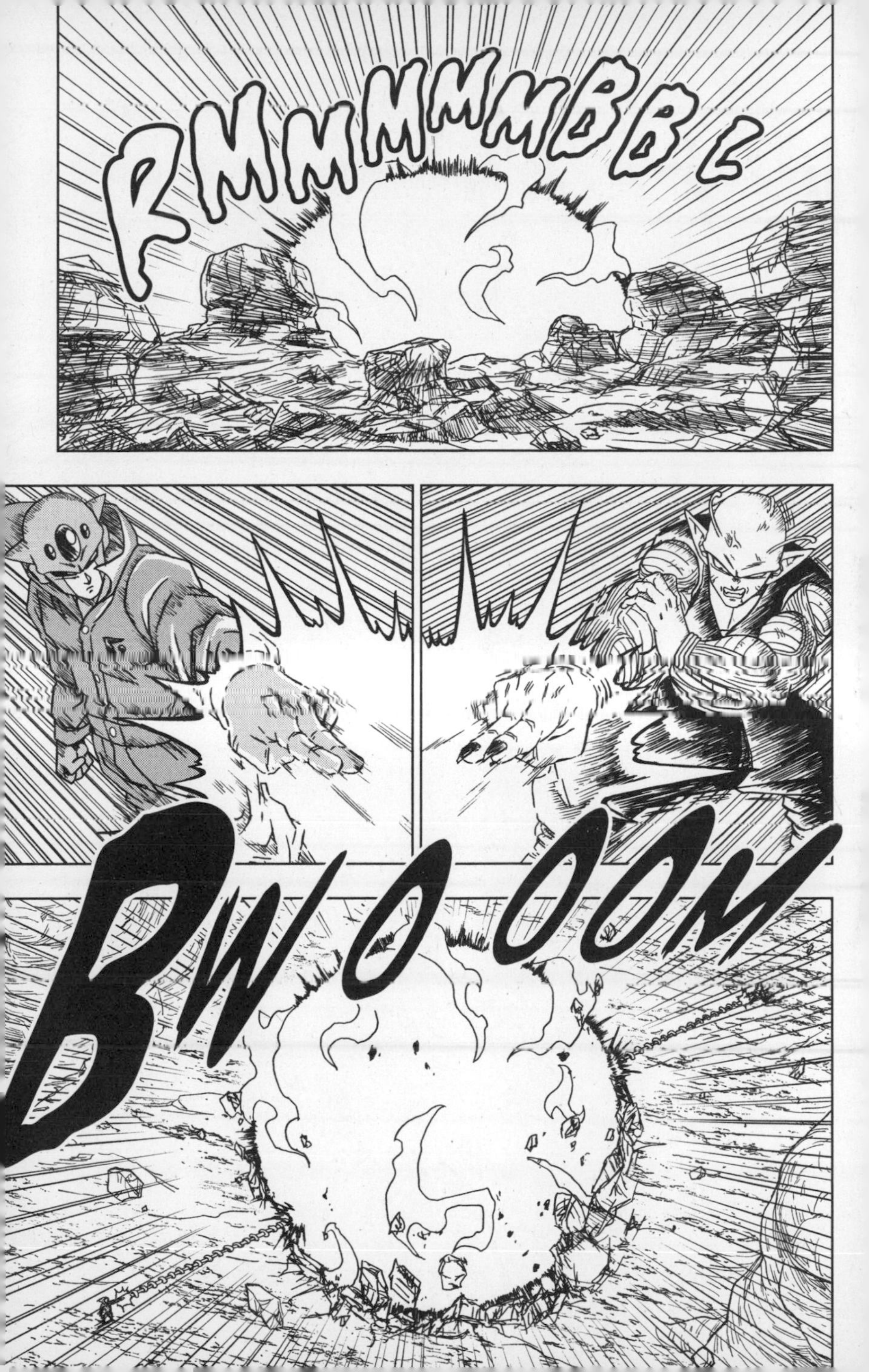
RMMMMMBBL
BWOOOM

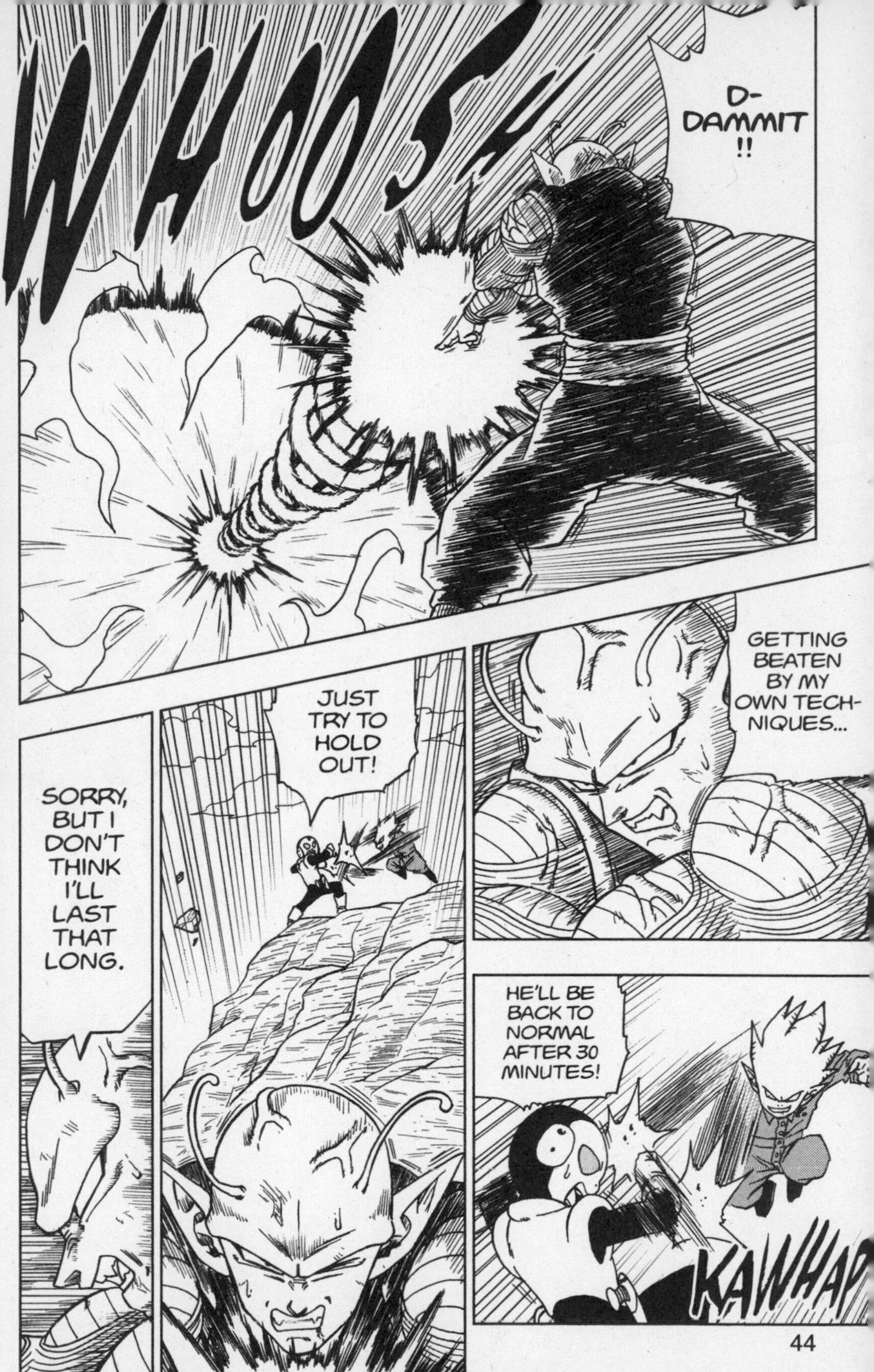
WHOOSH
D-DAMMIT!!
GETTING BEATEN BY MY OWN TECHNIQUES...
HE'LL BE BACK TO NORMAL AFTER 30 MINUTES!
KAWHAP
JUST TRY TO HOLD OUT!
SORRY, BUT I DON'T THINK I'LL LAST THAT LONG.

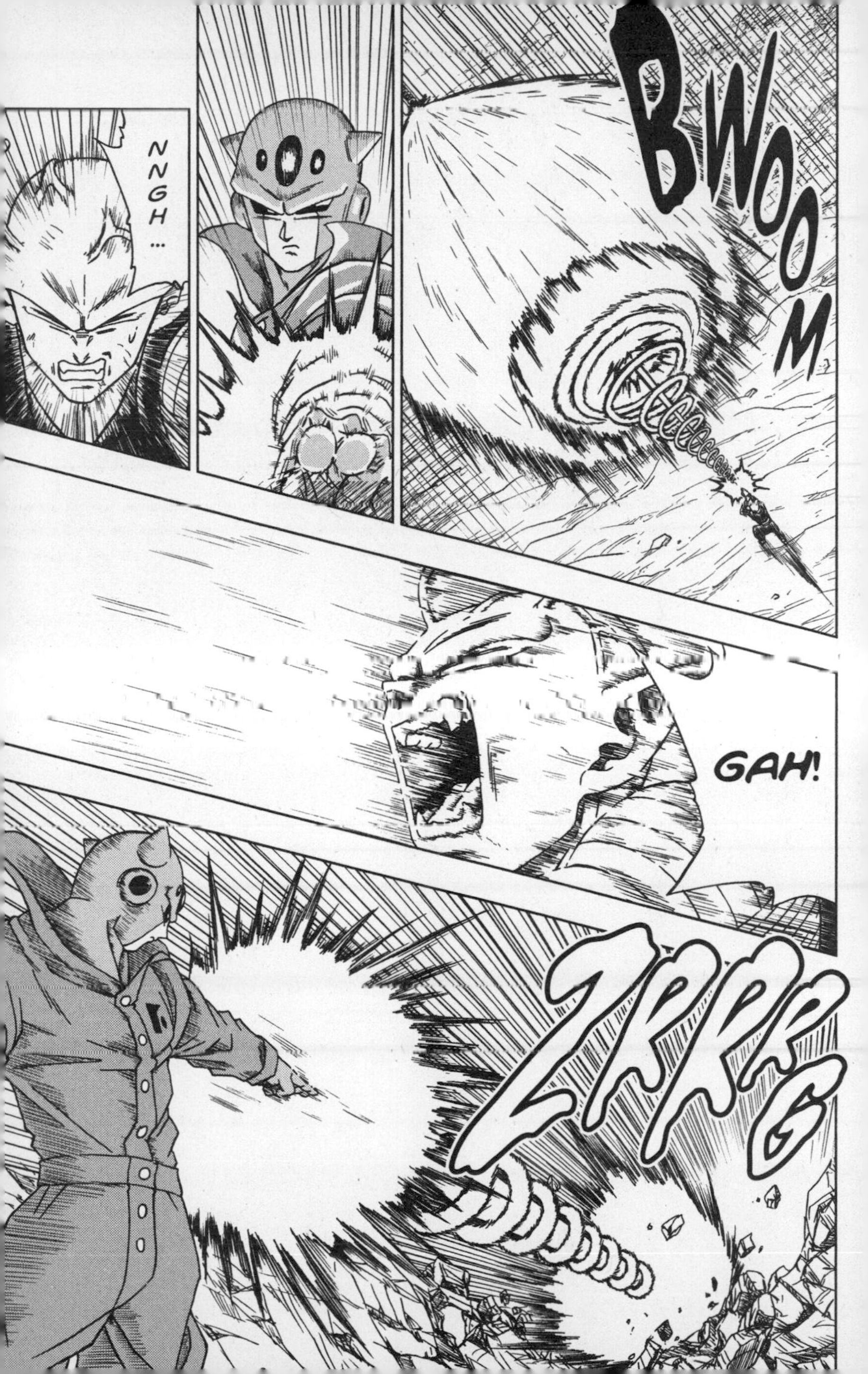
BWOOM
NNGH ...
GAH!

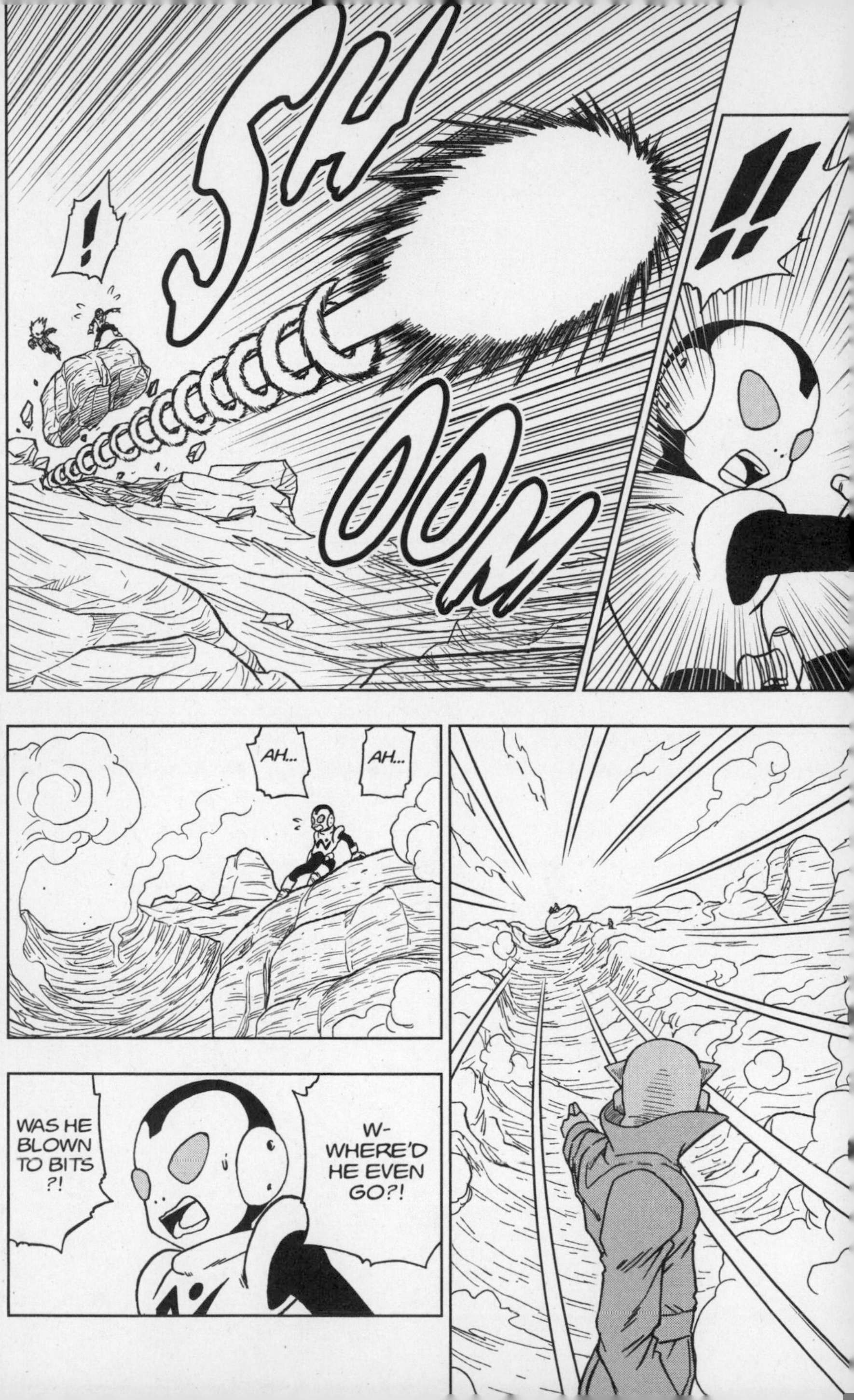
!!
SHOOOM
!
AH...
AH...
W- WHERE'D HE EVEN GO?!
WAS HE BLOWN TO BITS ?!

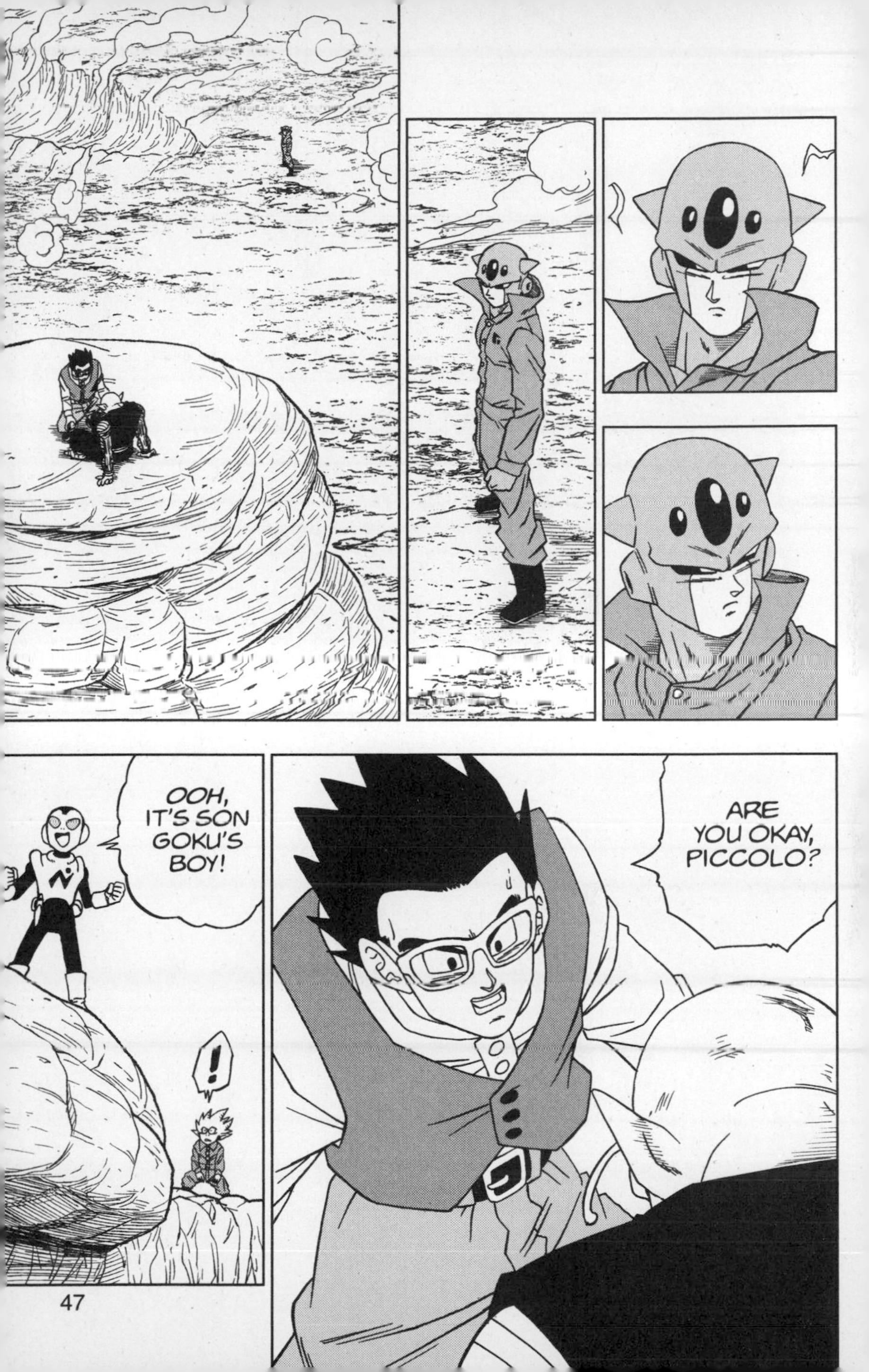
ARE YOU OKAY, PICCOLO?
OOH, IT'S SON GOKU'S BOY!
!

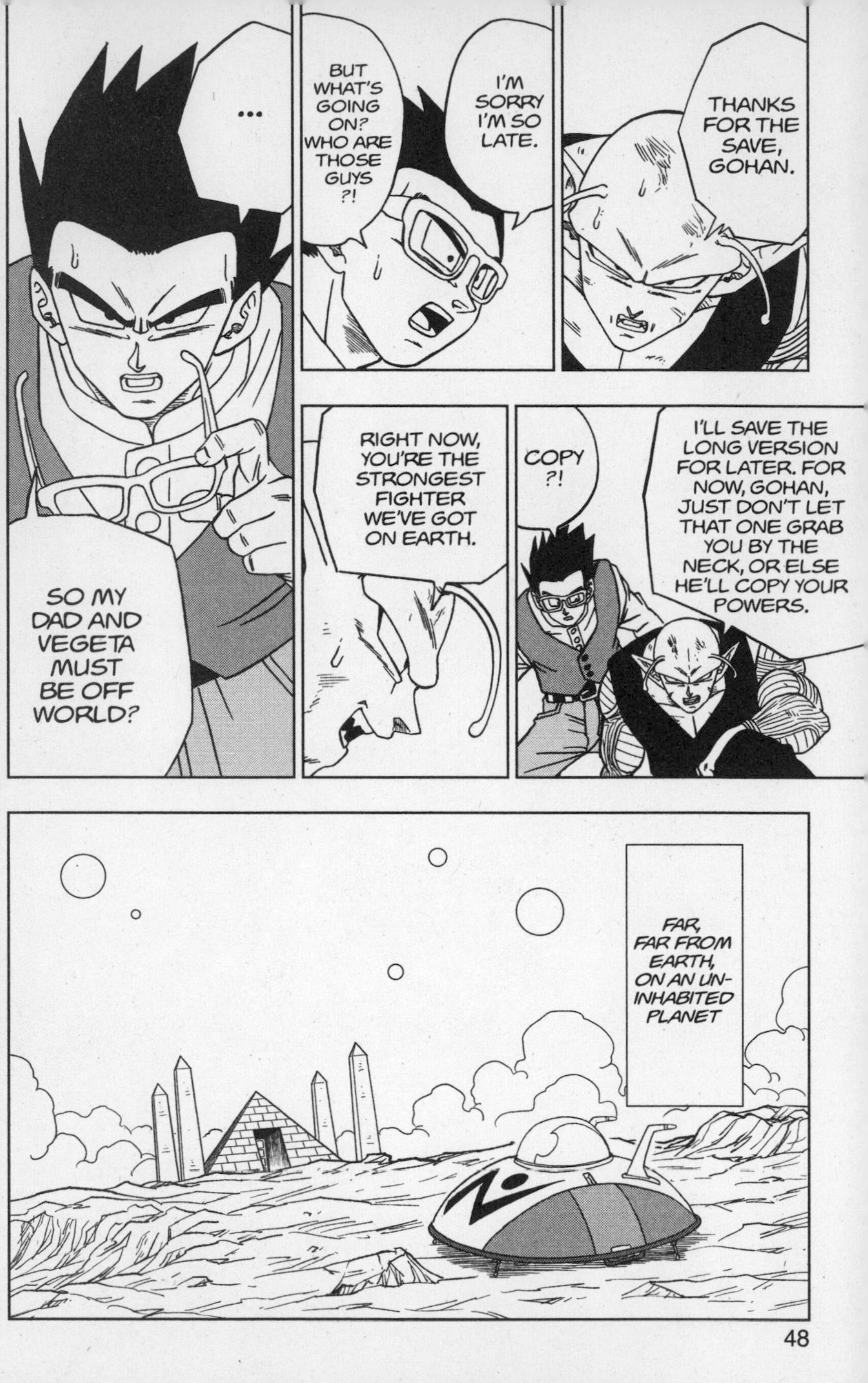
THANKS FOR THE SAVE, GOHAN.
I'M SORRY I'M SO LATE.
BUT WHAT'S GOING ON? WHO ARE THOSE GUYS?!
I'LL SAVE THE LONG VERSION FOR LATER. FOR NOW, GOHAN, JUST DON'T LET THAT ONE GRAB YOU BY THE NECK, OR ELSE HE'LL COPY YOUR POWERS.
COPY?!
RIGHT NOW, YOU'RE THE STRONGEST FIGHTER WE'VE GOT ON EARTH.
...
SO MY DAD AND VEGETA MUST BE OFF WORLD?
FAR, FAR FROM EARTH, ON AN UN-INHABITED PLANET

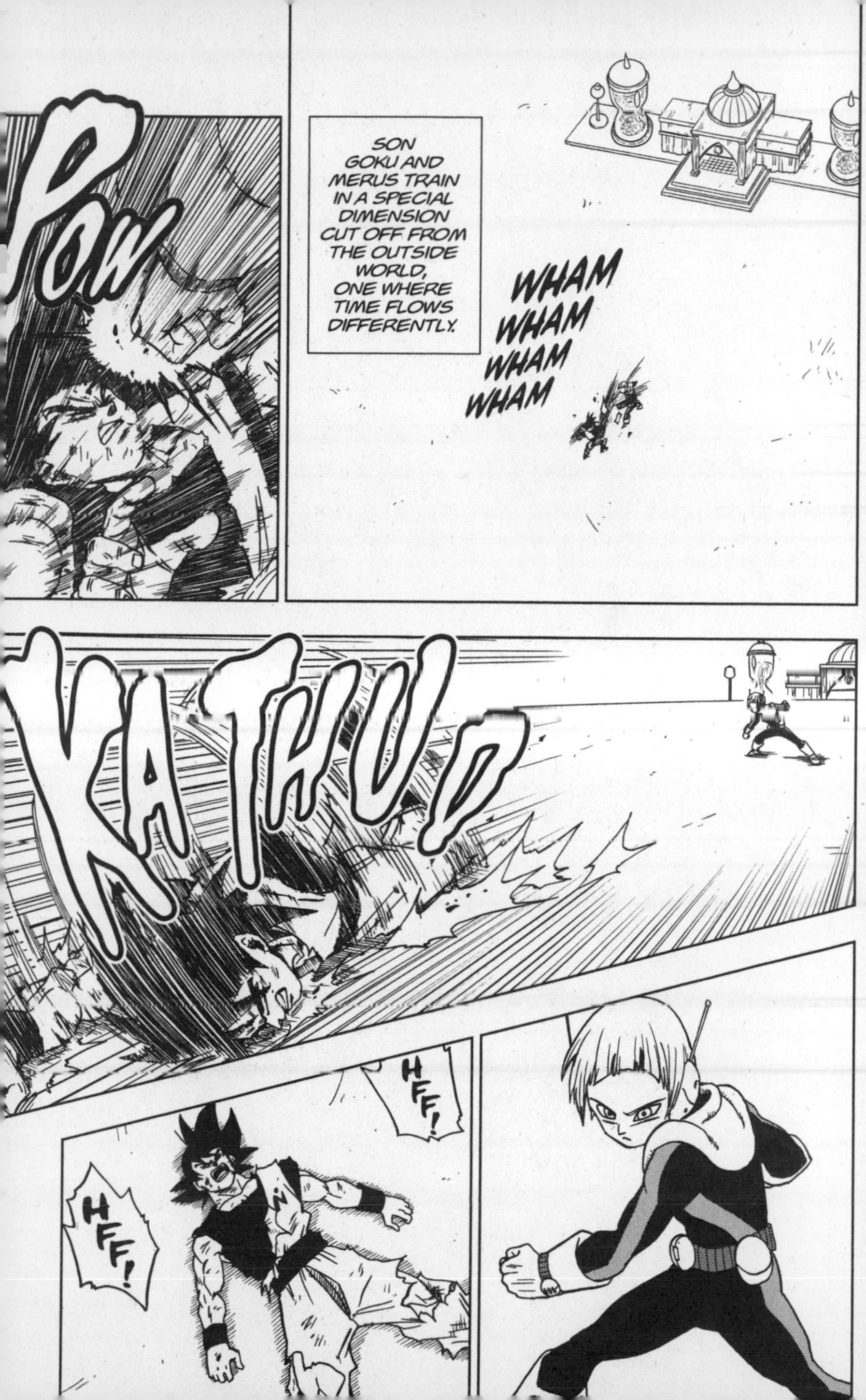
SON GOKU AND MERUS TRAIN IN A SPECIAL DIMENSION CUT OFF FROM THE OUTSIDE WORLD, ONE WHERE TIME FLOWS DIFFERENTLY.
WHAM WHAM WHAM WHAM
POW
KATHUD
HFF!
HFF!

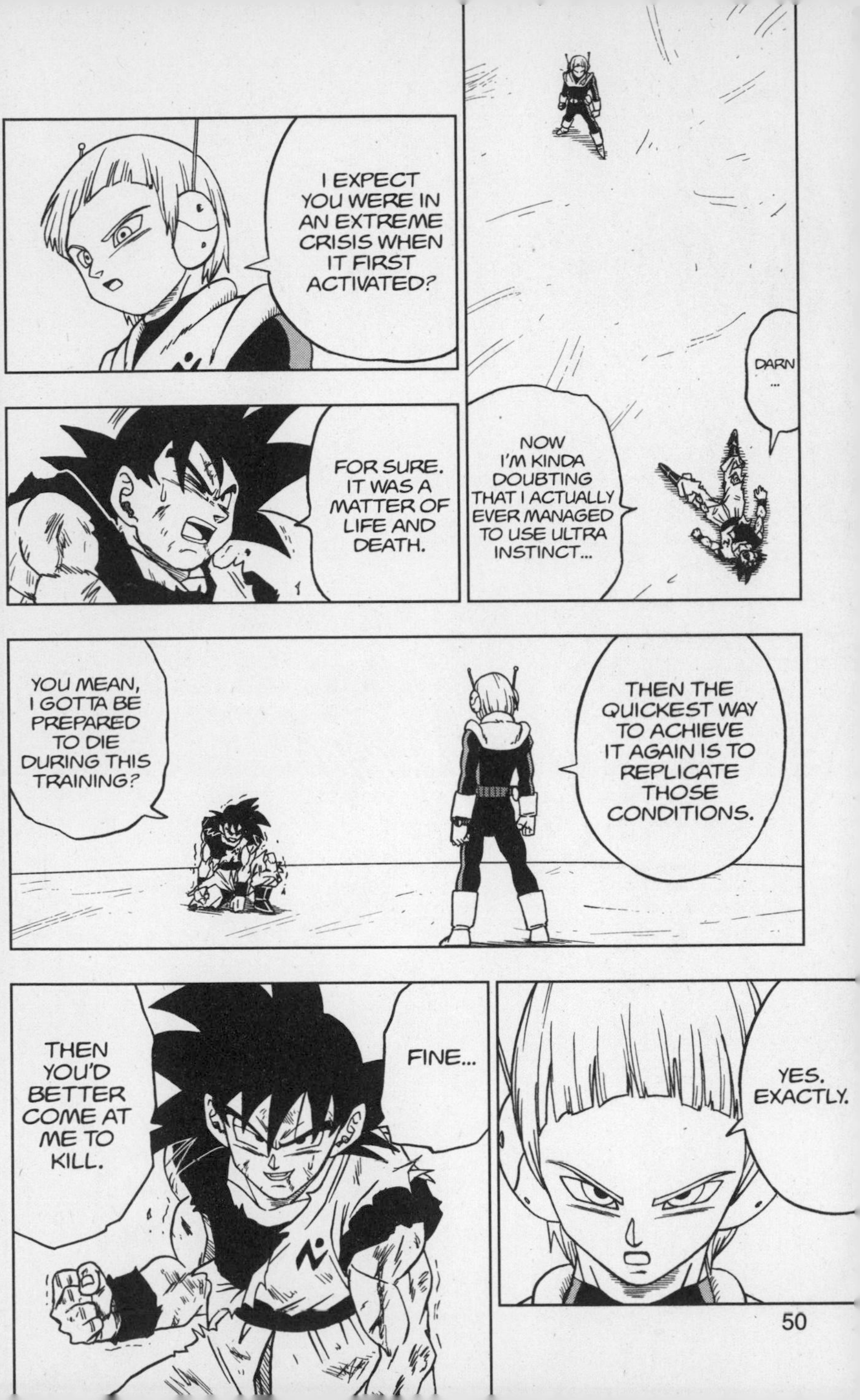
DARN...
NOW I'M KINDA DOUBTING THAT I ACTUALLY EVER MANAGED TO USE ULTRA INSTINCT...
I EXPECT YOU WERE IN AN EXTREME CRISIS WHEN IT FIRST ACTIVATED?
FOR SURE. IT WAS A MATTER OF LIFE AND DEATH.
THEN THE QUICKEST WAY TO ACHIEVE IT AGAIN IS TO REPLICATE THOSE CONDITIONS.
YOU MEAN, I GOTTA BE PREPARED TO DIE DURING THIS TRAINING?
YES. EXACTLY.
FINE...
THEN YOU'D BETTER COME AT ME TO KILL.

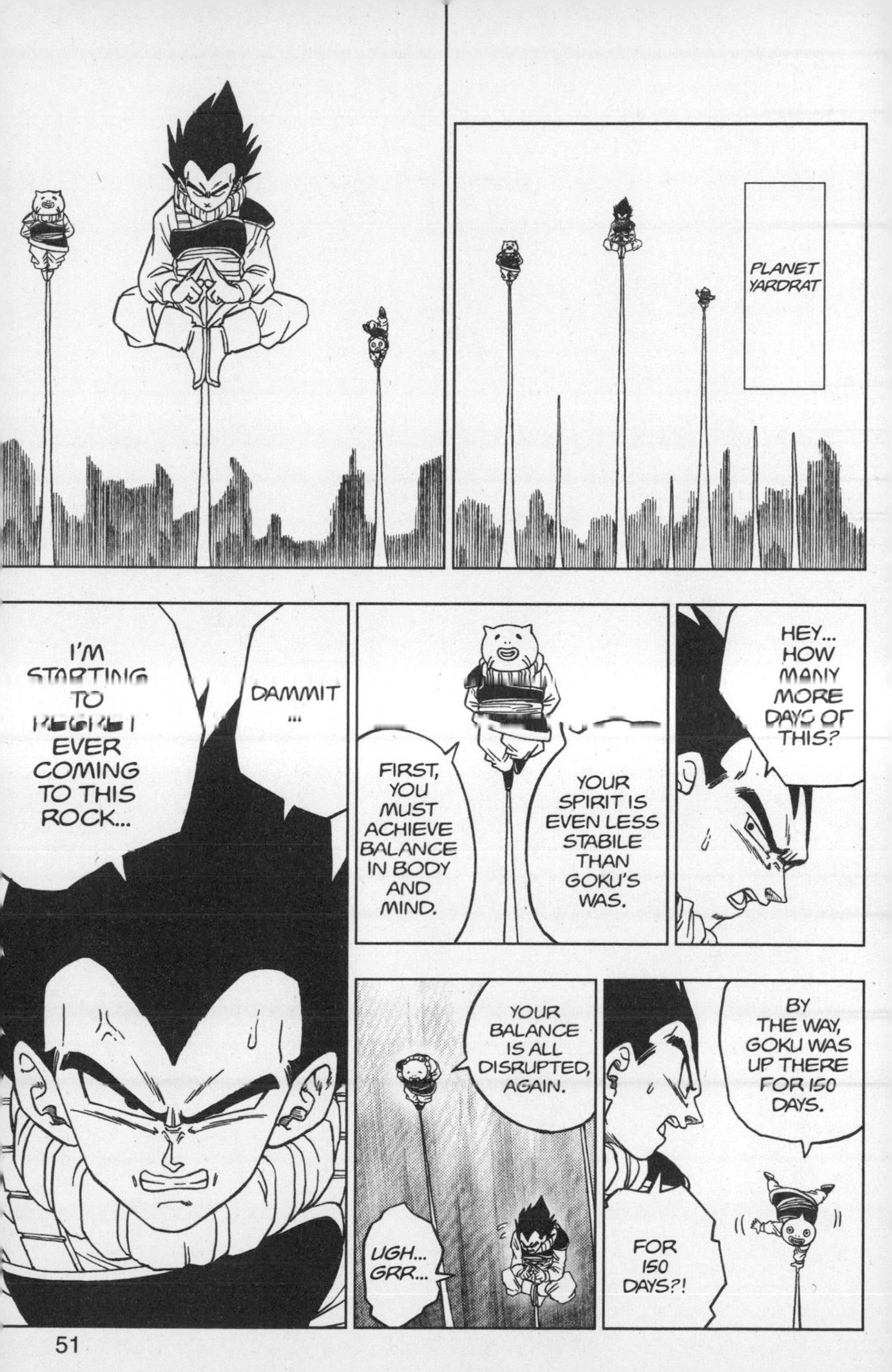
PLANET YARDRAT
HEY... HOW MANY MORE DAYS OF THIS?
YOUR SPIRIT IS EVEN LESS STABILE THAN GOKU'S WAS.
FIRST, YOU MUST ACHIEVE BALANCE IN BODY AND MIND.
BY THE WAY, GOKU WAS UP THERE FOR 150 DAYS.
FOR 150 DAYS?!
YOUR BALANCE IS ALL DISRUPTED, AGAIN.
UGH... GRR...
DAMMIT...
I'M STARTING TO REGRET EVER COMING TO THIS ROCK...

SAGANBO'S GALACTIC
BANDIT BRIGADE
MEMBER:
SHIMOREKKA

SAGANBO'S GALACTIC
BANDIT BRIGADE
MEMBER:
OG73-I

SAGANBO'S GALACTIC
BANDIT BRIGADE
MEMBER:
YUNBA

CHAPTER 54:
GOHAN VS. SEVEN-THREE

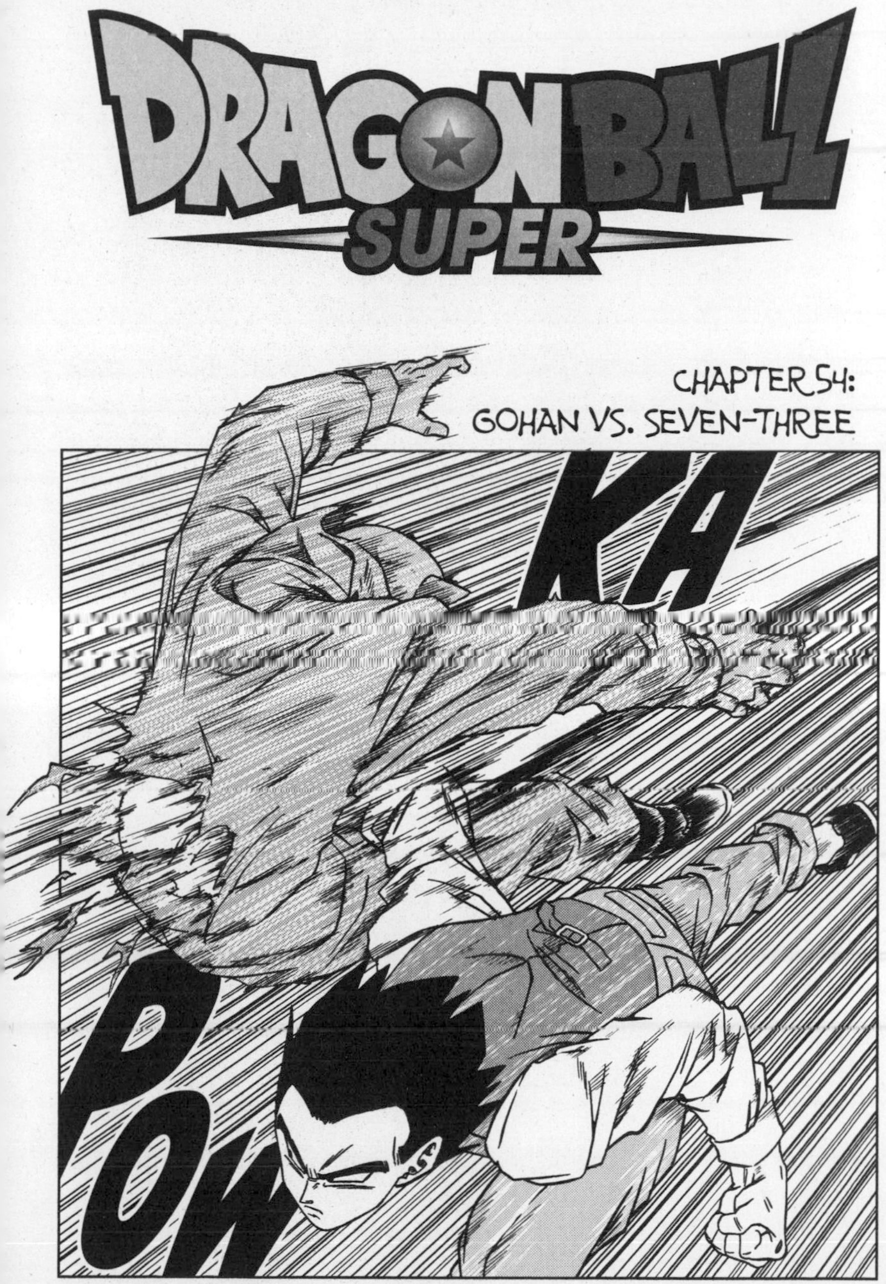
KA
DOM

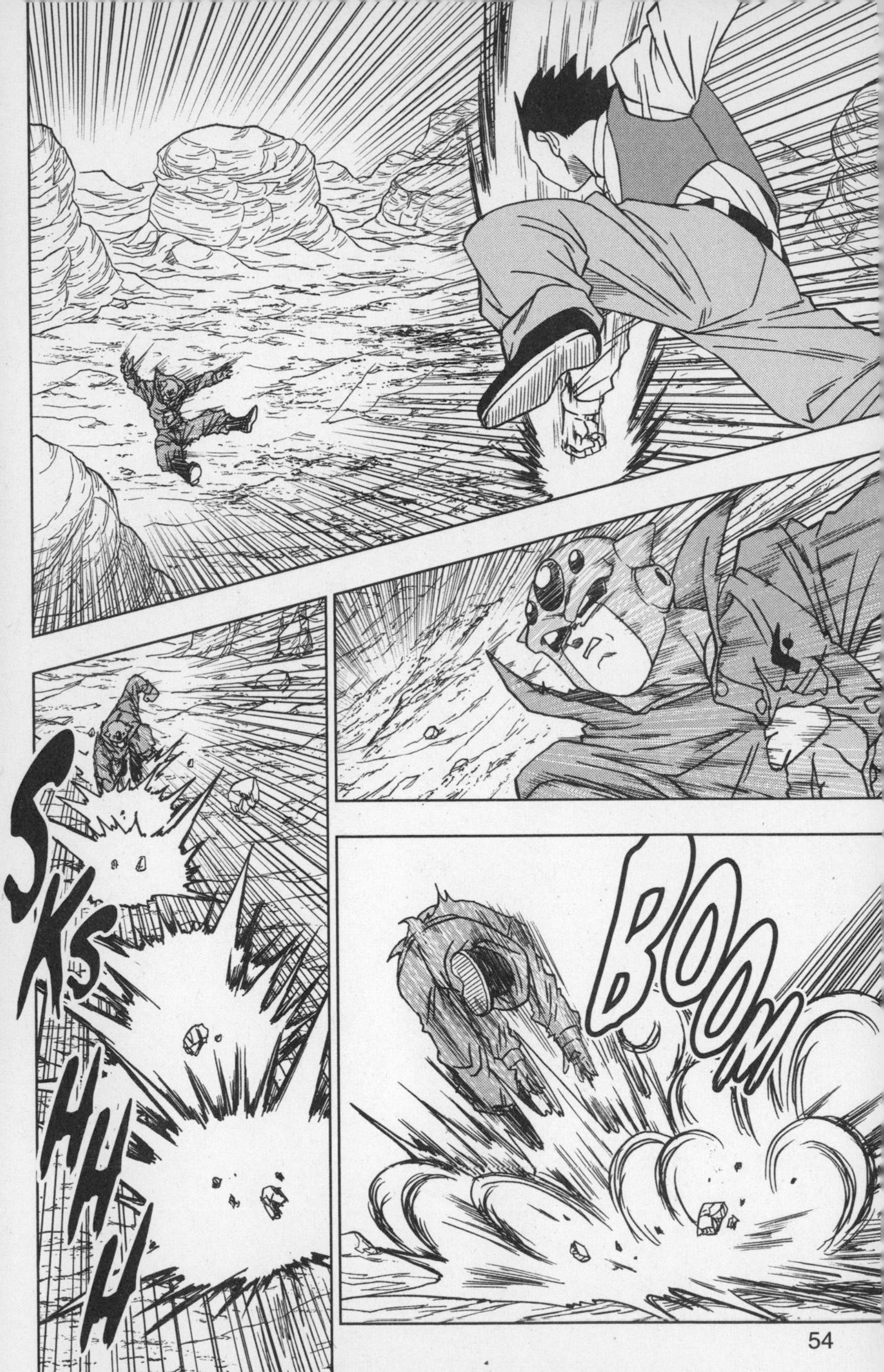
BOOM
SKSHHHH

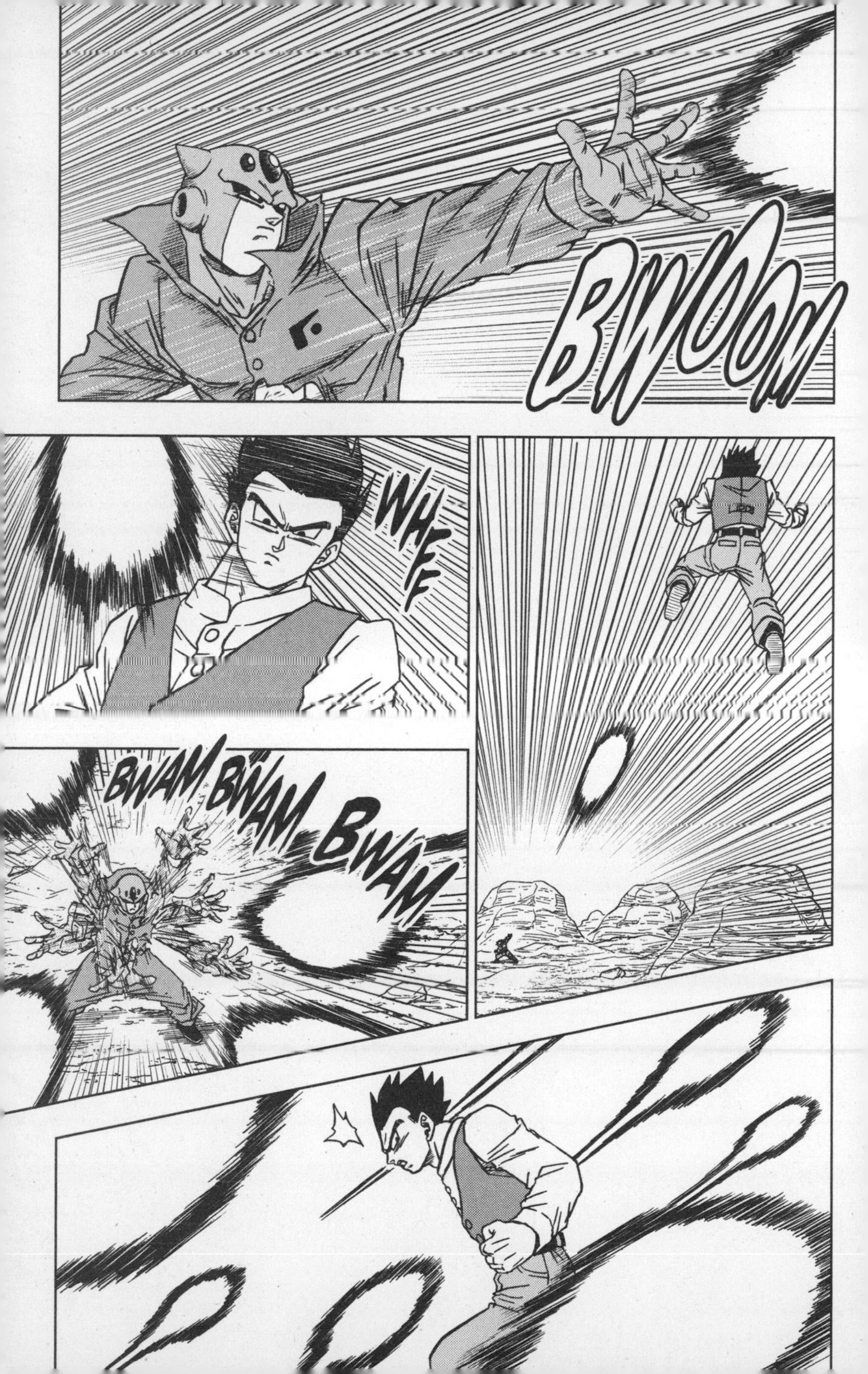
BWOOM
WHFF
BWAM BWAM BWAM

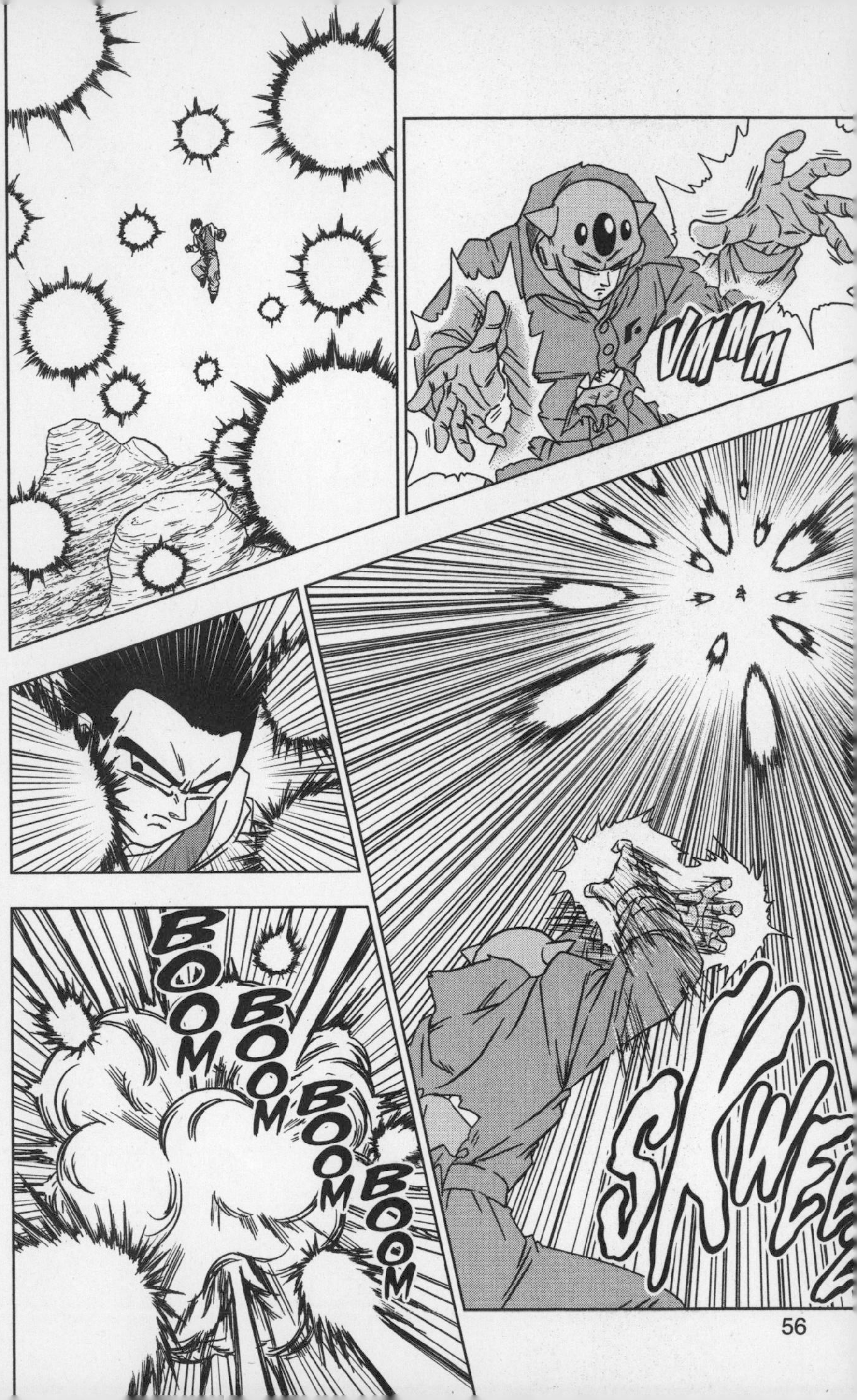
VMMMM
SHWE
BOOM
BOOM
BOOM
BOOM

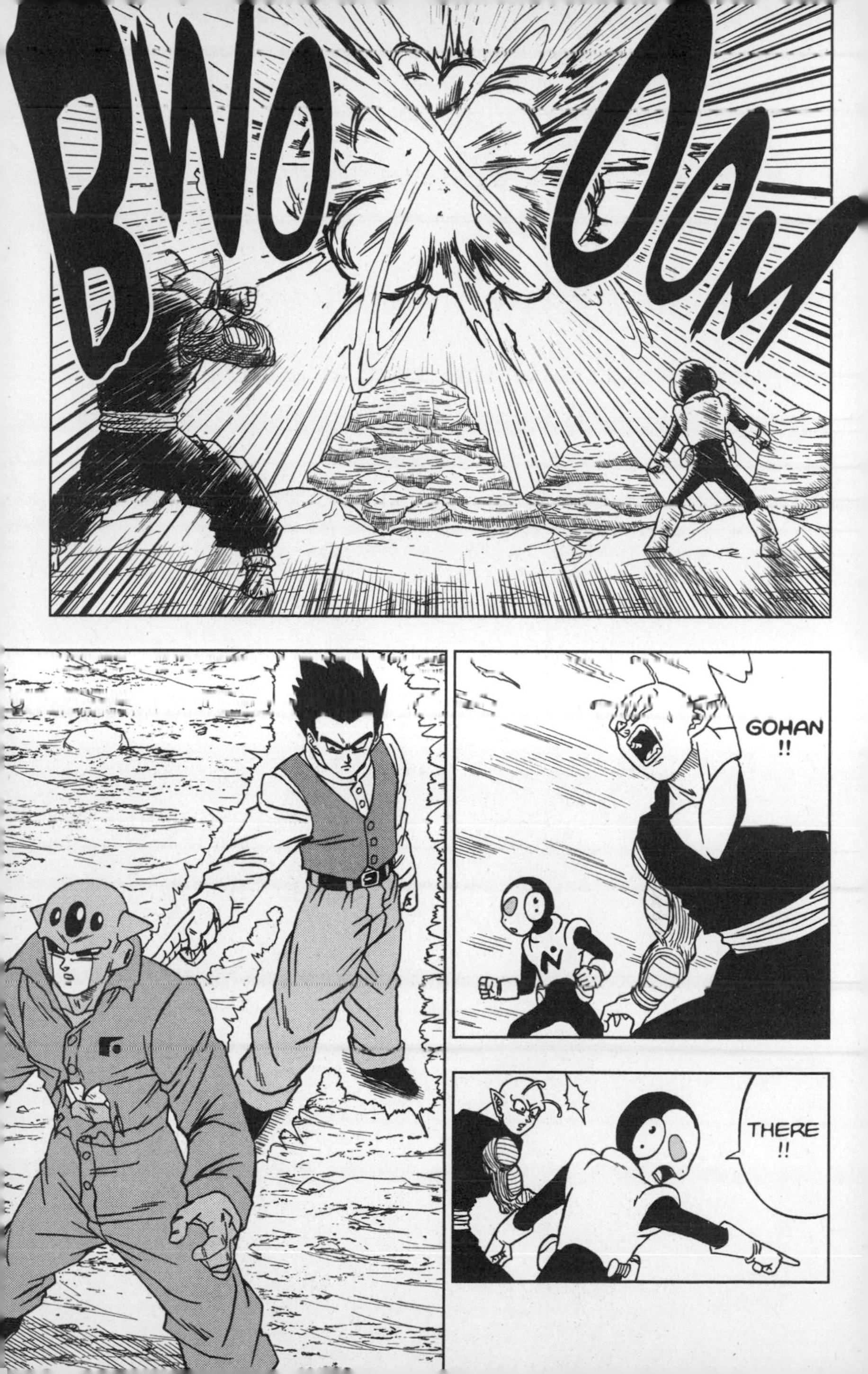
BWOOOM
GOHAN !!
THERE !!

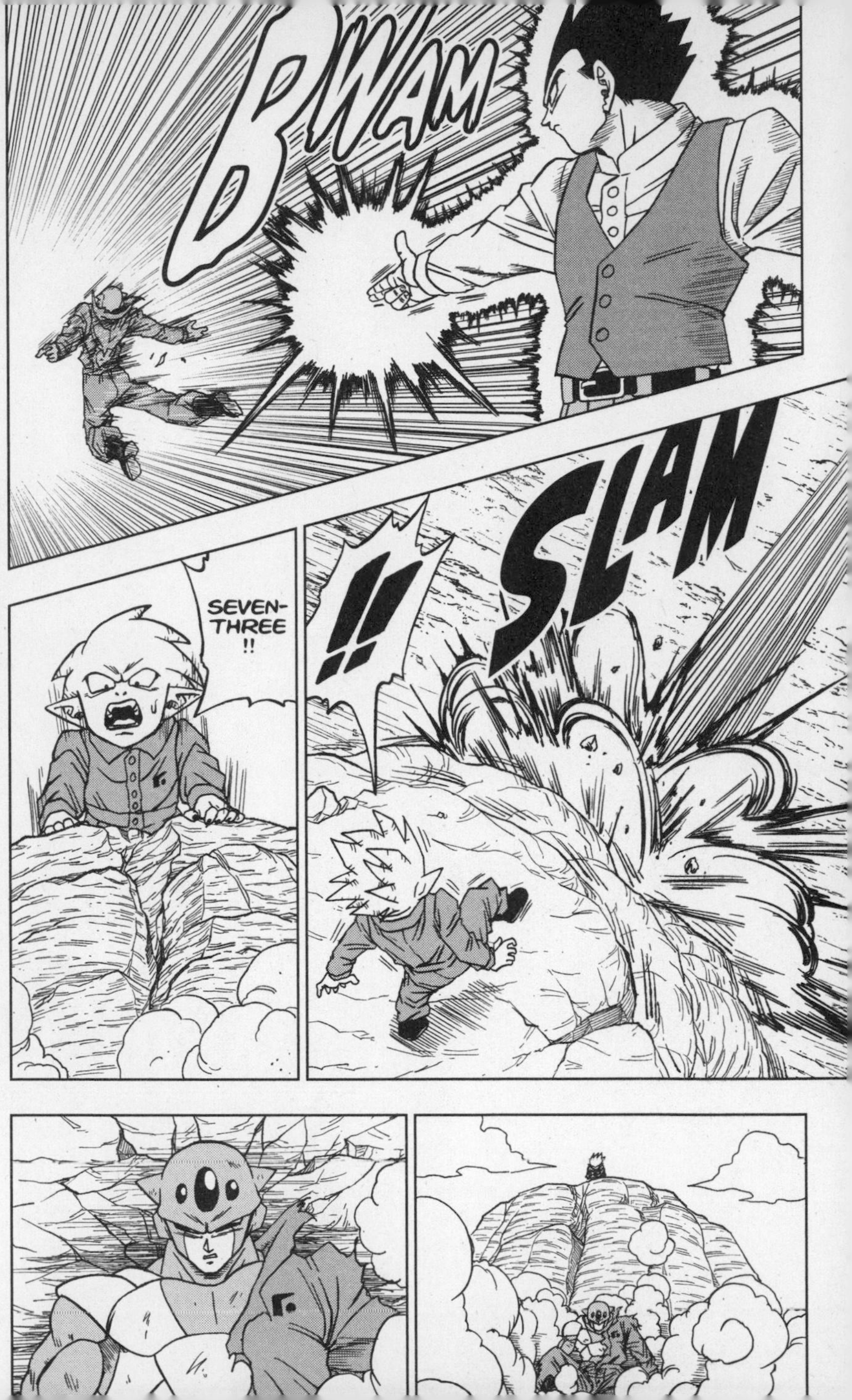
BWAM
SLAM
!!
SEVEN-THREE !!

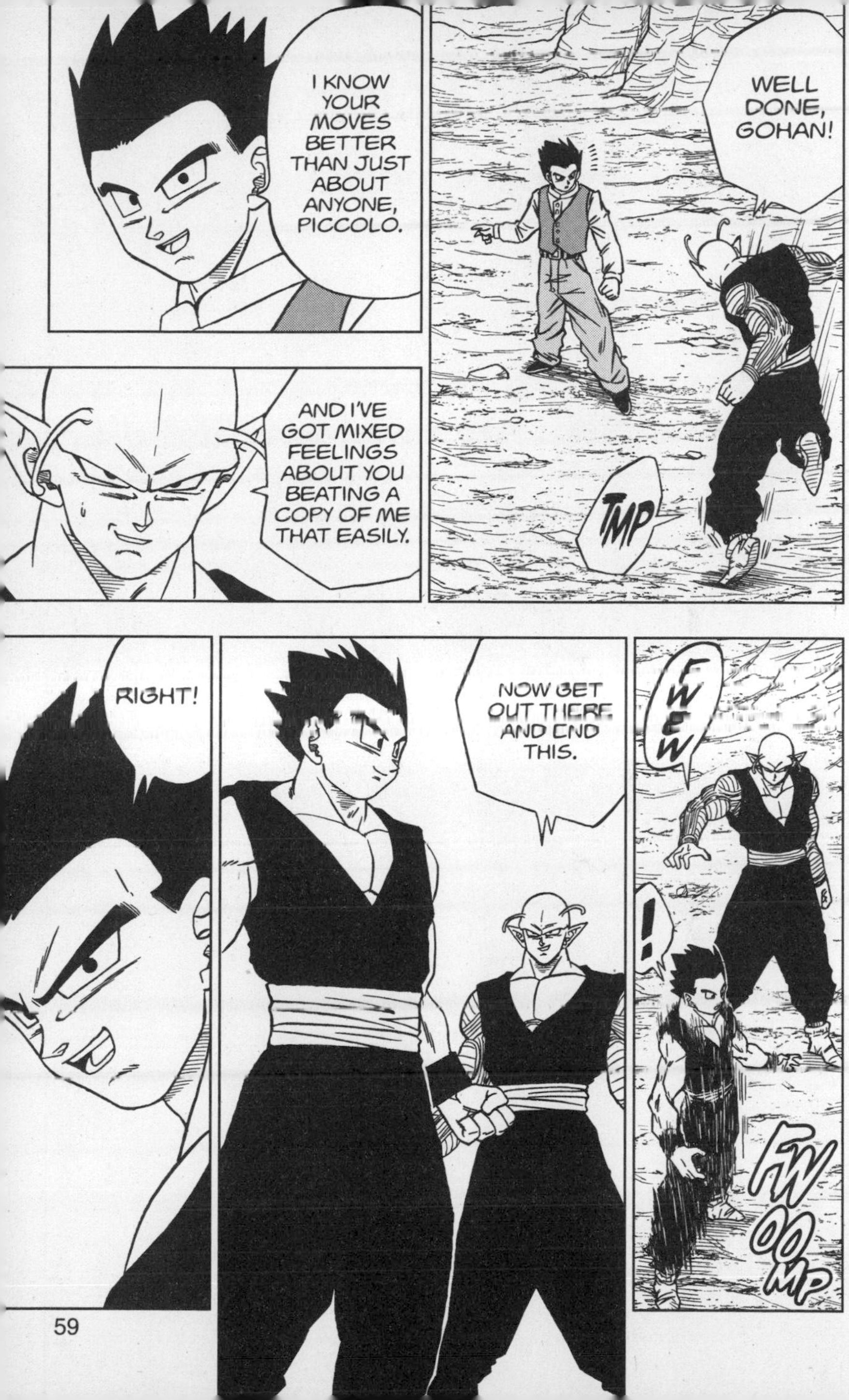
WELL DONE, GOHAN!
TMP
I KNOW YOUR MOVES BETTER THAN JUST ABOUT ANYONE, PICCOLO.
AND I'VE GOT MIXED FEELINGS ABOUT YOU BEATING A COPY OF ME THAT EASILY.
FWEW
!
FWOOMP
NOW GET OUT THERE AND END THIS.
RIGHT!

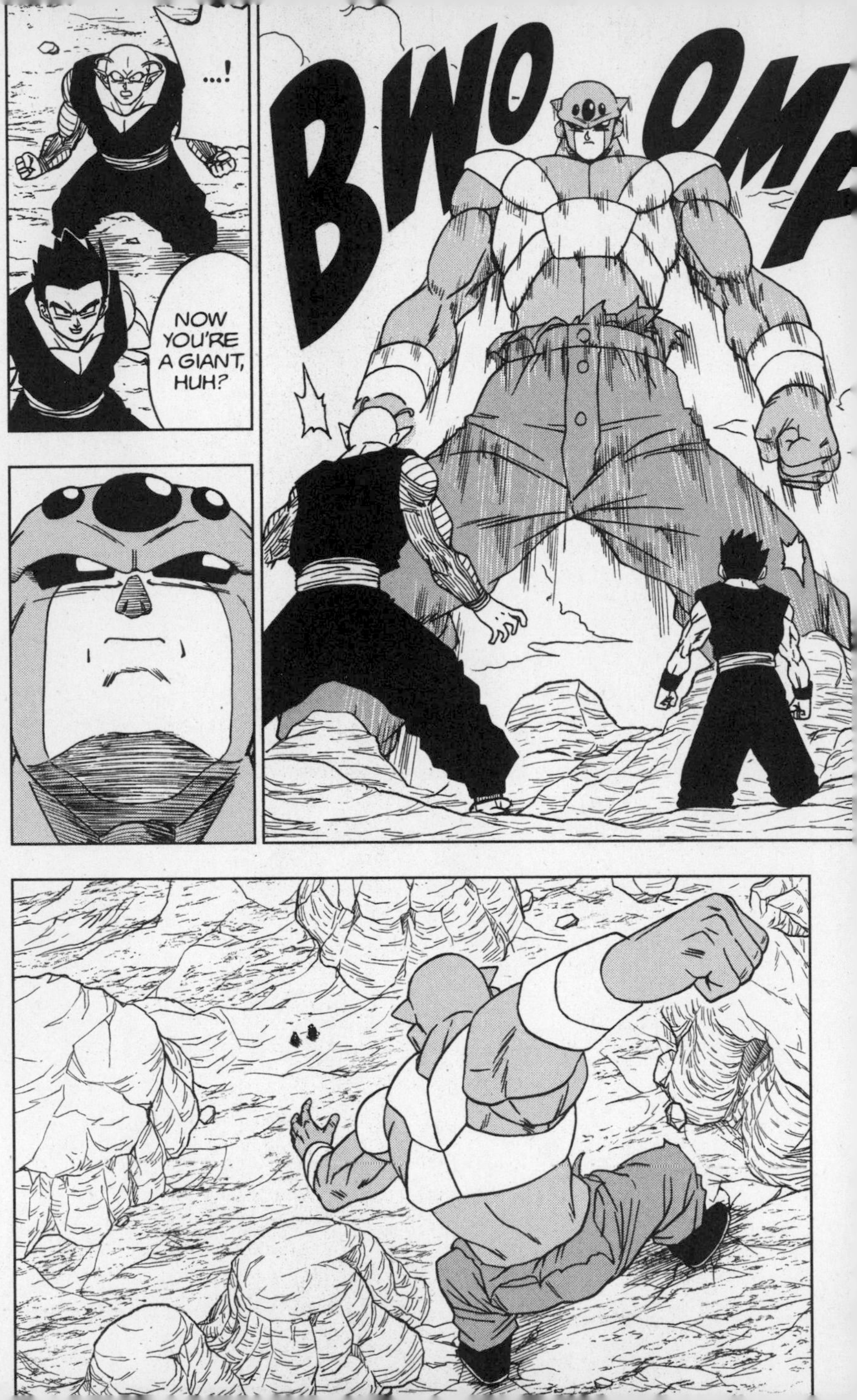
BWOOM
...!
NOW YOU'RE A GIANT, HUH?

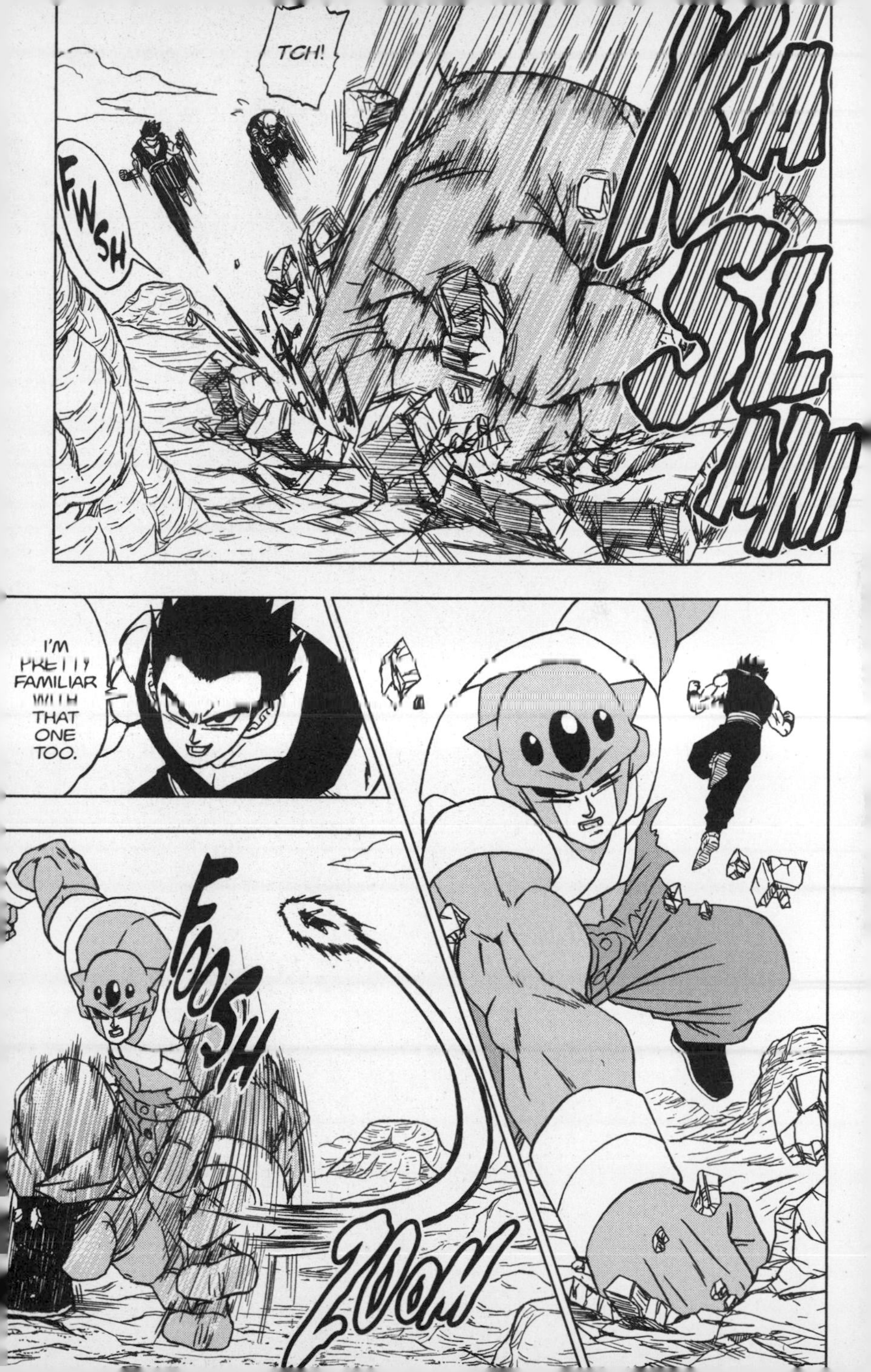
KA SLAM
TCH!
FWSH
ZOOM
I'M PRETTY FAMILIAR WITH THAT ONE TOO.
FOOSH

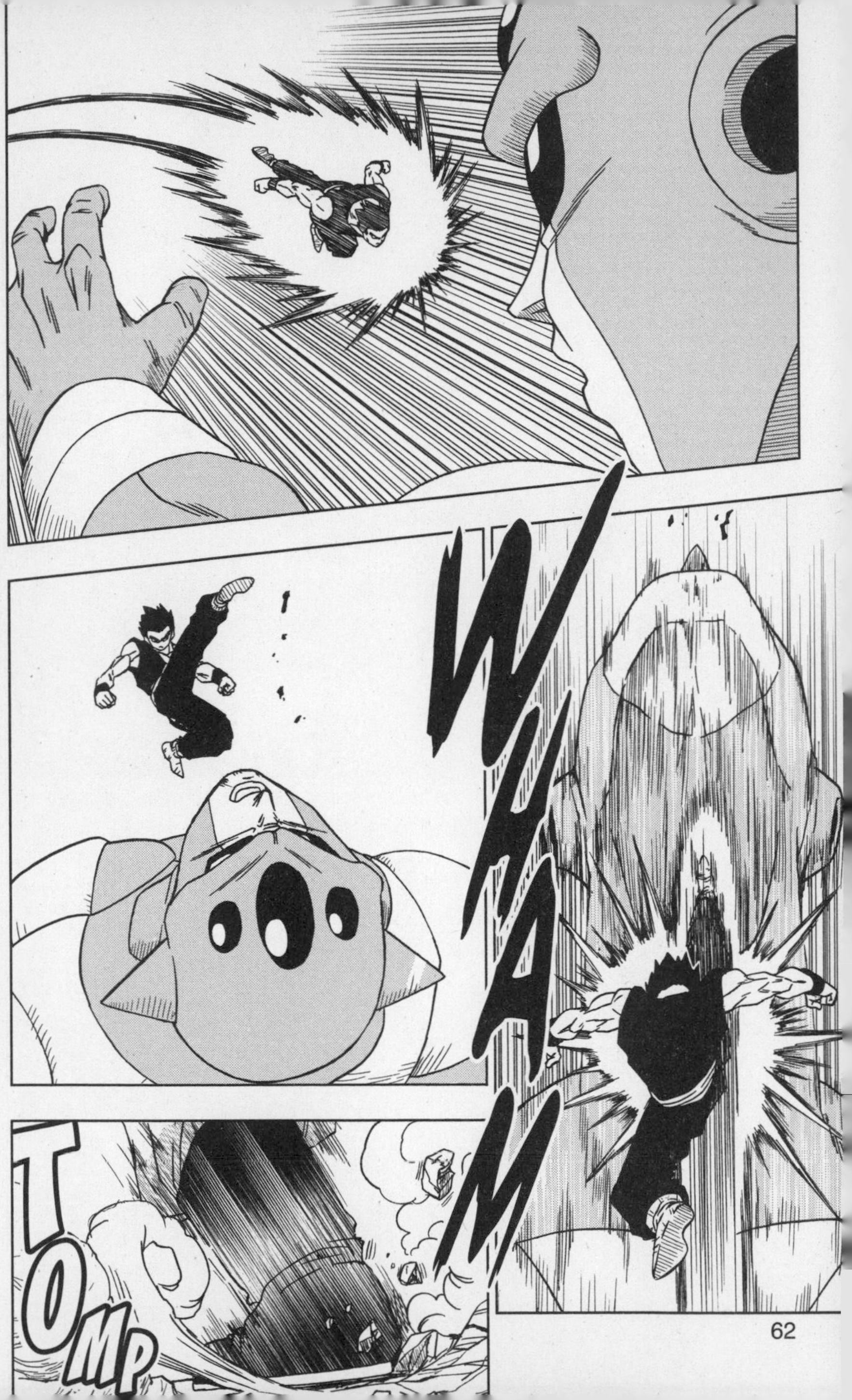
WHAM
TOMP

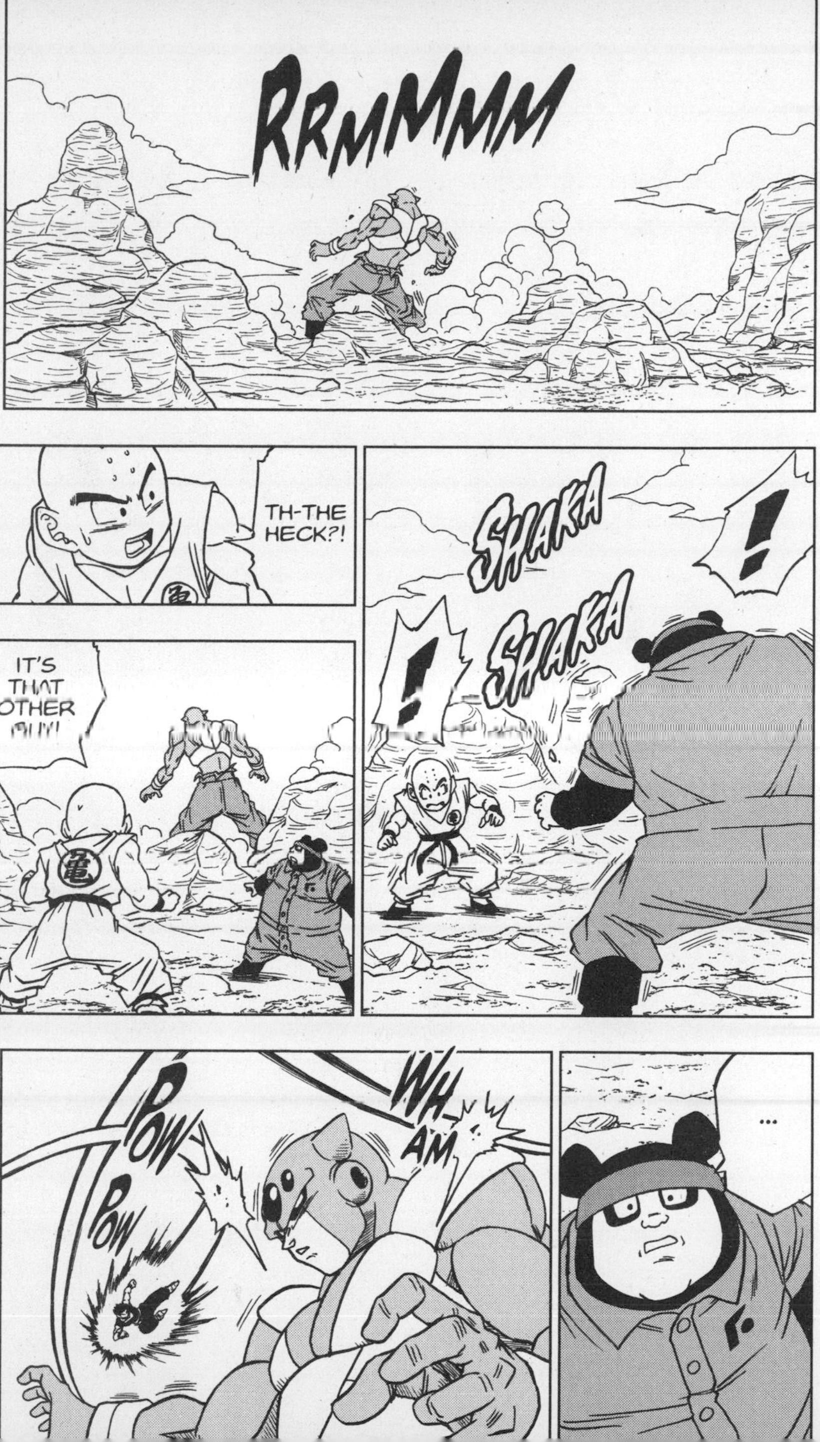
RRMMMM
SHAKA
SHAKA
!
!
TH-THE HECK?!
IT'S THAT OTHER GUY!
...
WH-AM
POW
POW

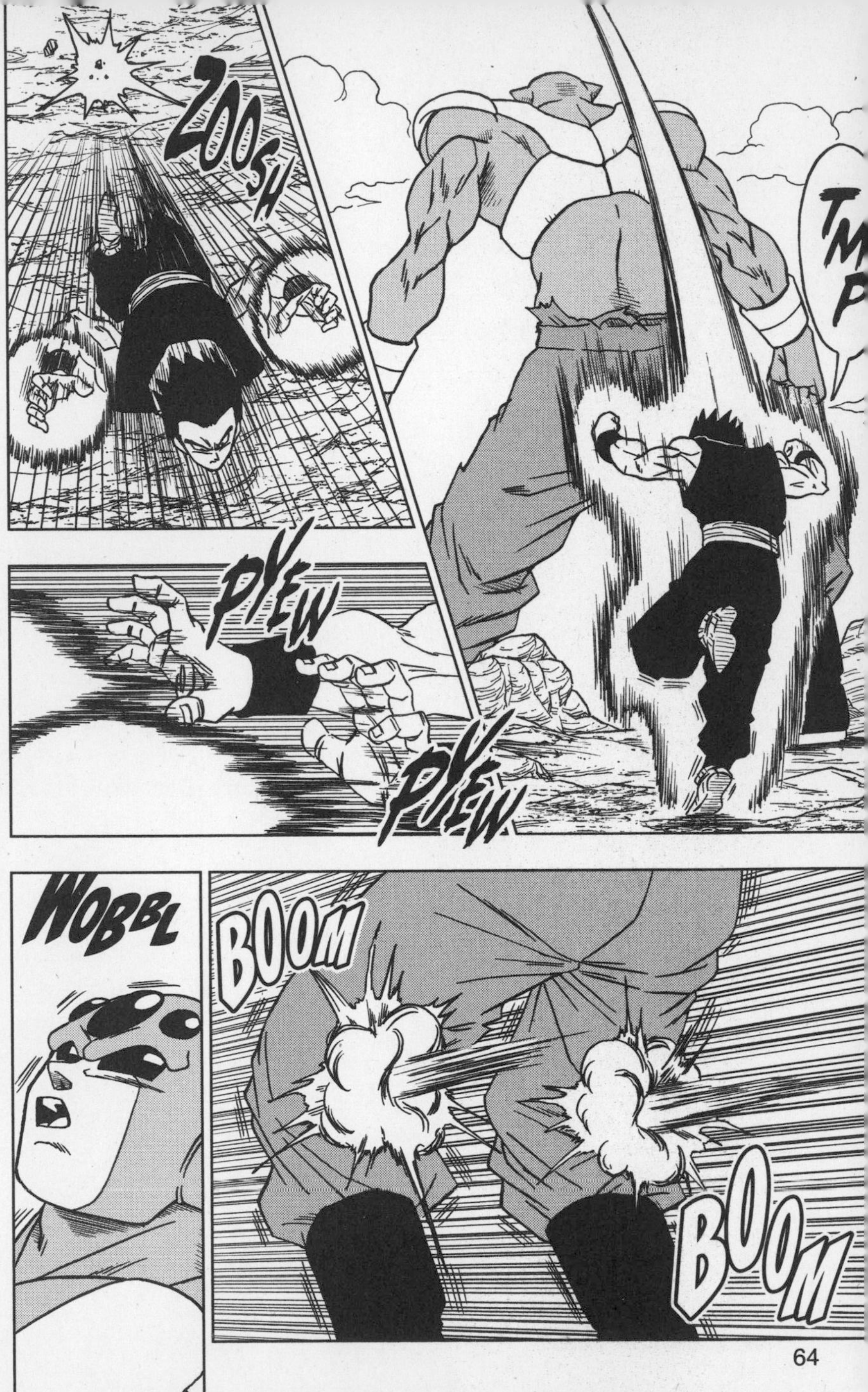
TMP
ZOOSH
PYEW
PYEW
BOOM
BOOM
WOBBL

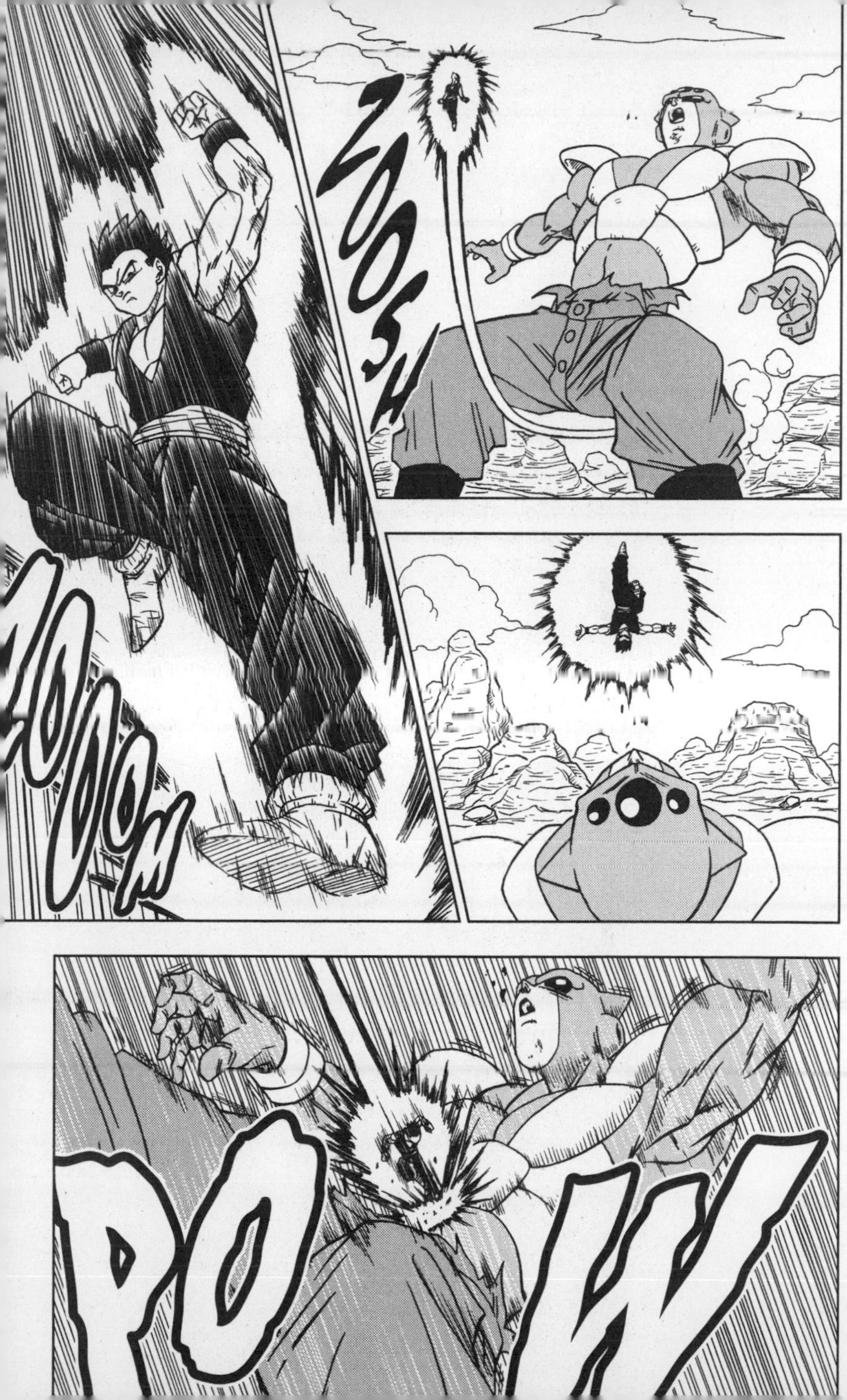
ZOOSH
OOOOM
POW

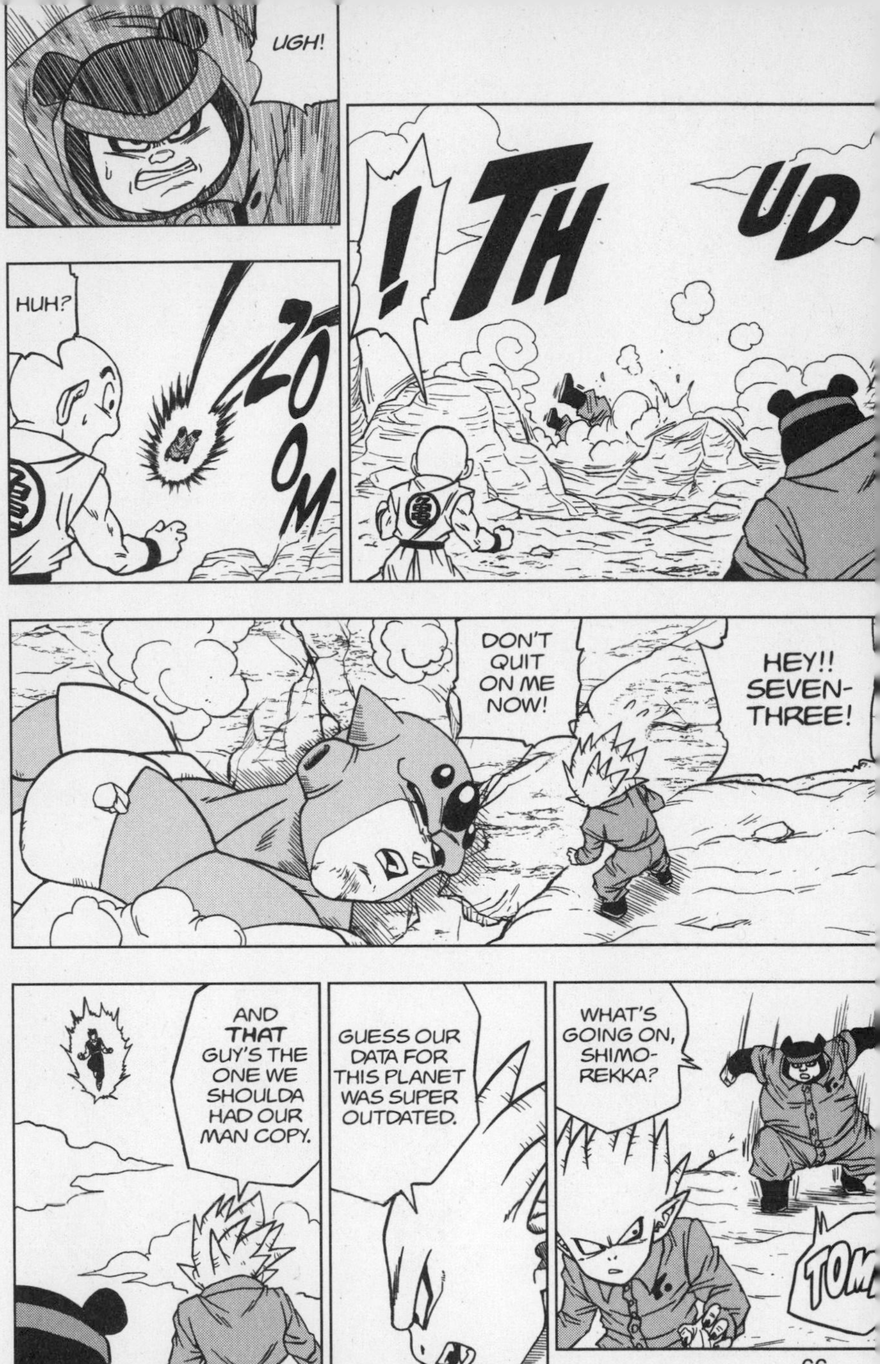

UGH!
HUH?
ZOOM
!
THUD
HEY!! SEVEN-THREE!
DON'T QUIT ON ME NOW!
TOM
WHAT'S GOING ON, SHIMO-REKKA?
GUESS OUR DATA FOR THIS PLANET WAS SUPER OUTDATED.
AND **THAT** GUY'S THE ONE WE SHOULDA HAD OUR MAN COPY.

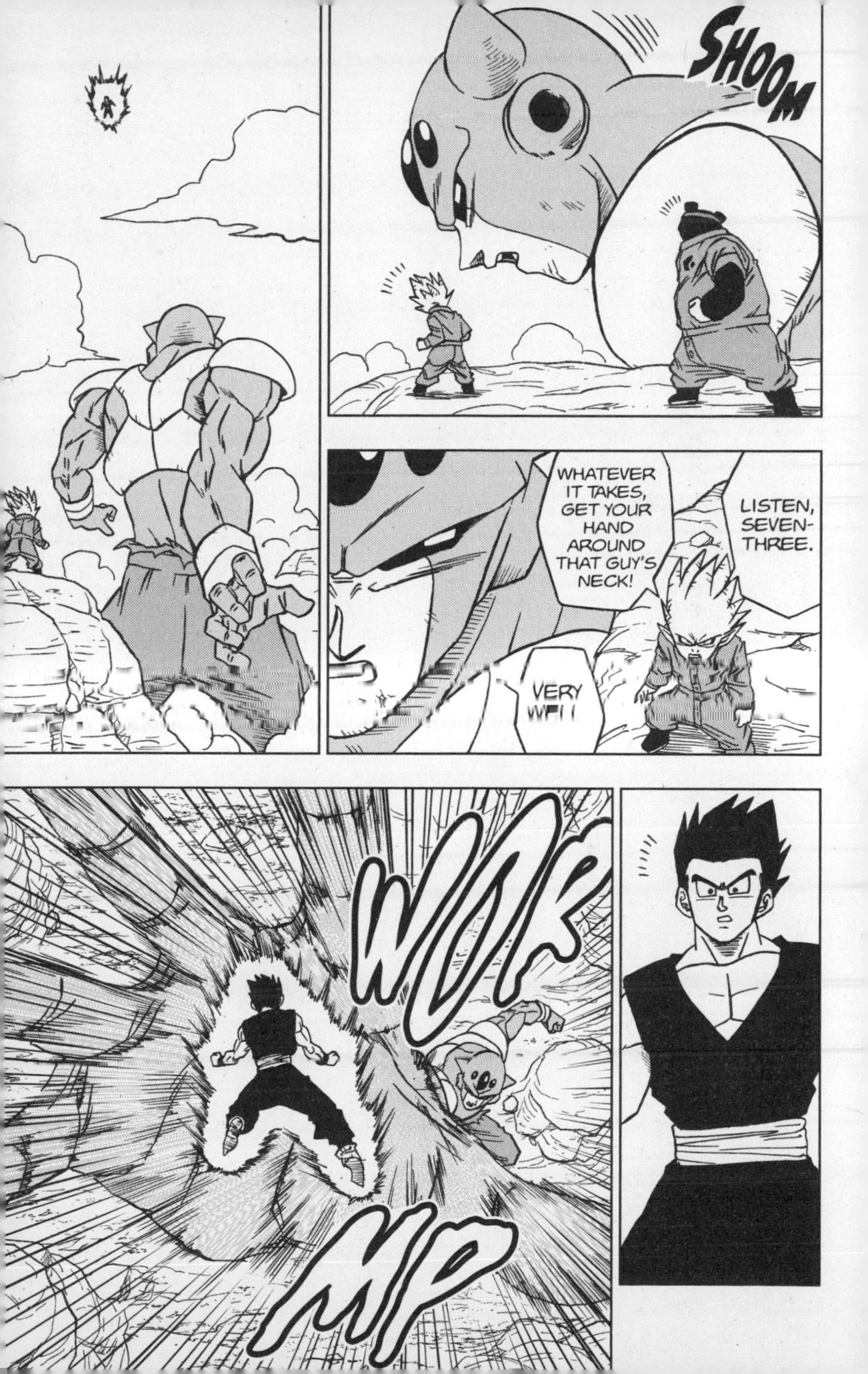
SHOOM
LISTEN, SEVEN-THREE.
WHATEVER IT TAKES, GET YOUR HAND AROUND THAT GUY'S NECK!
VERY WELL

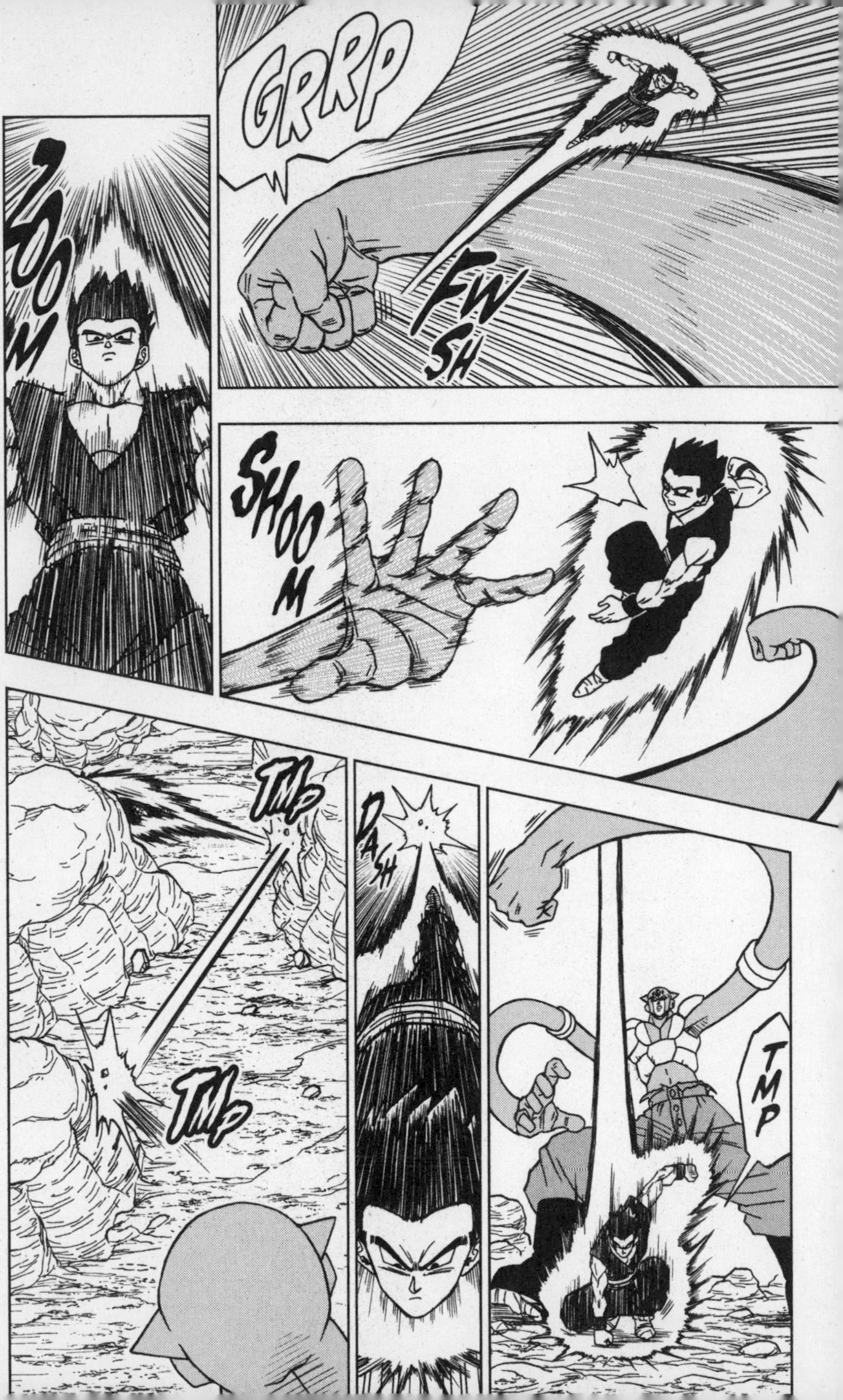
GRRP
FWSH
SHOOOM
ZOOOM
TMP
DASH
TMP
TMP

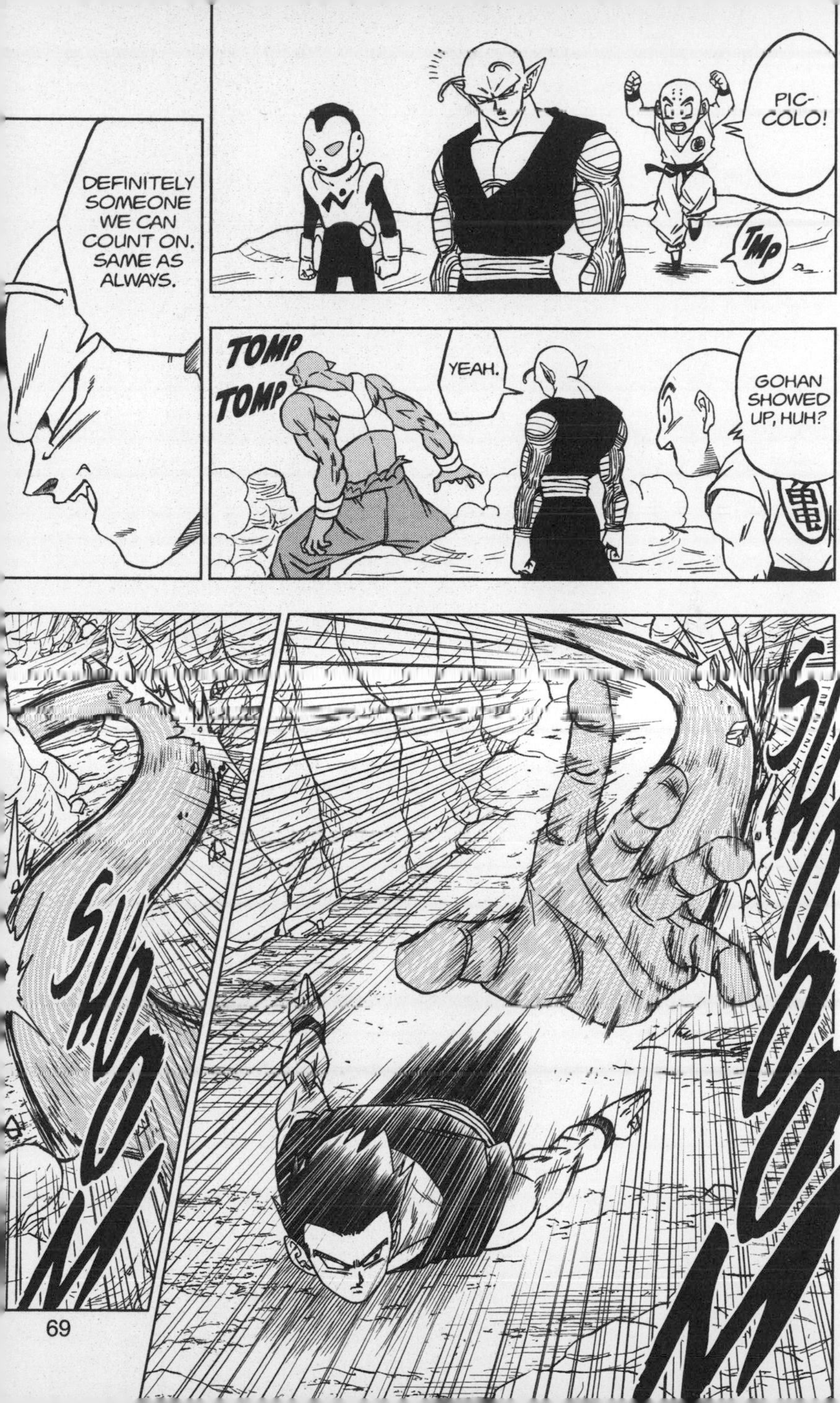
PIC-COLO!
TMP
GOHAN SHOWED UP, HUH?
YEAH.
TOMP TOMP
DEFINITELY SOMEONE WE CAN COUNT ON. SAME AS ALWAYS.
SHOOOM
SHOOM

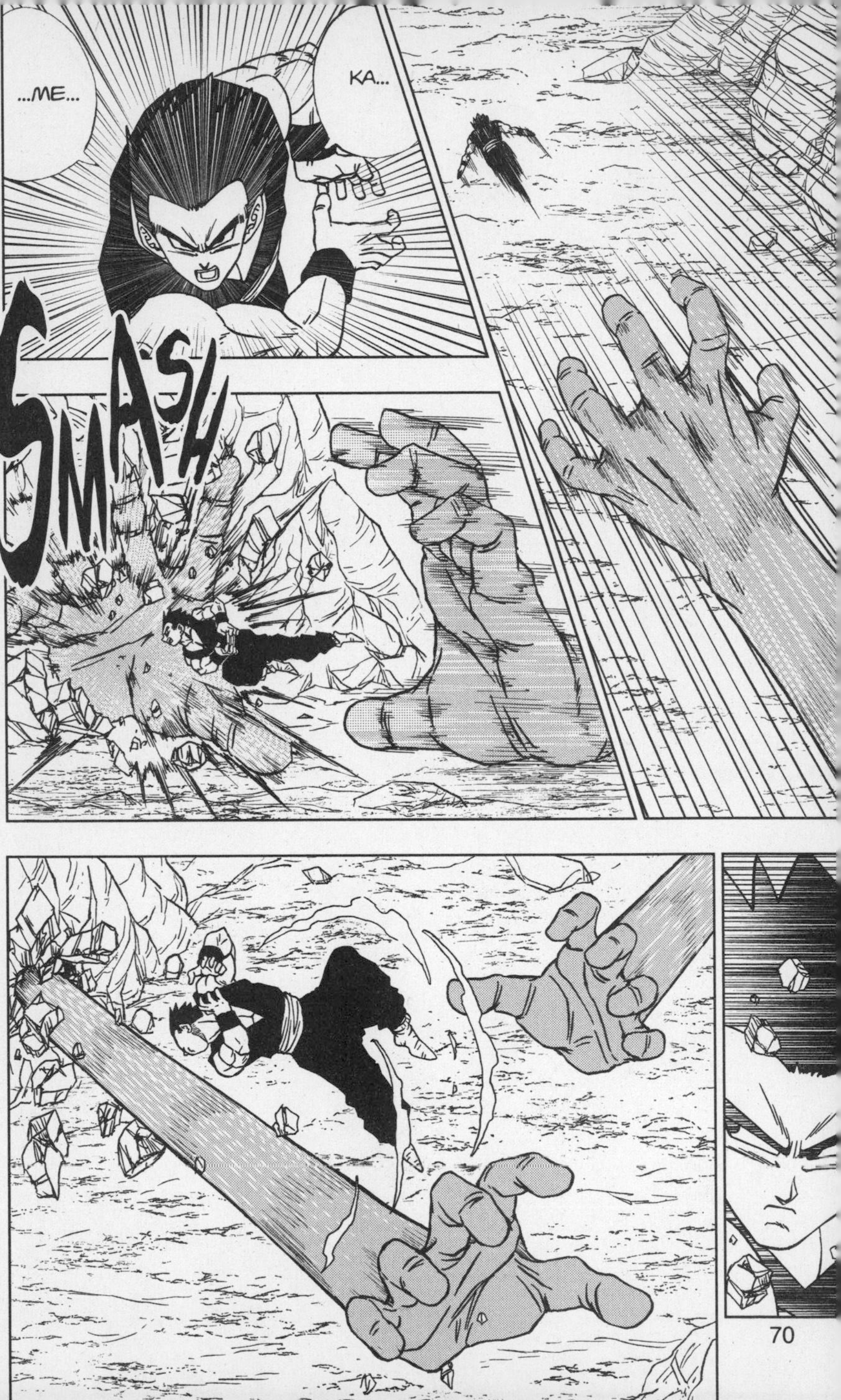
KA...
...ME...
SMASH

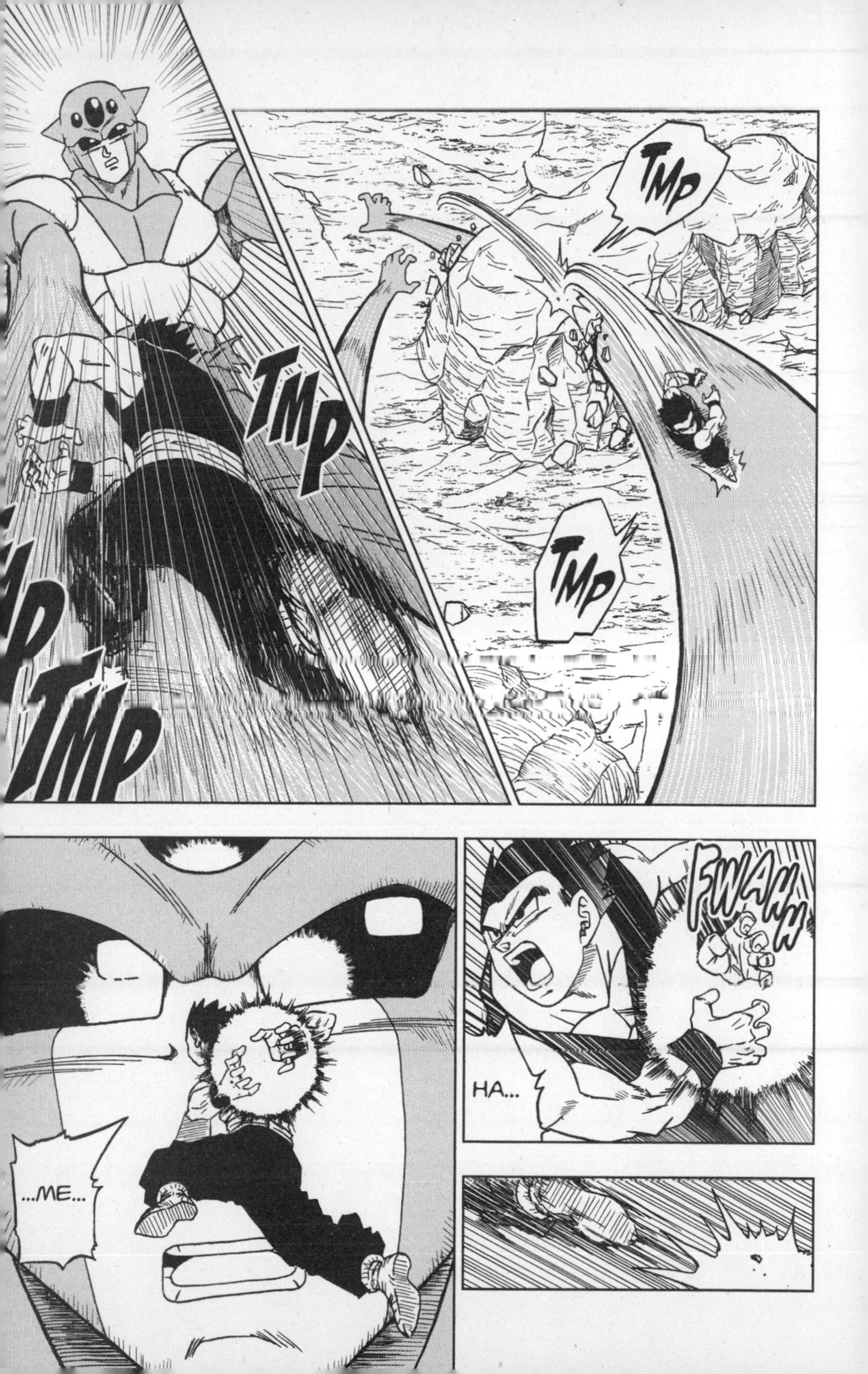

TMP
TMP
TMP
TMP
FWAHH
HA...
...ME...

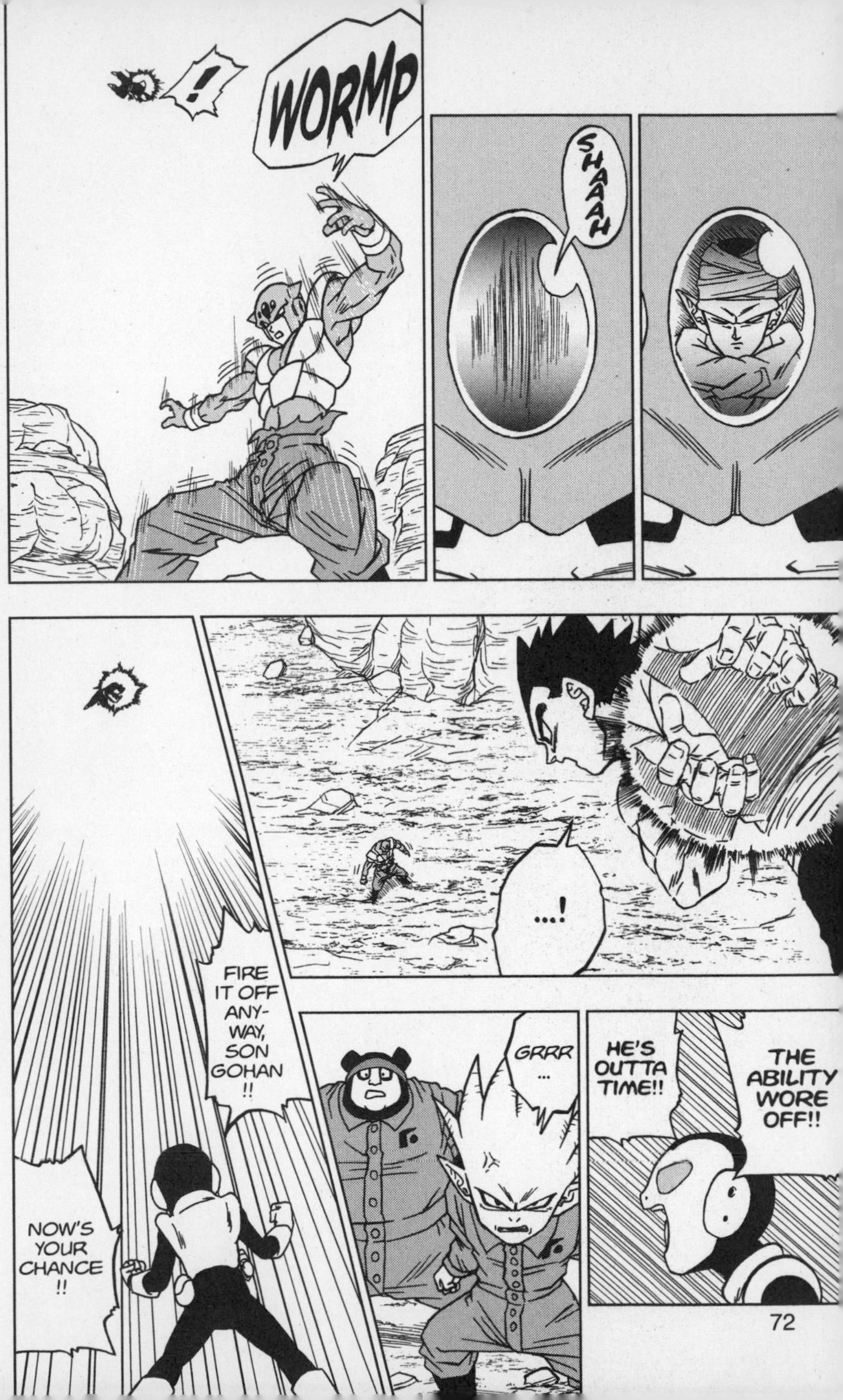
SHAAAH
WORMP
!
...!
THE ABILITY WORE OFF!!
HE'S OUTTA TIME!!
GRRR ...
FIRE IT OFF ANYWAY, SON GOHAN!!
NOW'S YOUR CHANCE!!

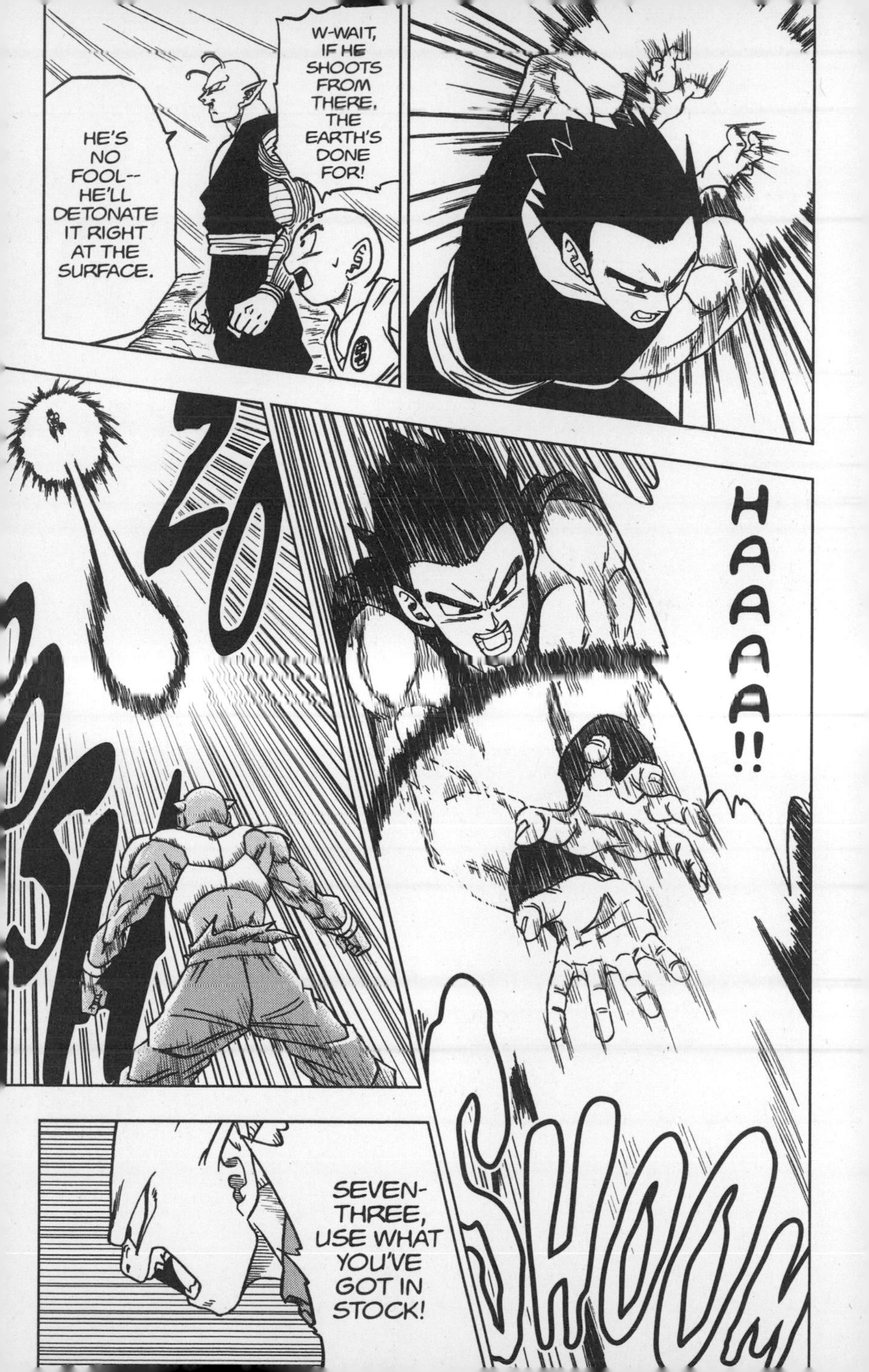

W-WAIT, IF HE SHOOTS FROM THERE, THE EARTH'S DONE FOR!
HE'S NO FOOL-- HE'LL DETONATE IT RIGHT AT THE SURFACE.
HAAAAA!!
SEVEN-THREE, USE WHAT YOU'VE GOT IN STOCK!

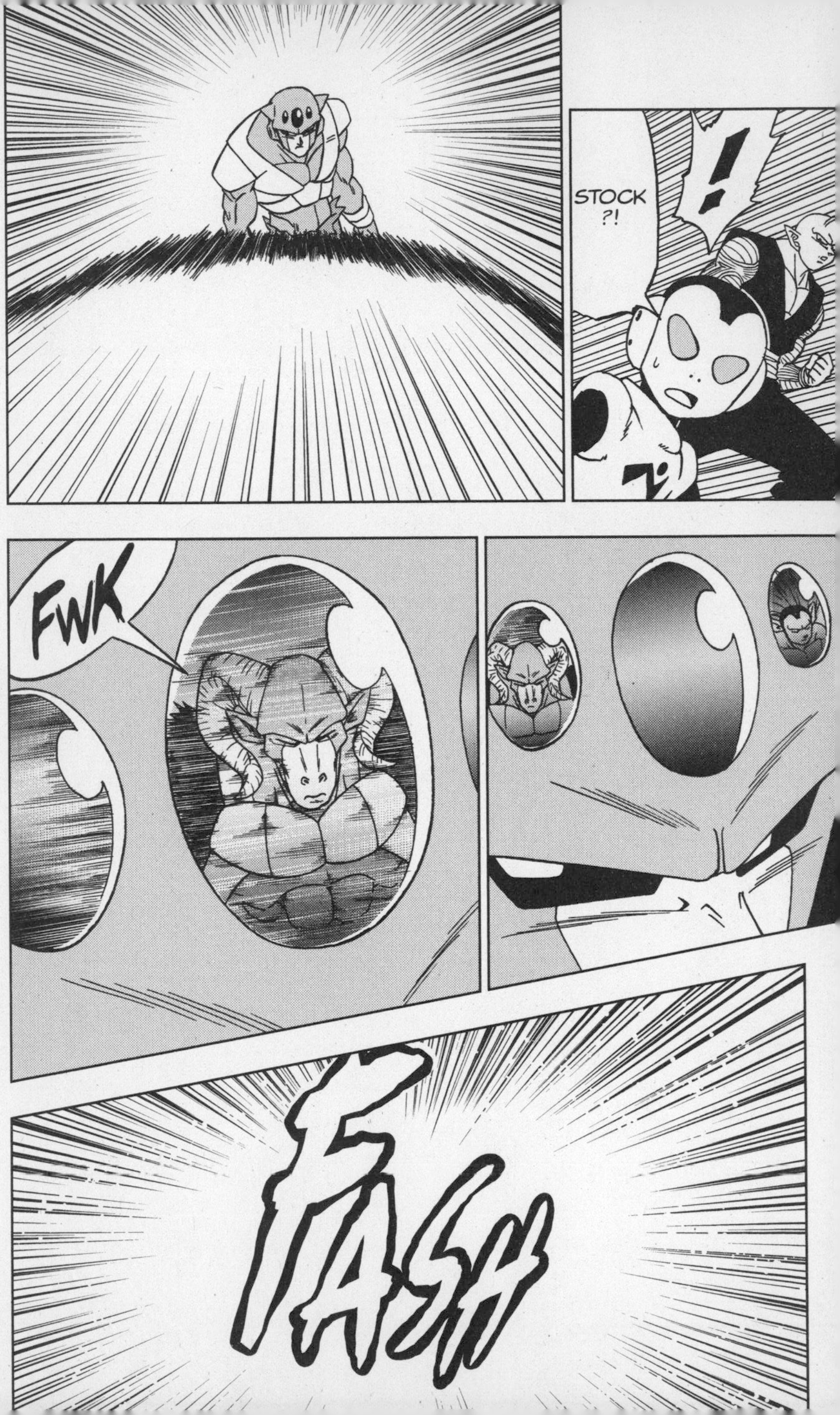
STOCK ?!
!
FWK
FASH

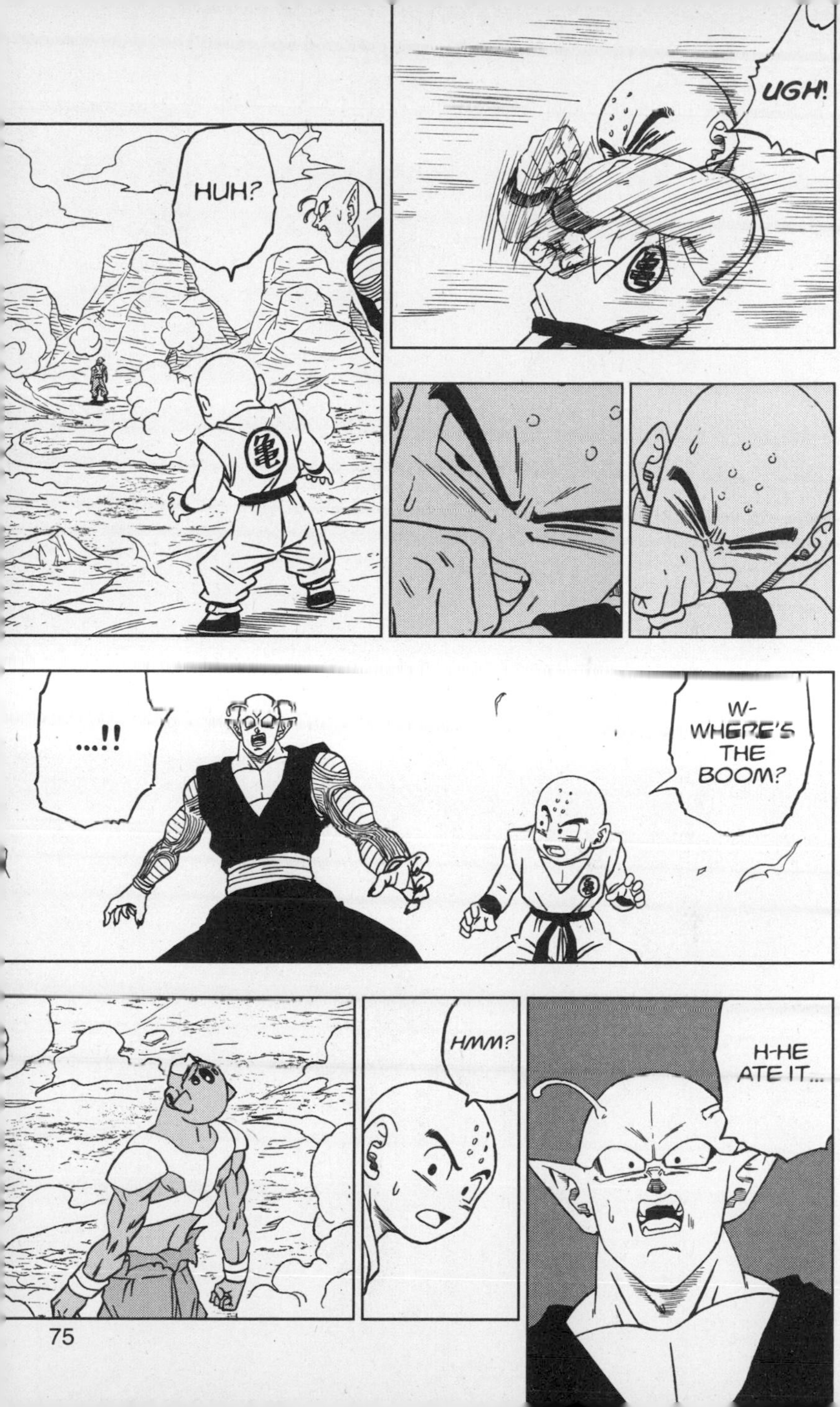
UGH!
HUH?
W-WHERE'S THE BOOM?
...!!
H-HE ATE IT...
HMM?

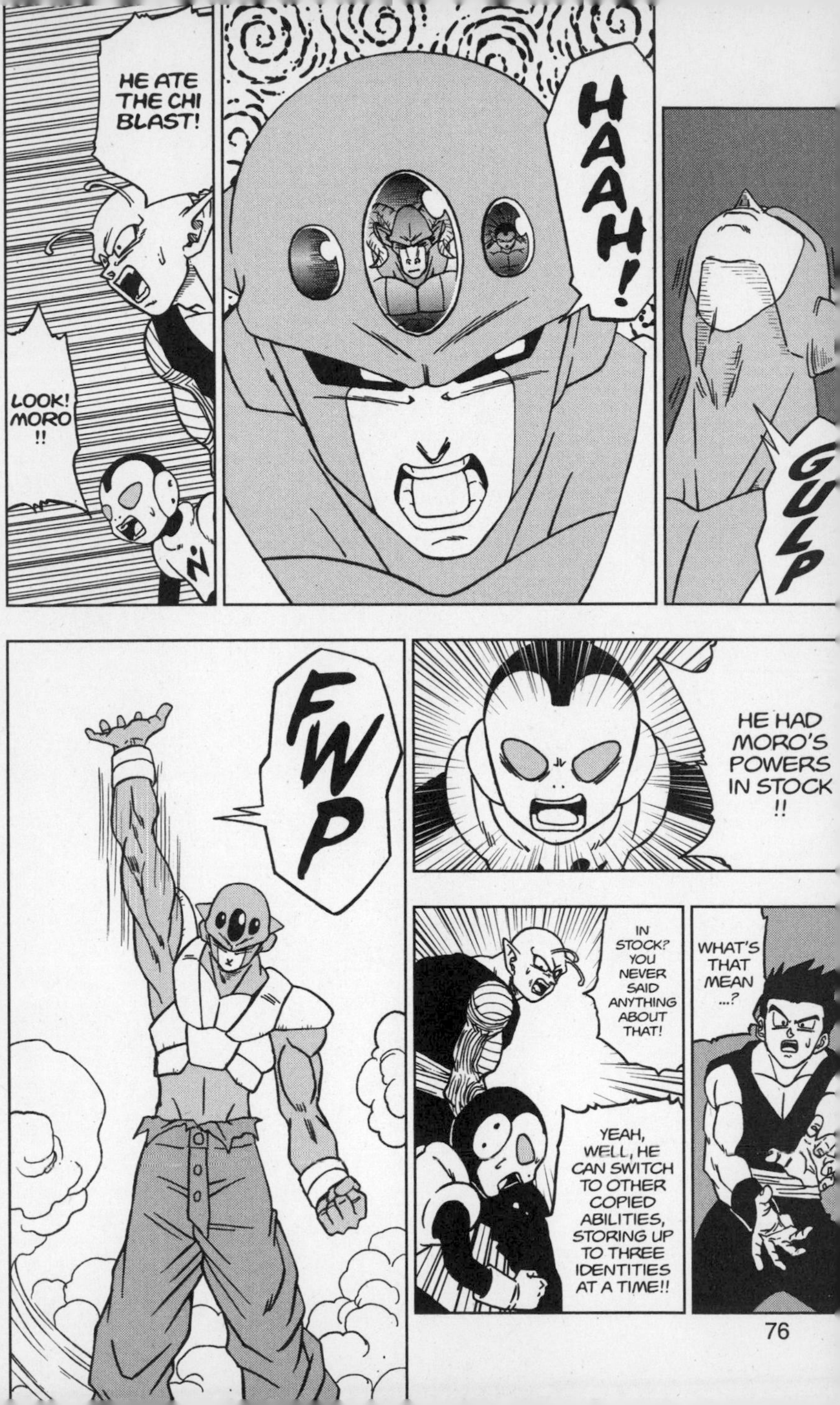
GULP
HAAAH!
HE ATE THE CHI BLAST!
LOOK! MORO !!
HE HAD MORO'S POWERS IN STOCK !!
WHAT'S THAT MEAN ...?
IN STOCK? YOU NEVER SAID ANYTHING ABOUT THAT!
YEAH, WELL, HE CAN SWITCH TO OTHER COPIED ABILITIES, STORING UP TO THREE IDENTITIES AT A TIME!!
FWP

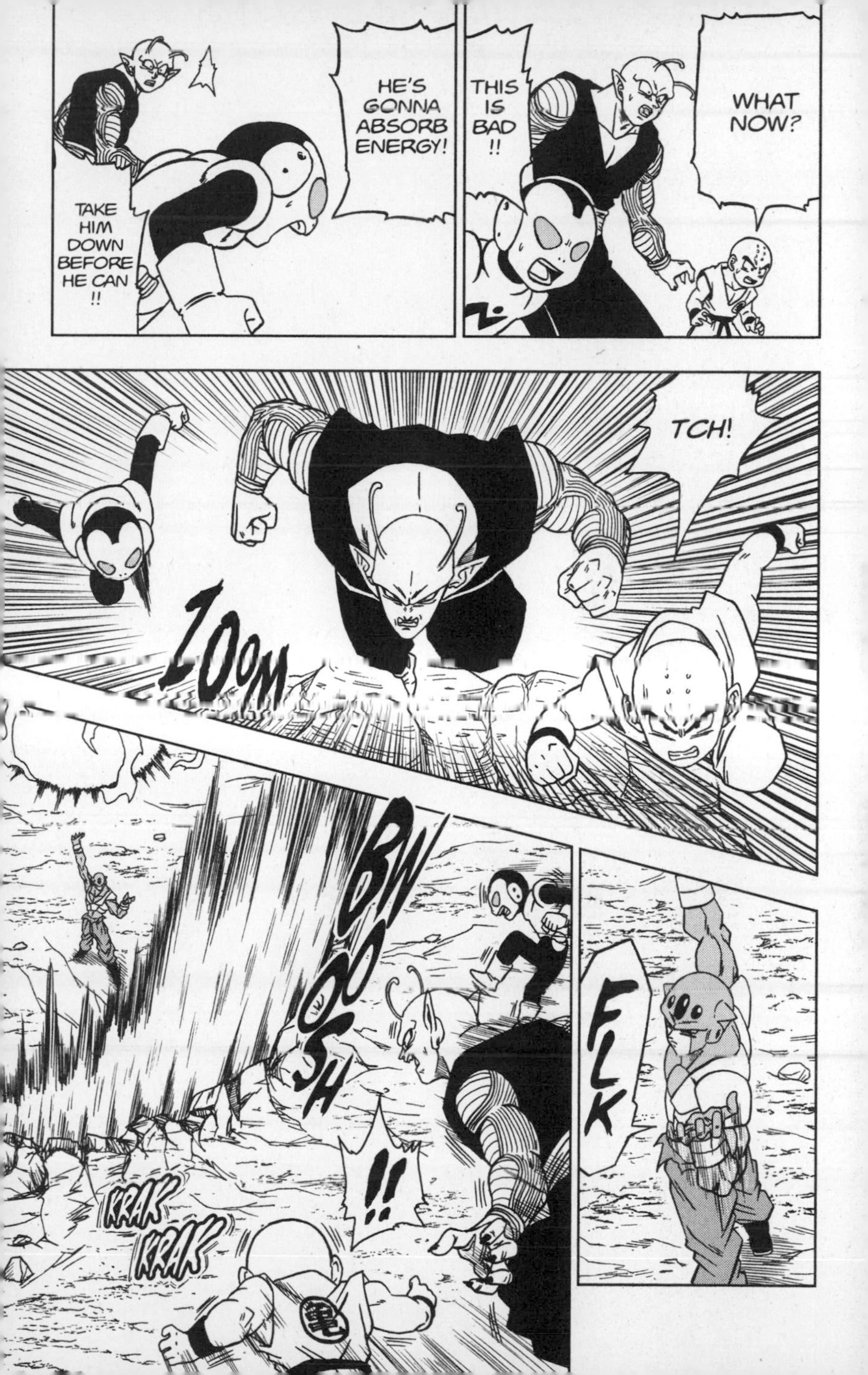
WHAT NOW?
THIS IS BAD !!
HE'S GONNA ABSORB ENERGY!
TAKE HIM DOWN BEFORE HE CAN !!
TCH!
ZOOM
FLK
BWOOOSH
!!
KRAK KRAK

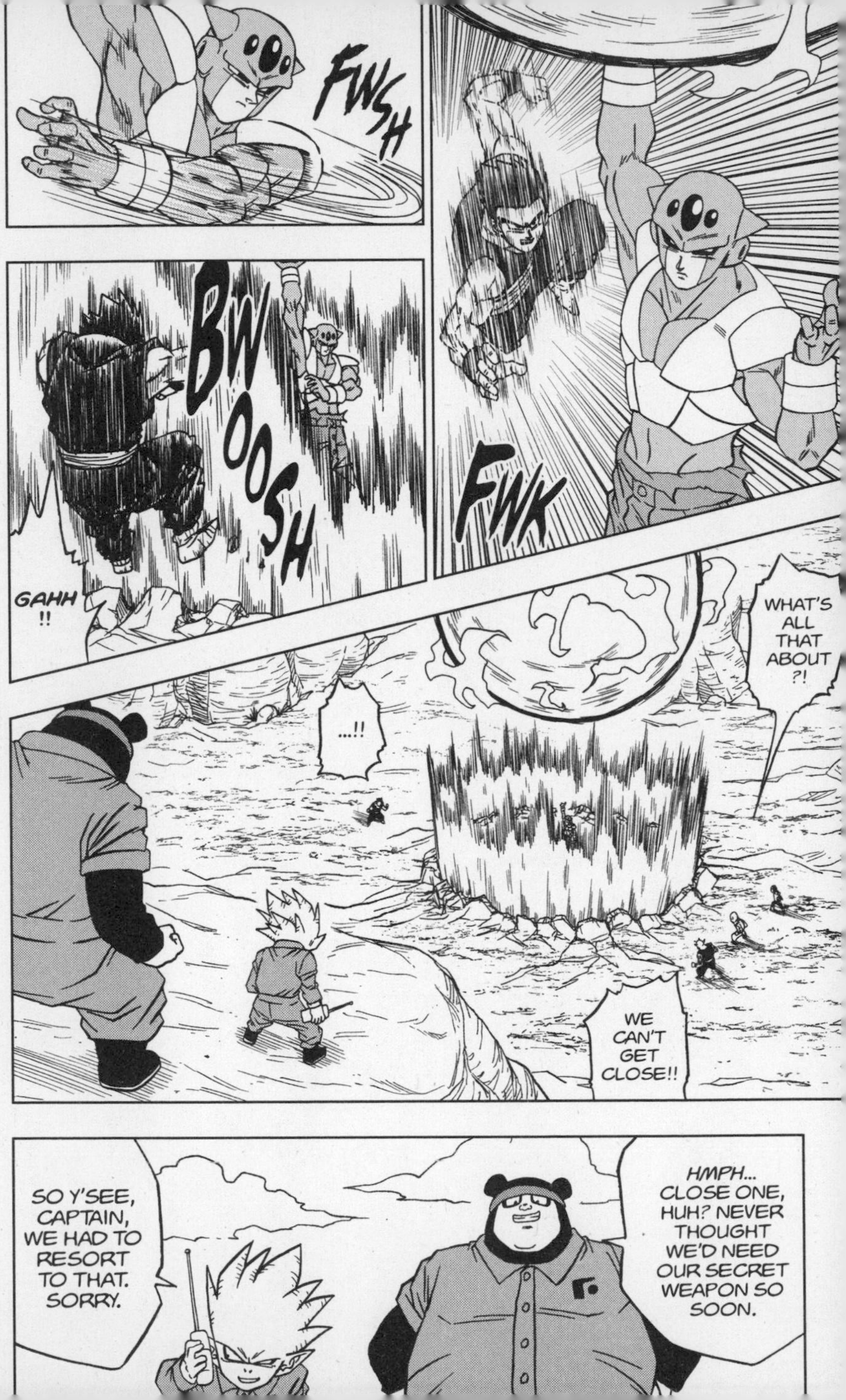
FWK
FWSH
BWOOSH
GAHH!!
WHAT'S ALL THAT ABOUT?!
...!!
WE CAN'T GET CLOSE!!
HMPH... CLOSE ONE, HUH? NEVER THOUGHT WE'D NEED OUR SECRET WEAPON SO SOON.
SO Y'SEE, CAPTAIN, WE HAD TO RESORT TO THAT. SORRY.

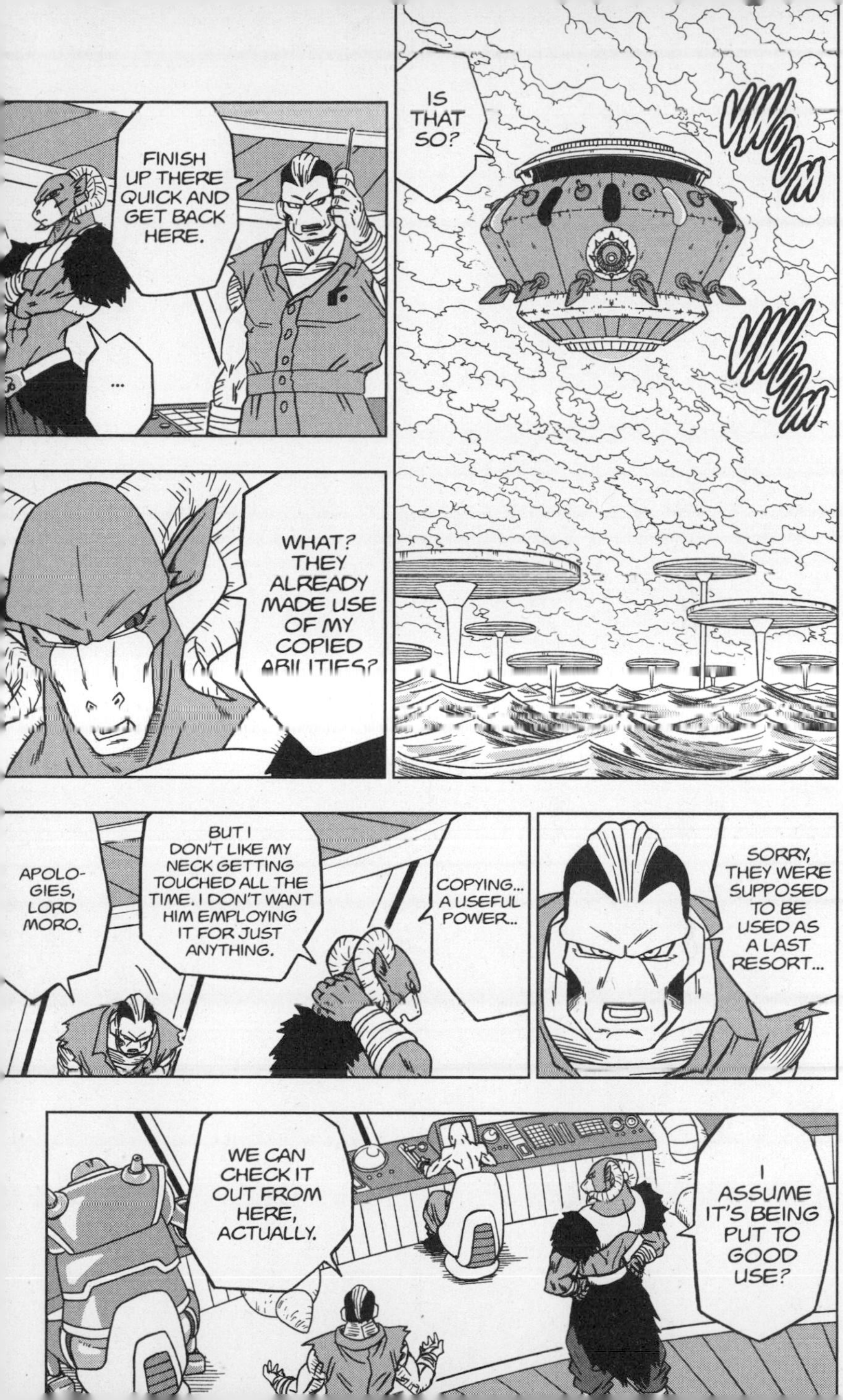
IS THAT SO?
VWOOM
VWOOM
FINISH UP THERE QUICK AND GET BACK HERE.
...
WHAT? THEY ALREADY MADE USE OF MY COPIED ABILITIES?
SORRY, THEY WERE SUPPOSED TO BE USED AS A LAST RESORT...
COPYING... A USEFUL POWER..
BUT I DON'T LIKE MY NECK GETTING TOUCHED ALL THE TIME. I DON'T WANT HIM EMPLOYING IT FOR JUST ANYTHING.
APOLOGIES, LORD MORO.
I ASSUME IT'S BEING PUT TO GOOD USE?
WE CAN CHECK IT OUT FROM HERE, ACTUALLY.

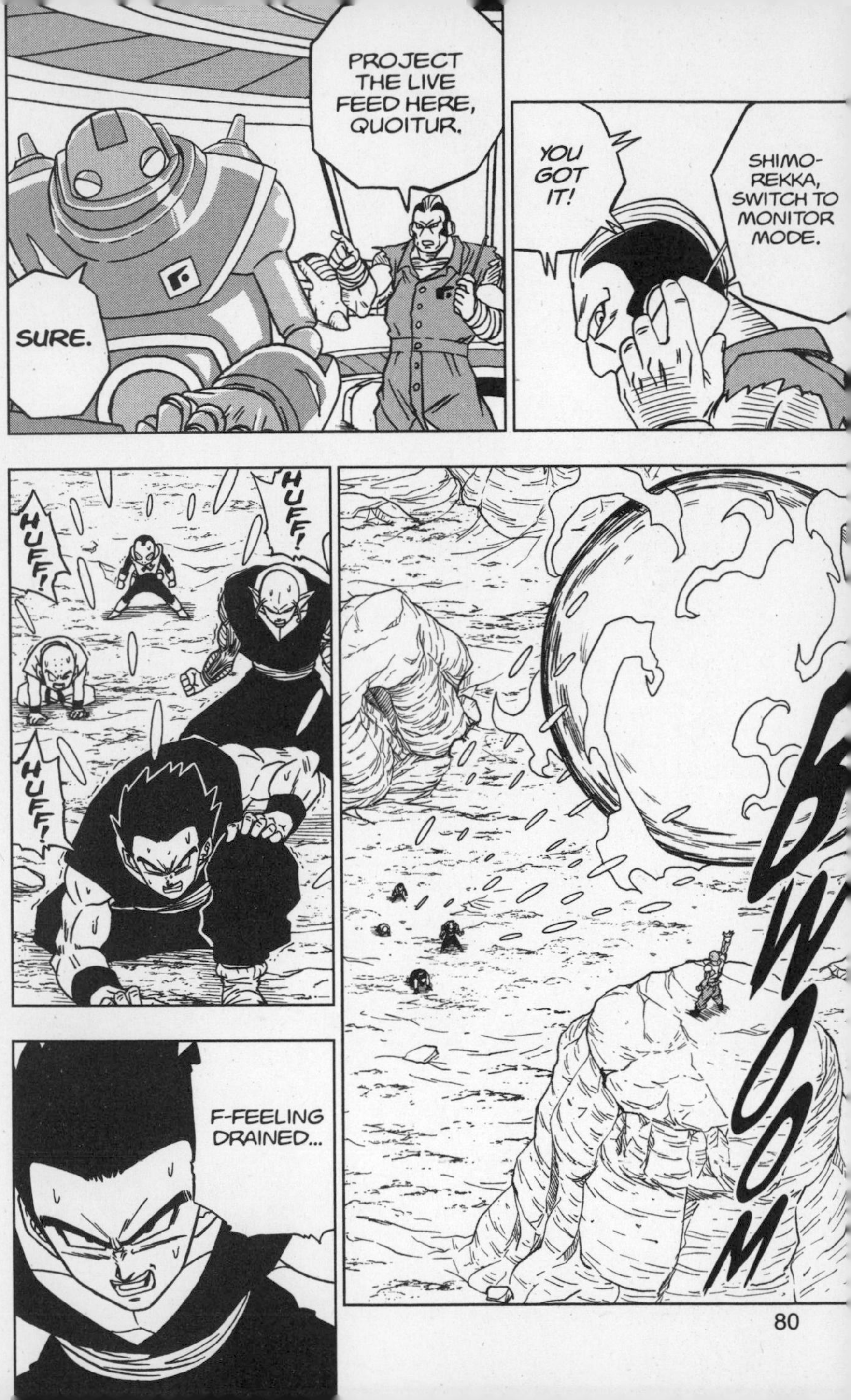
SHIMO-REKKA, SWITCH TO MONITOR MODE.
YOU GOT IT!
PROJECT THE LIVE FEED HERE, QUOITUR.
SURE.
HUFF!
HUFF!
HUFF!
F-FEELING DRAINED...

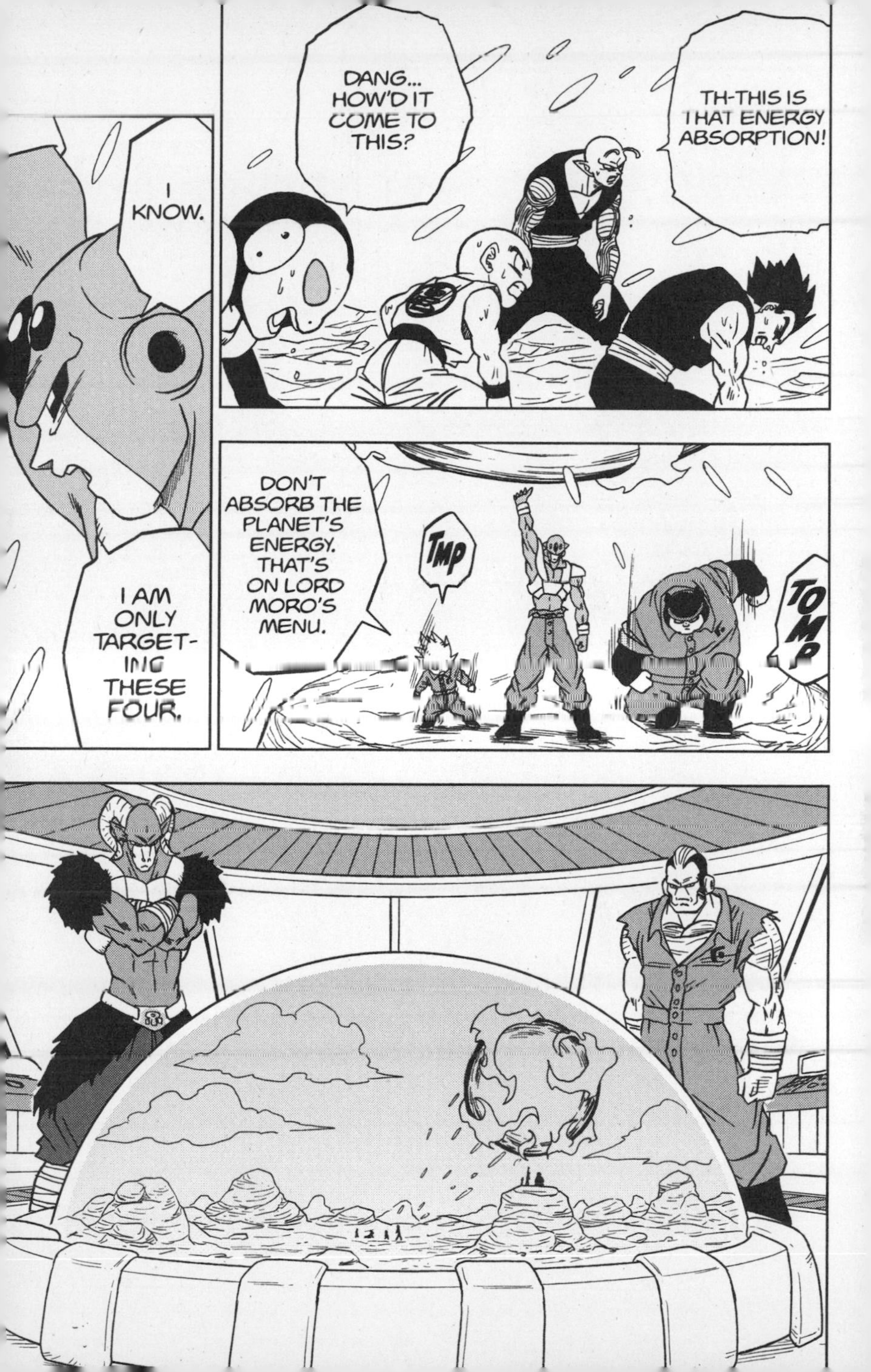
TH-THIS IS THAT ENERGY ABSORPTION!
DANG... HOW'D IT COME TO THIS?
TOMP
TMP
DON'T ABSORB THE PLANET'S ENERGY. THAT'S ON LORD MORO'S MENU.
I KNOW.
I AM ONLY TARGET-ING THESE FOUR.

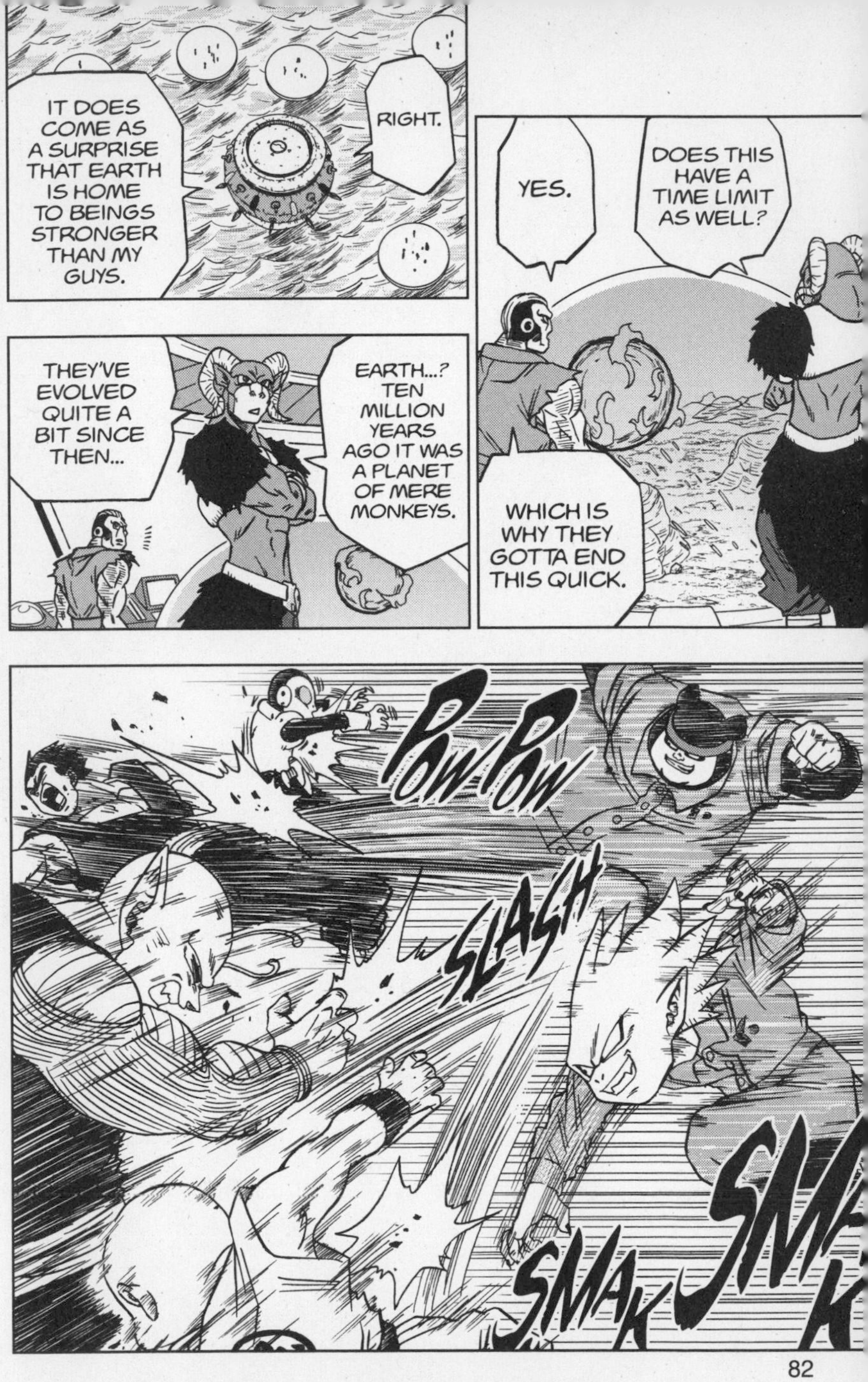

DOES THIS HAVE A TIME LIMIT AS WELL?
YES.
WHICH IS WHY THEY GOTTA END THIS QUICK.
RIGHT.
IT DOES COME AS A SURPRISE THAT EARTH IS HOME TO BEINGS STRONGER THAN MY GUYS.
EARTH...? TEN MILLION YEARS AGO IT WAS A PLANET OF MERE MONKEYS.
THEY'VE EVOLVED QUITE A BIT SINCE THEN...
POW POW
SLASH
SMA
SMAK

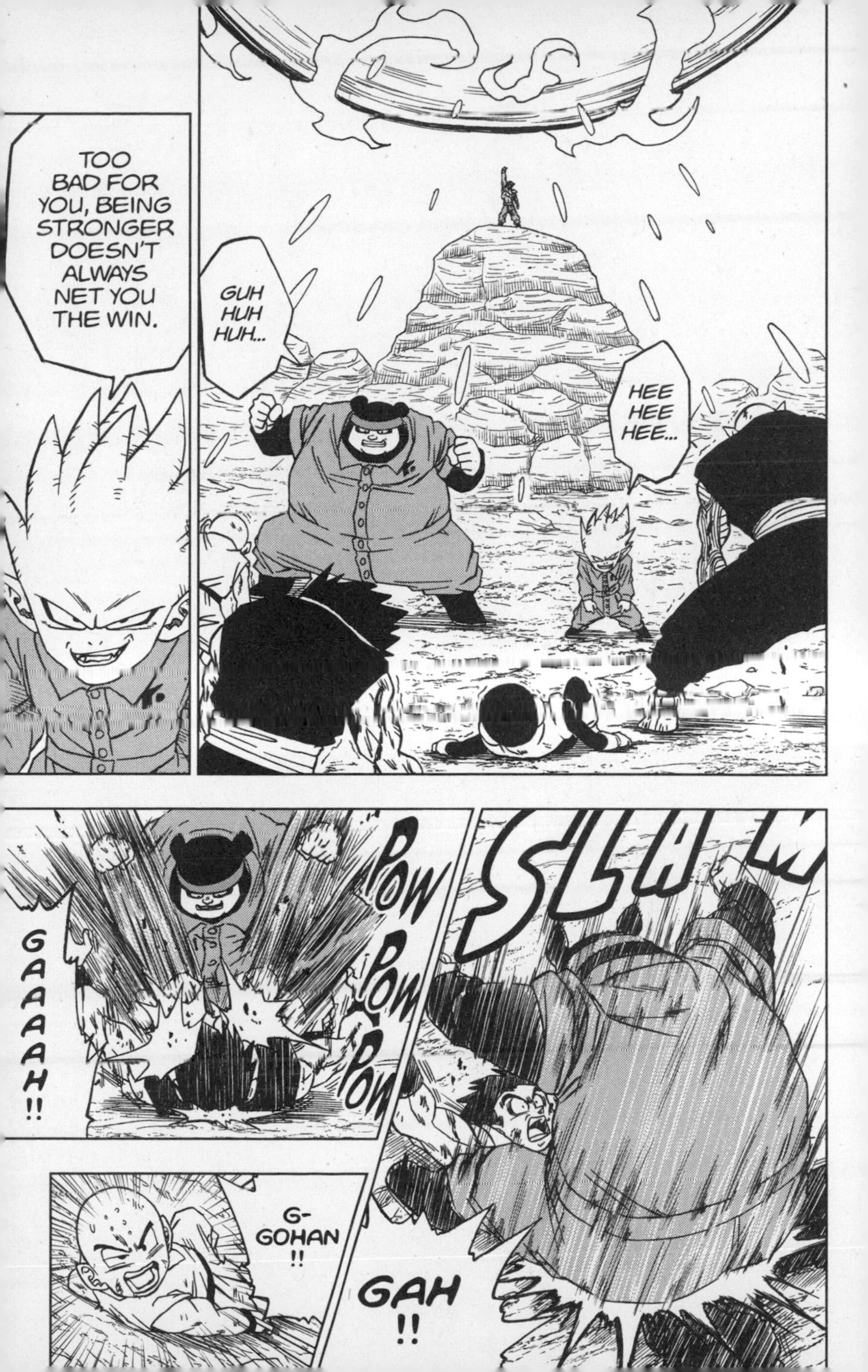
HEE HEE HEE...
GUH HUH HUH...
TOO BAD FOR YOU, BEING STRONGER DOESN'T ALWAYS NET YOU THE WIN.
SLAM
GAH!!
POW POW POW POW
GAAAAAH!!
G-GOHAN!!

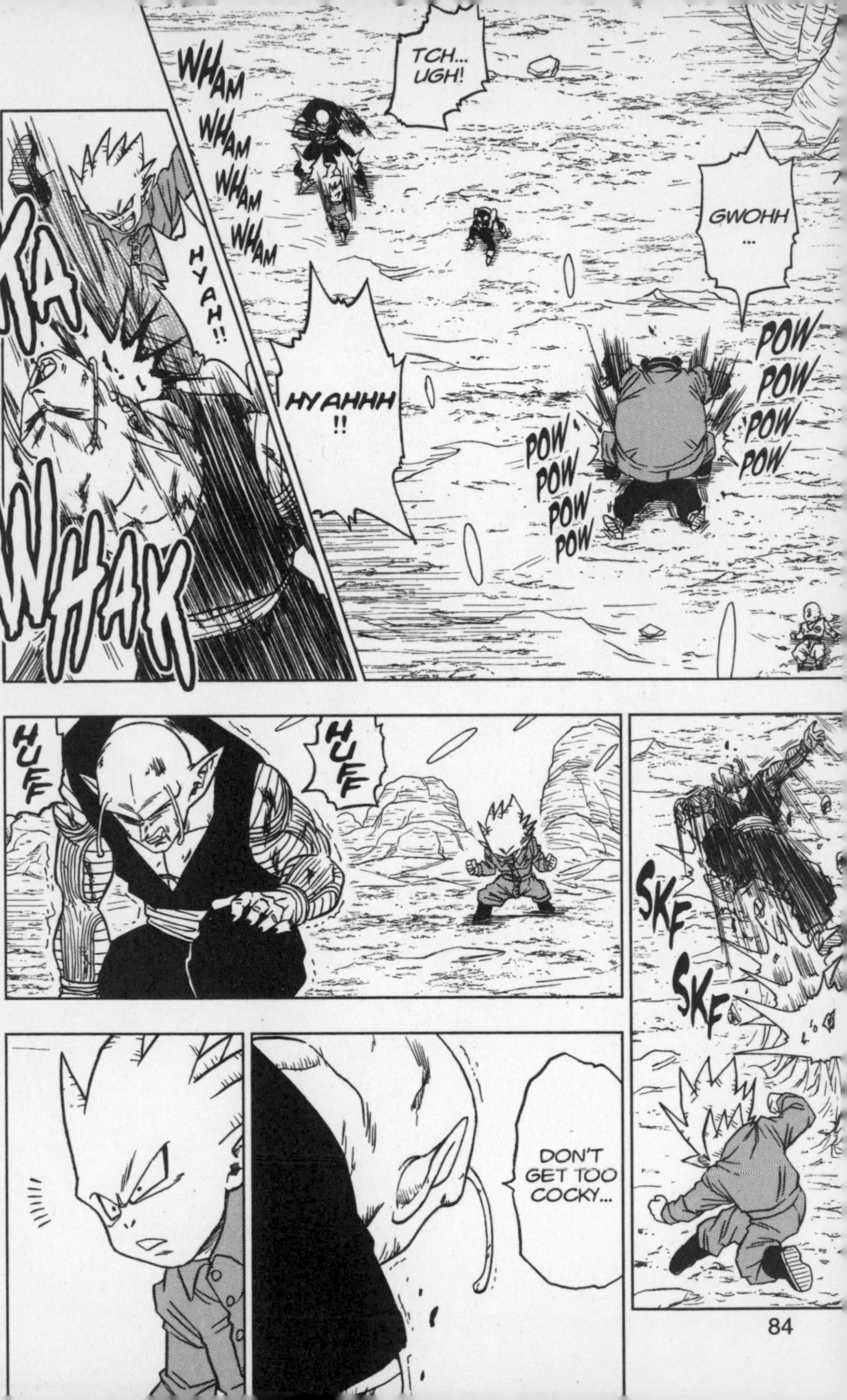
GWOHH ...
POW POW POW POW
POW POW POW POW
TCH... UGH!
WHAM WHAM WHAM WHAM WHAM
HYAHHH !!
HYAH!!
KA
WHAK
SKF
SKF
HUFF
HUFF
DON'T GET TOO COCKY...

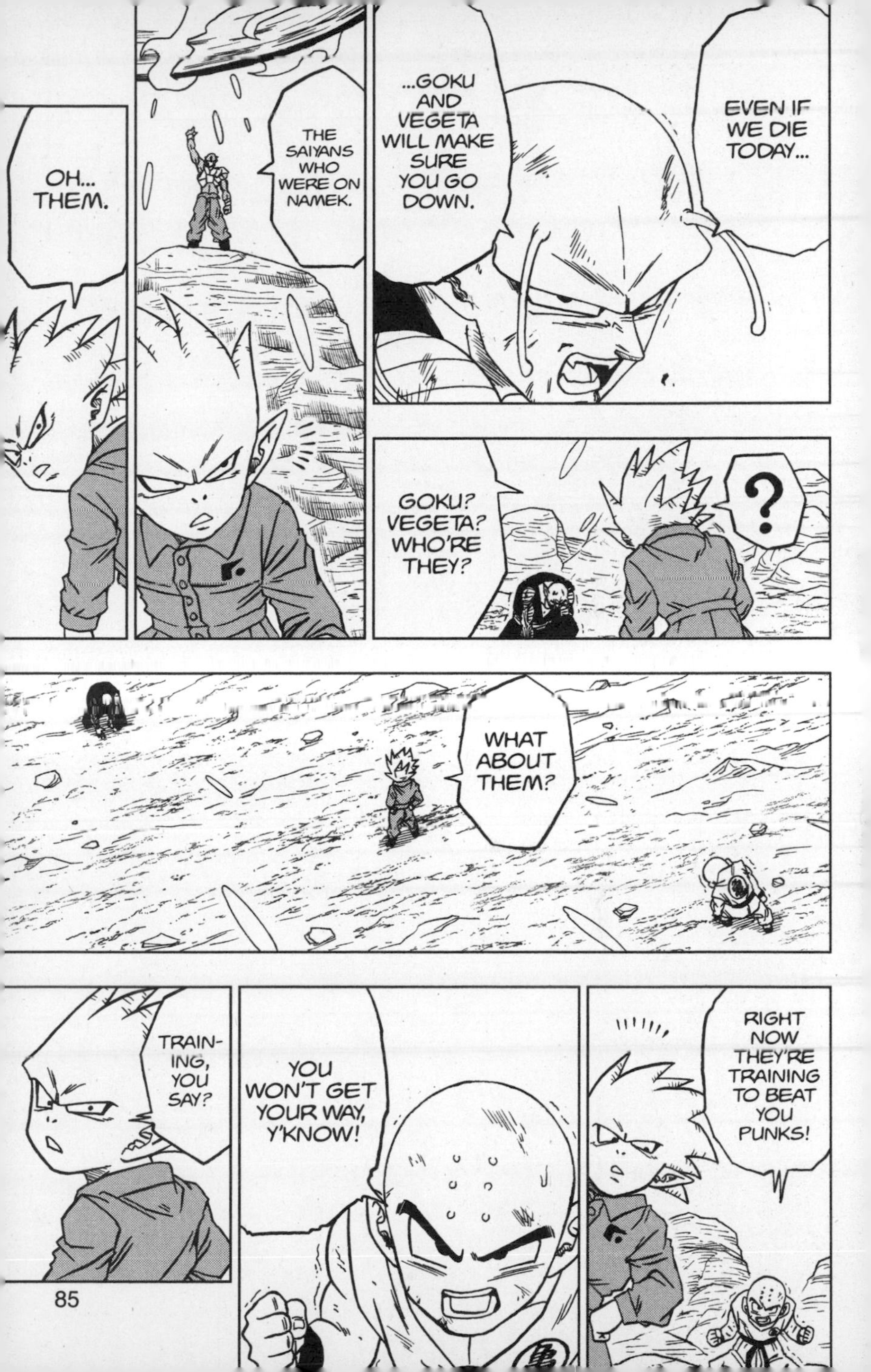
EVEN IF WE DIE TODAY...
...GOKU AND VEGETA WILL MAKE SURE YOU GO DOWN.
?
GOKU? VEGETA? WHO'RE THEY?
THE SAIYANS WHO WERE ON NAMEK.
OH... THEM.
WHAT ABOUT THEM?
RIGHT NOW THEY'RE TRAINING TO BEAT YOU PUNKS!
YOU WON'T GET YOUR WAY, Y'KNOW!
TRAIN-ING, YOU SAY?

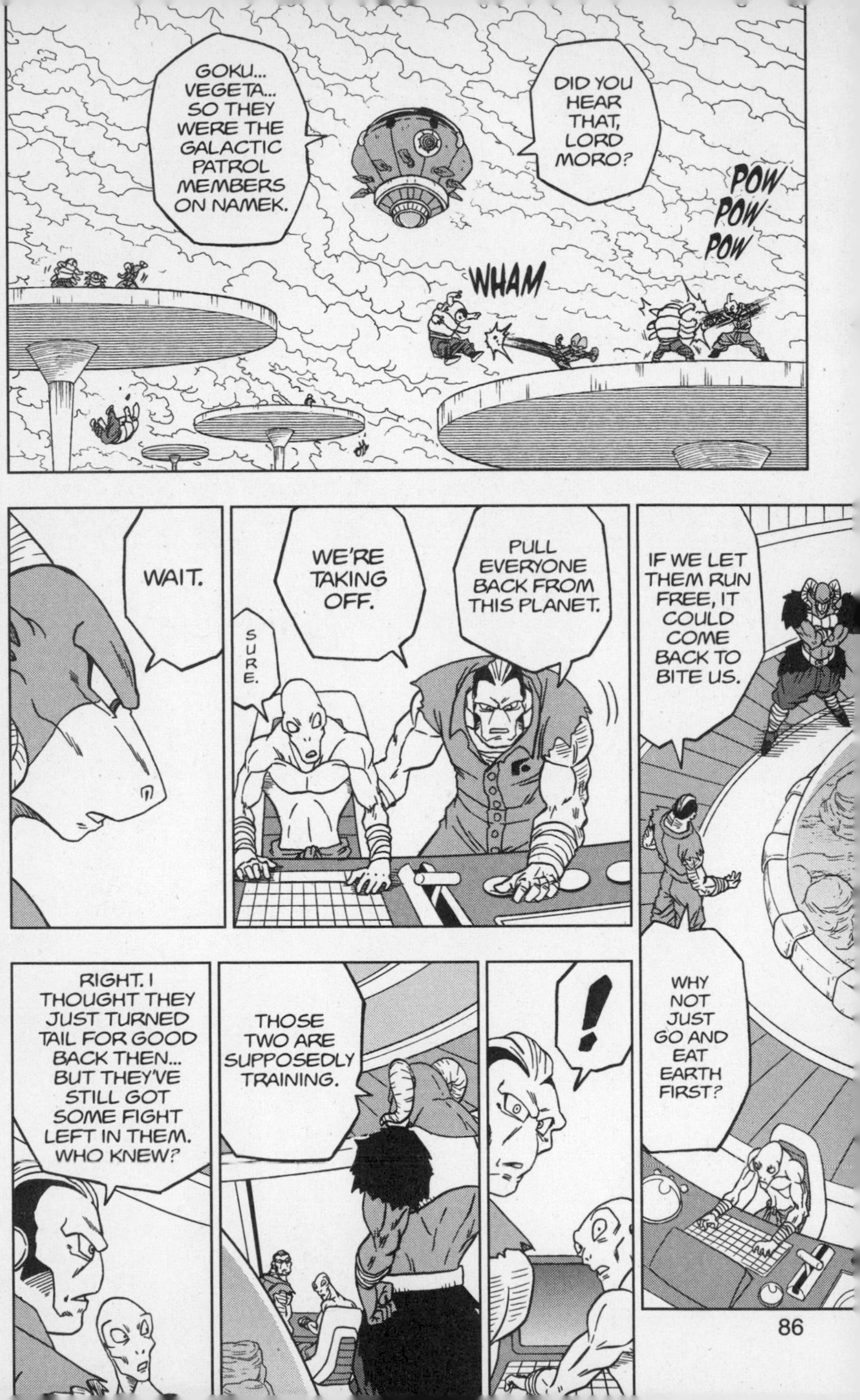

DID YOU HEAR THAT, LORD MORO?
POW POW POW
WHAM
GOKU... VEGETA... SO THEY WERE THE GALACTIC PATROL MEMBERS ON NAMEK.
IF WE LET THEM RUN FREE, IT COULD COME BACK TO BITE US.
WHY NOT JUST GO AND EAT EARTH FIRST?
PULL EVERYONE BACK FROM THIS PLANET.
WE'RE TAKING OFF.
SURE.
WAIT.
!
THOSE TWO ARE SUPPOSEDLY TRAINING.
RIGHT. I THOUGHT THEY JUST TURNED TAIL FOR GOOD BACK THEN... BUT THEY'VE STILL GOT SOME FIGHT LEFT IN THEM. WHO KNEW?

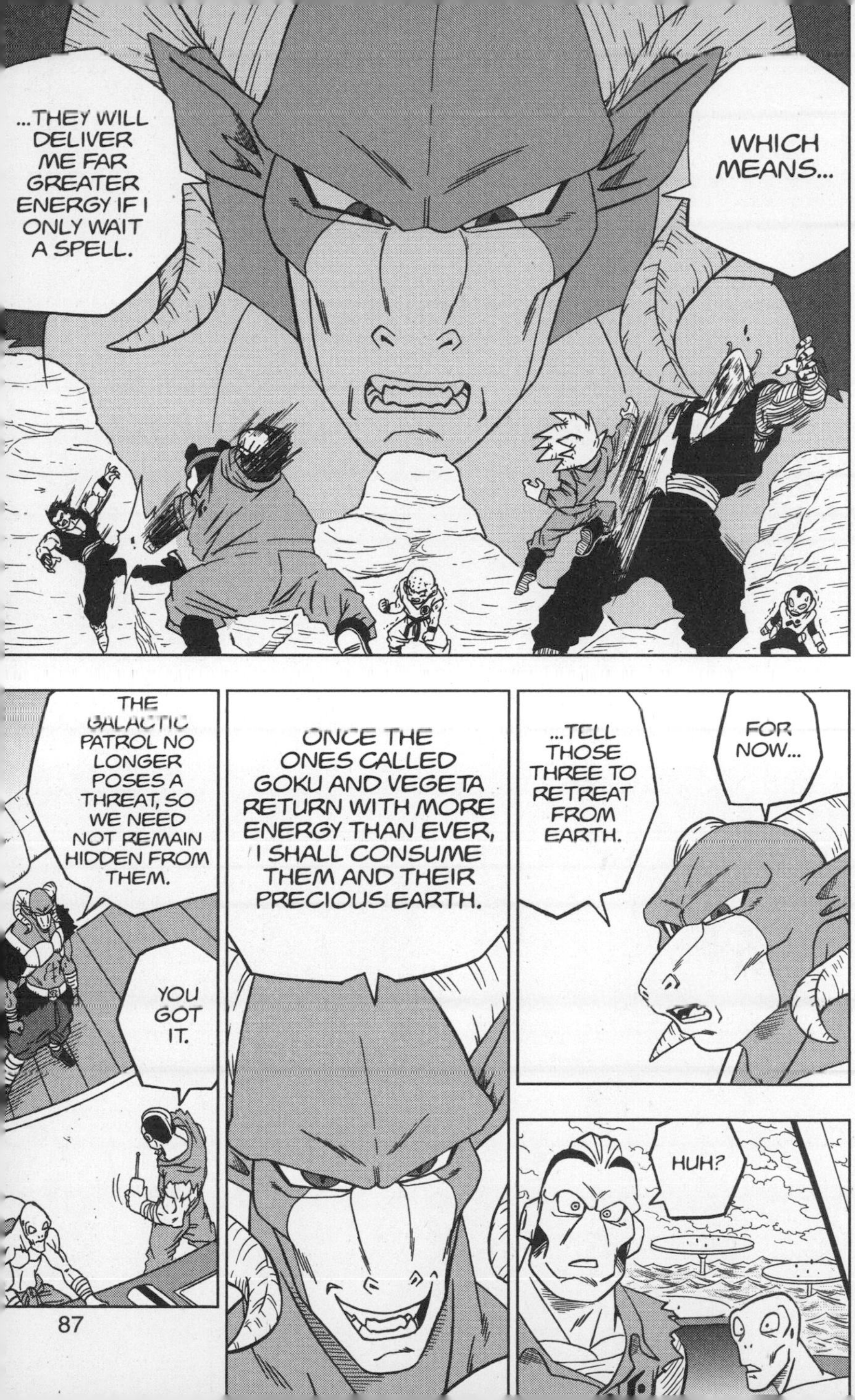
WHICH MEANS...
...THEY WILL DELIVER ME FAR GREATER ENERGY IF I ONLY WAIT A SPELL.
FOR NOW...
...TELL THOSE THREE TO RETREAT FROM EARTH.
HUH?
ONCE THE ONES CALLED GOKU AND VEGETA RETURN WITH MORE ENERGY THAN EVER, I SHALL CONSUME THEM AND THEIR PRECIOUS EARTH.
THE GALACTIC PATROL NO LONGER POSES A THREAT, SO WE NEED NOT REMAIN HIDDEN FROM THEM.
YOU GOT IT.

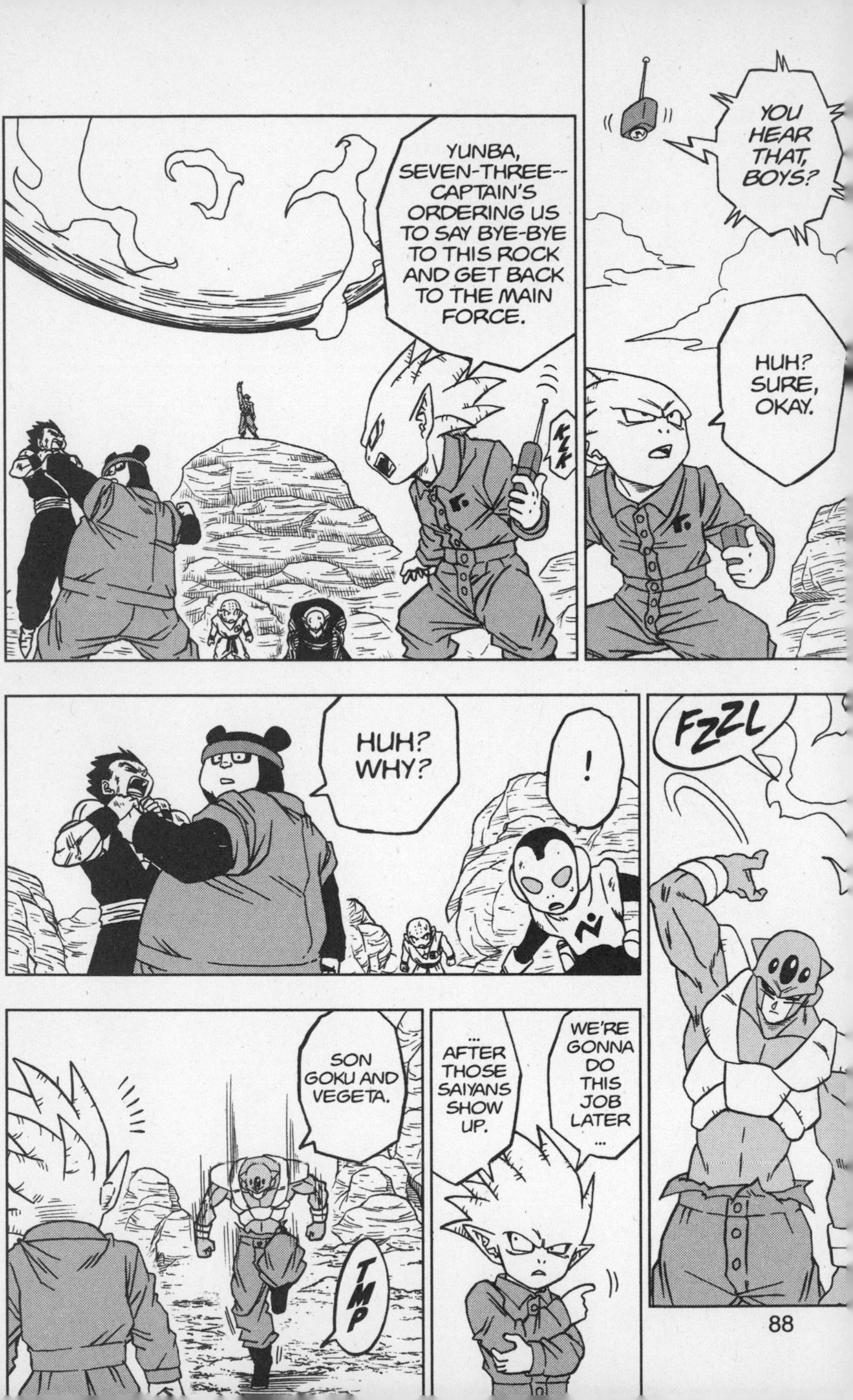
YOU HEAR THAT, BOYS?
HUH? SURE, OKAY.
YUNBA, SEVEN-THREE-- CAPTAIN'S ORDERING US TO SAY BYE-BYE TO THIS ROCK AND GET BACK TO THE MAIN FORCE.
KZK
FZZL
!
HUH? WHY?
WE'RE GONNA DO THIS JOB LATER ...
... AFTER THOSE SAIYANS SHOW UP.
SON GOKU AND VEGETA.
TMP

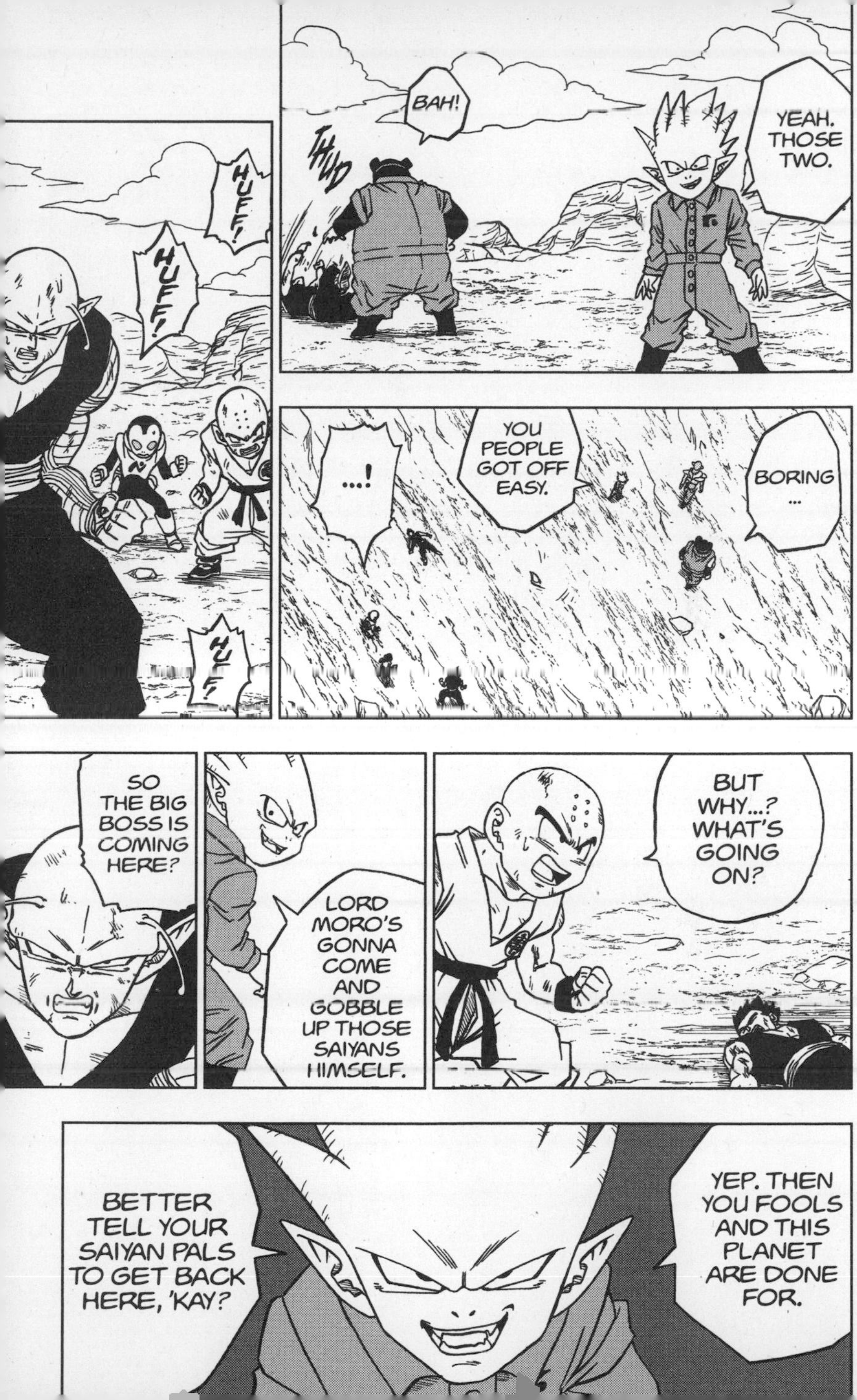
YEAH. THOSE TWO.
BAH!
THUD
BORING...
YOU PEOPLE GOT OFF EASY.
...!
HUFF!
HUFF!
HUFF!
BUT WHY...? WHAT'S GOING ON?
LORD MORO'S GONNA COME AND GOBBLE UP THOSE SAIYANS HIMSELF.
SO THE BIG BOSS IS COMING HERE?
YEP. THEN YOU FOOLS AND THIS PLANET ARE DONE FOR.
BETTER TELL YOUR SAIYAN PALS TO GET BACK HERE, 'KAY?

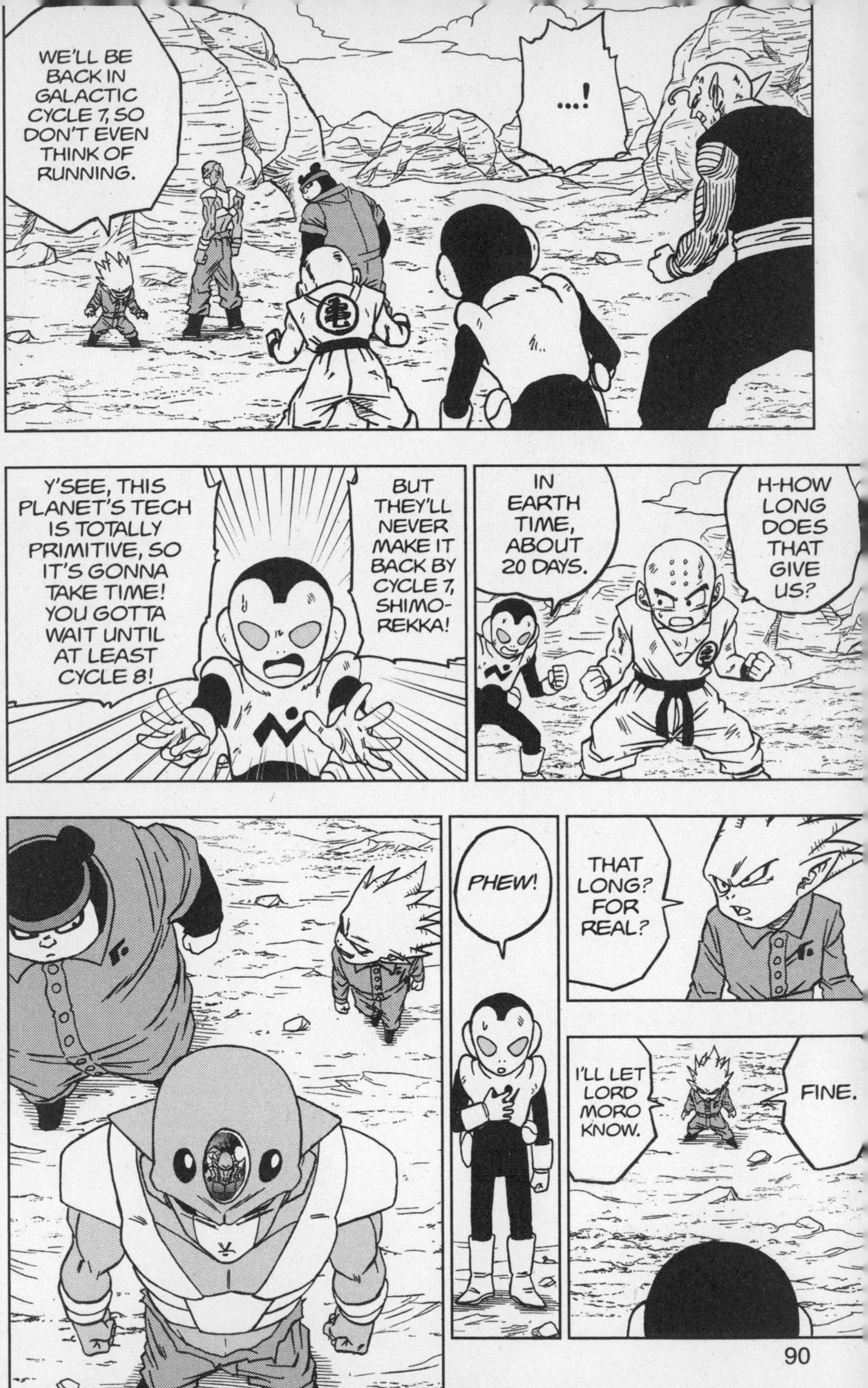
WE'LL BE BACK IN GALACTIC CYCLE 7, SO DON'T EVEN THINK OF RUNNING.
...!
H-HOW LONG DOES THAT GIVE US?
IN EARTH TIME, ABOUT 20 DAYS.
BUT THEY'LL NEVER MAKE IT BACK BY CYCLE 7, SHIMO-REKKA!
Y'SEE, THIS PLANET'S TECH IS TOTALLY PRIMITIVE, SO IT'S GONNA TAKE TIME! YOU GOTTA WAIT UNTIL AT LEAST CYCLE 8!
THAT LONG? FOR REAL?
FINE.
I'LL LET LORD MORO KNOW.
PHEW!

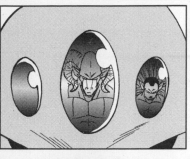

ZWOOM

KACHK

SKWEEZ

POP

SHOOP

TMP

LATER.

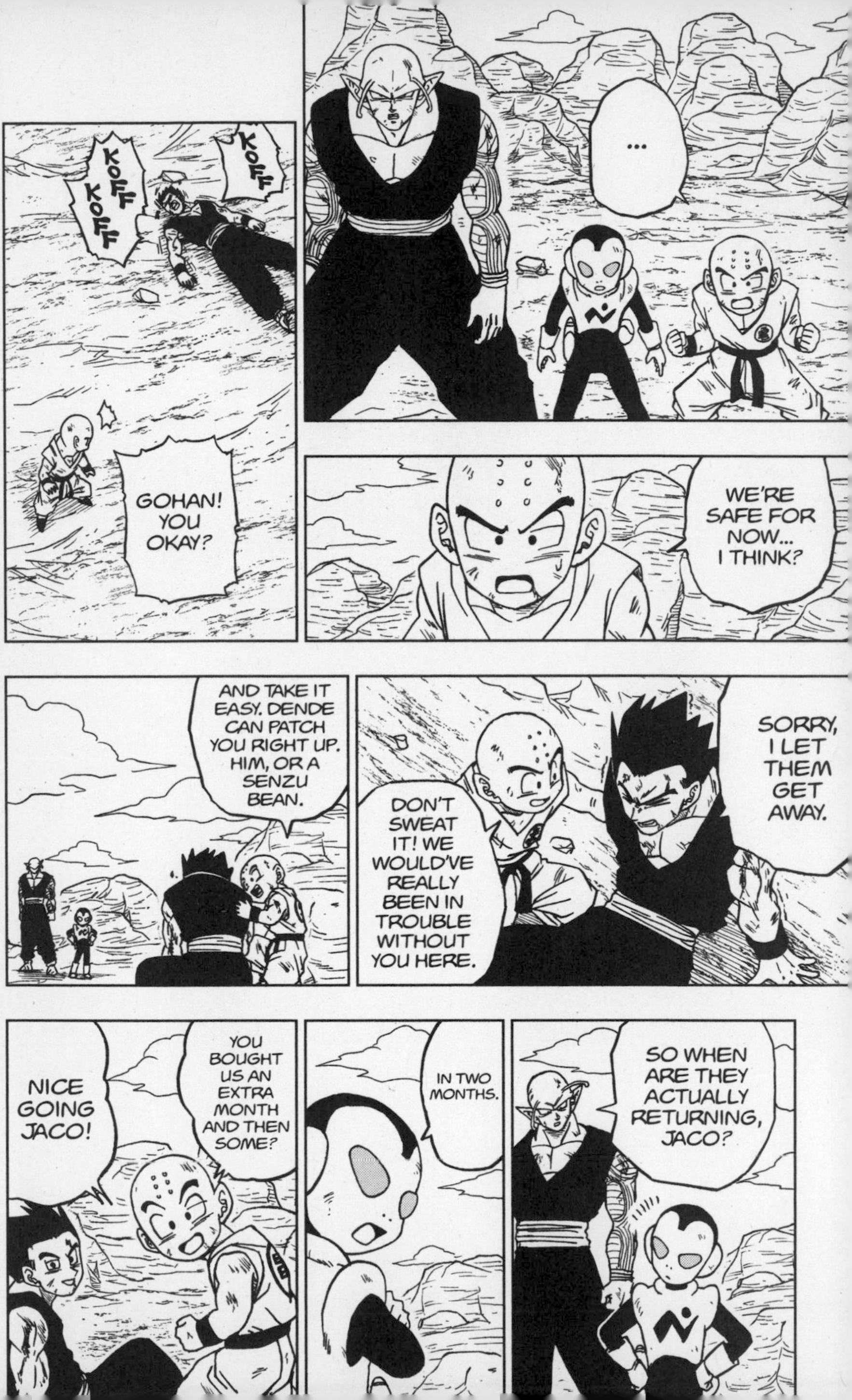

...
WE'RE SAFE FOR NOW... I THINK?
KOFF
KOFF KOFF
GOHAN! YOU OKAY?
SORRY, I LET THEM GET AWAY.
DON'T SWEAT IT! WE WOULD'VE REALLY BEEN IN TROUBLE WITHOUT YOU HERE.
AND TAKE IT EASY. DENDE CAN PATCH YOU RIGHT UP. HIM, OR A SENZU BEAN.
SO WHEN ARE THEY ACTUALLY RETURNING, JACO?
IN TWO MONTHS.
YOU BOUGHT US AN EXTRA MONTH AND THEN SOME?
NICE GOING JACO!

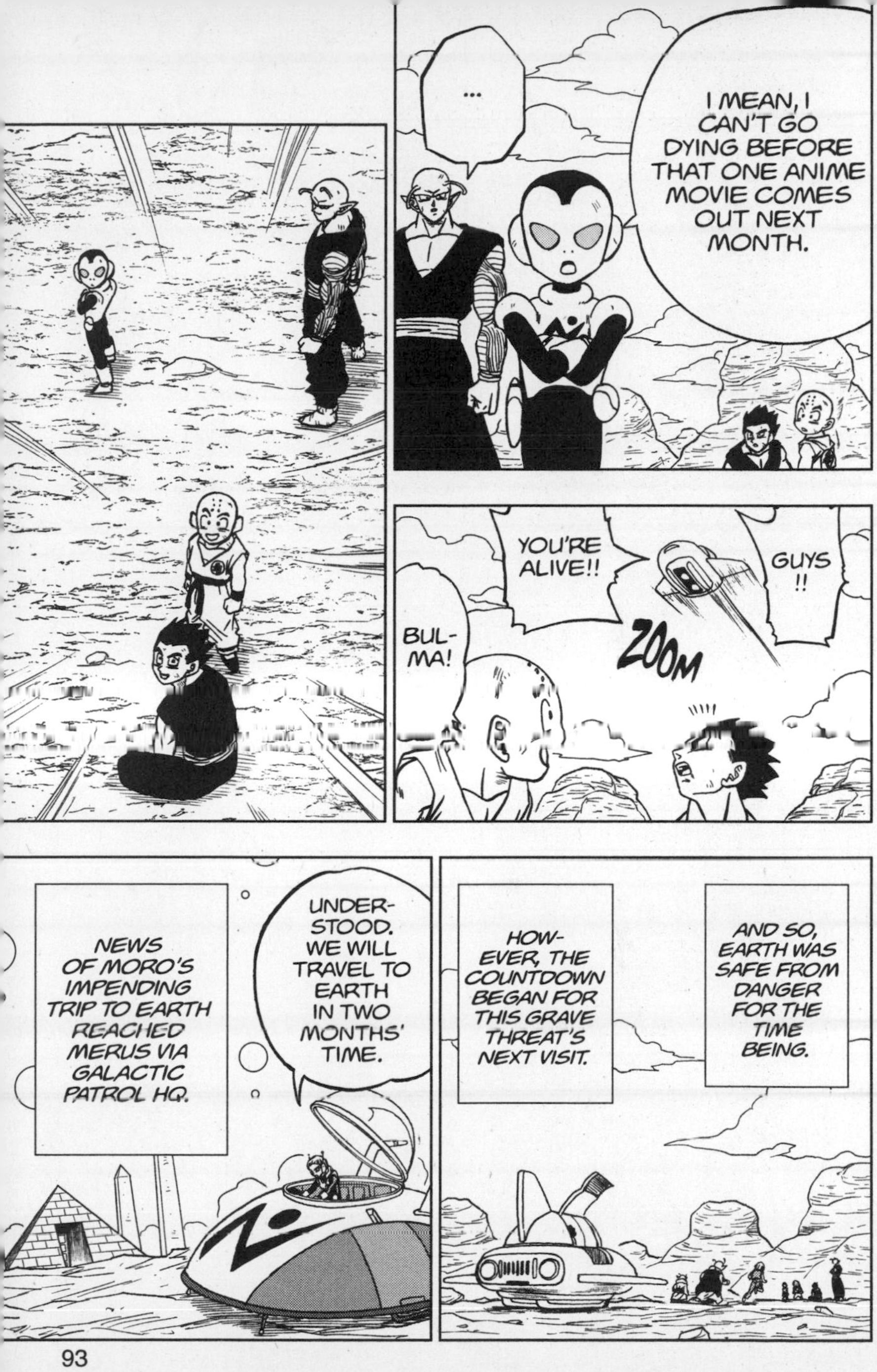

I MEAN, I CAN'T GO DYING BEFORE THAT ONE ANIME MOVIE COMES OUT NEXT MONTH.
...
GUYS !!
YOU'RE ALIVE!!
ZOOM
BUL-MA!
AND SO, EARTH WAS SAFE FROM DANGER FOR THE TIME BEING.
HOW-EVER, THE COUNTDOWN BEGAN FOR THIS GRAVE THREAT'S NEXT VISIT.
UNDER-STOOD. WE WILL TRAVEL TO EARTH IN TWO MONTHS' TIME.
NEWS OF MORO'S IMPENDING TRIP TO EARTH REACHED MERUS VIA GALACTIC PATROL HQ.

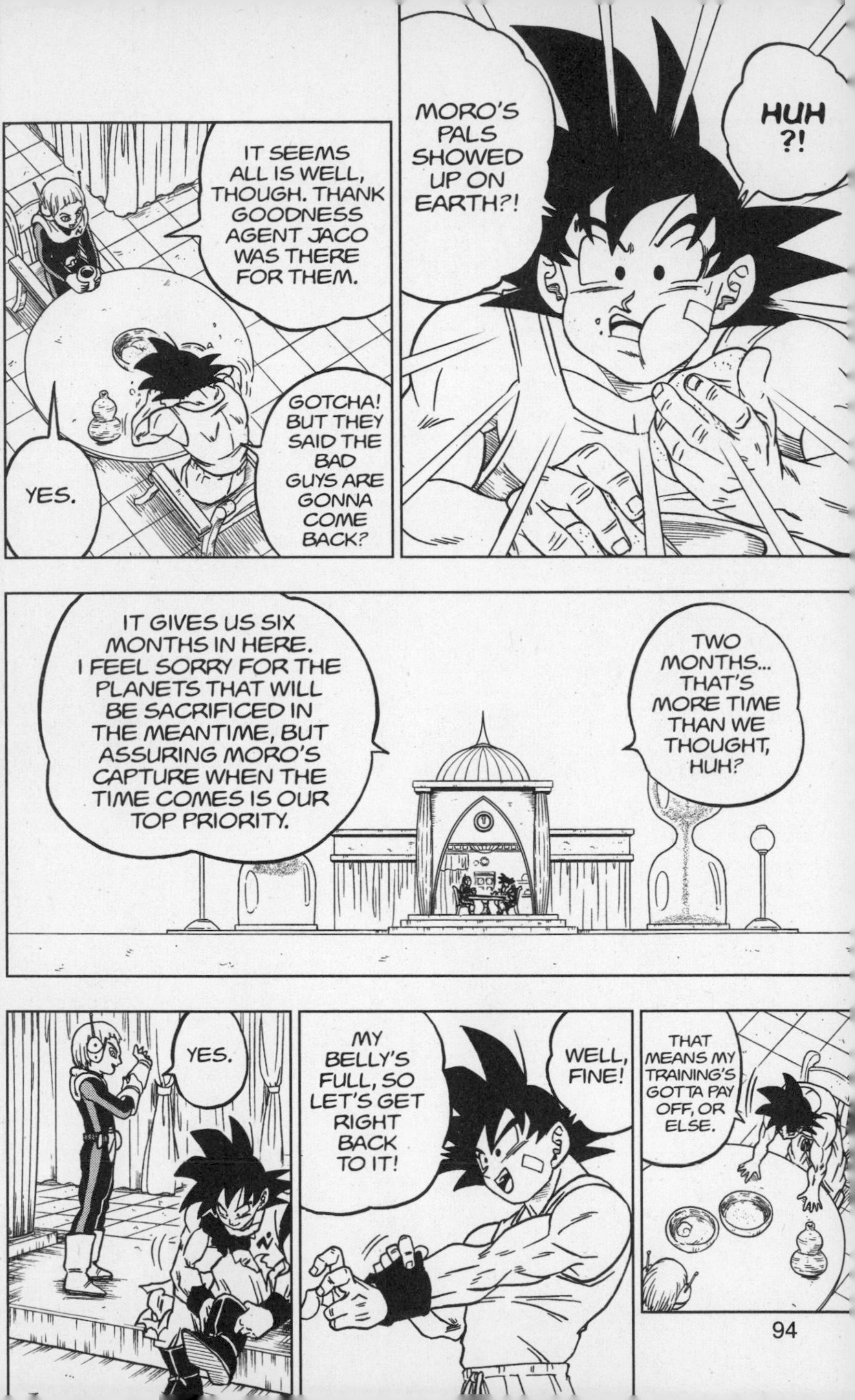
HUH ?!
MORO'S PALS SHOWED UP ON EARTH?!
IT SEEMS ALL IS WELL, THOUGH. THANK GOODNESS AGENT JACO WAS THERE FOR THEM.
GOTCHA! BUT THEY SAID THE BAD GUYS ARE GONNA COME BACK?
YES.
TWO MONTHS... THAT'S MORE TIME THAN WE THOUGHT, HUH?
IT GIVES US SIX MONTHS IN HERE. I FEEL SORRY FOR THE PLANETS THAT WILL BE SACRIFICED IN THE MEANTIME, BUT ASSURING MORO'S CAPTURE WHEN THE TIME COMES IS OUR TOP PRIORITY.
THAT MEANS MY TRAINING'S GOTTA PAY OFF, OR ELSE.
WELL, FINE!
MY BELLY'S FULL, SO LET'S GET RIGHT BACK TO IT!
YES.

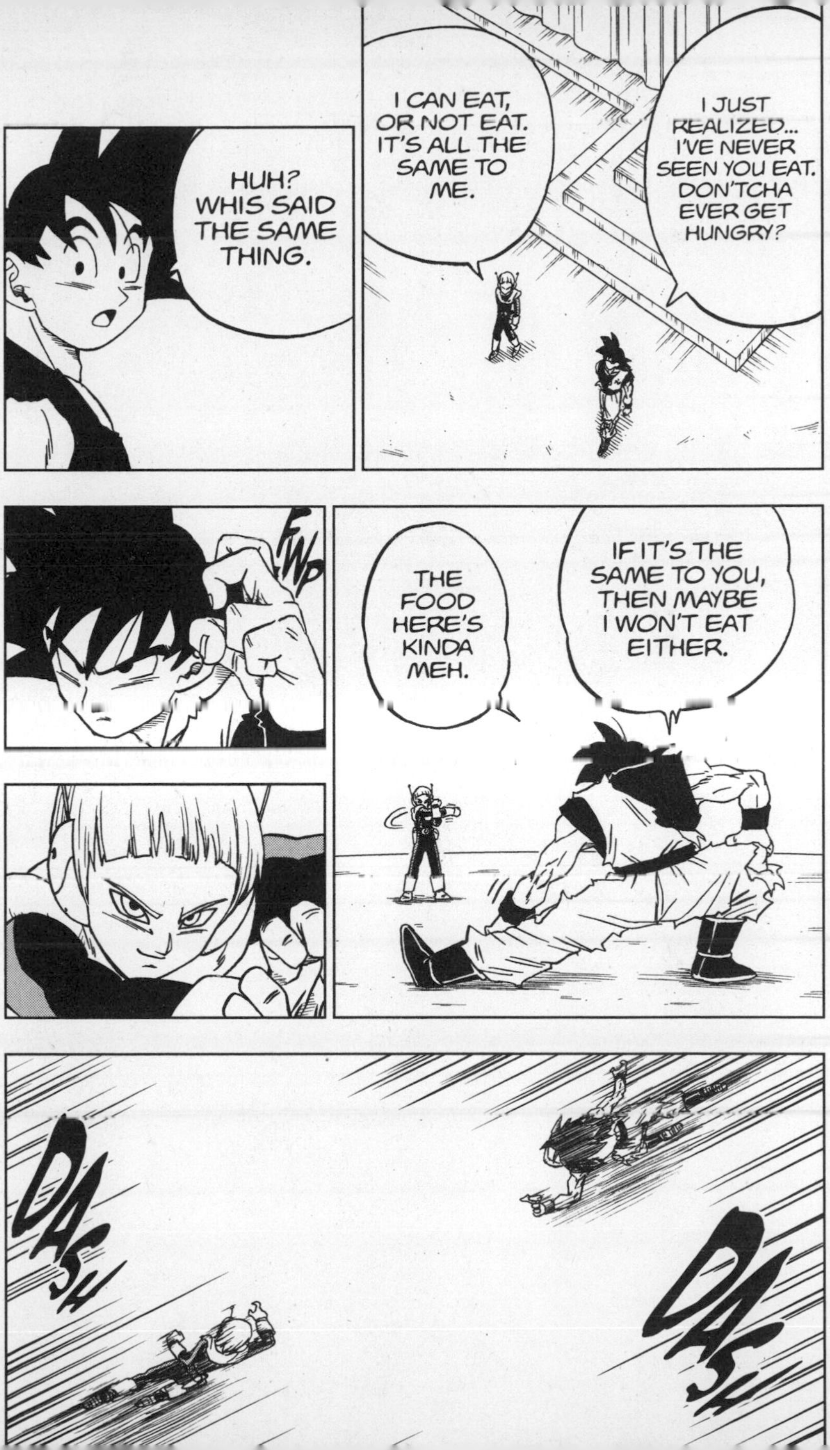
I JUST REALIZED... I'VE NEVER SEEN YOU EAT. DON'TCHA EVER GET HUNGRY?
I CAN EAT, OR NOT EAT. IT'S ALL THE SAME TO ME.
HUH? WHIS SAID THE SAME THING.
IF IT'S THE SAME TO YOU, THEN MAYBE I WON'T EAT EITHER.
THE FOOD HERE'S KINDA MEH.
FWP
DASH
DASH

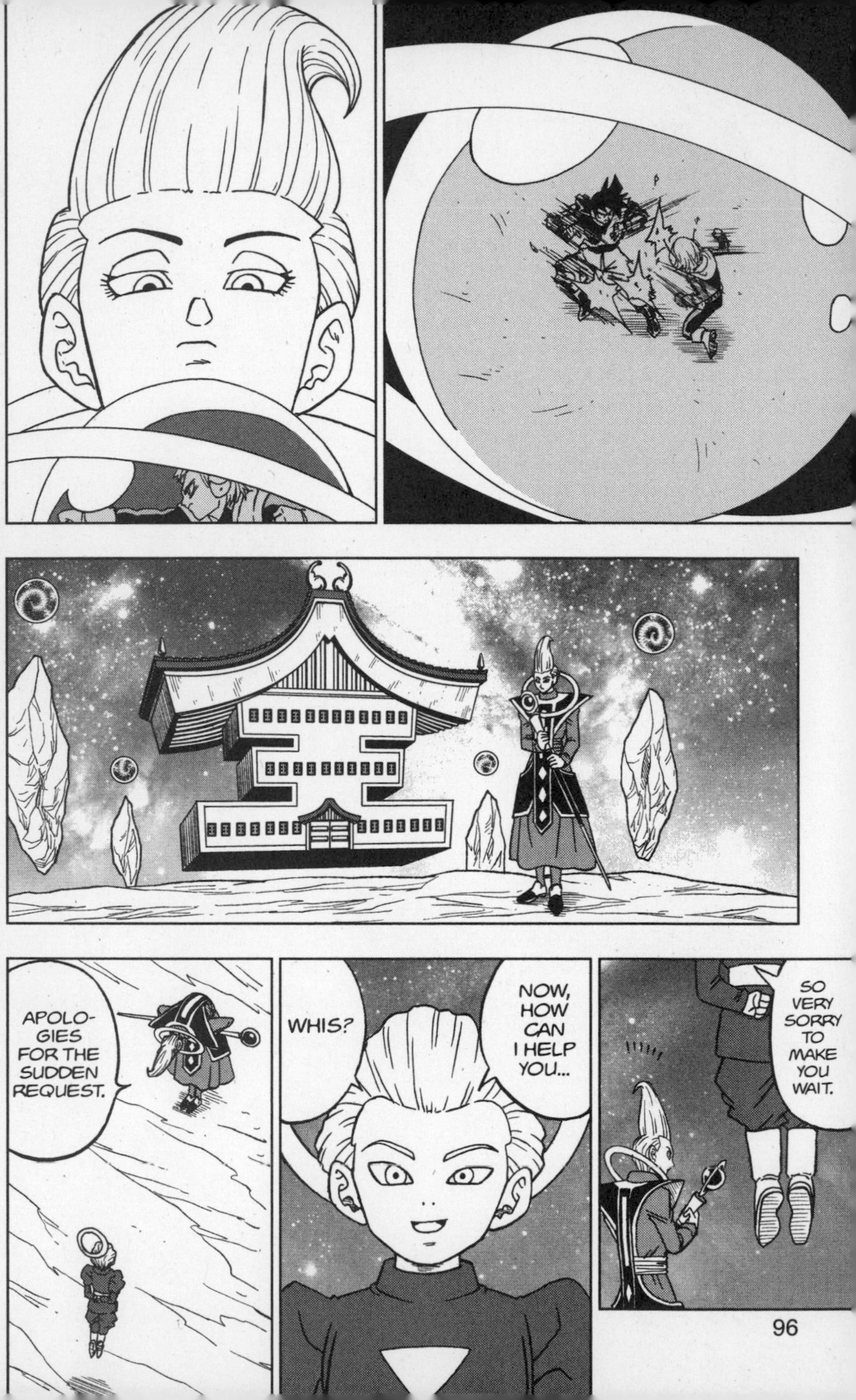
SO VERY SORRY TO MAKE YOU WAIT.
!!!!!
NOW, HOW CAN I HELP YOU...
WHIS?
APOLO-GIES FOR THE SUDDEN REQUEST.

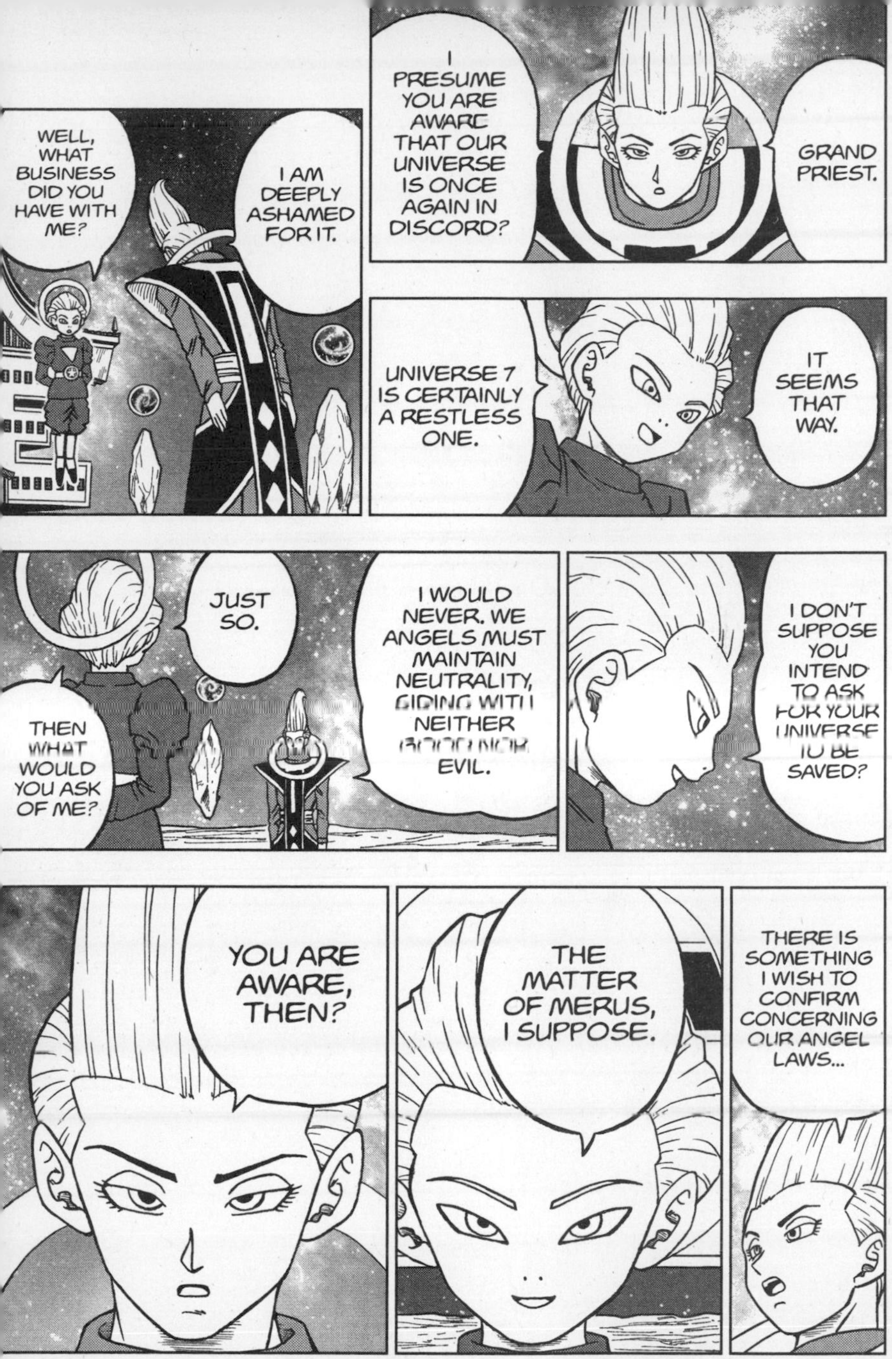
GRAND PRIEST.
I PRESUME YOU ARE AWARE THAT OUR UNIVERSE IS ONCE AGAIN IN DISCORD?
IT SEEMS THAT WAY.
UNIVERSE 7 IS CERTAINLY A RESTLESS ONE.
I AM DEEPLY ASHAMED FOR IT.
WELL, WHAT BUSINESS DID YOU HAVE WITH ME?
I DON'T SUPPOSE YOU INTEND TO ASK FOR YOUR UNIVERSE TO BE SAVED?
I WOULD NEVER. WE ANGELS MUST MAINTAIN NEUTRALITY, SIDING WITH NEITHER GOOD NOR EVIL.
JUST SO.
THEN WHAT WOULD YOU ASK OF ME?
THERE IS SOMETHING I WISH TO CONFIRM CONCERNING OUR ANGEL LAWS...
THE MATTER OF MERUS, I SUPPOSE.
YOU ARE AWARE, THEN?

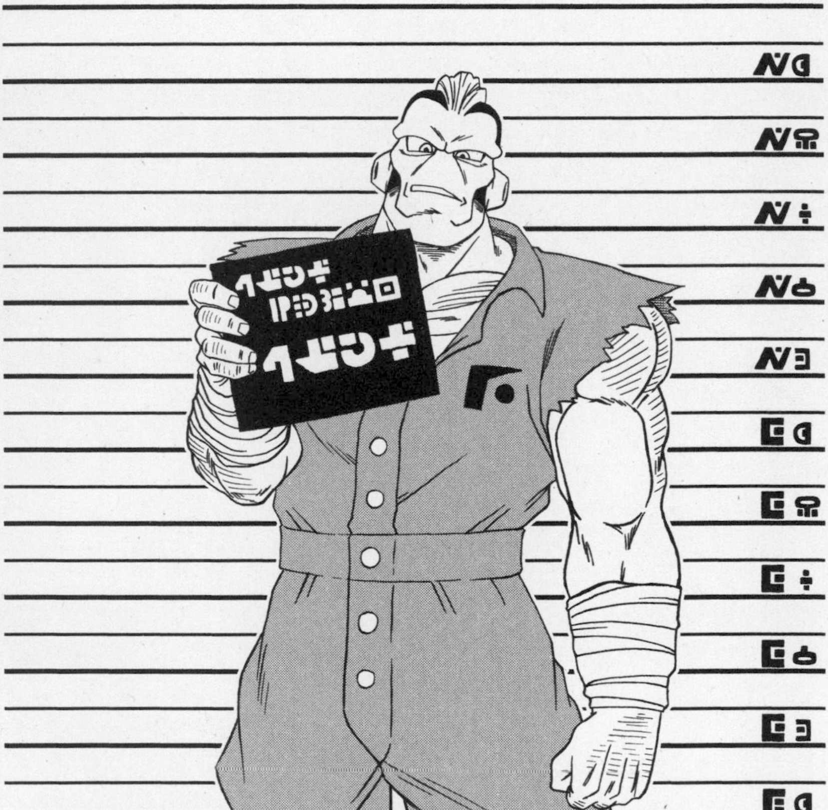

SAGANBO'S
GALACTIC BANDIT
BRIGADE LEADER:
SAGANBO

DRAGON BALL SUPER

CHAPTER 55: MERUS'S TRUE IDENTITY

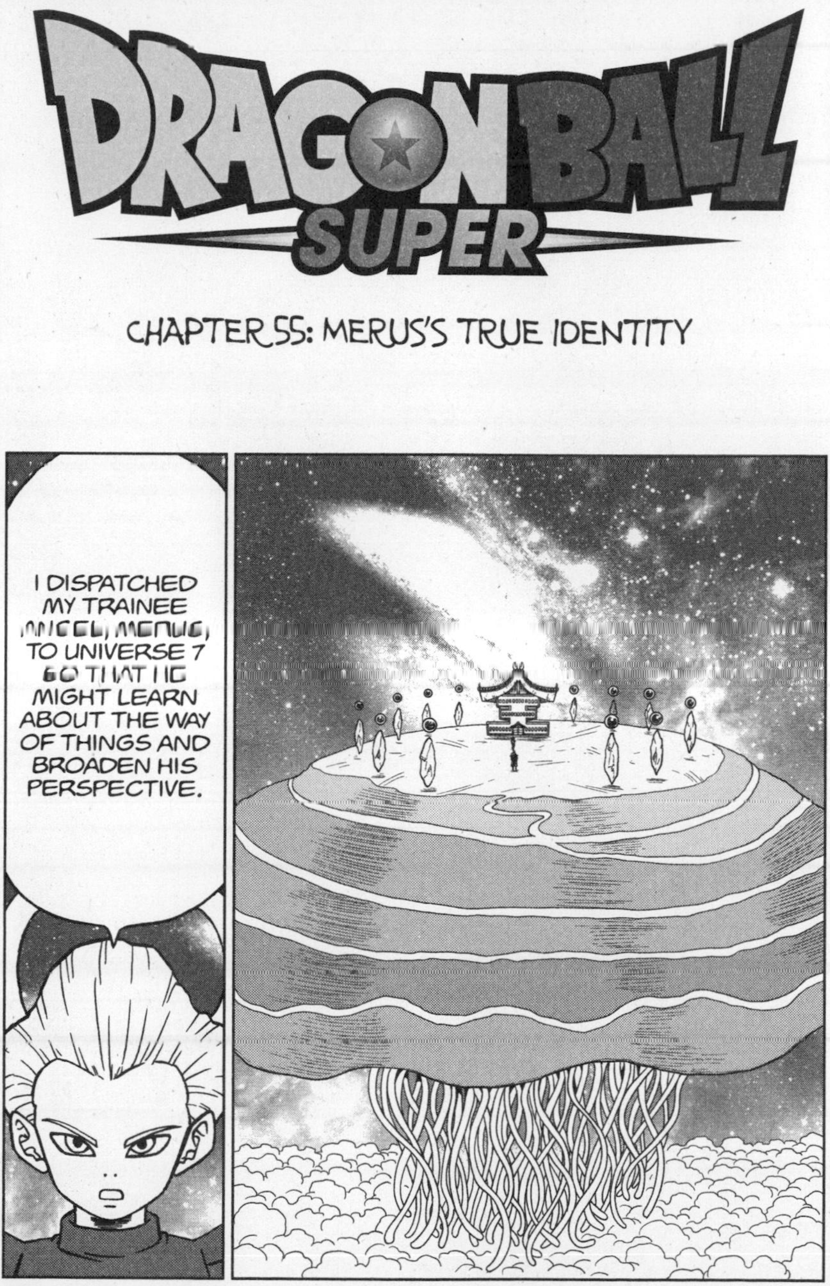
I DISPATCHED MY TRAINEE ANGEL, MERUS, TO UNIVERSE 7 SO THAT HE MIGHT LEARN ABOUT THE WAY OF THINGS AND BROADEN HIS PERSPECTIVE.

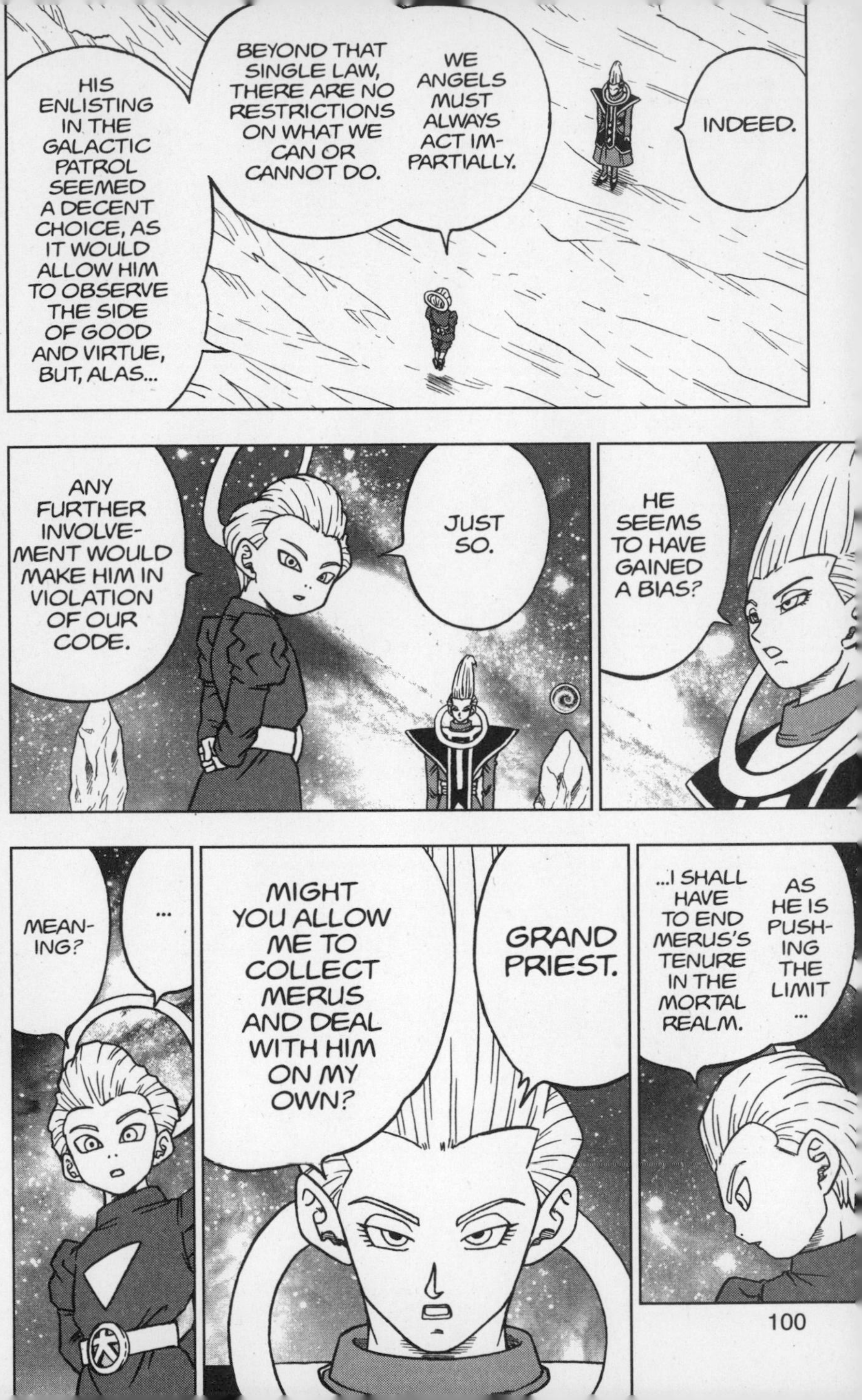
INDEED.
WE ANGELS MUST ALWAYS ACT IMPARTIALLY.
BEYOND THAT SINGLE LAW, THERE ARE NO RESTRICTIONS ON WHAT WE CAN OR CANNOT DO.
HIS ENLISTING IN THE GALACTIC PATROL SEEMED A DECENT CHOICE, AS IT WOULD ALLOW HIM TO OBSERVE THE SIDE OF GOOD AND VIRTUE, BUT, ALAS...
HE SEEMS TO HAVE GAINED A BIAS?
JUST SO.
ANY FURTHER INVOLVEMENT WOULD MAKE HIM IN VIOLATION OF OUR CODE.
AS HE IS PUSHING THE LIMIT...
...I SHALL HAVE TO END MERUS'S TENURE IN THE MORTAL REALM.
GRAND PRIEST.
MIGHT YOU ALLOW ME TO COLLECT MERUS AND DEAL WITH HIM ON MY OWN?
...
MEANING?

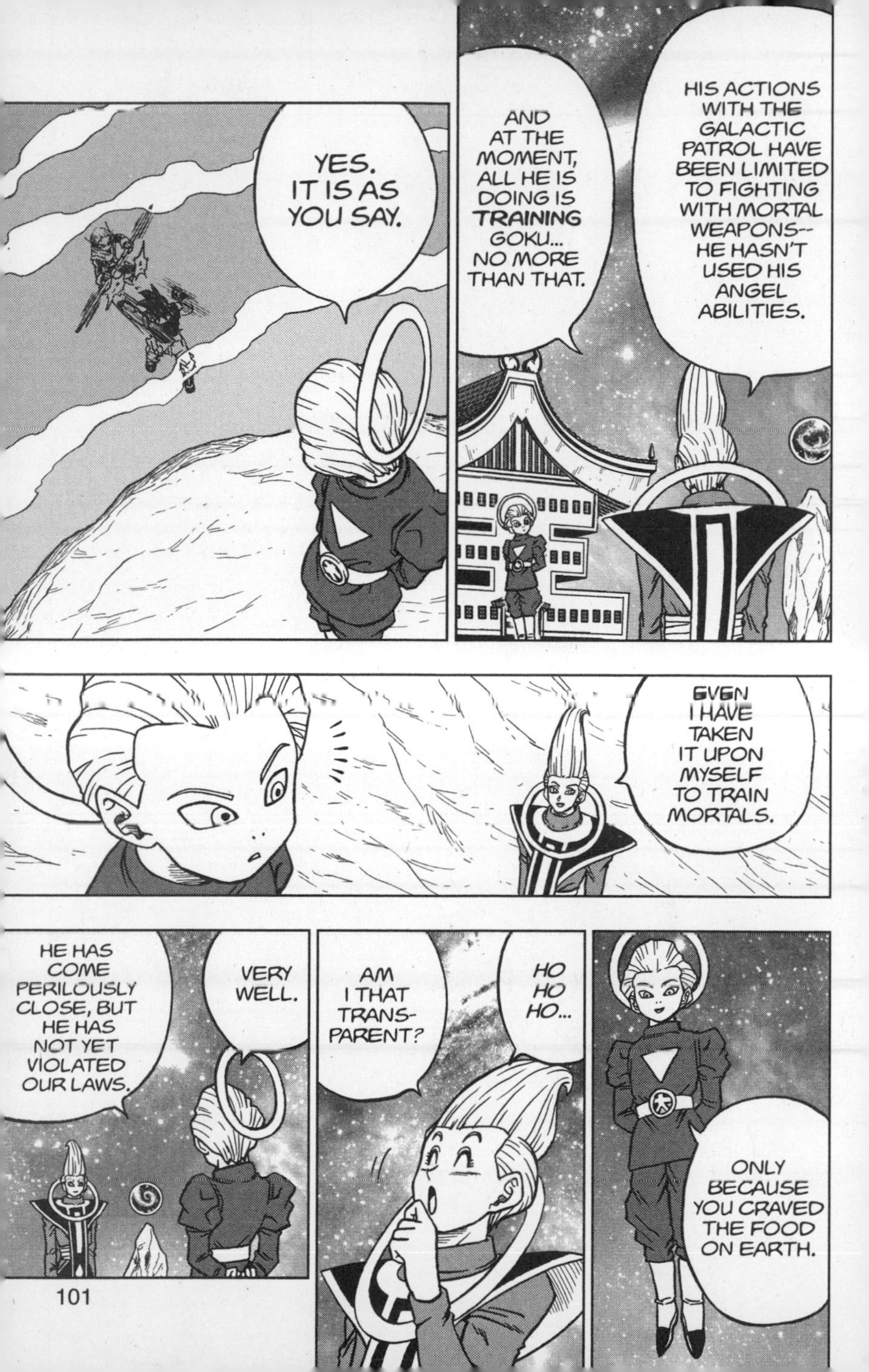
HIS ACTIONS WITH THE GALACTIC PATROL HAVE BEEN LIMITED TO FIGHTING WITH MORTAL WEAPONS-- HE HASN'T USED HIS ANGEL ABILITIES.
AND AT THE MOMENT, ALL HE IS DOING IS **TRAINING** GOKU... NO MORE THAN THAT.
YES. IT IS AS YOU SAY.
EVEN I HAVE TAKEN IT UPON MYSELF TO TRAIN MORTALS.
ONLY BECAUSE YOU CRAVED THE FOOD ON EARTH.
HO HO HO...
AM I THAT TRANS-PARENT?
VERY WELL.
HE HAS COME PERILOUSLY CLOSE, BUT HE HAS NOT YET VIOLATED OUR LAWS.

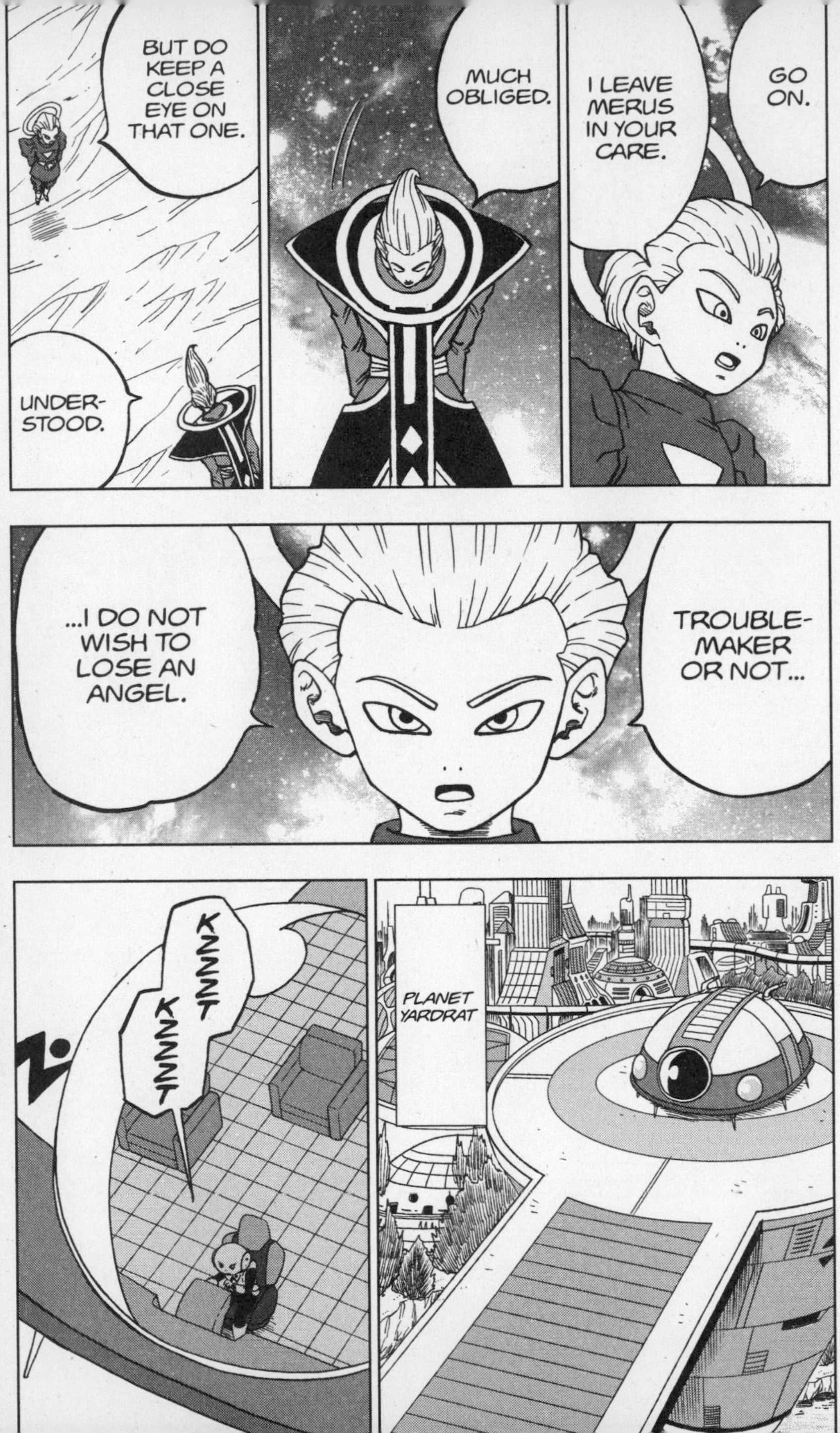
GO ON.
I LEAVE MERUS IN YOUR CARE.
MUCH OBLIGED.
BUT DO KEEP A CLOSE EYE ON THAT ONE.
UNDERSTOOD.
TROUBLE-MAKER OR NOT...
...I DO NOT WISH TO LOSE AN ANGEL.
PLANET YARDRAT
KZZZT
KZZZT

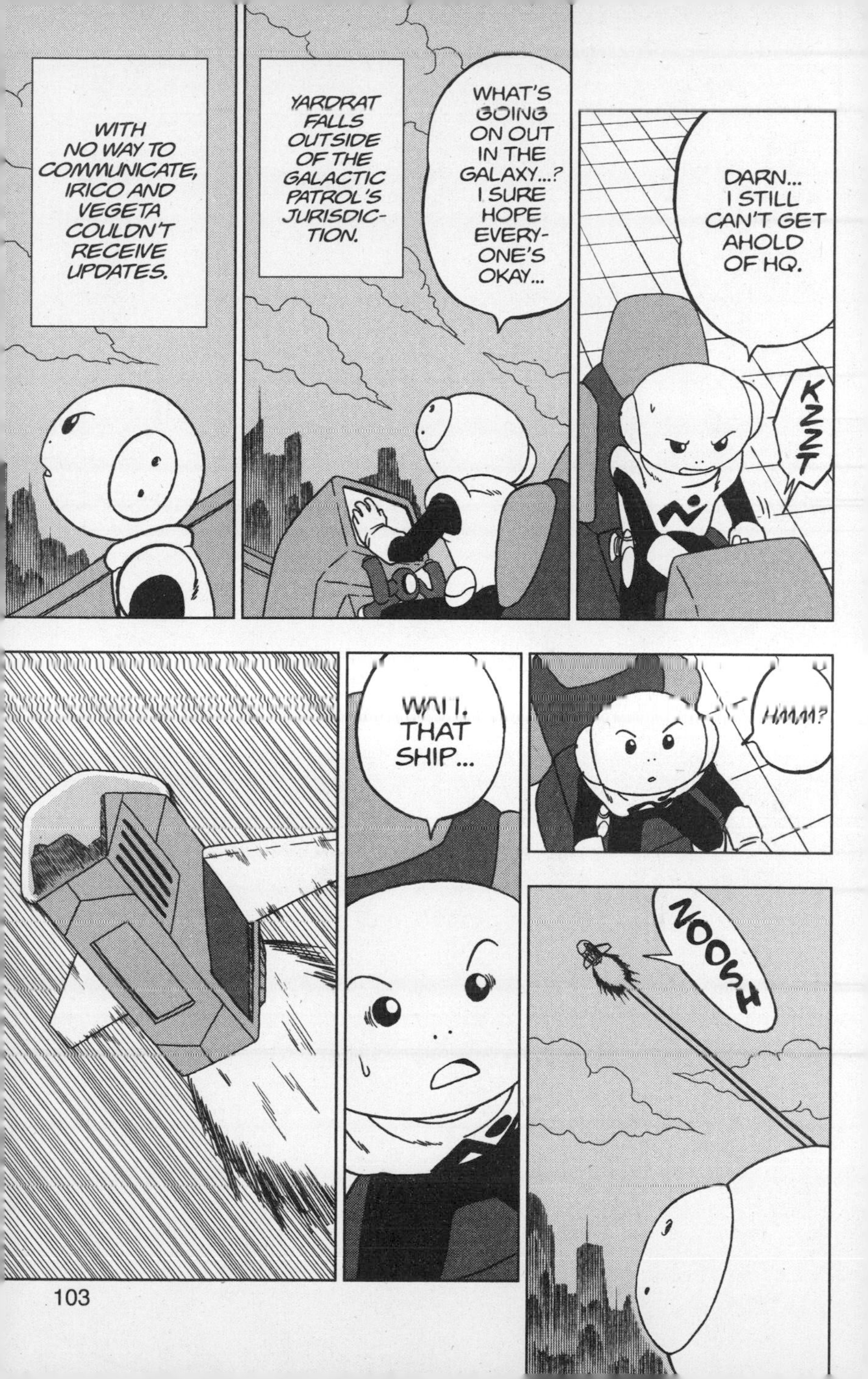
DARN... I STILL CAN'T GET AHOLD OF HQ.
KZZT
WHAT'S GOING ON OUT IN THE GALAXY...? I SURE HOPE EVERYONE'S OKAY...
YARDRAT FALLS OUTSIDE OF THE GALACTIC PATROL'S JURISDICTION.
WITH NO WAY TO COMMUNICATE, IRICO AND VEGETA COULDN'T RECEIVE UPDATES.
HMM?
WOOSH
WAIT. THAT SHIP...

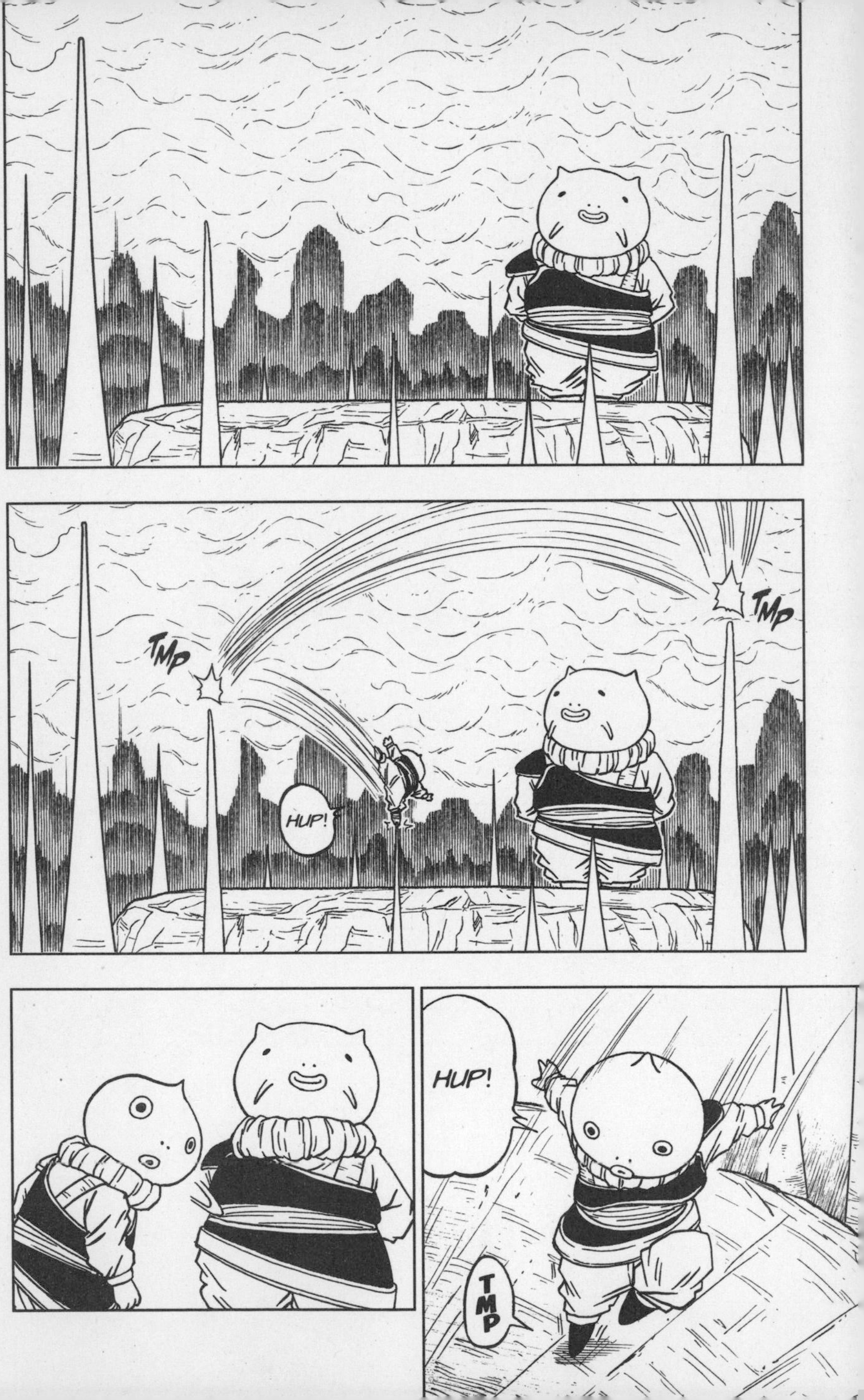
TMP
TMP
HUP!
HUP!
TMP

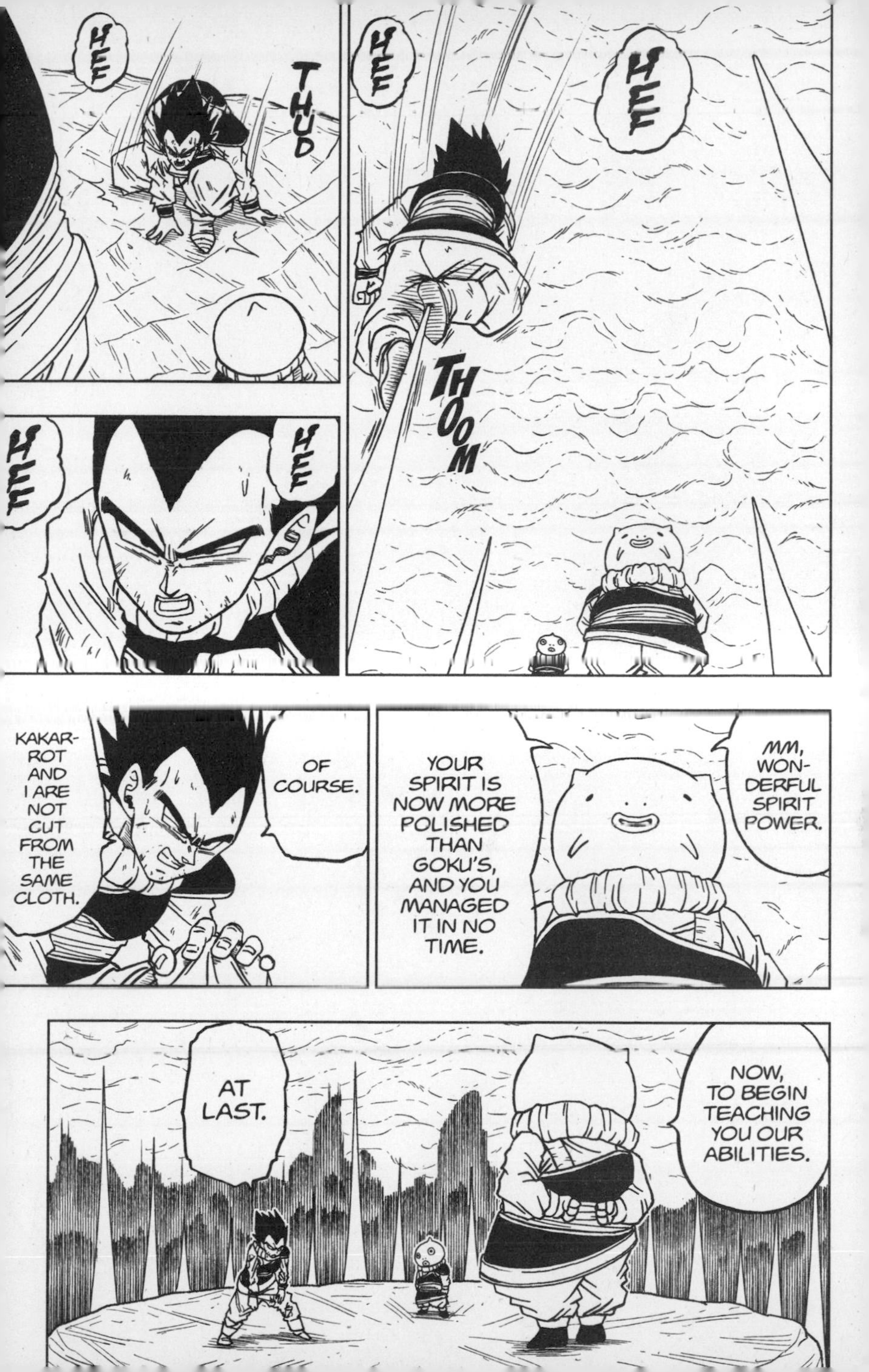
HEF
HEF
THOOM
THUD
HEF
HEF
HEF
MM, WON-DERFUL SPIRIT POWER.
YOUR SPIRIT IS NOW MORE POLISHED THAN GOKU'S, AND YOU MANAGED IT IN NO TIME.
OF COURSE.
KAKAR-ROT AND I ARE NOT CUT FROM THE SAME CLOTH.
NOW, TO BEGIN TEACHING YOU OUR ABILITIES.
AT LAST.

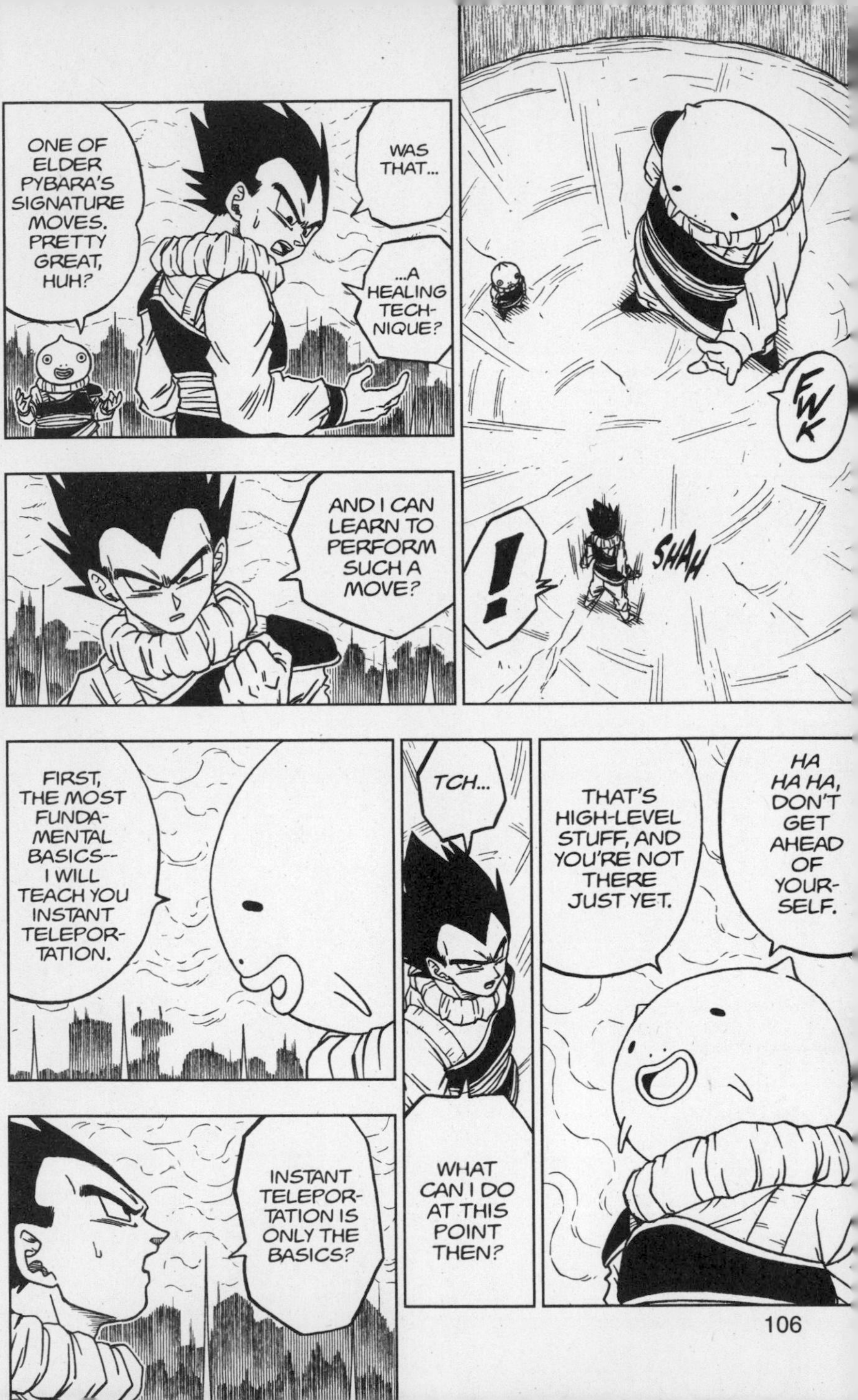
FWK
SHAH
!
WAS THAT...
...A HEALING TECH-NIQUE?
ONE OF ELDER PYBARA'S SIGNATURE MOVES. PRETTY GREAT, HUH?
AND I CAN LEARN TO PERFORM SUCH A MOVE?
FIRST, THE MOST FUNDA-MENTAL BASICS-- I WILL TEACH YOU INSTANT TELEPOR-TATION.
INSTANT TELEPOR-TATION IS ONLY THE BASICS?
WHAT CAN I DO AT THIS POINT THEN?
HA HA HA, DON'T GET AHEAD OF YOUR-SELF.
THAT'S HIGH-LEVEL STUFF, AND YOU'RE NOT THERE JUST YET.
TCH...

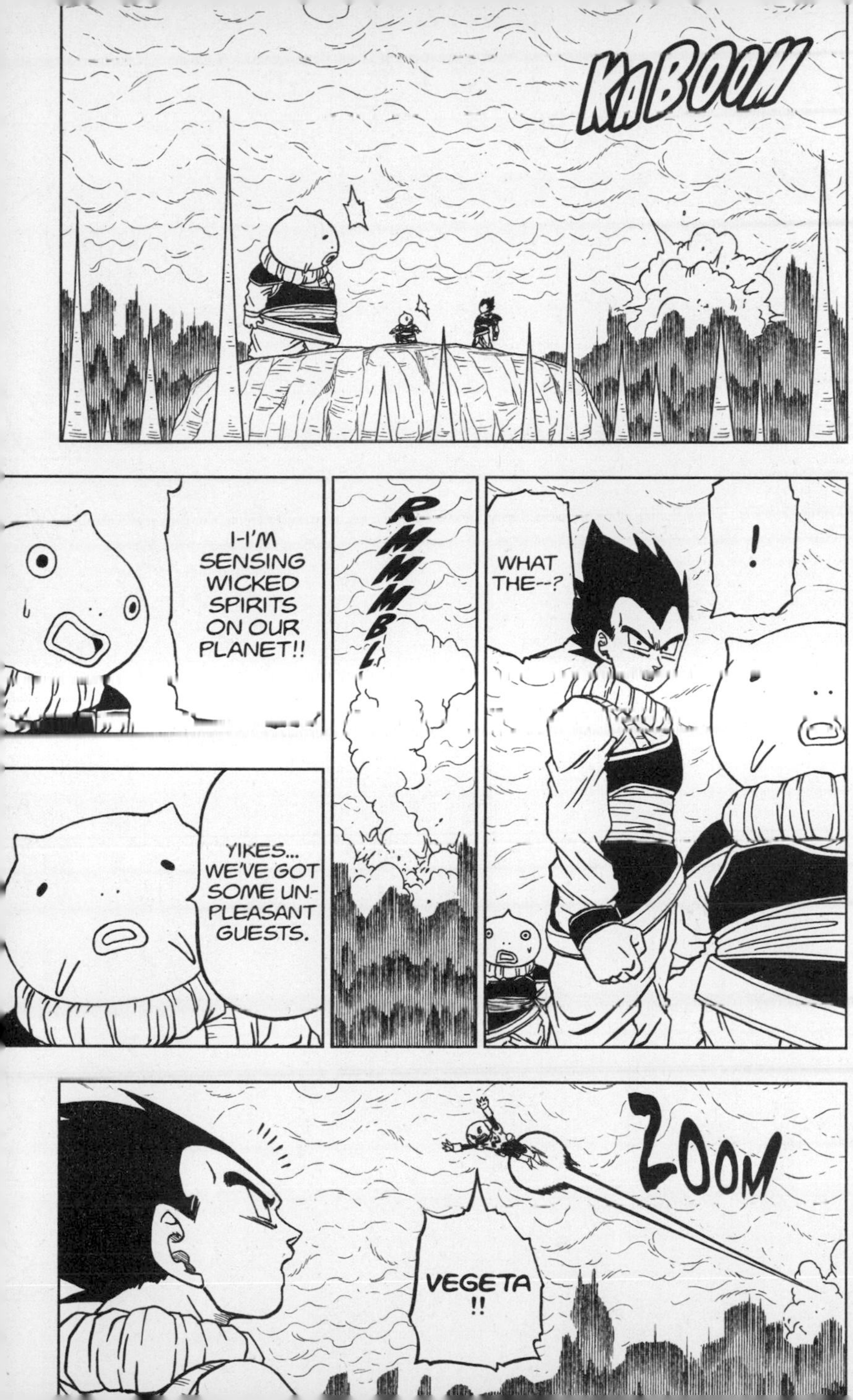
KABOOM
!
WHAT THE--?
RMMMBL
I-I'M SENSING WICKED SPIRITS ON OUR PLANET!!
YIKES... WE'VE GOT SOME UN-PLEASANT GUESTS.
ZOOM
VEGETA !!

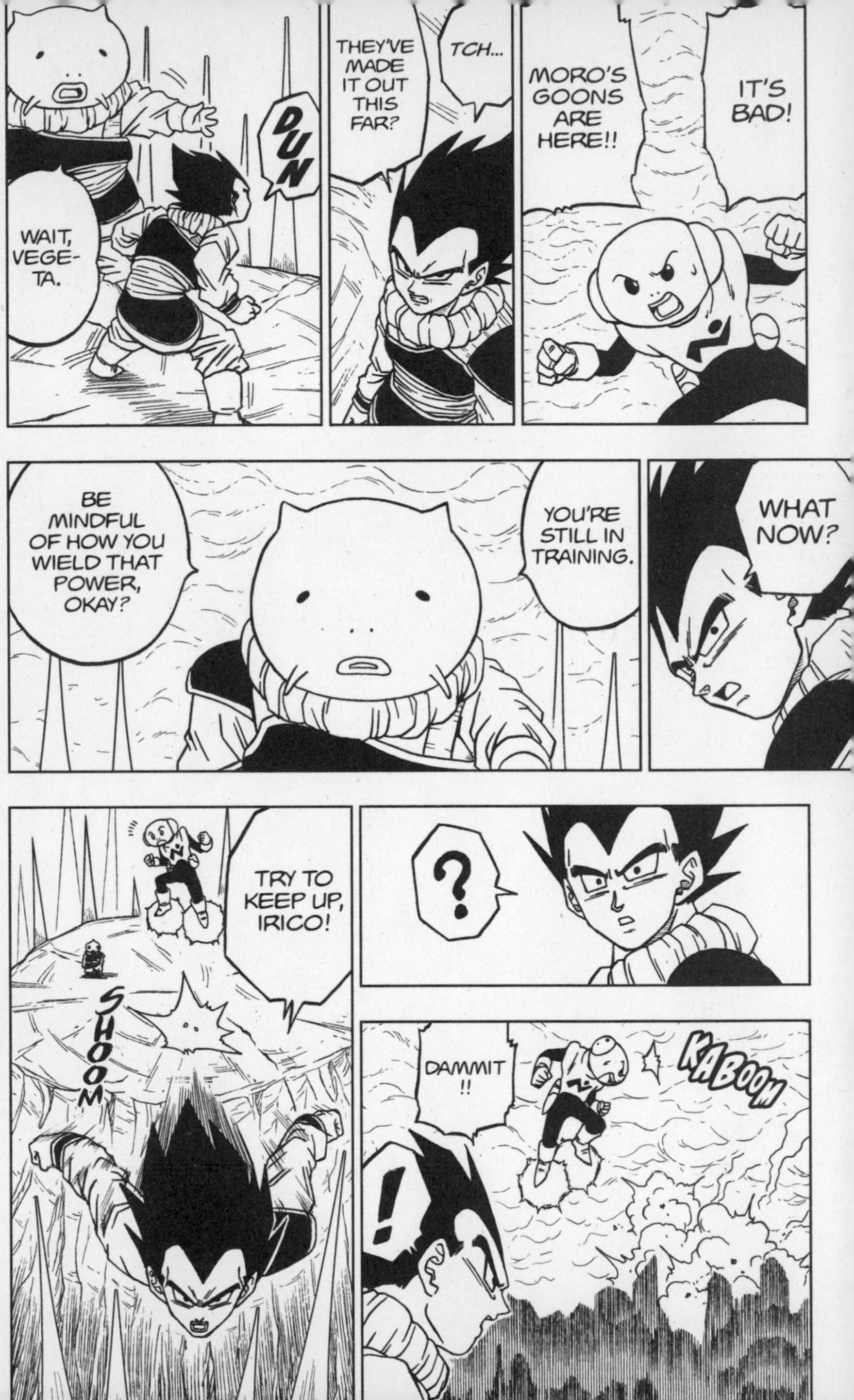
IT'S BAD!
MORO'S GOONS ARE HERE!!
TCH...
THEY'VE MADE IT OUT THIS FAR?
DUN
WAIT, VEGE-TA.
WHAT NOW?
YOU'RE STILL IN TRAINING.
BE MINDFUL OF HOW YOU WIELD THAT POWER, OKAY?
?
KABOOM
DAMMIT !!
!
TRY TO KEEP UP, IRICO!
SHOOOM

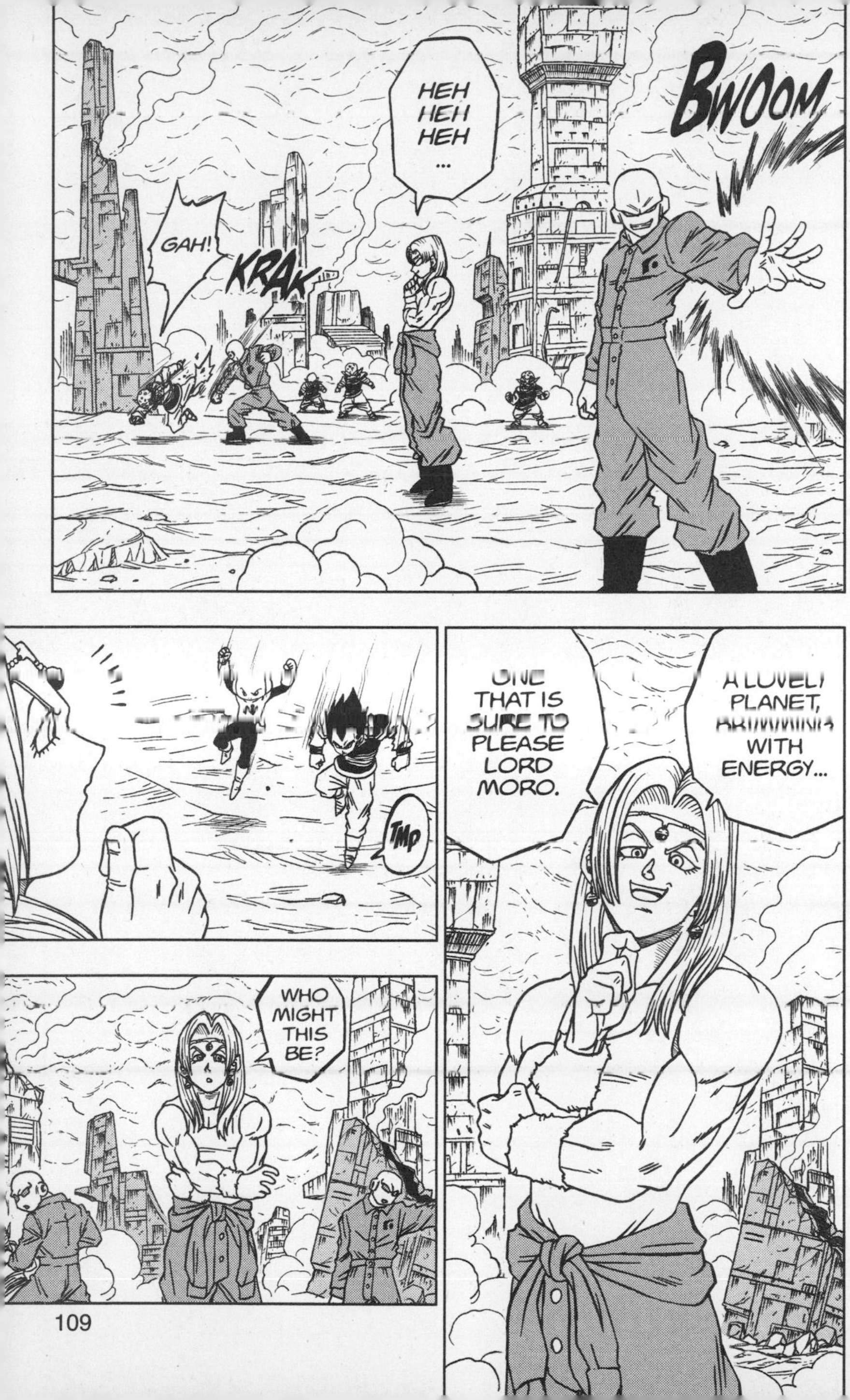
BWOOM
HEH HEH HEH ...
KRAK
GAH!
A LOVELY PLANET, WITH ENERGY...
ONE THAT IS SURE TO PLEASE LORD MORO.
TMP
WHO MIGHT THIS BE?

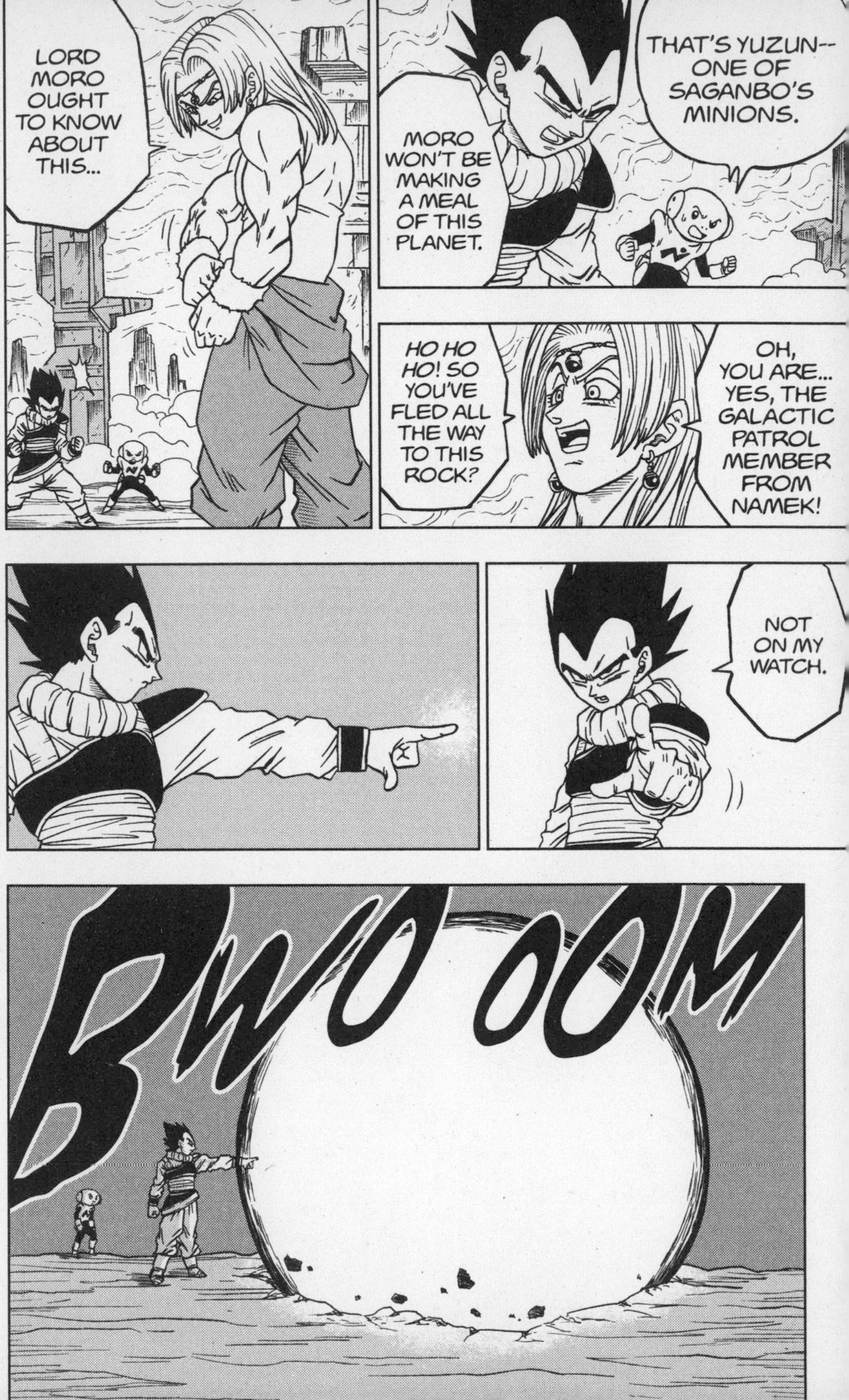
THAT'S YUZUN-- ONE OF SAGANBO'S MINIONS.
MORO WON'T BE MAKING A MEAL OF THIS PLANET.
OH, YOU ARE... YES, THE GALACTIC PATROL MEMBER FROM NAMEK!
HO HO HO! SO YOU'VE FLED ALL THE WAY TO THIS ROCK?
LORD MORO OUGHT TO KNOW ABOUT THIS...
NOT ON MY WATCH.
BWOOOM

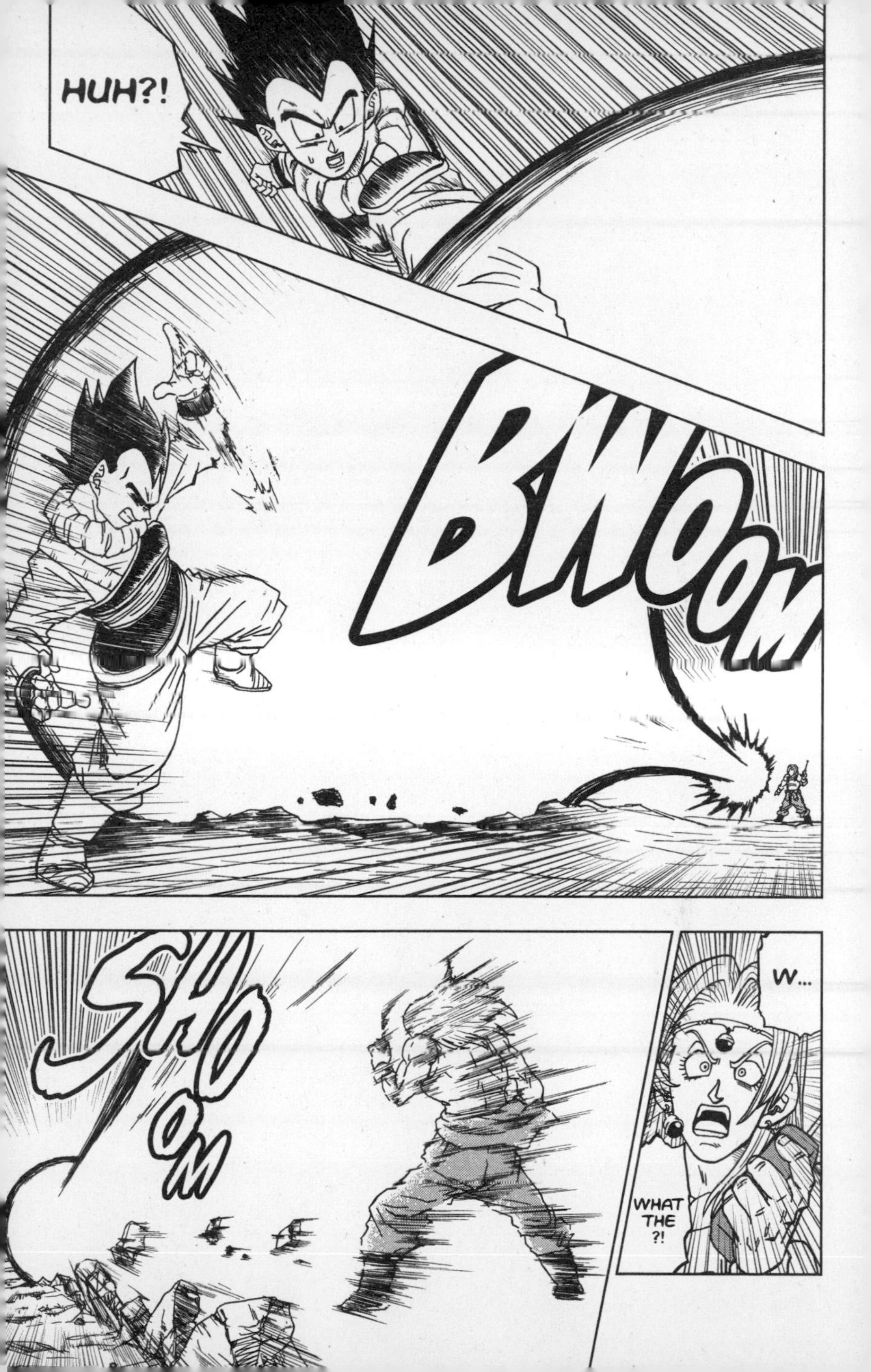
HUH?!
BWOOM
W...
WHAT THE ?!
SHOOM

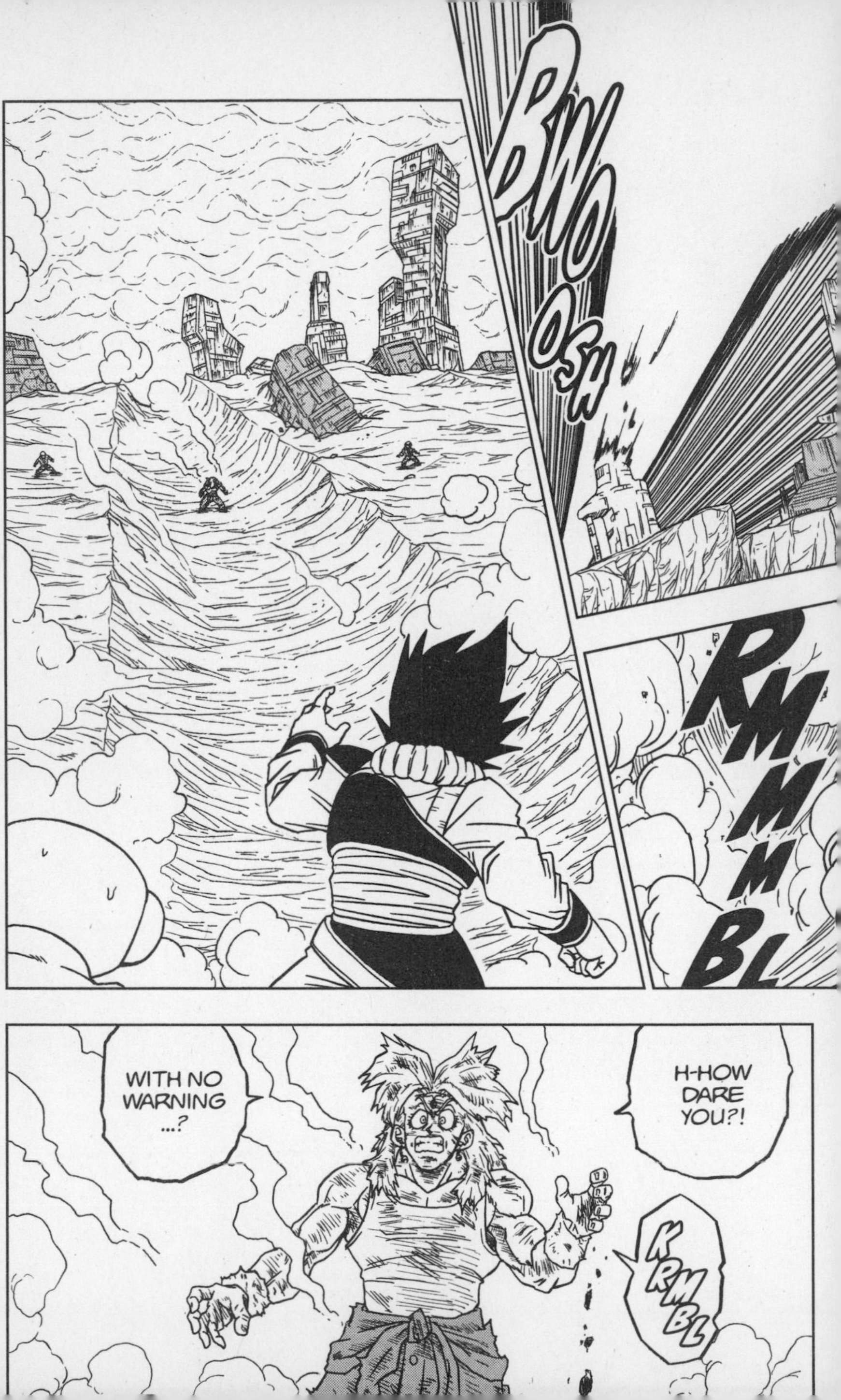
BWOOSH
RMMMBL
H-HOW DARE YOU?!
WITH NO WARNING ...?
KRMBL

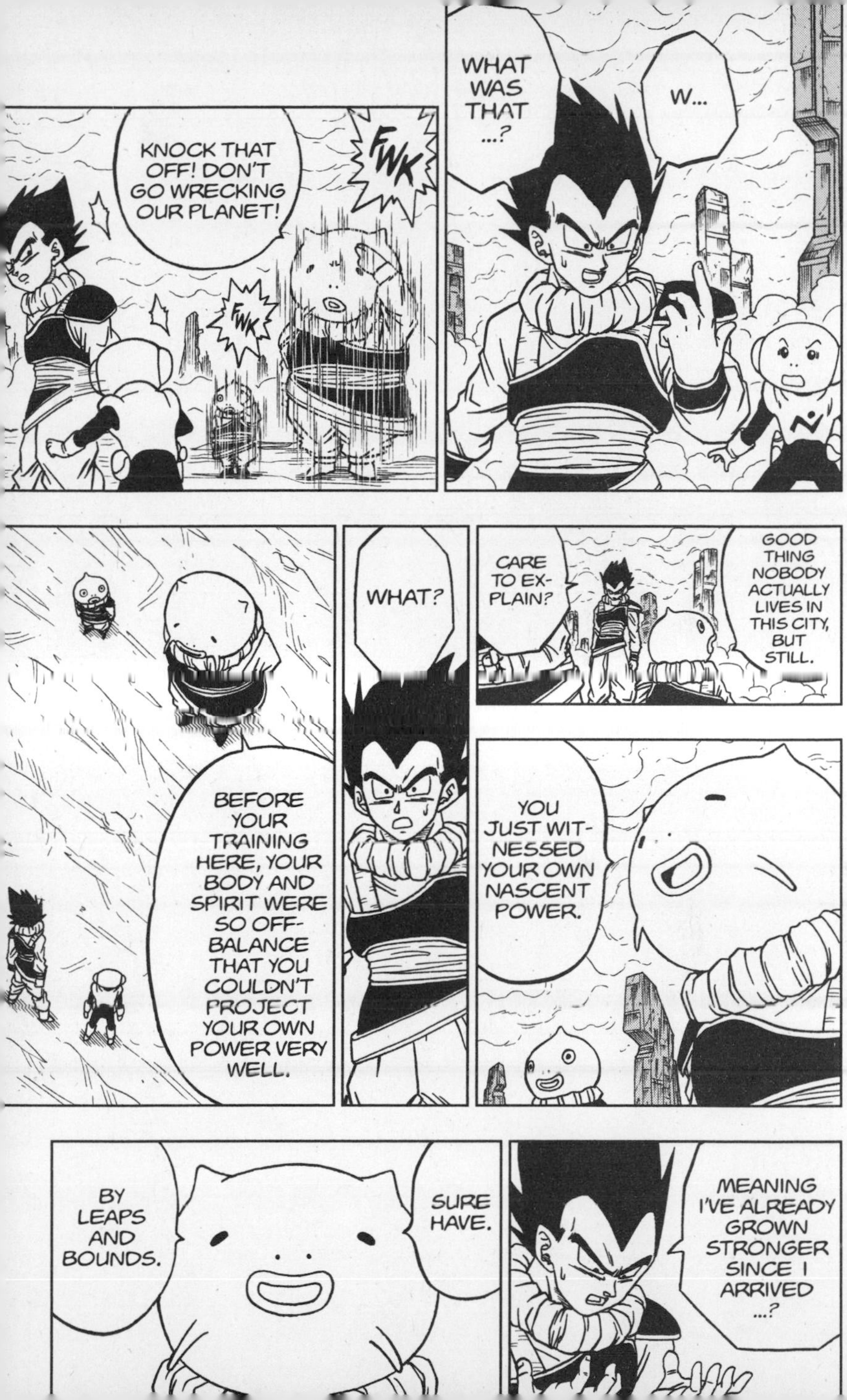
W...
WHAT WAS THAT ...?
FWK
KNOCK THAT OFF! DON'T GO WRECKING OUR PLANET!
FWK
GOOD THING NOBODY ACTUALLY LIVES IN THIS CITY, BUT STILL.
CARE TO EX-PLAIN?
YOU JUST WIT-NESSED YOUR OWN NASCENT POWER.
WHAT?
BEFORE YOUR TRAINING HERE, YOUR BODY AND SPIRIT WERE SO OFF-BALANCE THAT YOU COULDN'T PROJECT YOUR OWN POWER VERY WELL.
MEANING I'VE ALREADY GROWN STRONGER SINCE I ARRIVED ...?
SURE HAVE.
BY LEAPS AND BOUNDS.

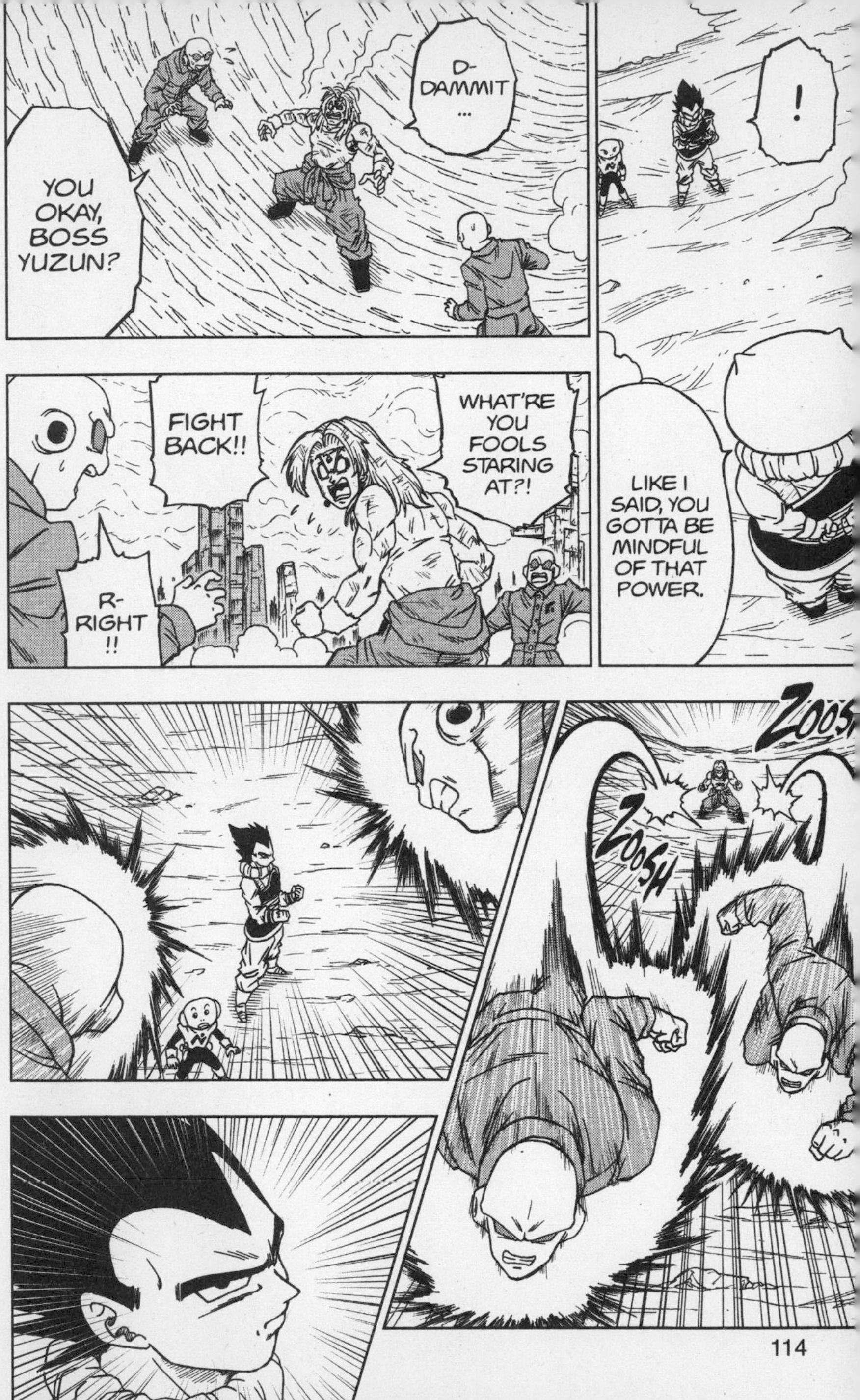
!
D-DAMMIT...
YOU OKAY, BOSS YUZUN?
LIKE I SAID, YOU GOTTA BE MINDFUL OF THAT POWER.
WHAT'RE YOU FOOLS STARING AT?!
FIGHT BACK!!
R-RIGHT!!
ZOOS
ZOOSH

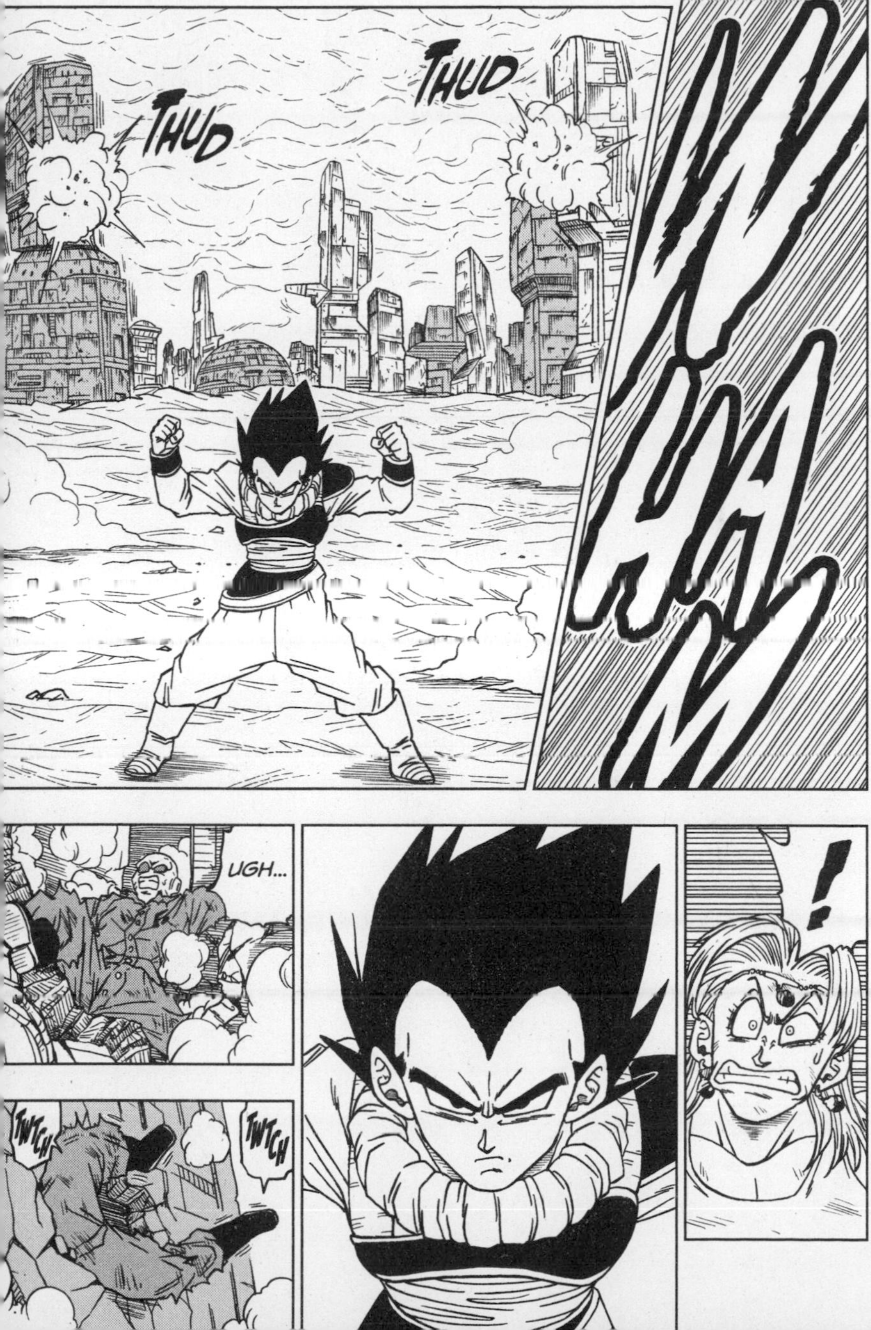
THUD
THUD
!
UGH...
TWITCH
TWITCH

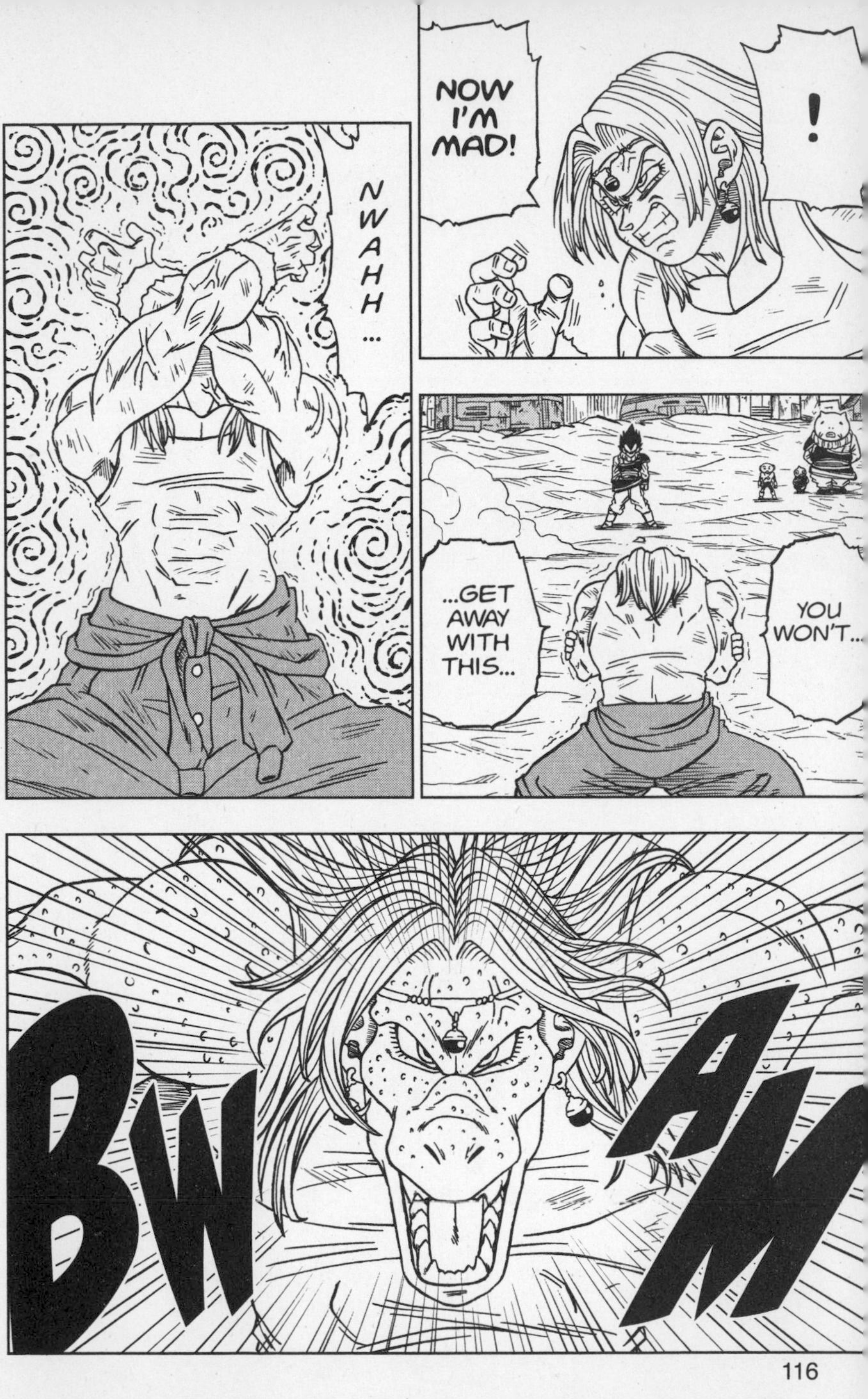
!
NOW I'M MAD!
YOU WON'T...
...GET AWAY WITH THIS...
NWAHH...
BWA

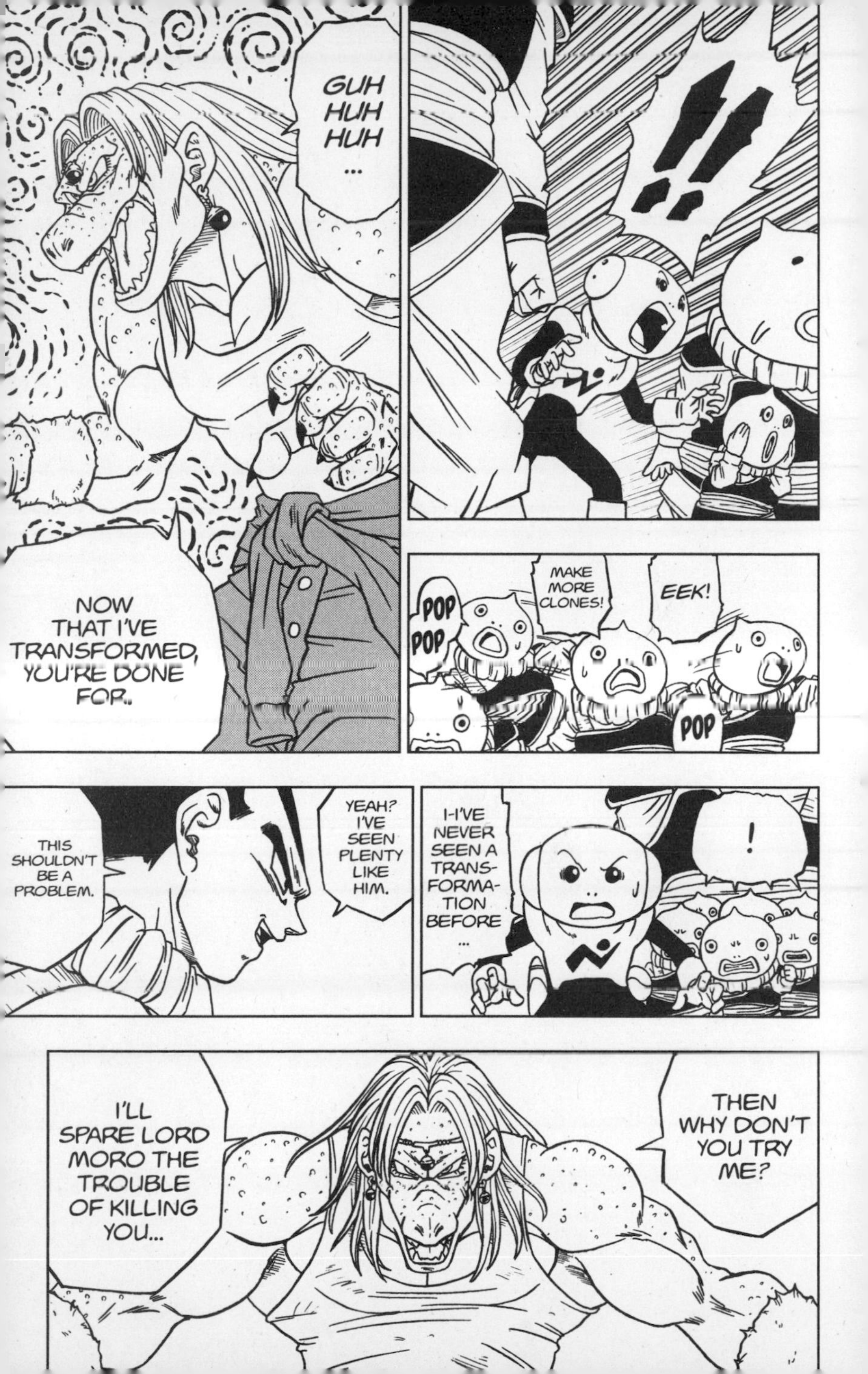
!!
EEK!
MAKE MORE CLONES!
POP POP
POP
GUH HUH HUH ...
NOW THAT I'VE TRANSFORMED, YOU'RE DONE FOR..
!
I-I'VE NEVER SEEN A TRANS-FORMA-TION BEFORE ...
YEAH? I'VE SEEN PLENTY LIKE HIM.
THIS SHOULDN'T BE A PROBLEM.
THEN WHY DON'T YOU TRY ME?
I'LL SPARE LORD MORO THE TROUBLE OF KILLING YOU...

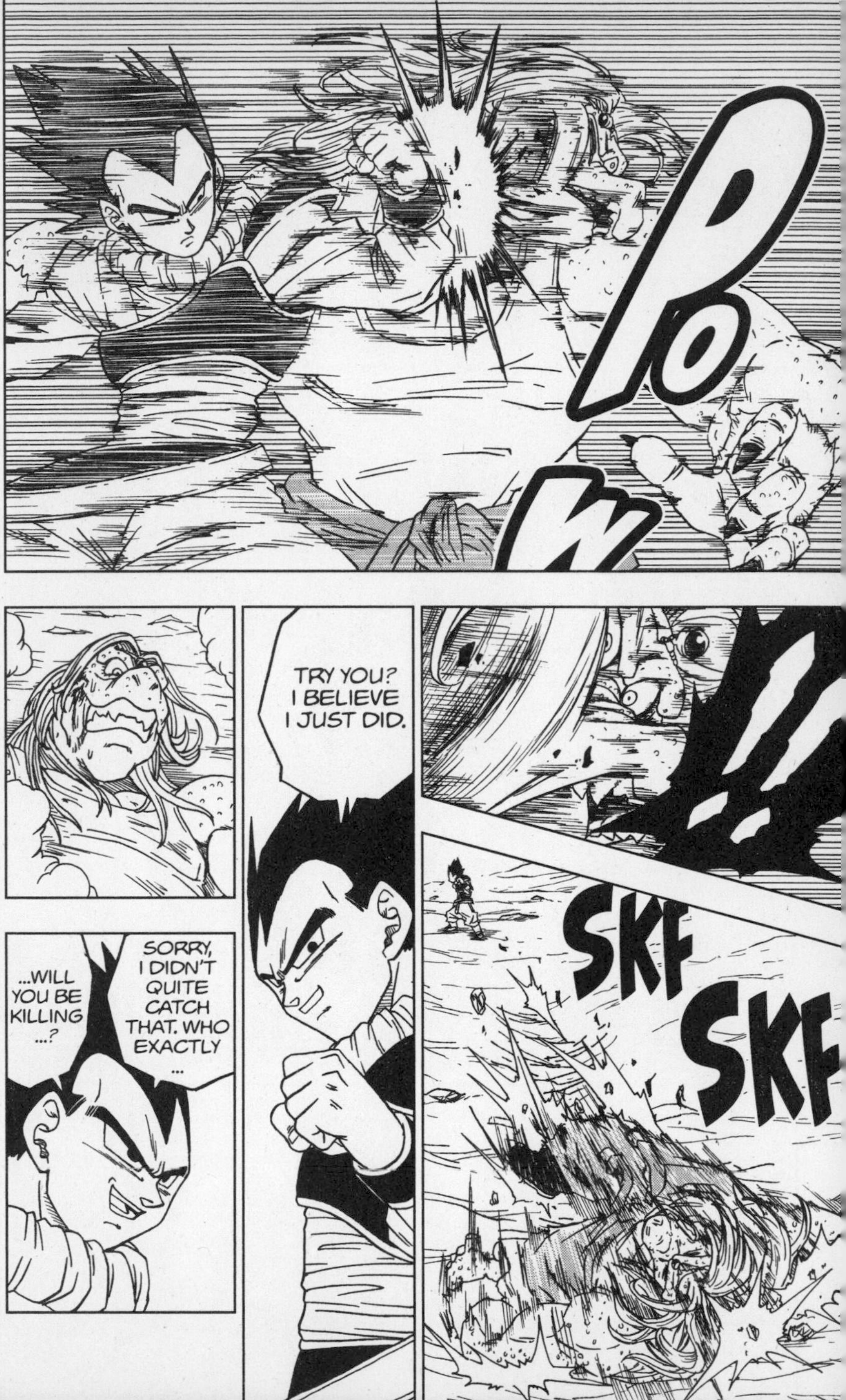
POW
!!
SKF
SKF
TRY YOU? I BELIEVE I JUST DID.
SORRY, I DIDN'T QUITE CATCH THAT. WHO EXACTLY ...
...WILL YOU BE KILLING ...?

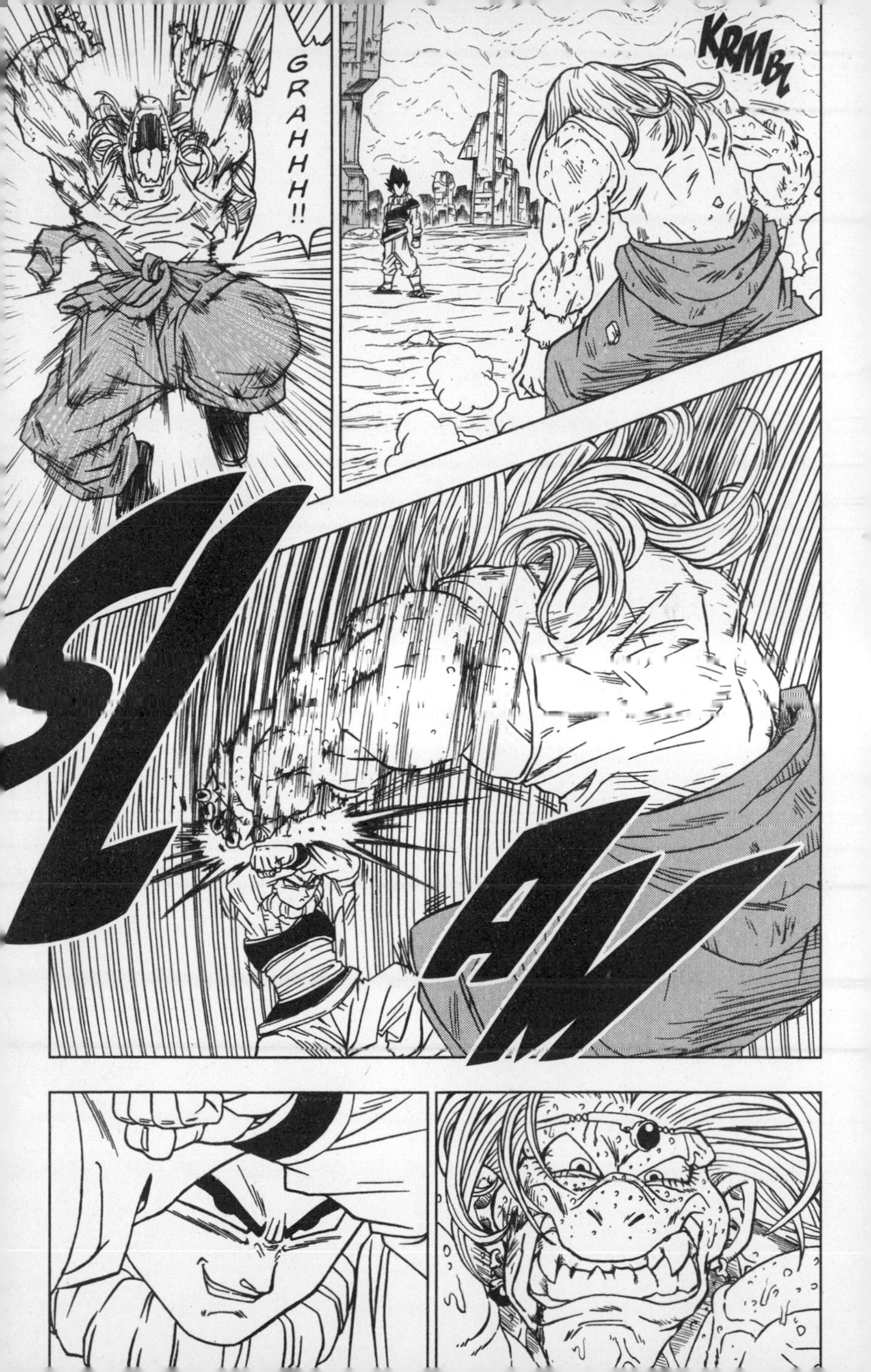
KRMBL
GRAHHHH!!
SLAM

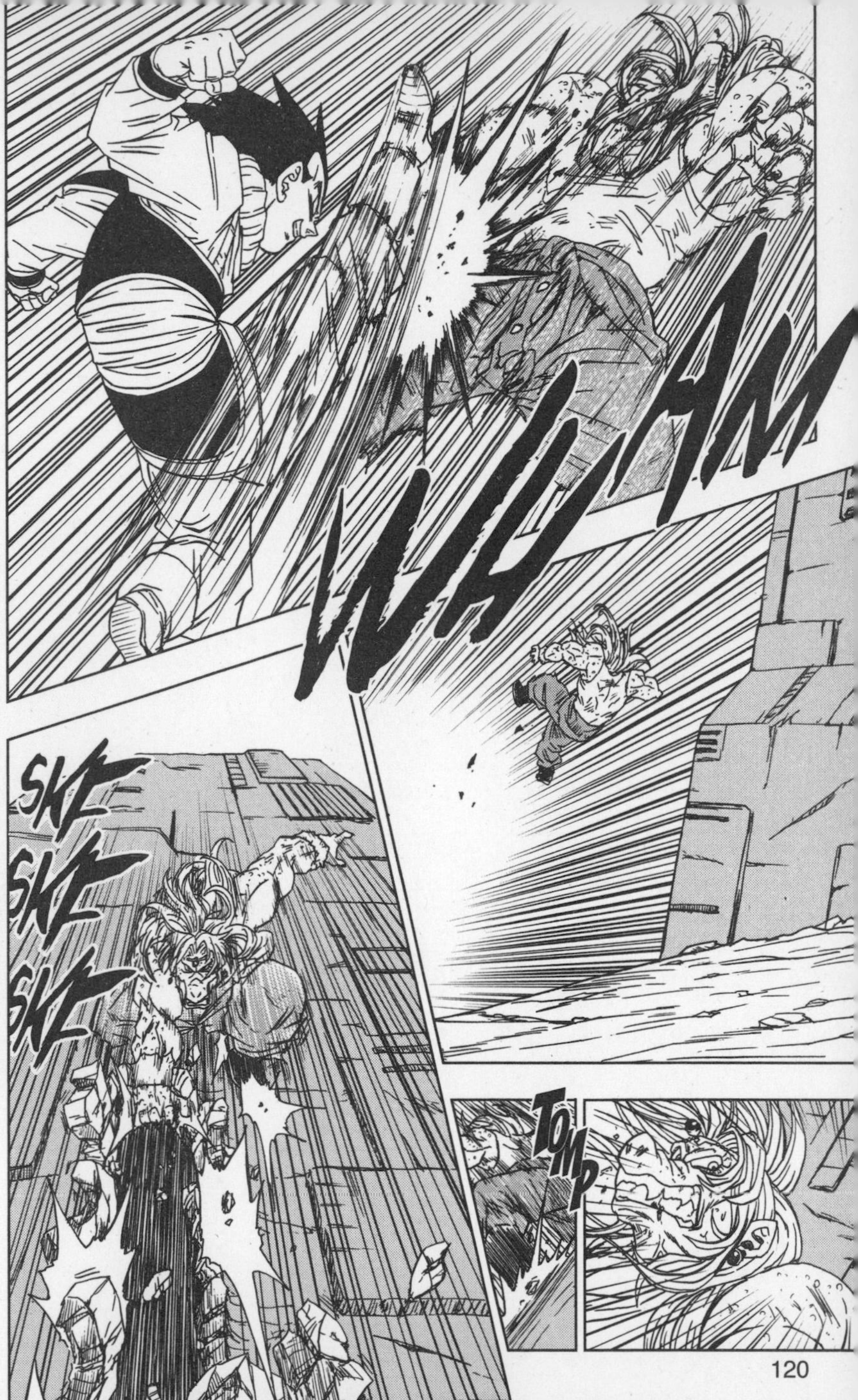
WHAM
SKI
SKI
SKI
TOMP

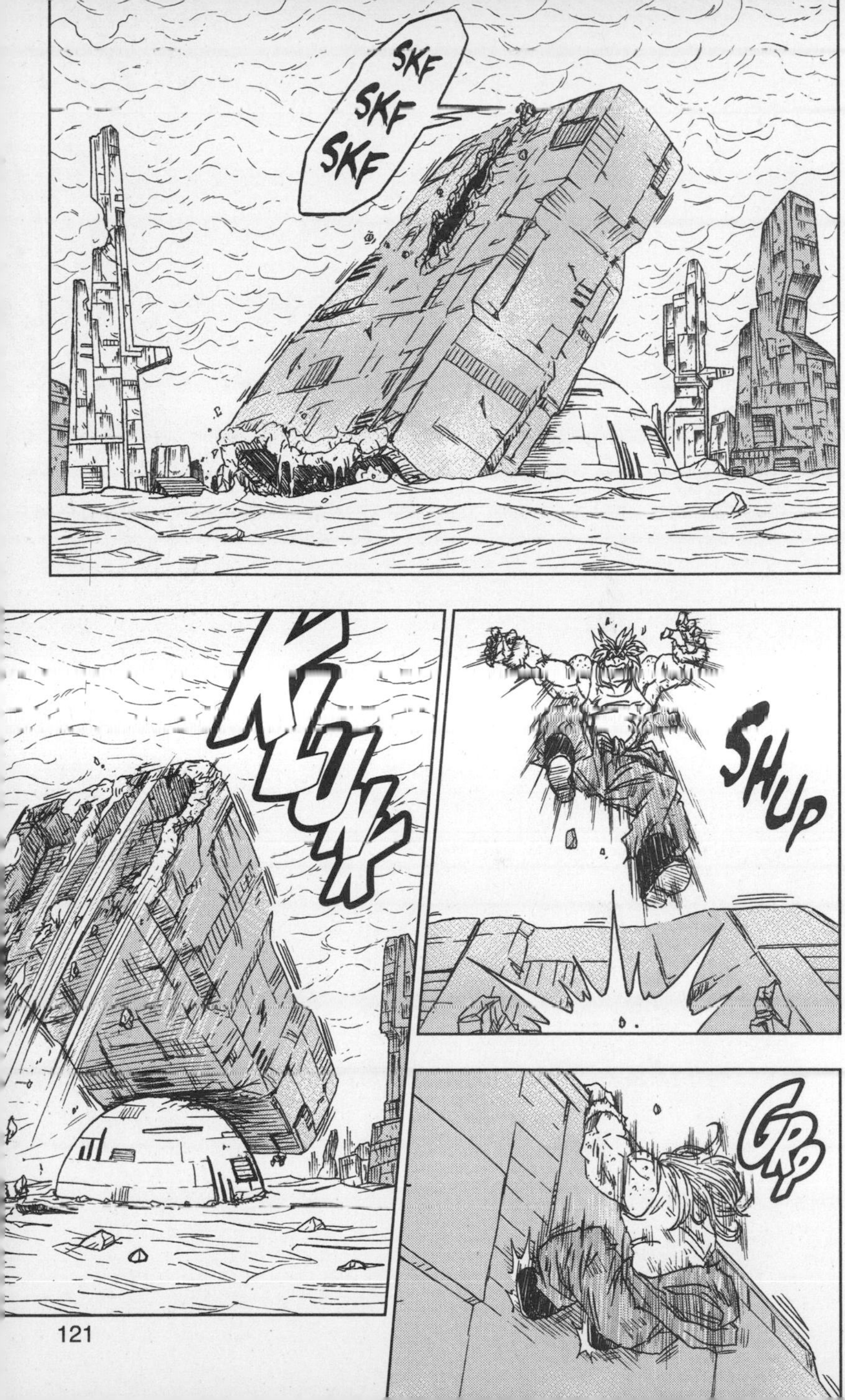
SKF
SKF
SKF
SHUP
GRP
KLUNK

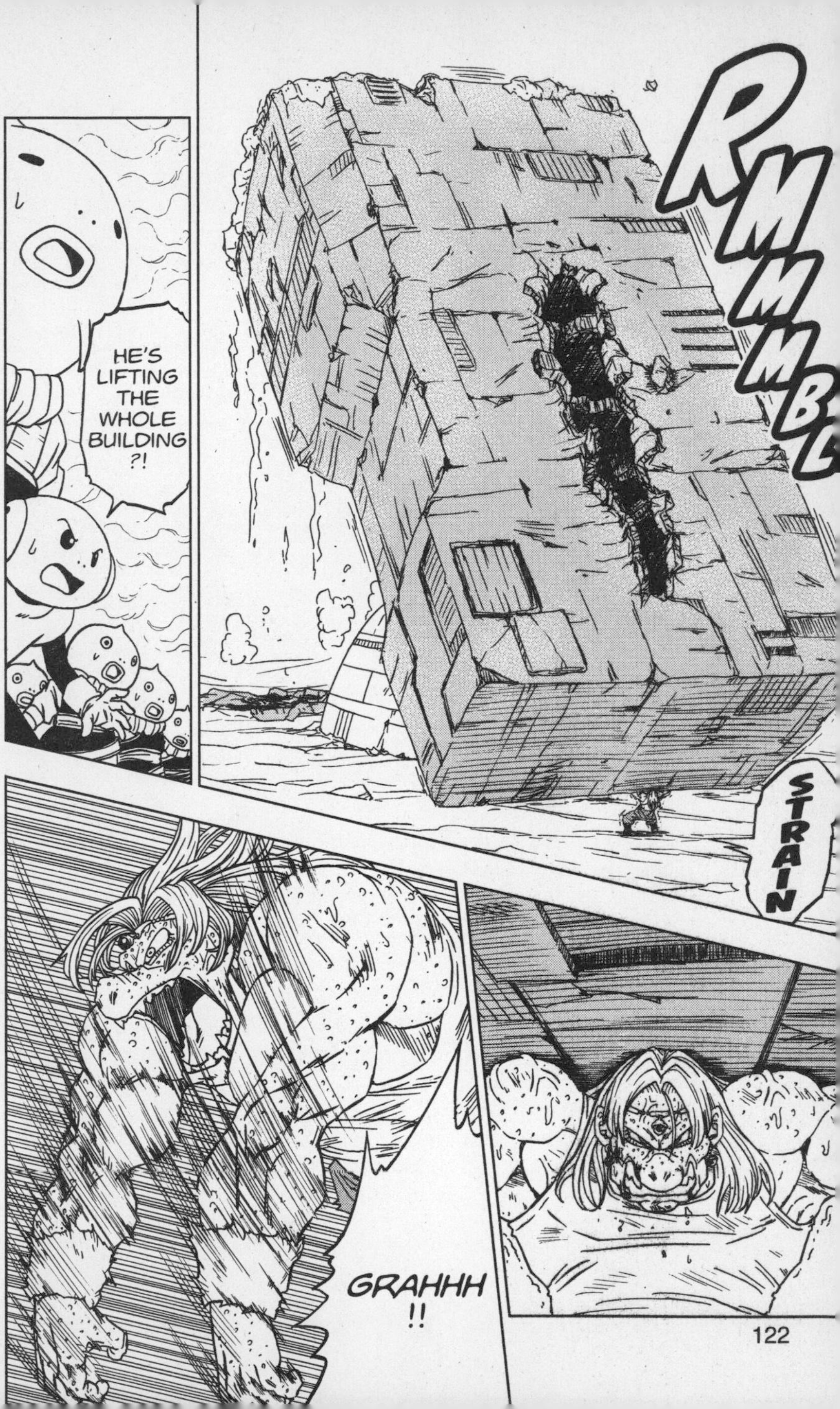
RMMMBL
STRAIN
HE'S LIFTING THE WHOLE BUILDING ?!
GRAHHH !!

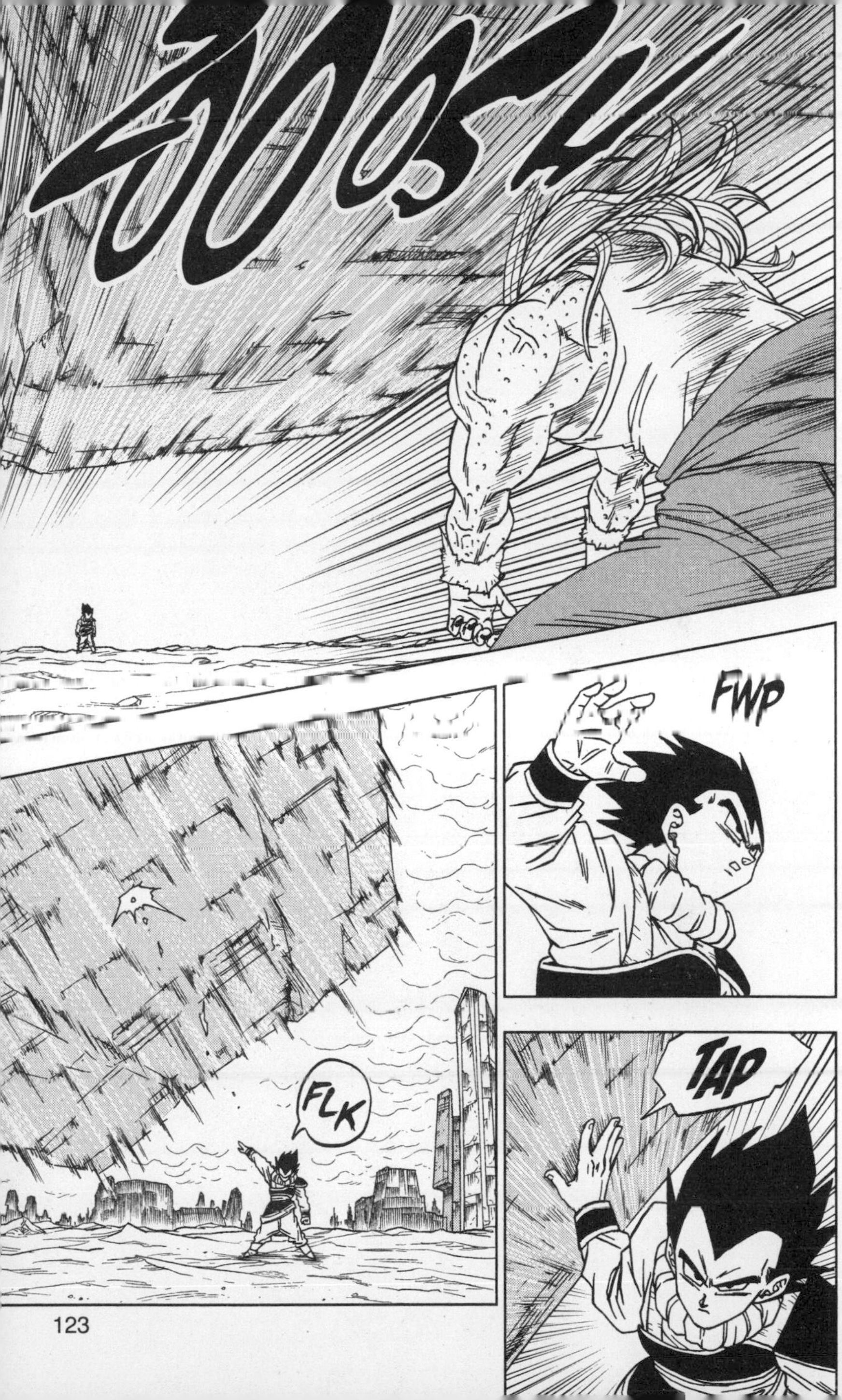
FWP
TAP
FLK

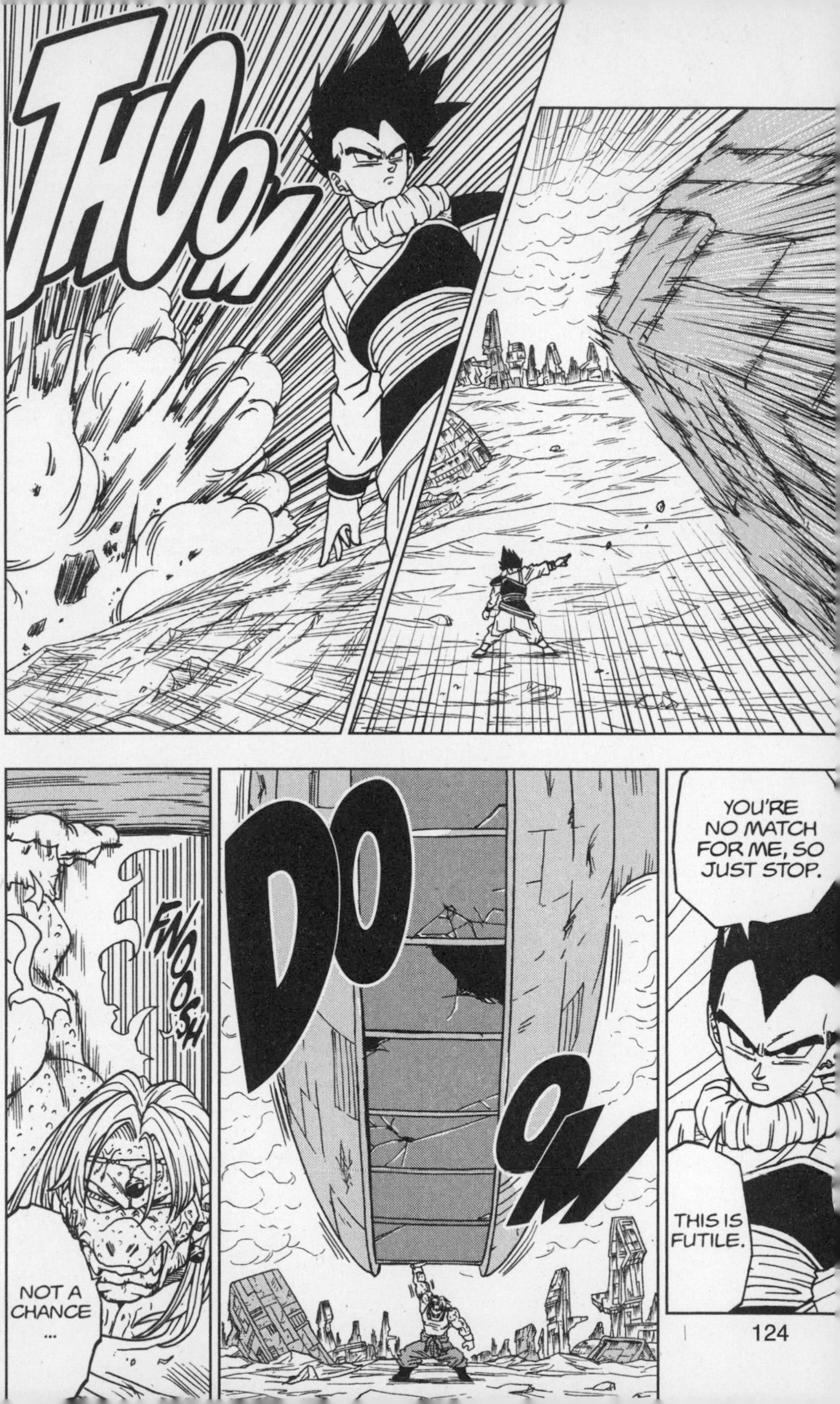
THOOM
YOU'RE NO MATCH FOR ME, SO JUST STOP.
THIS IS FUTILE.
DOOM
FWOOSH
NOT A CHANCE ...

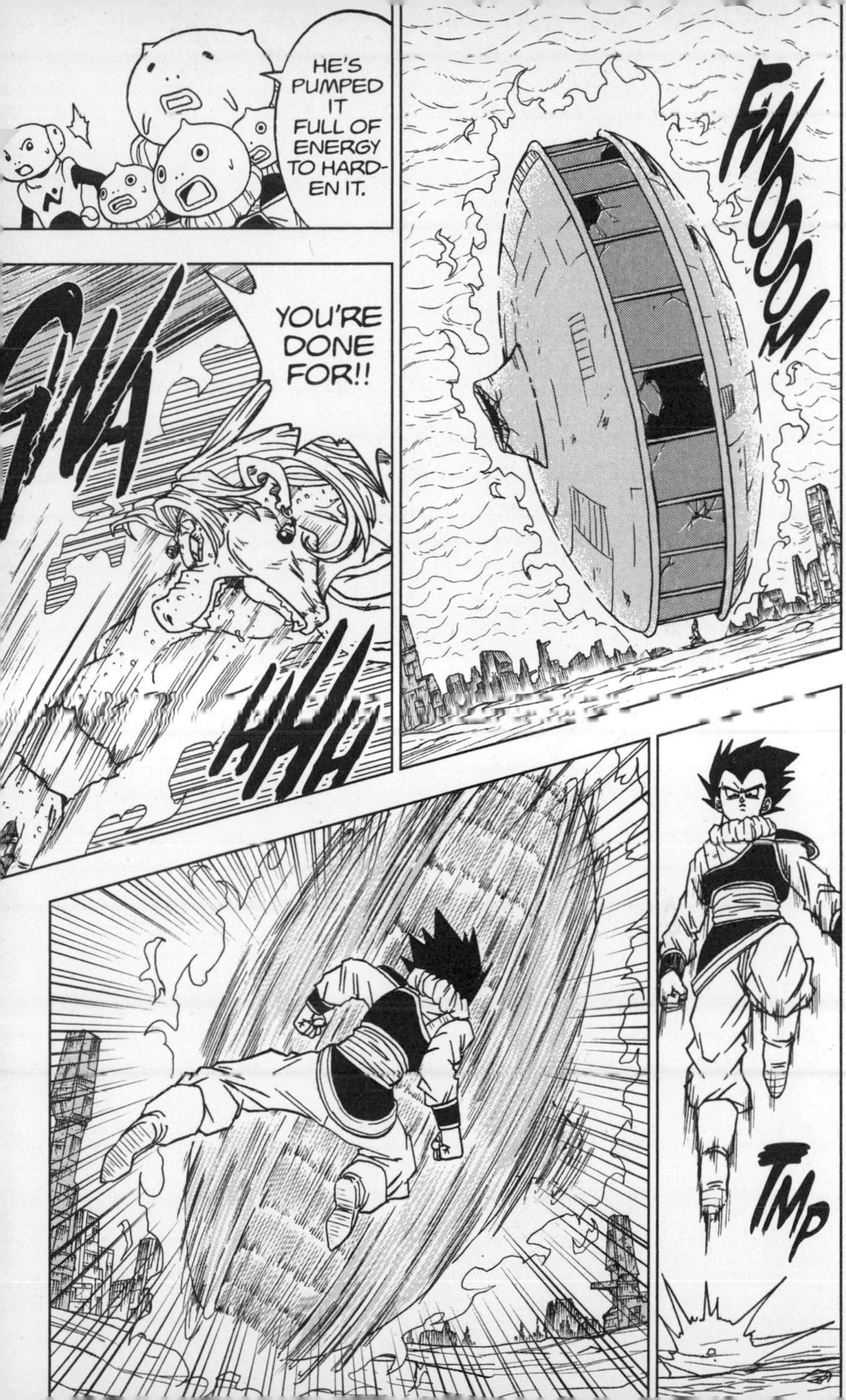
FWOOOM
HE'S PUMPED IT FULL OF ENERGY TO HARDEN IT.
GWAHHH
YOU'RE DONE FOR!!
TMP

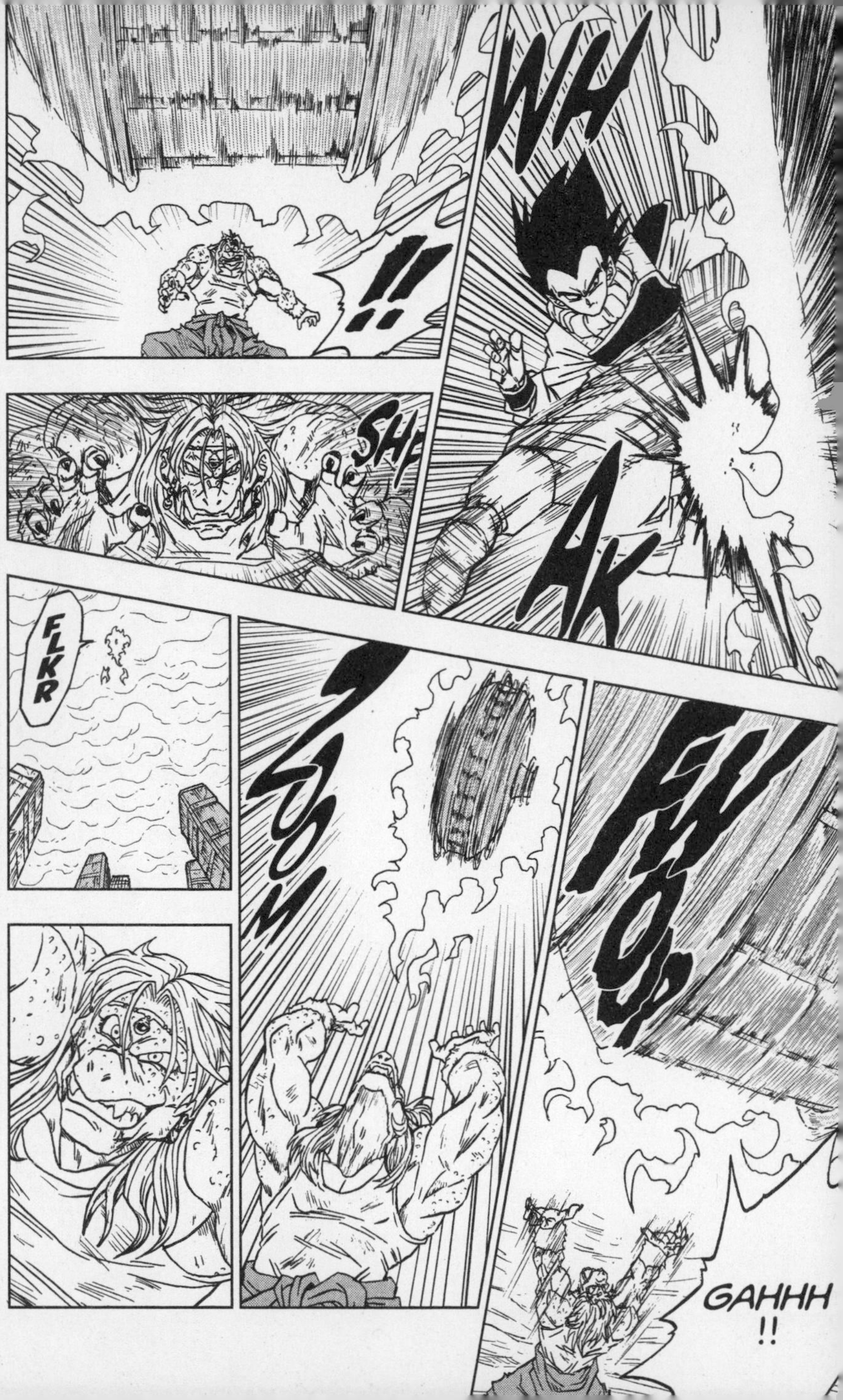
WH
AK
!!
SHF
WHOOP
GAHHH !!
VWOOM
FLKR

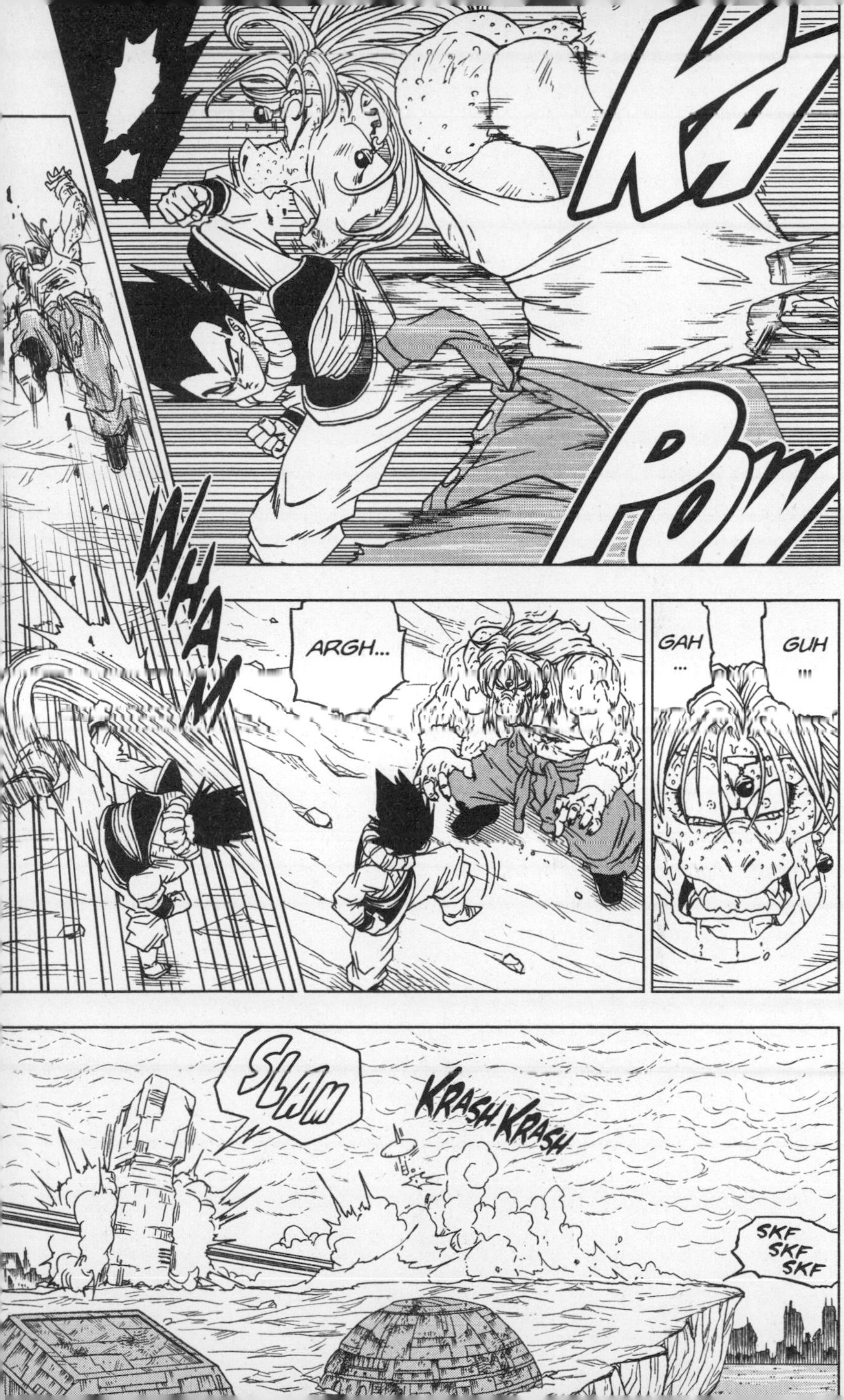
KA
POW
GAH...
GUH...
ARGH...
WHAM
SKF SKF SKF
KRASH KRASH
SLAM

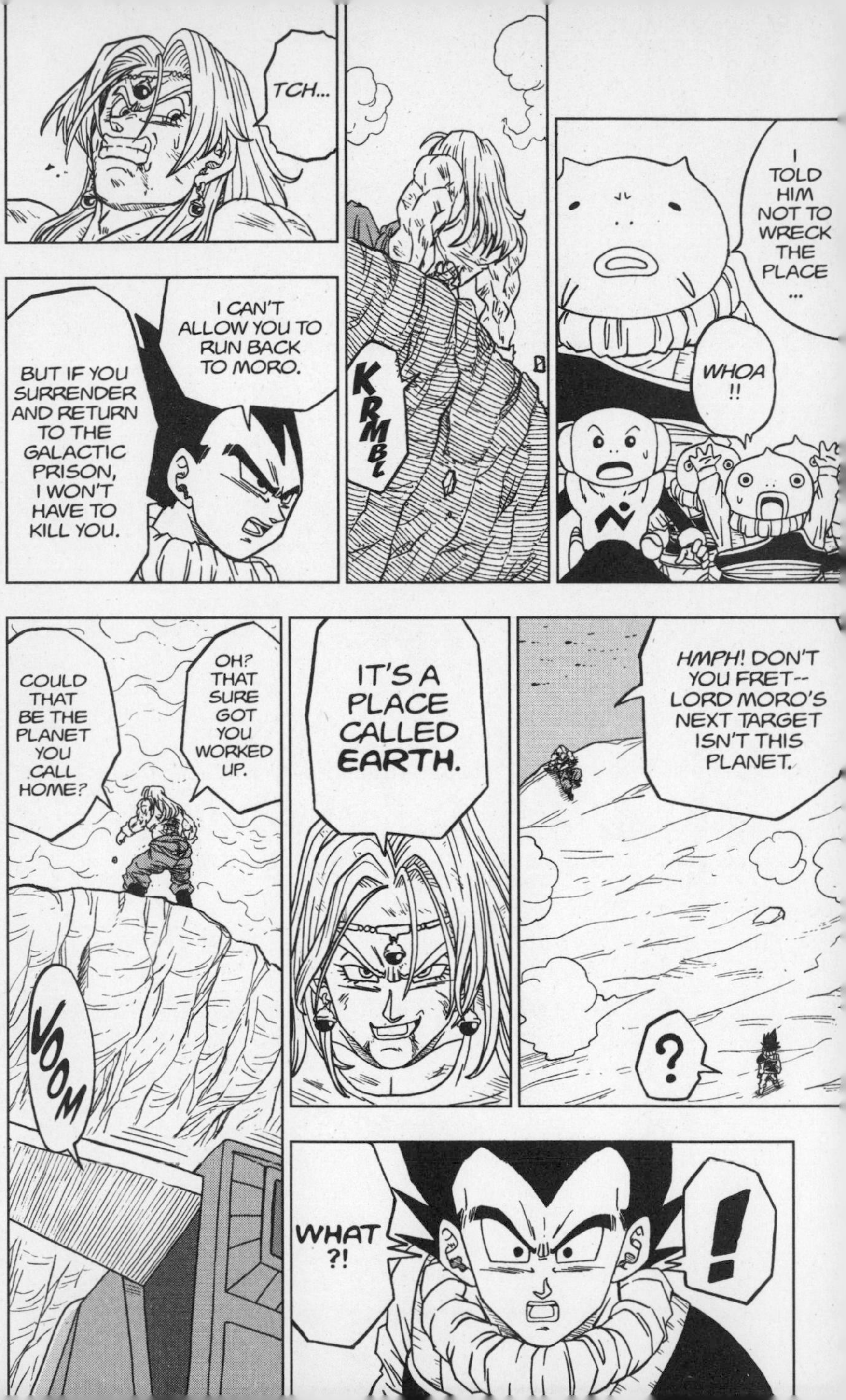
I TOLD HIM NOT TO WRECK THE PLACE ...
WHOA !!
KRMBL
TCH...
I CAN'T ALLOW YOU TO RUN BACK TO MORO.
BUT IF YOU SURRENDER AND RETURN TO THE GALACTIC PRISON, I WON'T HAVE TO KILL YOU.
HMPH! DON'T YOU FRET-- LORD MORO'S NEXT TARGET ISN'T THIS PLANET.
?
IT'S A PLACE CALLED EARTH.
!
WHAT ?!
OH? THAT SURE GOT YOU WORKED UP.
COULD THAT BE THE PLANET YOU CALL HOME?
VOOM

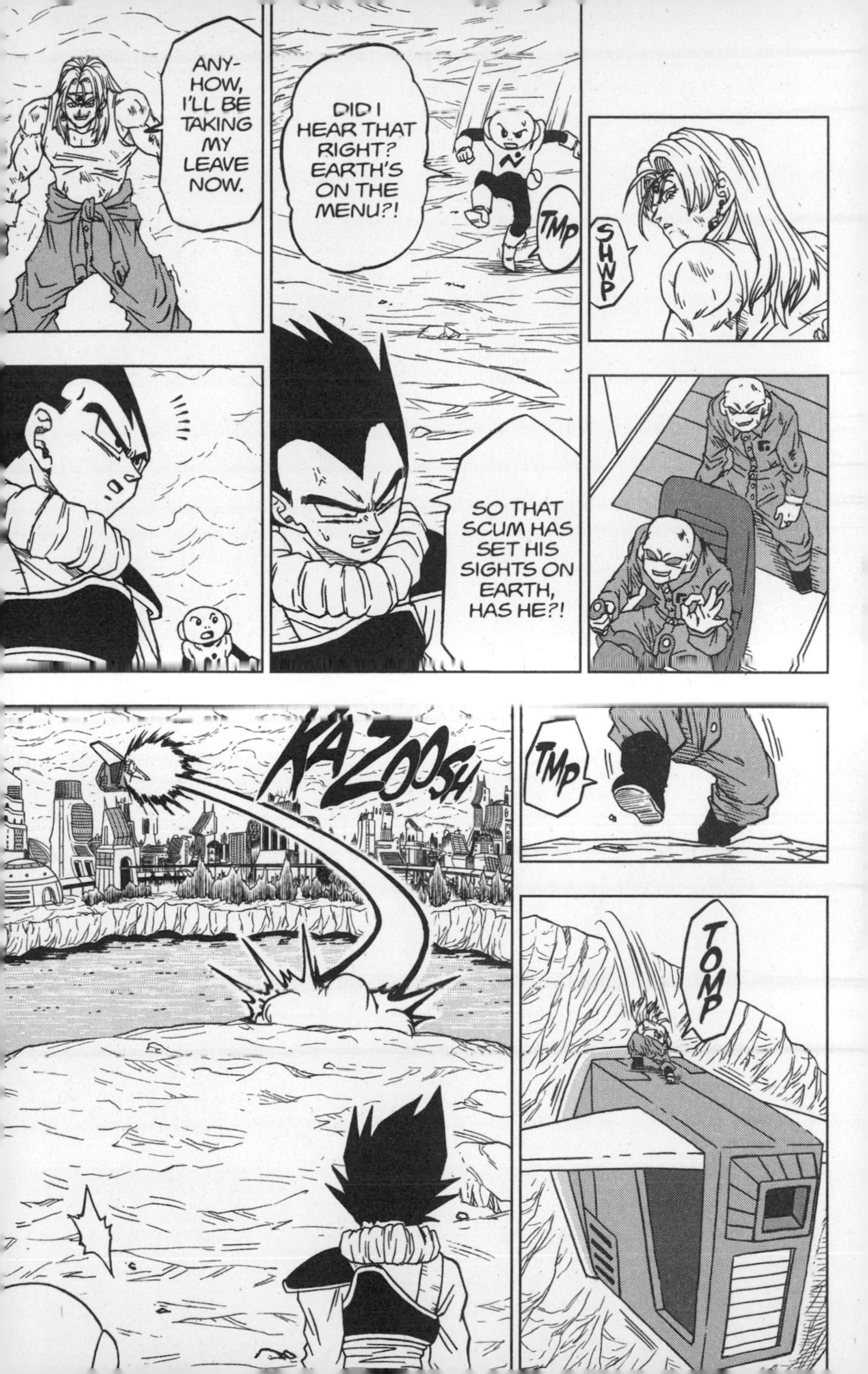
SHWP
DID I HEAR THAT RIGHT? EARTH'S ON THE MENU?!
TMP
ANY-HOW, I'LL BE TAKING MY LEAVE NOW.
SO THAT SCUM HAS SET HIS SIGHTS ON EARTH, HAS HE?!
TMP
TOMP
KAZOOSH

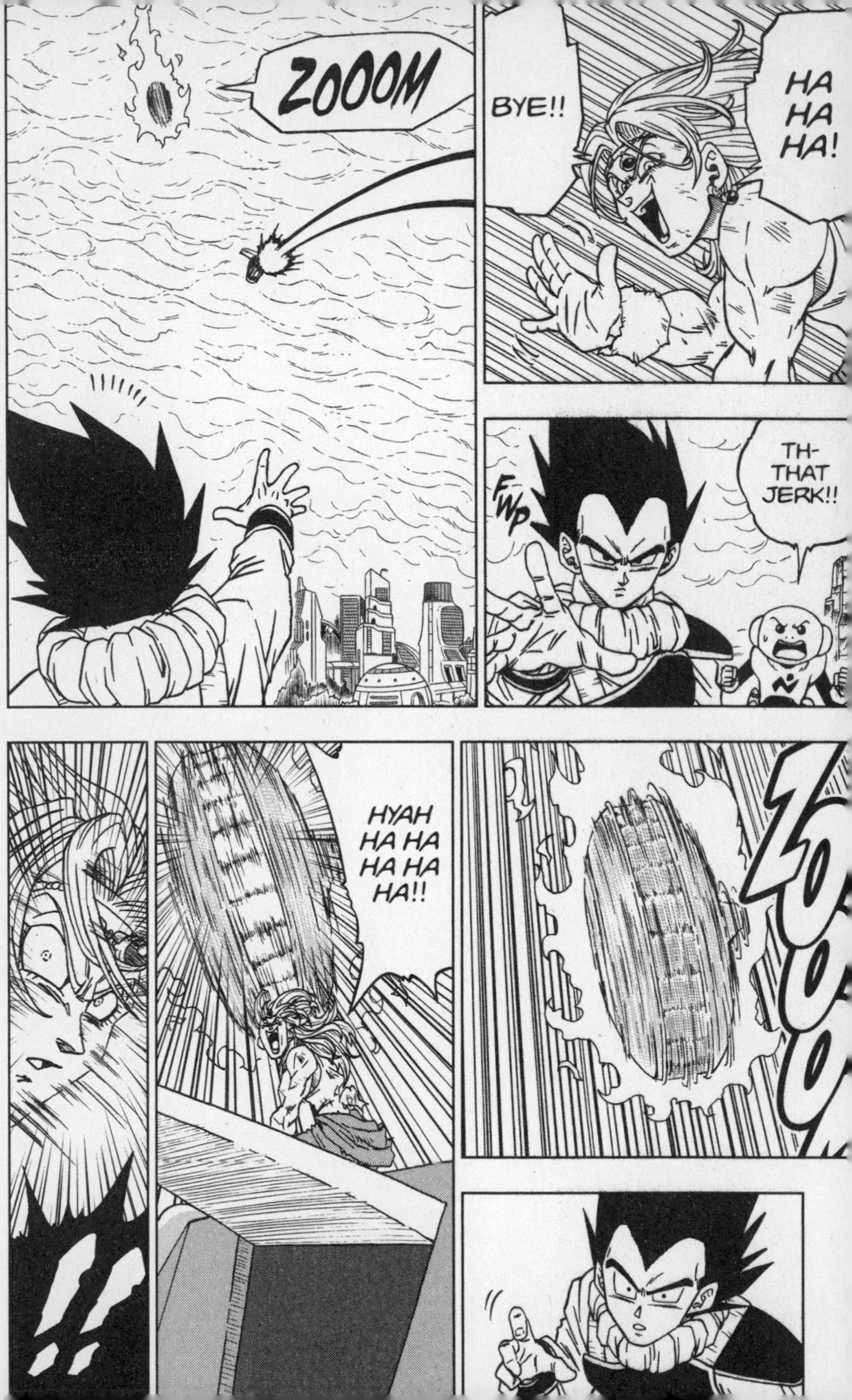
HA HA HA!
BYE!!
TH- THAT JERK!!
FWP
ZOOOM
HYAH HA HA HA HA HA HA!!

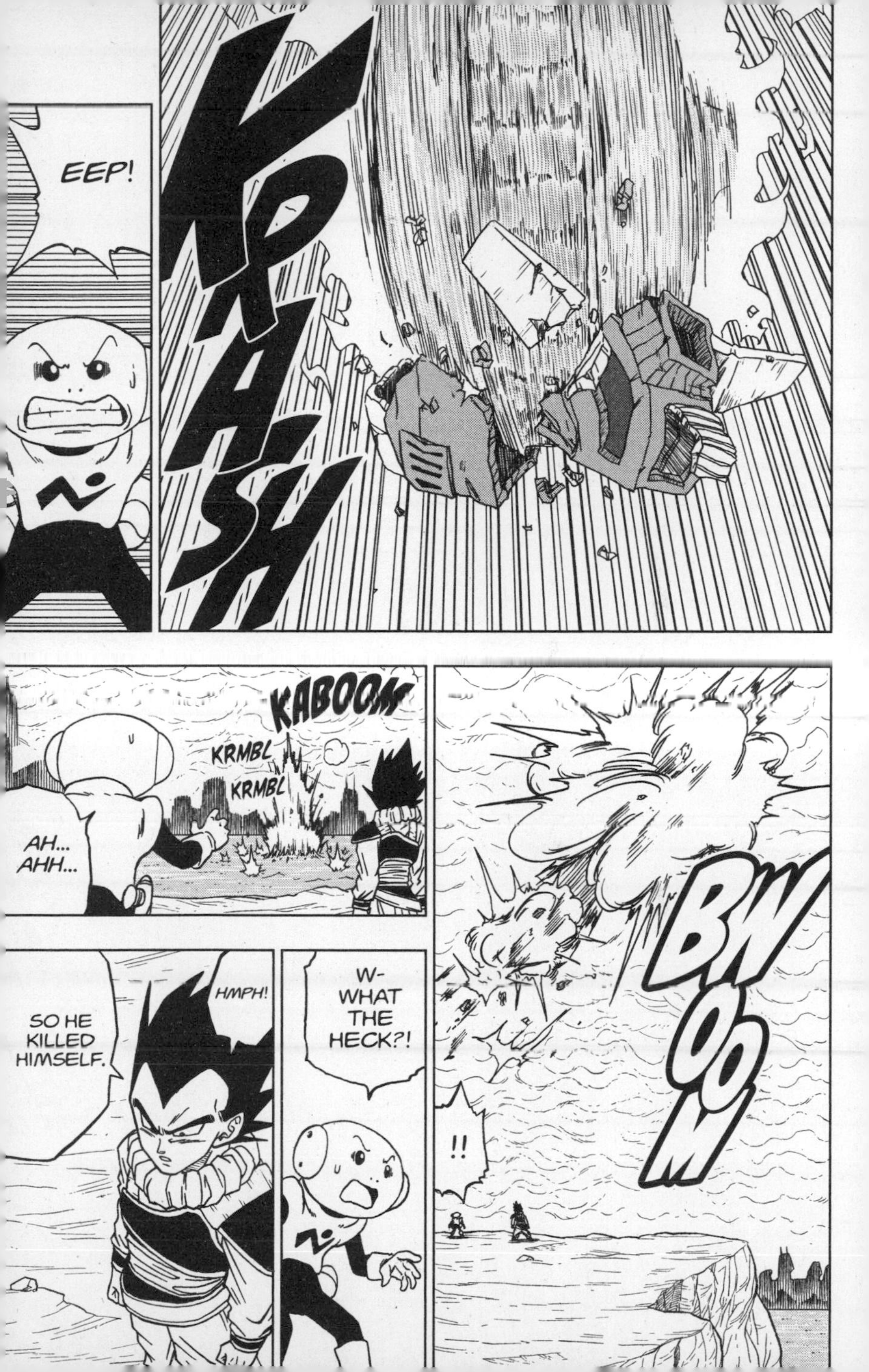
KRASH
EEP!
BWOOOM
!!
KABOOM
KRMBL
KRMBL
AH... AHH...
W- WHAT THE HECK?!
HMPH!
SO HE KILLED HIMSELF.

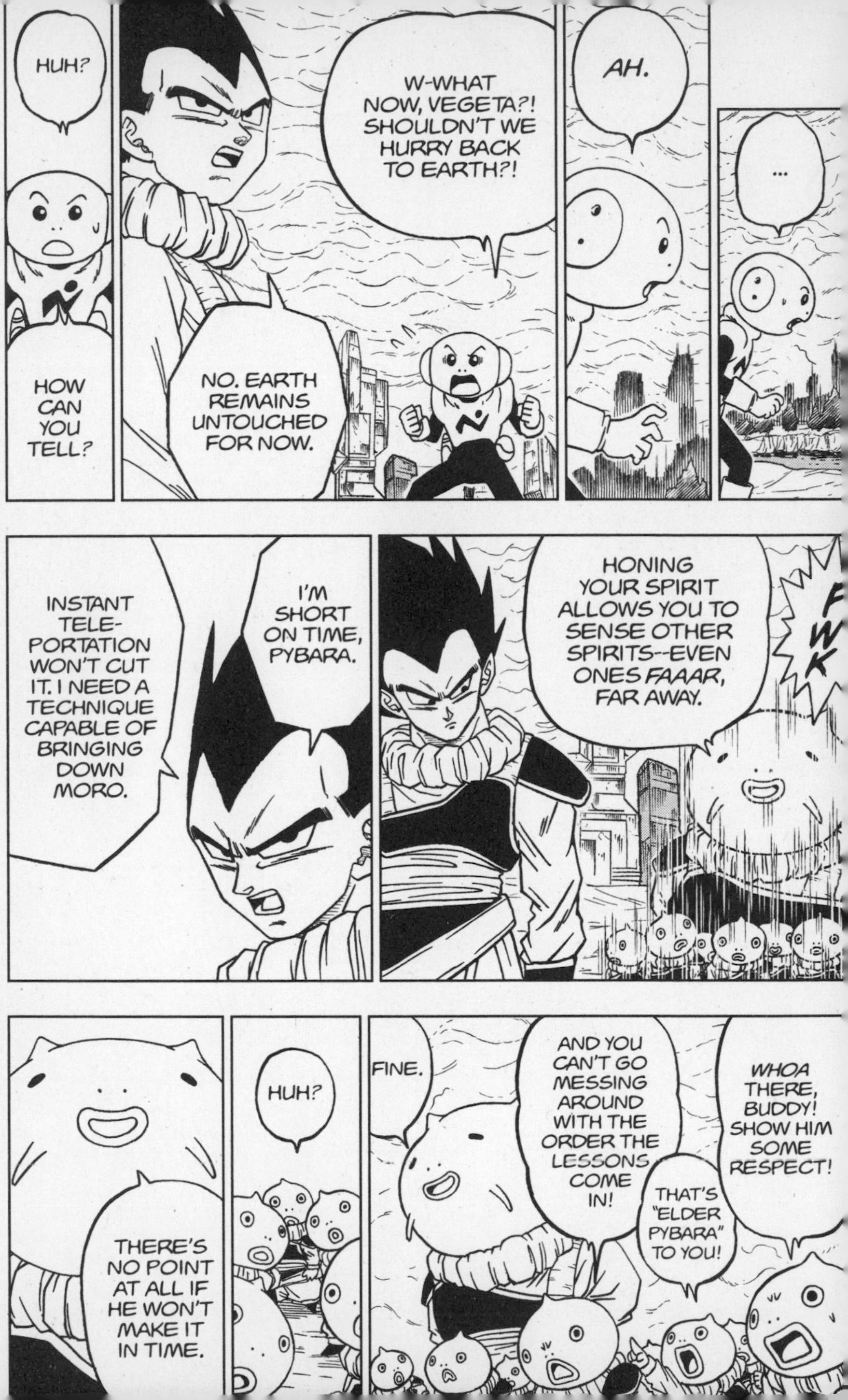
...
AH.
W-WHAT NOW, VEGETA?! SHOULDN'T WE HURRY BACK TO EARTH?!
NO. EARTH REMAINS UNTOUCHED FOR NOW.
HUH?
HOW CAN YOU TELL?
HONING YOUR SPIRIT ALLOWS YOU TO SENSE OTHER SPIRITS--EVEN ONES *FAAAR*, FAR AWAY.
FWK
I'M SHORT ON TIME, PYBARA.
INSTANT TELE-PORTATION WON'T CUT IT. I NEED A TECHNIQUE CAPABLE OF BRINGING DOWN MORO.
WHOA THERE, BUDDY! SHOW HIM SOME RESPECT!
THAT'S "ELDER PYBARA" TO YOU!
AND YOU CAN'T GO MESSING AROUND WITH THE ORDER THE LESSONS COME IN!
FINE.
HUH?
THERE'S NO POINT AT ALL IF HE WON'T MAKE IT IN TIME.

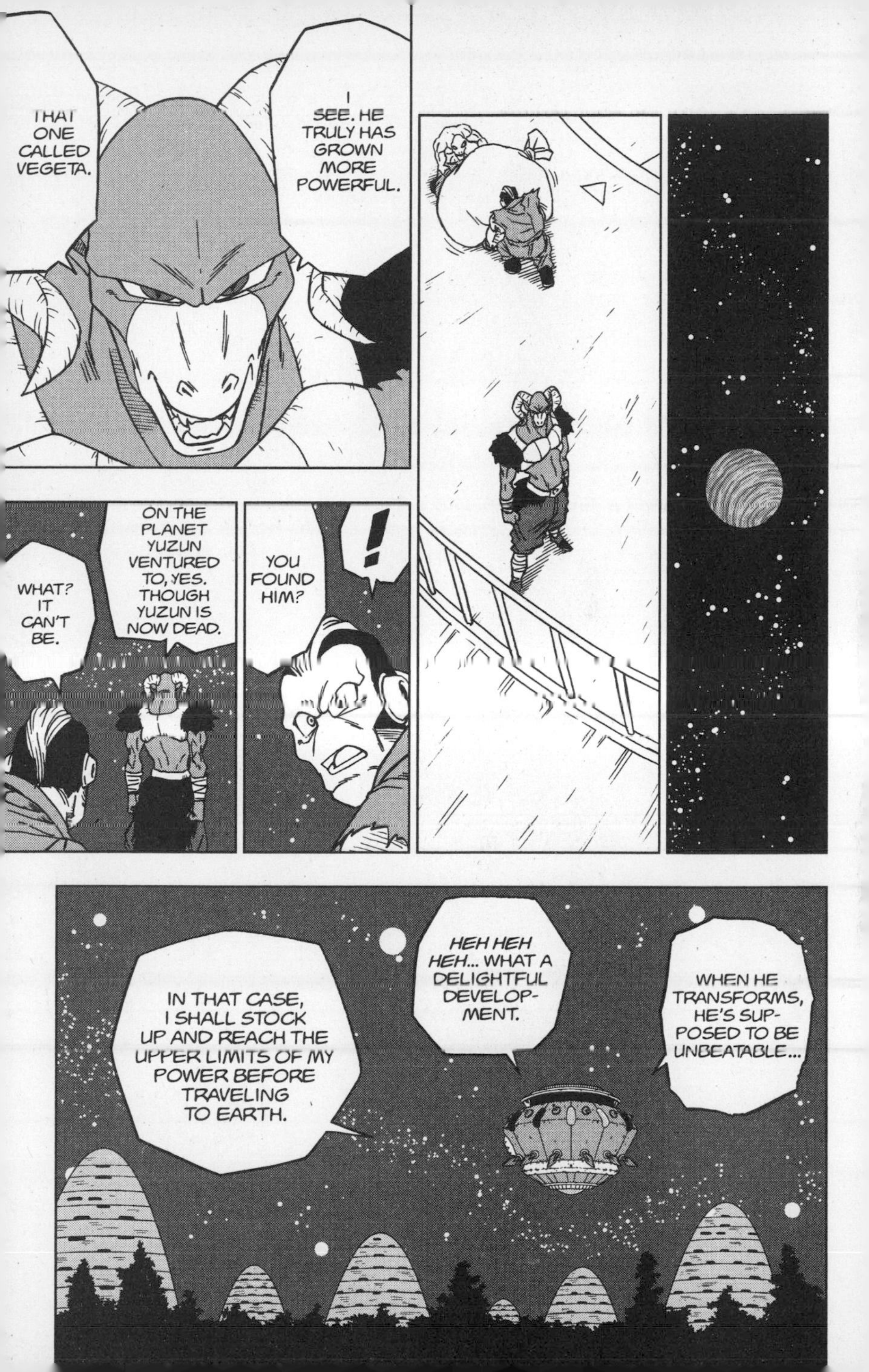
I SEE. HE TRULY HAS GROWN MORE POWERFUL.
THAT ONE CALLED VEGETA.
!
YOU FOUND HIM?
ON THE PLANET YUZUN VENTURED TO, YES. THOUGH YUZUN IS NOW DEAD.
WHAT? IT CAN'T BE.
WHEN HE TRANSFORMS, HE'S SUP-POSED TO BE UNBEATABLE...
HEH HEH HEH... WHAT A DELIGHTFUL DEVELOP-MENT.
IN THAT CASE, I SHALL STOCK UP AND REACH THE UPPER LIMITS OF MY POWER BEFORE TRAVELING TO EARTH.

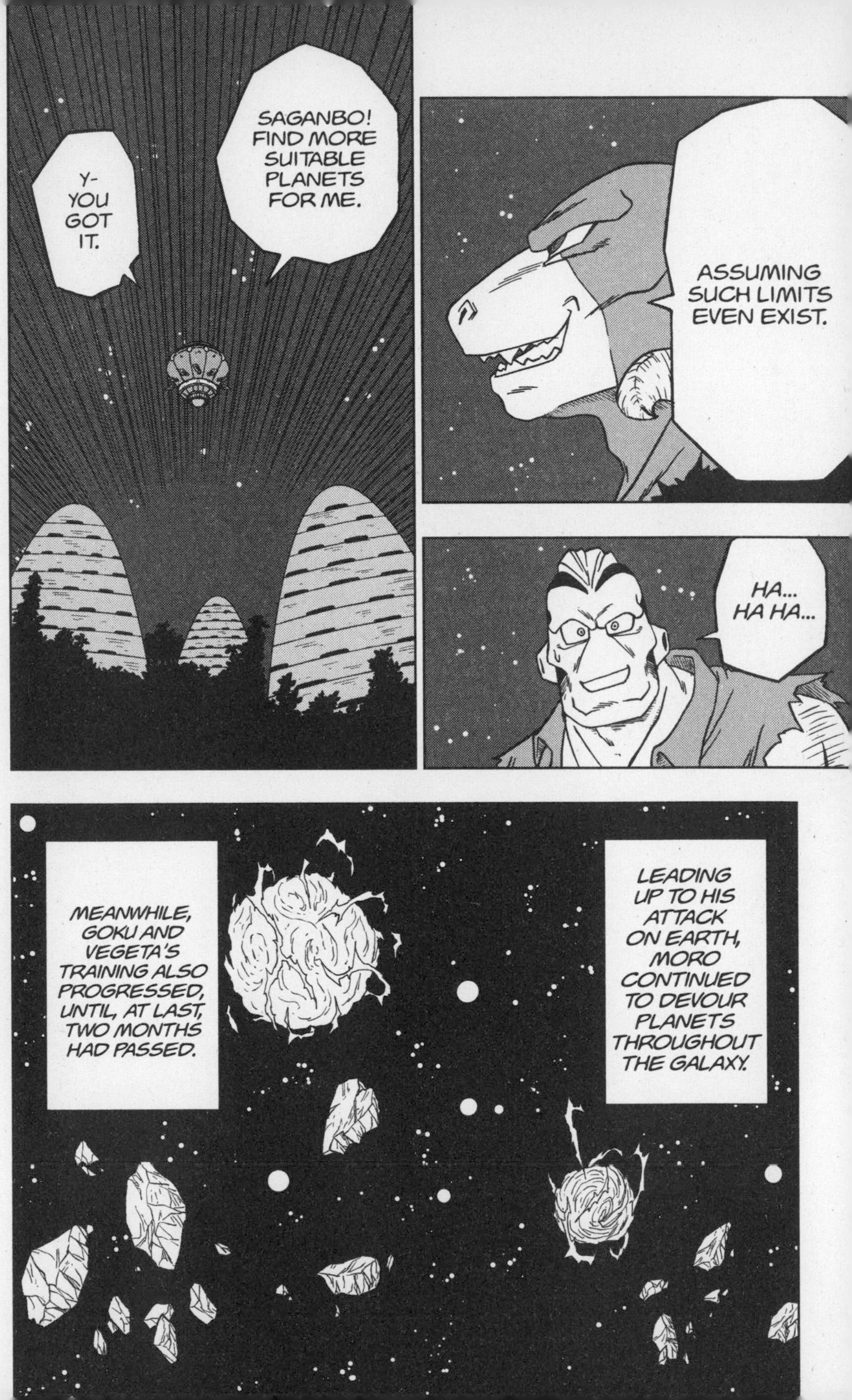
ASSUMING SUCH LIMITS EVEN EXIST.
HA... HA HA...
SAGANBO! FIND MORE SUITABLE PLANETS FOR ME.
Y- YOU GOT IT.
LEADING UP TO HIS ATTACK ON EARTH, MORO CONTINUED TO DEVOUR PLANETS THROUGHOUT THE GALAXY.
MEANWHILE, GOKU AND VEGETA'S TRAINING ALSO PROGRESSED, UNTIL, AT LAST, TWO MONTHS HAD PASSED.

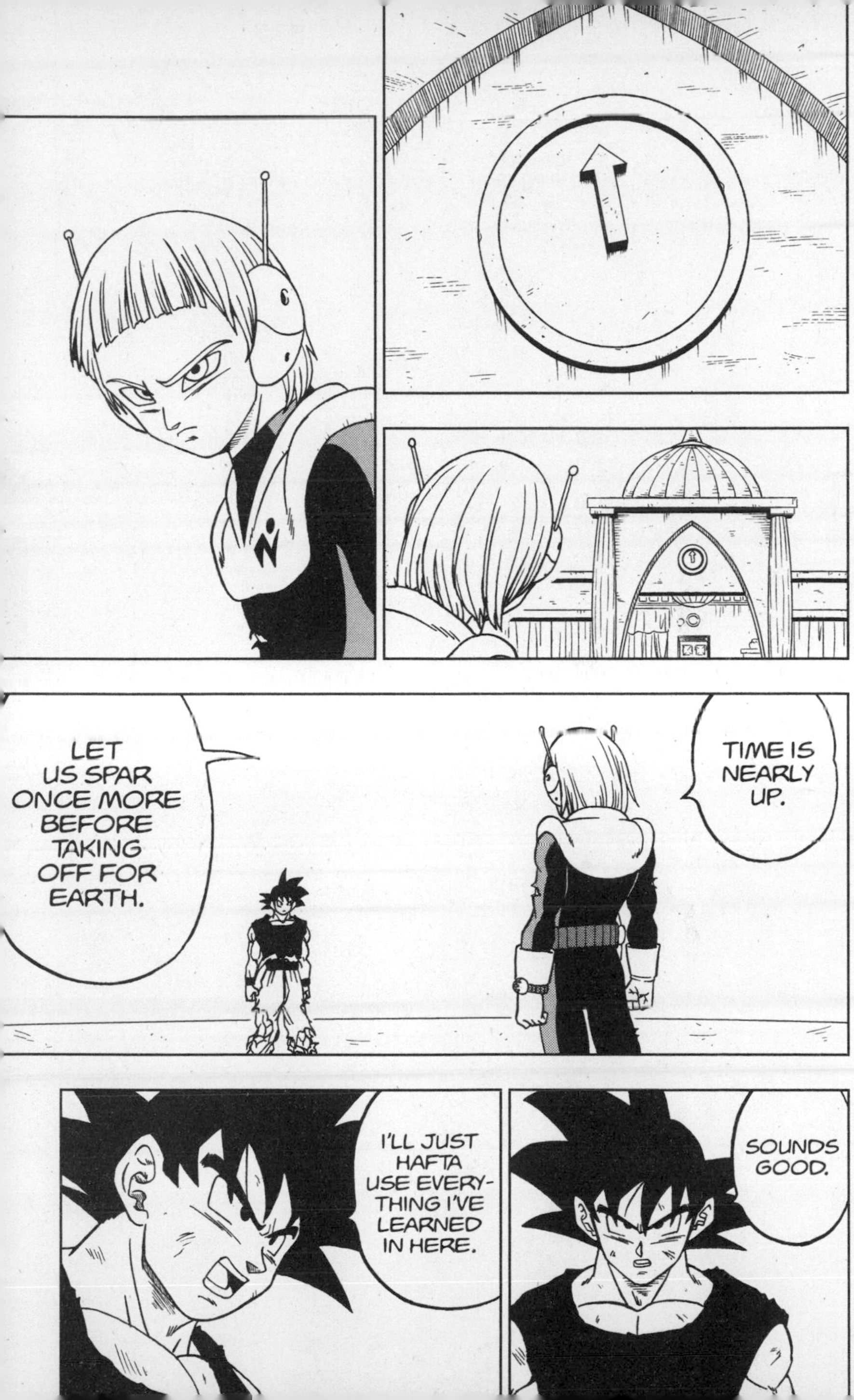
TIME IS NEARLY UP.
LET US SPAR ONCE MORE BEFORE TAKING OFF FOR EARTH.
SOUNDS GOOD.
I'LL JUST HAFTA USE EVERY-THING I'VE LEARNED IN HERE.

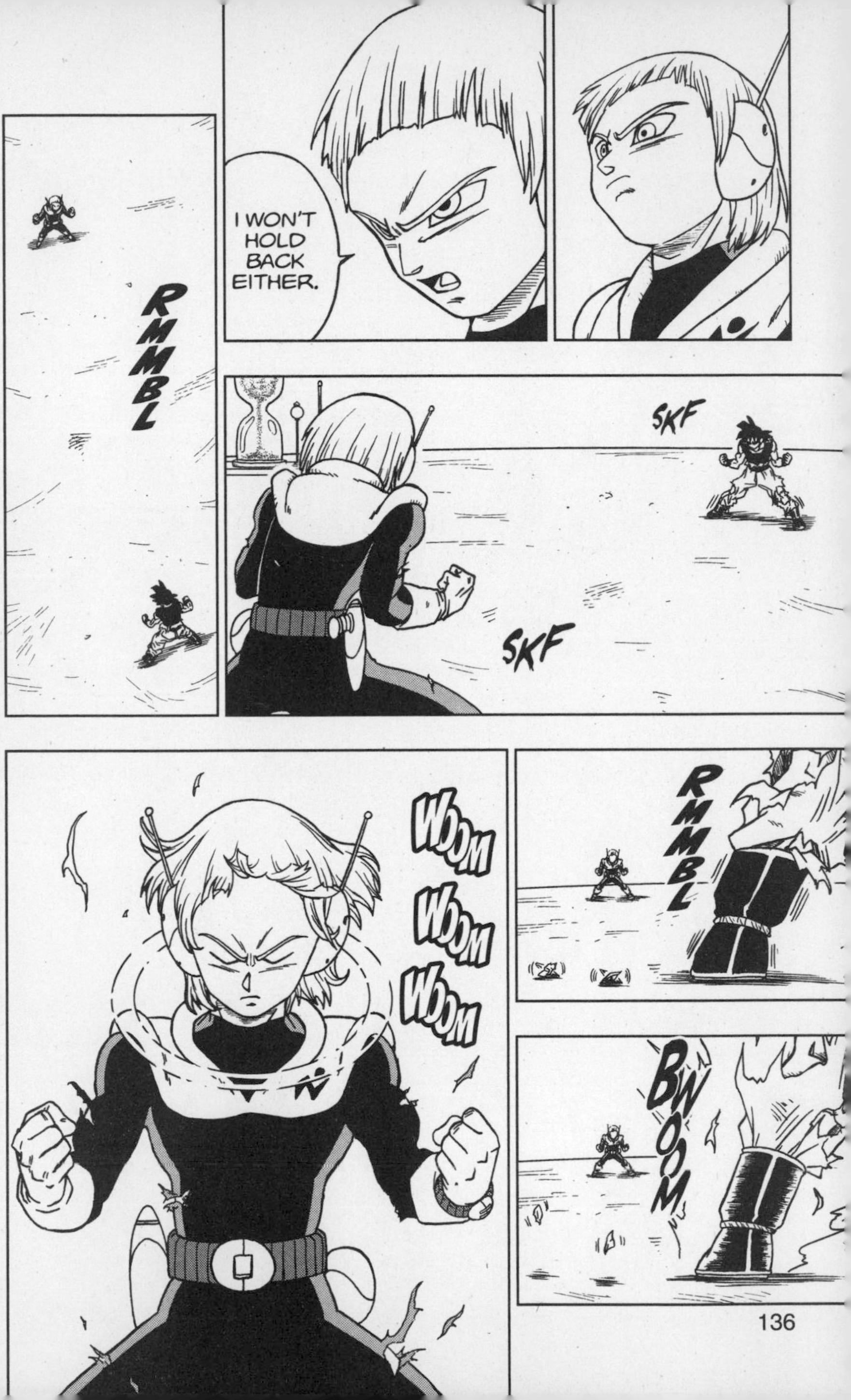
I WON'T HOLD BACK EITHER.
SKF
SKF
RMMBL
RMMBL
BWOOM
WOOM WOOM WOOM

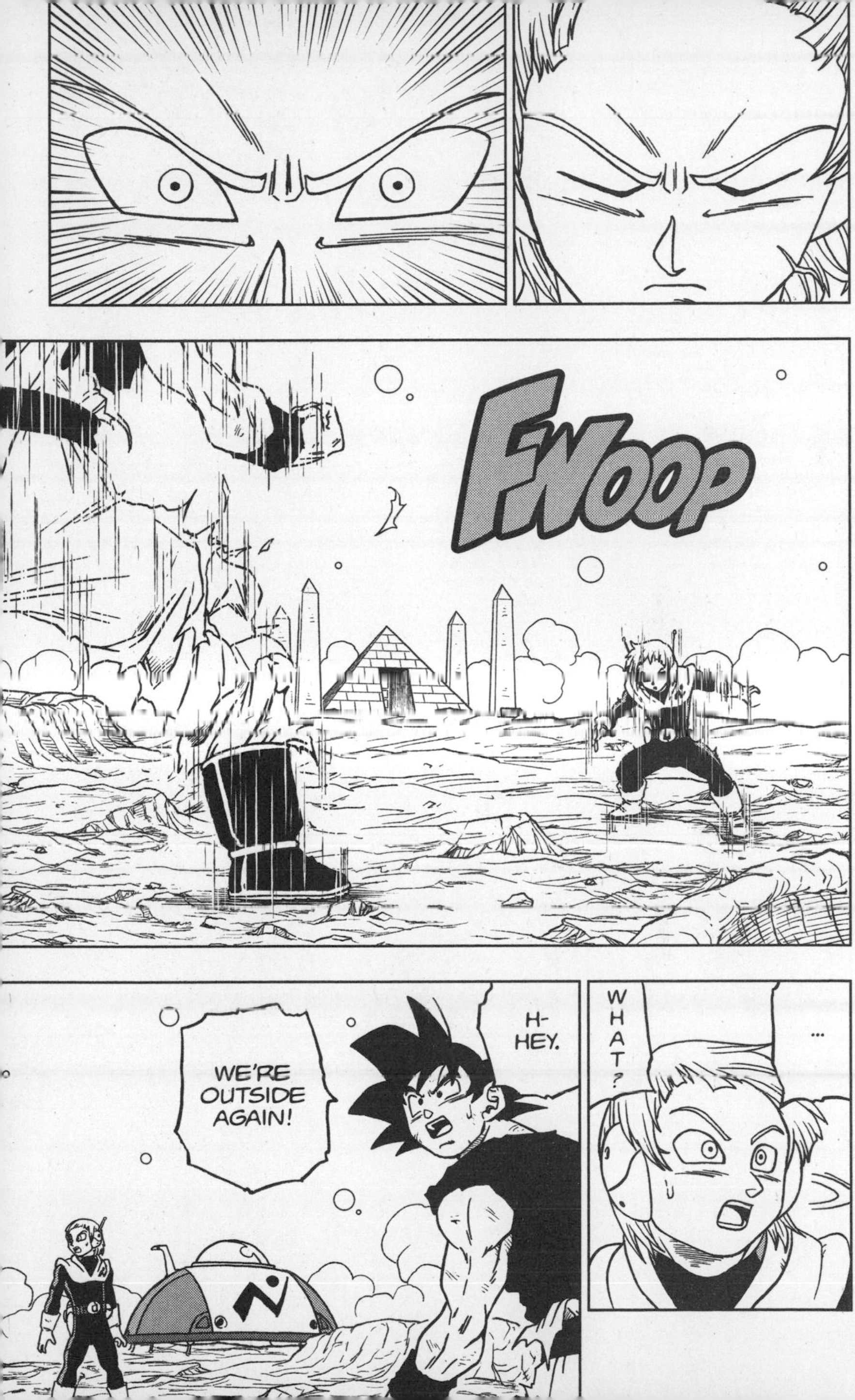
FWOOP
WHAT?
...
H-HEY.
WE'RE OUTSIDE AGAIN!

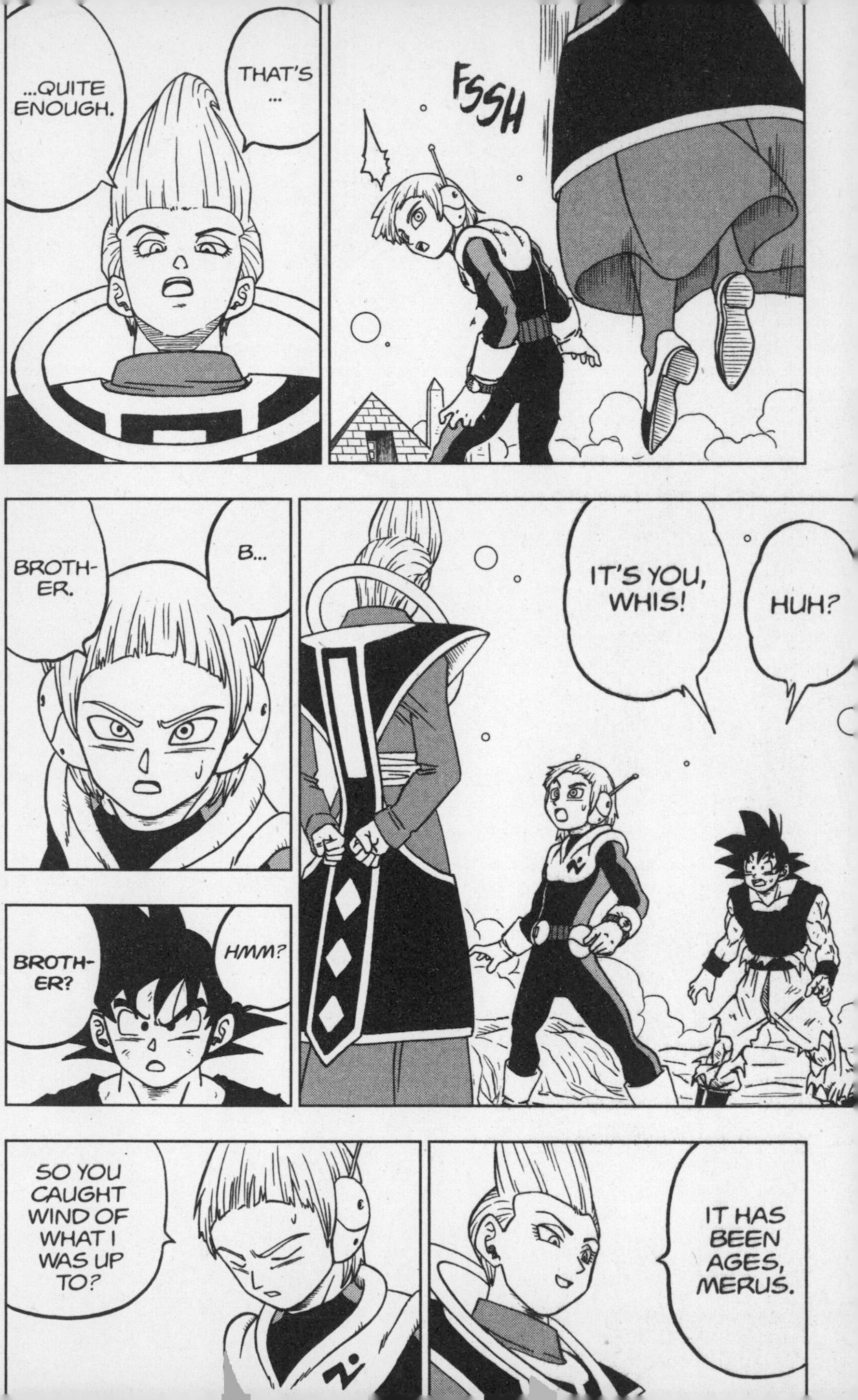
FSSH
THAT'S ...
...QUITE ENOUGH.
HUH?
IT'S YOU, WHIS!
B...
BROTHER-ER.
HMM?
BROTHER?
IT HAS BEEN AGES, MERUS.
SO YOU CAUGHT WIND OF WHAT I WAS UP TO?

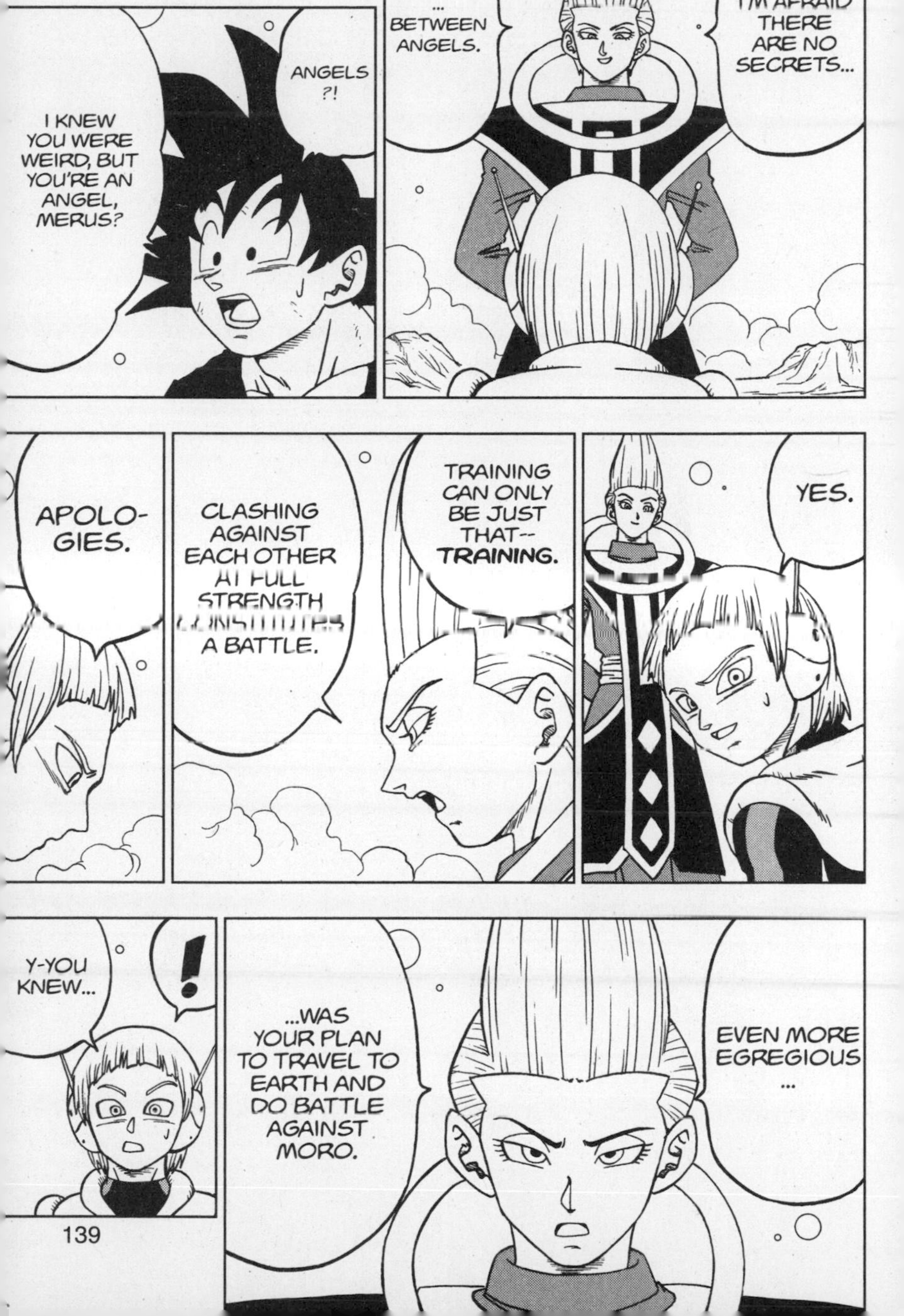
I'M AFRAID THERE ARE NO SECRETS...
...BETWEEN ANGELS.
ANGELS?!
I KNEW YOU WERE WEIRD, BUT YOU'RE AN ANGEL, MERUS?
YES.
TRAINING CAN ONLY BE JUST THAT-- TRAINING.
CLASHING AGAINST EACH OTHER AT FULL STRENGTH CONSTITUTES A BATTLE.
APOLOGIES.
EVEN MORE EGREGIOUS...
...WAS YOUR PLAN TO TRAVEL TO EARTH AND DO BATTLE AGAINST MORO.
!
Y-YOU KNEW...

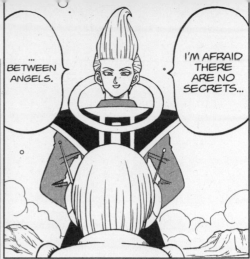

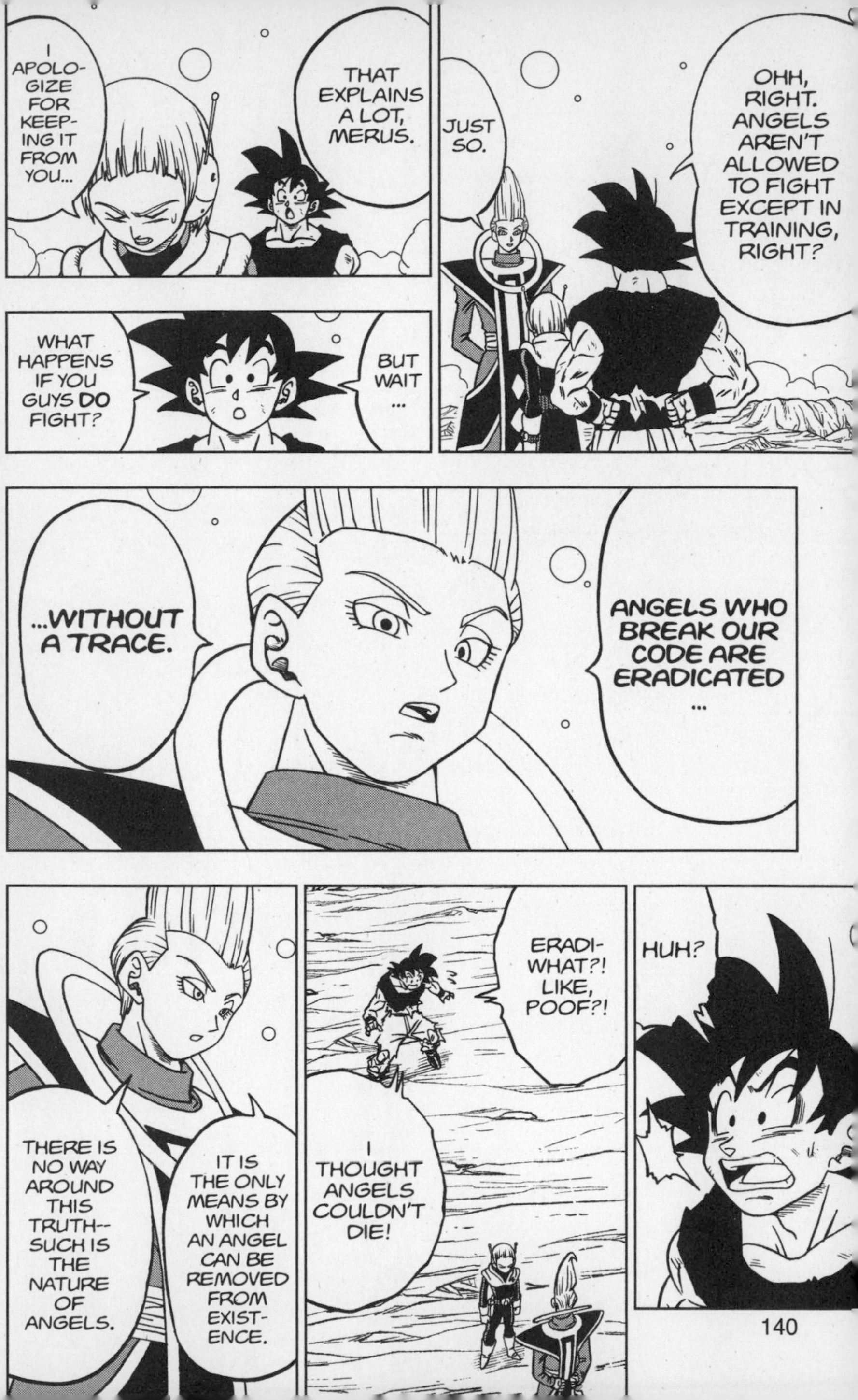
OHH, RIGHT. ANGELS AREN'T ALLOWED TO FIGHT EXCEPT IN TRAINING, RIGHT?
JUST SO.
THAT EXPLAINS A LOT, MERUS.
I APOLOGIZE FOR KEEPING IT FROM YOU...
BUT WAIT...
WHAT HAPPENS IF YOU GUYS DO FIGHT?
ANGELS WHO BREAK OUR CODE ARE ERADICATED...
...WITHOUT A TRACE.
HUH?
ERADI-WHAT?! LIKE, POOF?!
I THOUGHT ANGELS COULDN'T DIE!
IT IS THE ONLY MEANS BY WHICH AN ANGEL CAN BE REMOVED FROM EXISTENCE.
THERE IS NO WAY AROUND THIS TRUTH-- SUCH IS THE NATURE OF ANGELS.

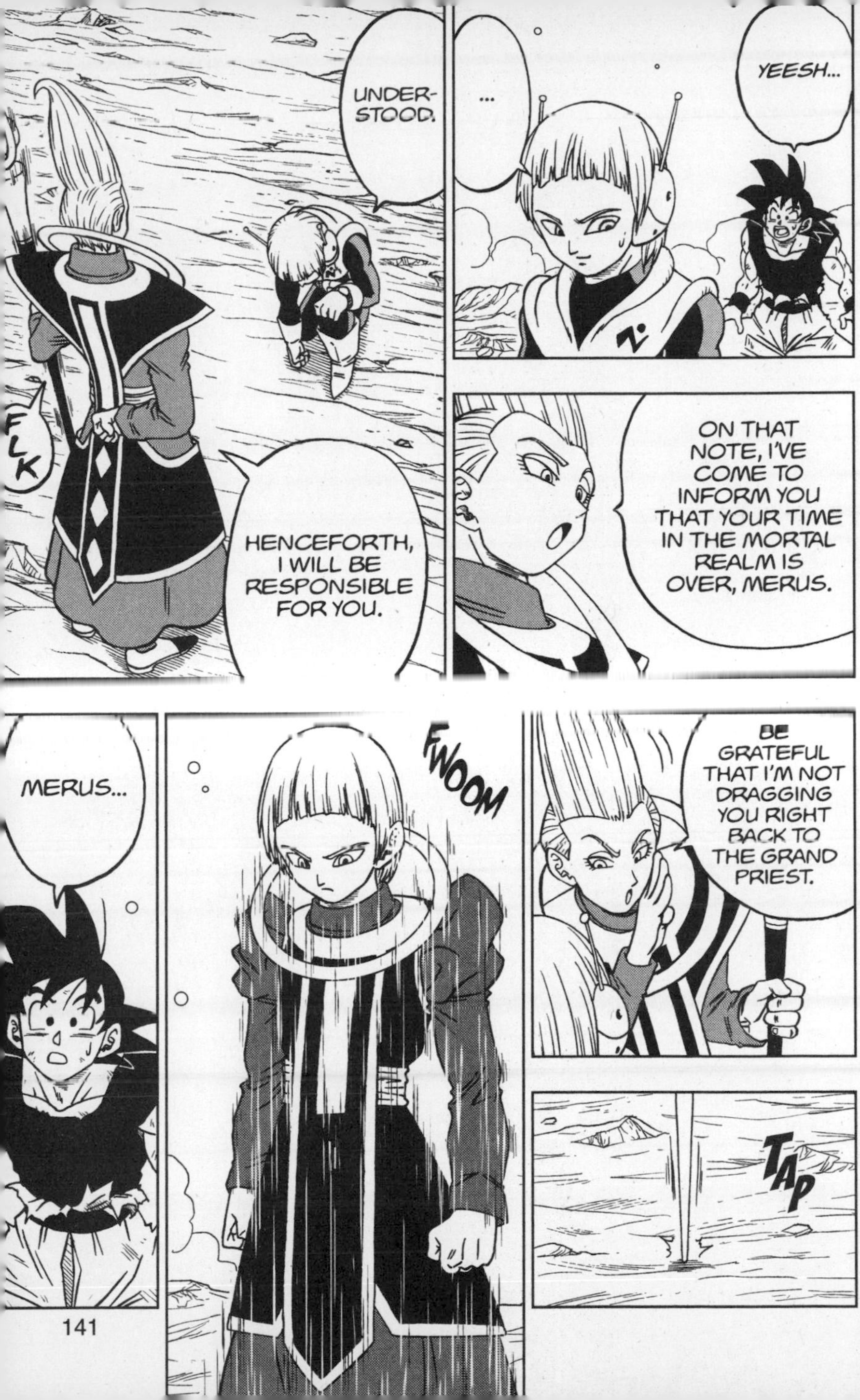
YEESH...
...
ON THAT NOTE, I'VE COME TO INFORM YOU THAT YOUR TIME IN THE MORTAL REALM IS OVER, MERUS.
UNDER-STOOD.
HENCEFORTH, I WILL BE RESPONSIBLE FOR YOU.
FLK
BE GRATEFUL THAT I'M NOT DRAGGING YOU RIGHT BACK TO THE GRAND PRIEST.
TAP
FWOOM
MERUS...

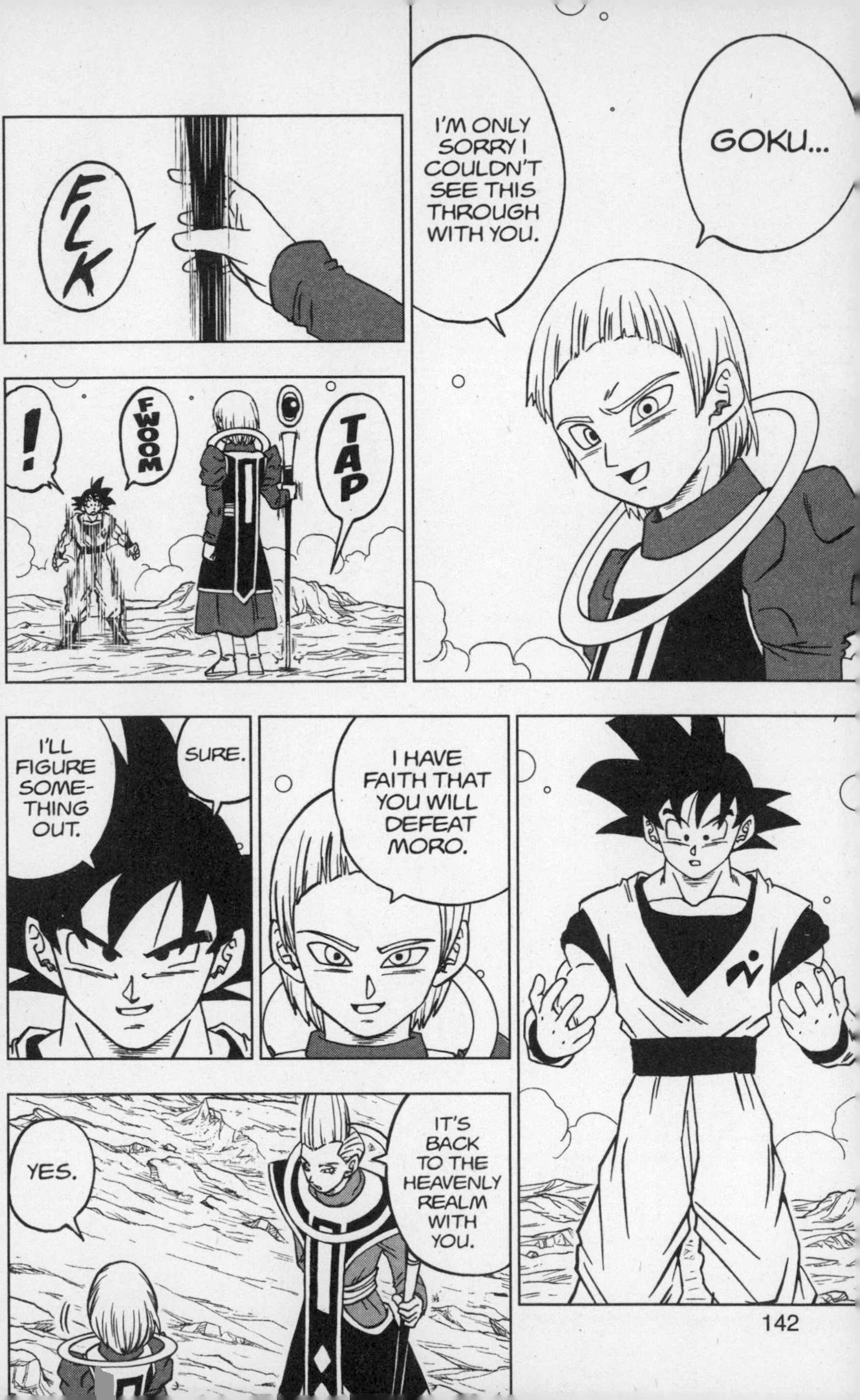
GOKU...
I'M ONLY SORRY I COULDN'T SEE THIS THROUGH WITH YOU.
FLK
TAP
FWOOM
!
I HAVE FAITH THAT YOU WILL DEFEAT MORO.
SURE.
I'LL FIGURE SOME-THING OUT.
IT'S BACK TO THE HEAVENLY REALM WITH YOU.
YES.

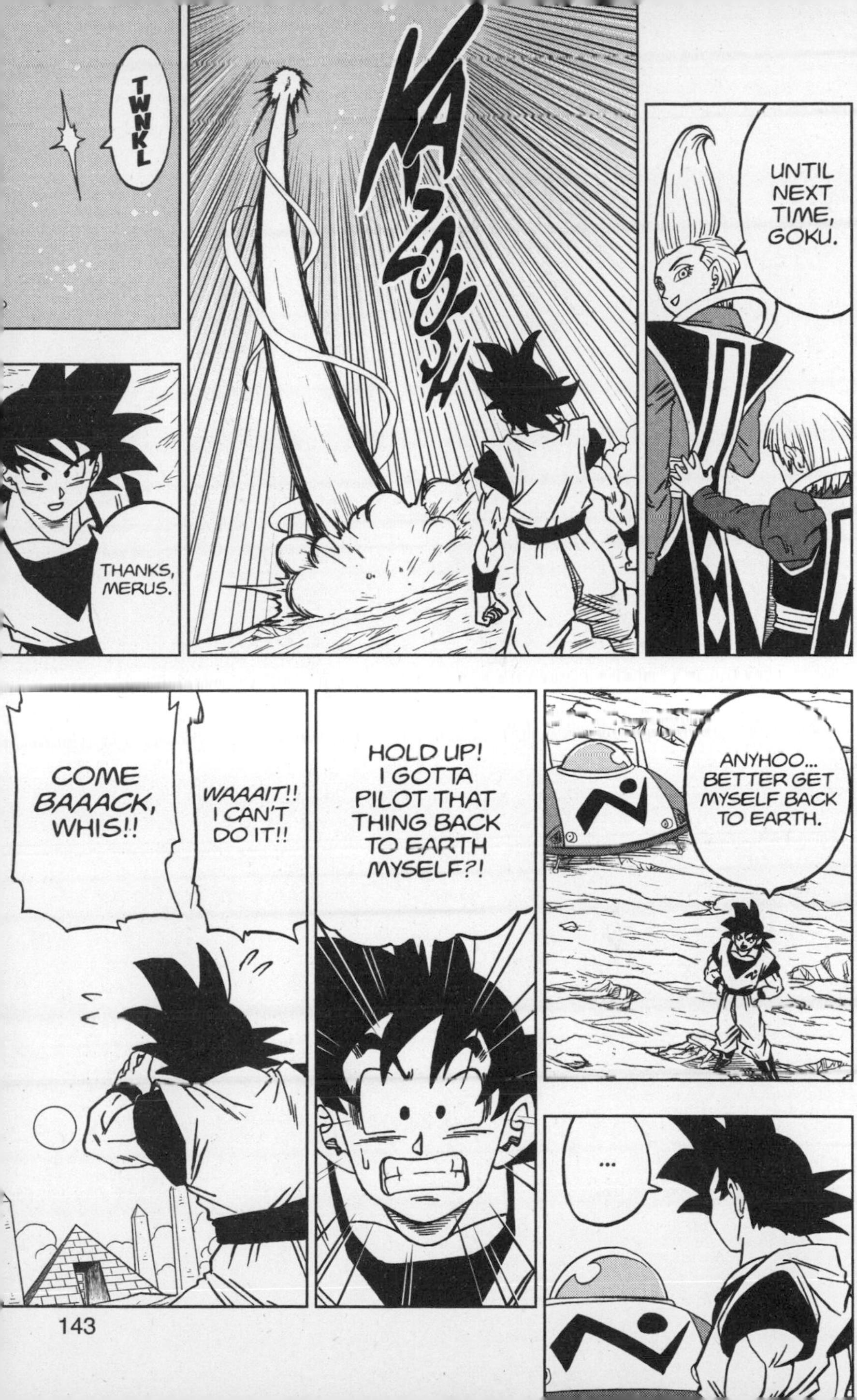
UNTIL NEXT TIME, GOKU.
KAZOOSH
TWNKL
THANKS, MERUS.
ANYHOO... BETTER GET MYSELF BACK TO EARTH.
...
HOLD UP! I GOTTA PILOT THAT THING BACK TO EARTH MYSELF?!
WAAAIT!! I CAN'T DO IT!!
COME BAAACK, WHIS!!

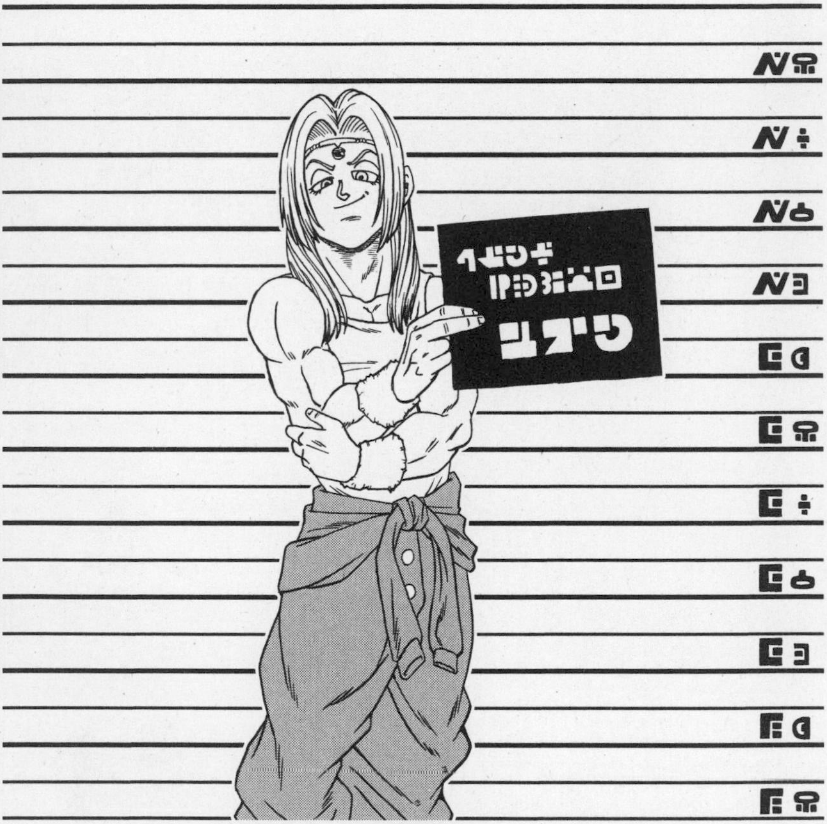

SAGANBO'S
GALACTIC BANDIT
BRIGADE MEMBER:
YUZUN

DRAGON BALL SUPER

CHAPTER 56: WARRIORS OF EARTH ASSEMBLE

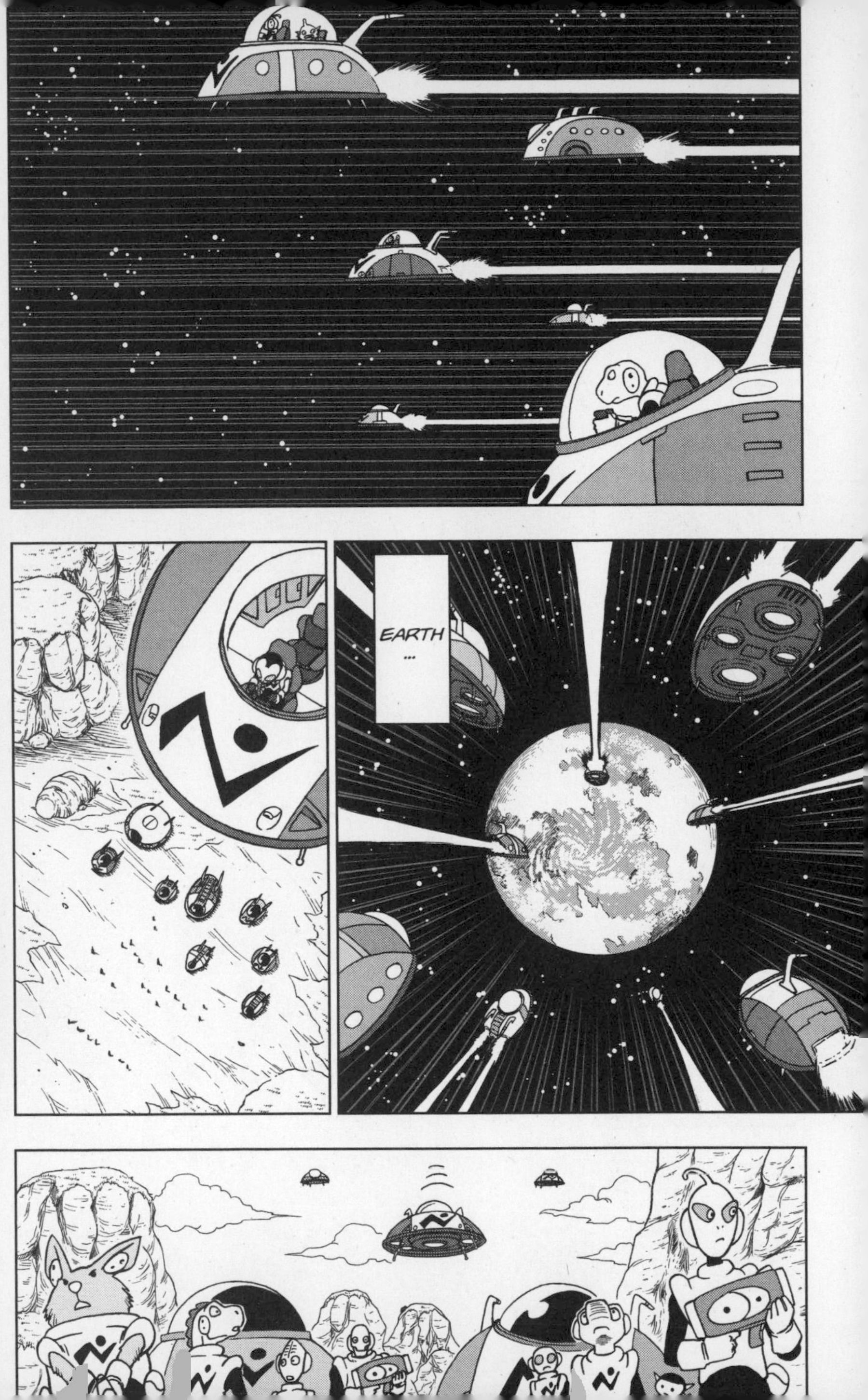
EARTH ...

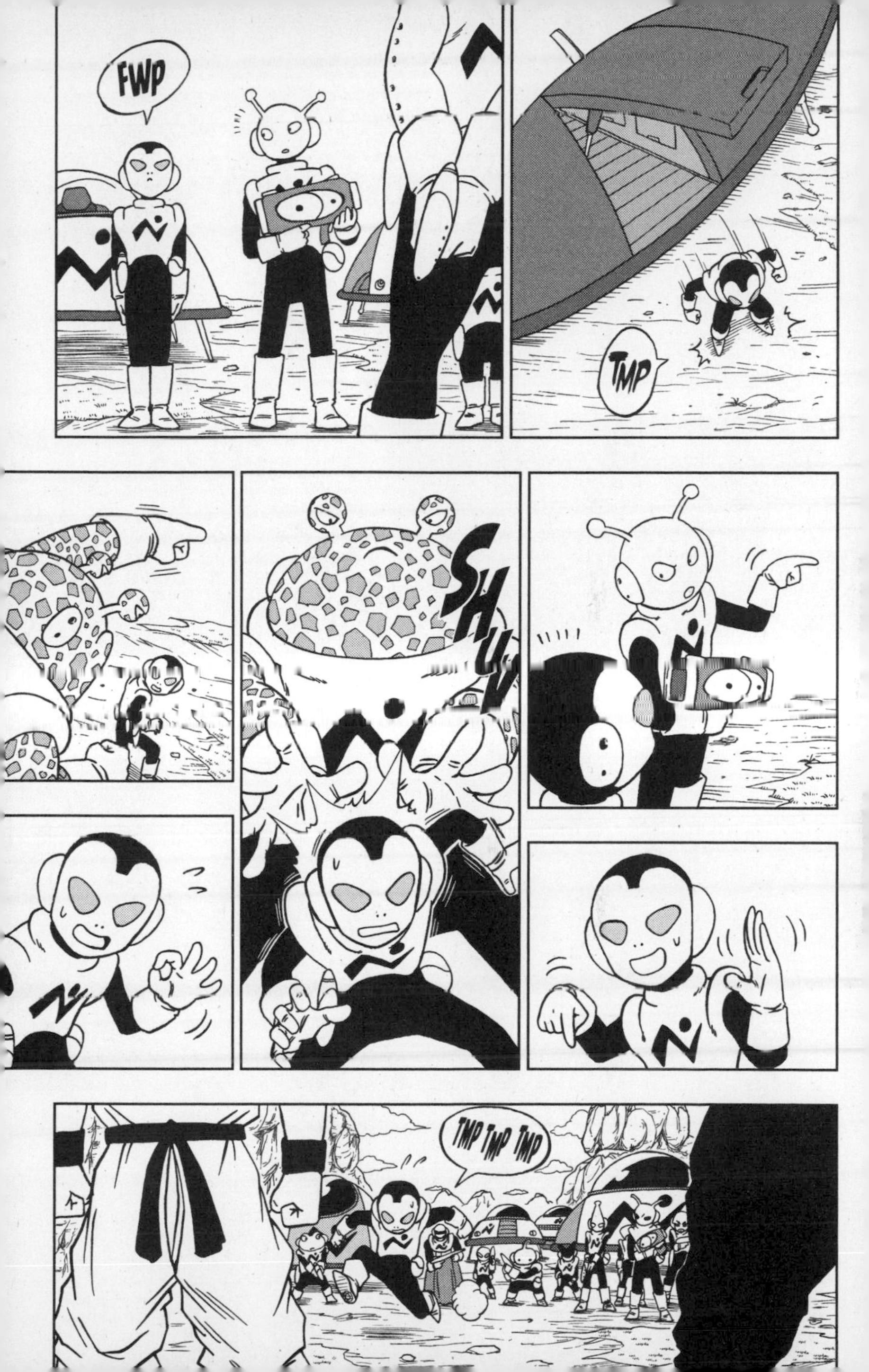
TMP
FWP
SHUV
TMP TMP TMP

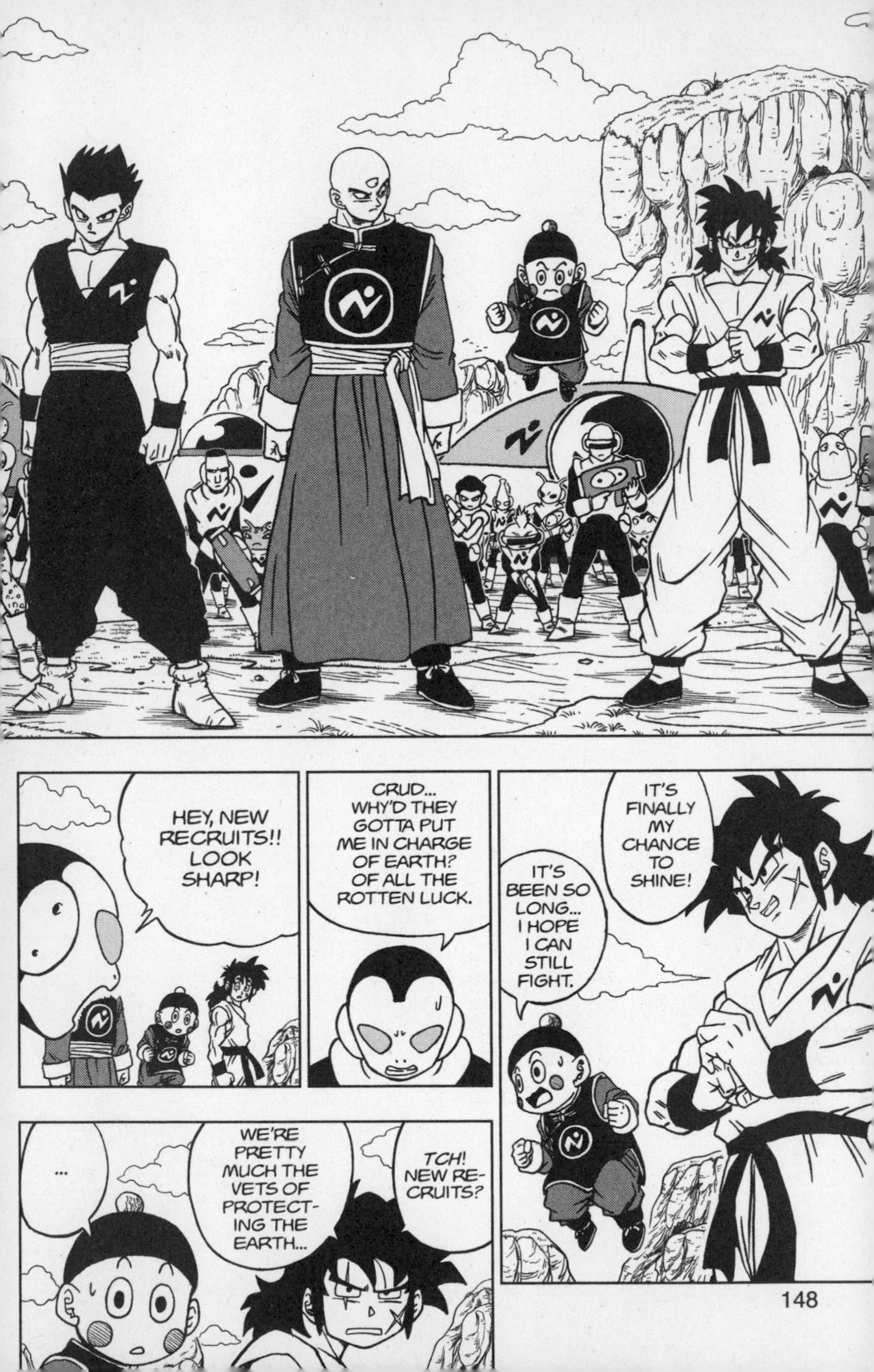
IT'S FINALLY MY CHANCE TO SHINE!
IT'S BEEN SO LONG... I HOPE I CAN STILL FIGHT.
CRUD... WHY'D THEY GOTTA PUT ME IN CHARGE OF EARTH? OF ALL THE ROTTEN LUCK.
HEY, NEW RECRUITS!! LOOK SHARP!
TCH! NEW RE-CRUITS?
WE'RE PRETTY MUCH THE VETS OF PROTECT-ING THE EARTH...
...

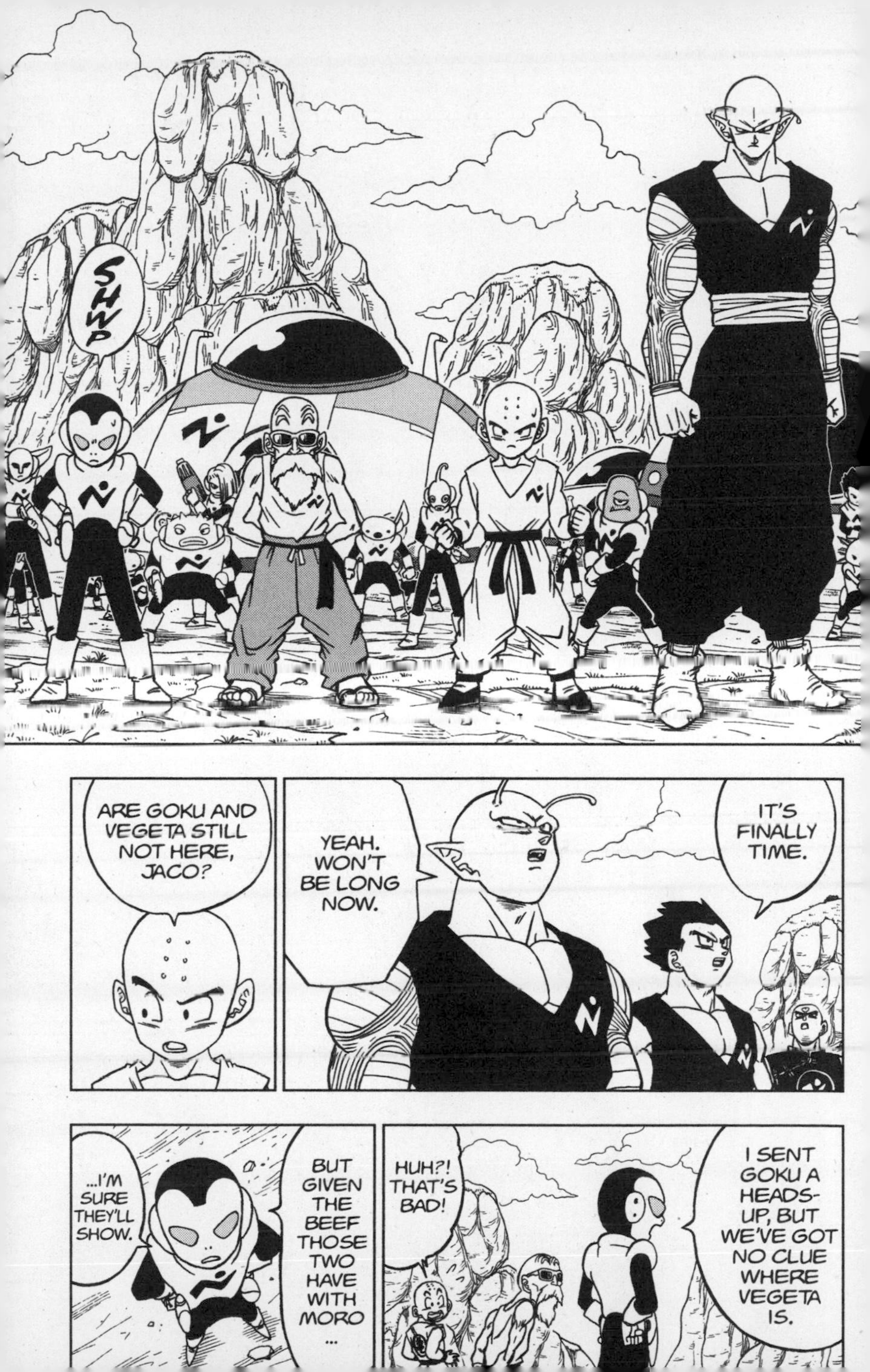
SHWP
IT'S FINALLY TIME.
YEAH. WON'T BE LONG NOW.
ARE GOKU AND VEGETA STILL NOT HERE, JACO?
I SENT GOKU A HEADS-UP, BUT WE'VE GOT NO CLUE WHERE VEGETA IS.
HUH?! THAT'S BAD!
BUT GIVEN THE BEEF THOSE TWO HAVE WITH MORO ...
...I'M SURE THEY'LL SHOW.

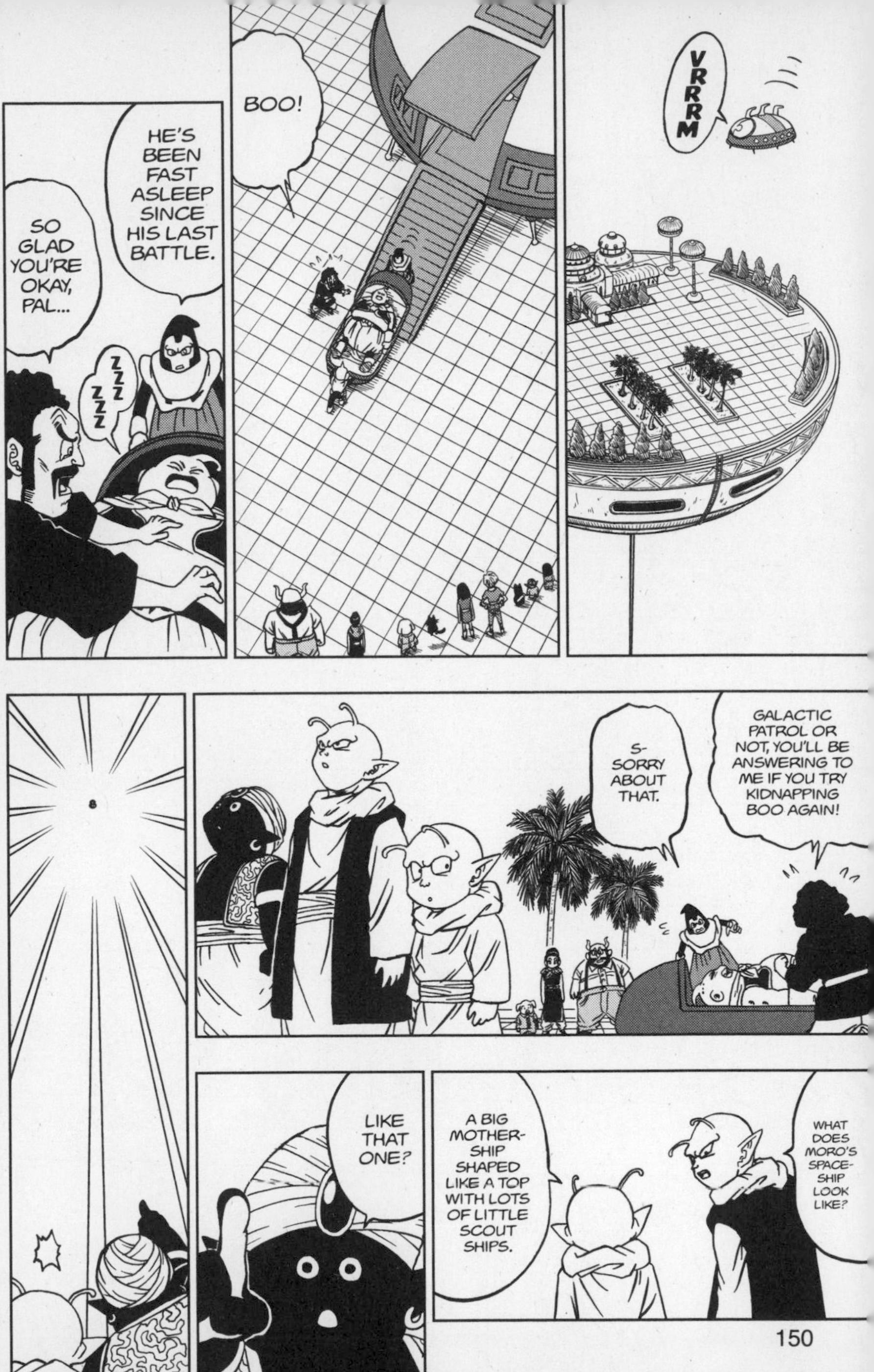
VRRRM
BOO!
HE'S BEEN FAST ASLEEP SINCE HIS LAST BATTLE.
SO GLAD YOU'RE OKAY, PAL...
ZZZ ZZZ ZZZ
GALACTIC PATROL OR NOT, YOU'LL BE ANSWERING TO ME IF YOU TRY KIDNAPPING BOO AGAIN!
S-SORRY ABOUT THAT.
WHAT DOES MORO'S SPACESHIP LOOK LIKE?
A BIG MOTHERSHIP SHAPED LIKE A TOP WITH LOTS OF LITTLE SCOUT SHIPS.
LIKE THAT ONE?

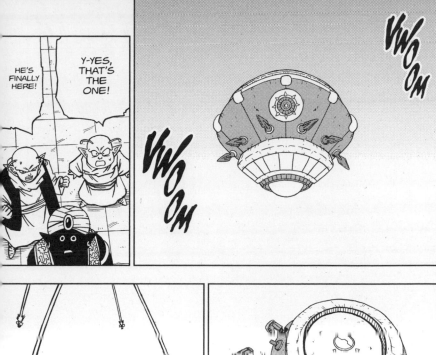

VWOOM
VWOOM
Y-YES, THAT'S THE ONE!
HE'S FINALLY HERE!
WHRRR
?!
FWISH
FWISH
SHOOOM

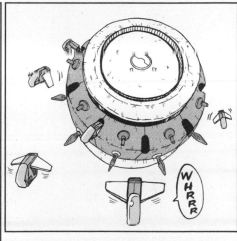

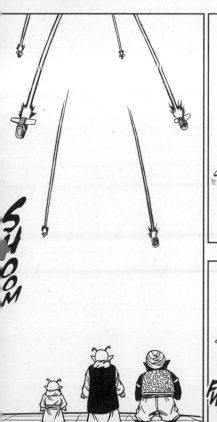

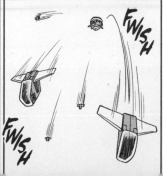

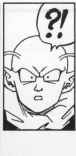

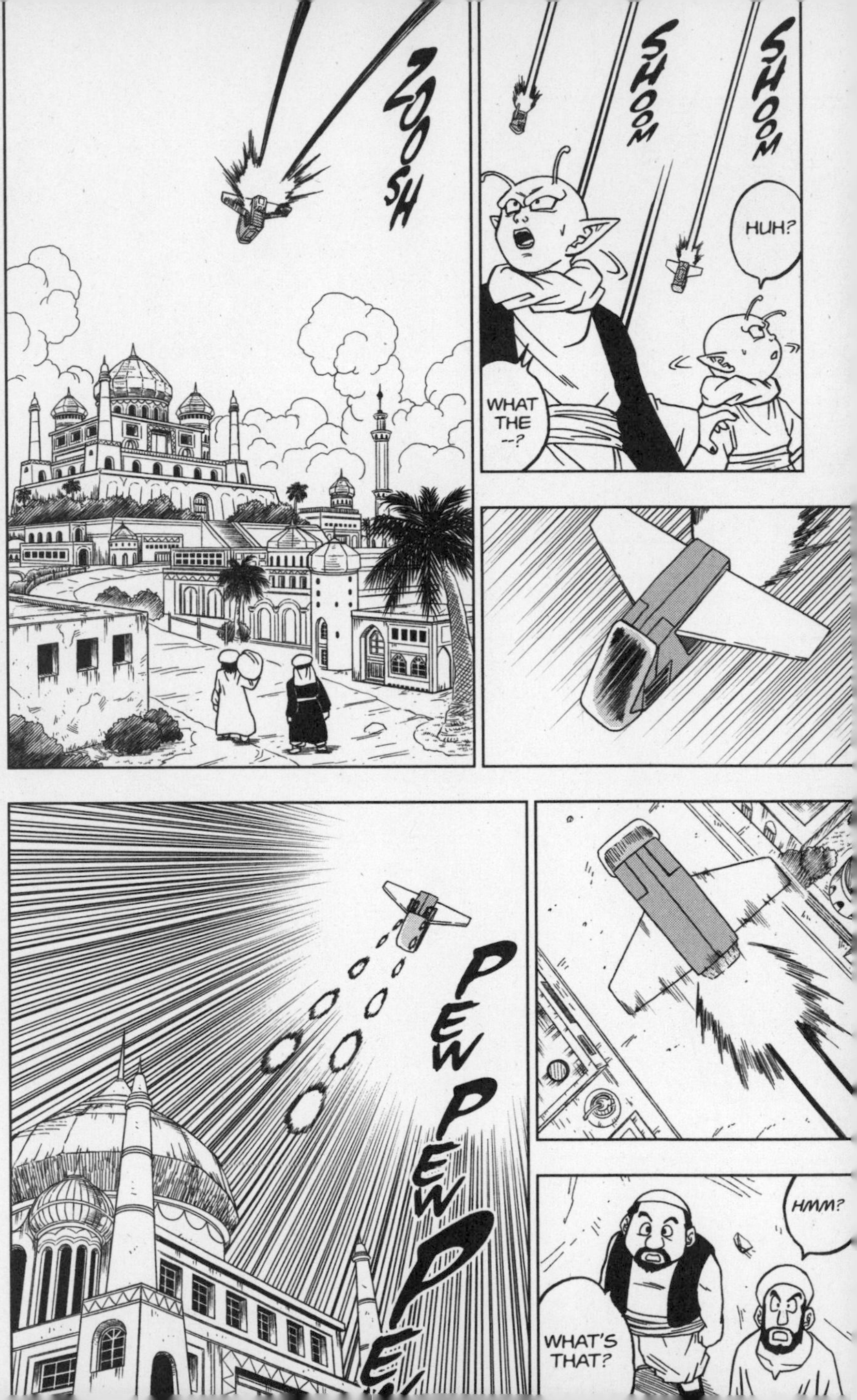
SHOOM
SHOOM
HUH?
WHAT THE --?
ZOOOSH
HMM?
WHAT'S THAT?
PEW PEW PEW

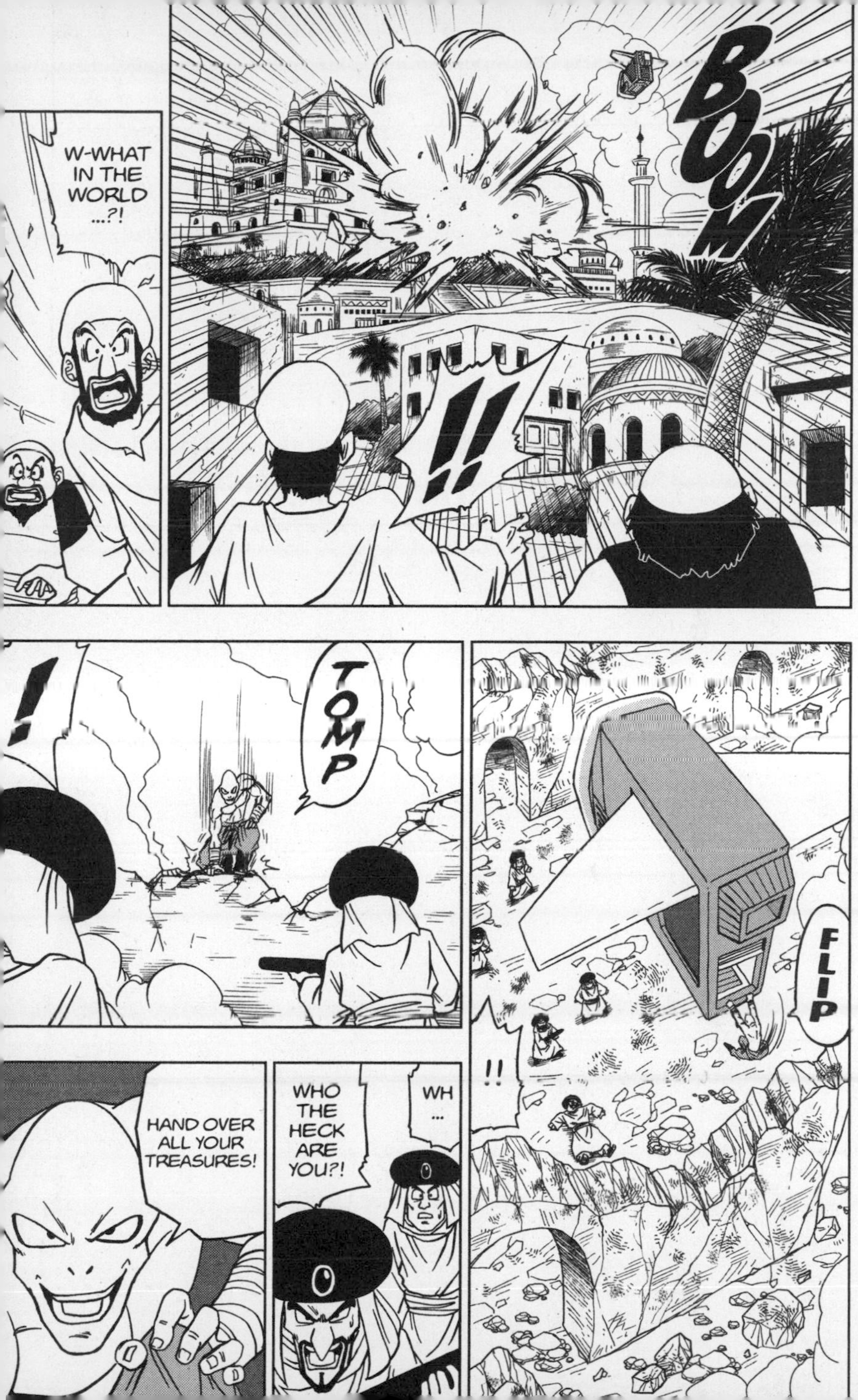
BOOM
!!
W-WHAT IN THE WORLD ...?!
FLIP
!!
TOMP
!
WH ...
WHO THE HECK ARE YOU?!
HAND OVER ALL YOUR TREASURES!

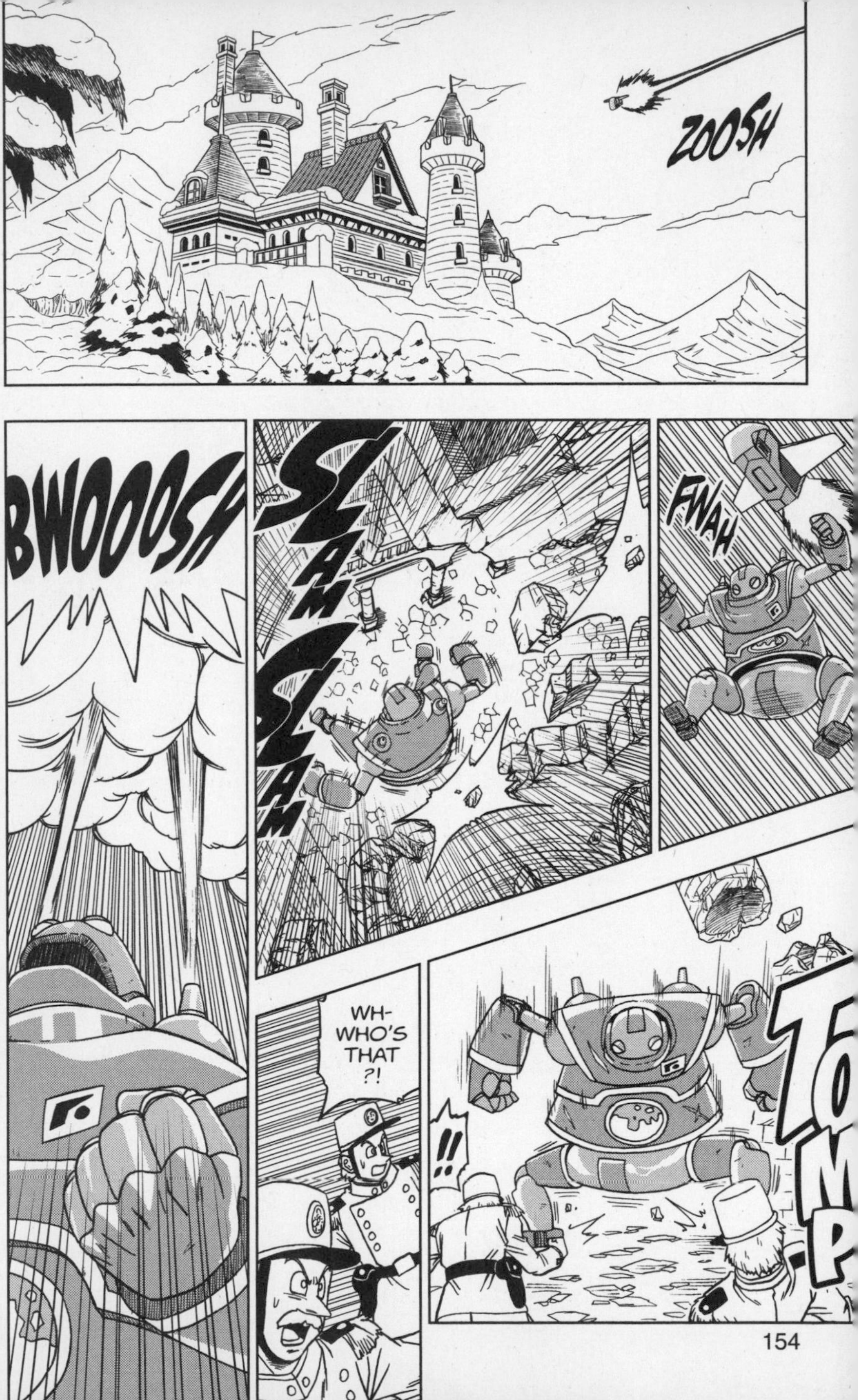
ZOOSH
FWAH
SLAM SLAM
TOMP
!!
WH- WHO'S THAT ?!
BWOOOSH

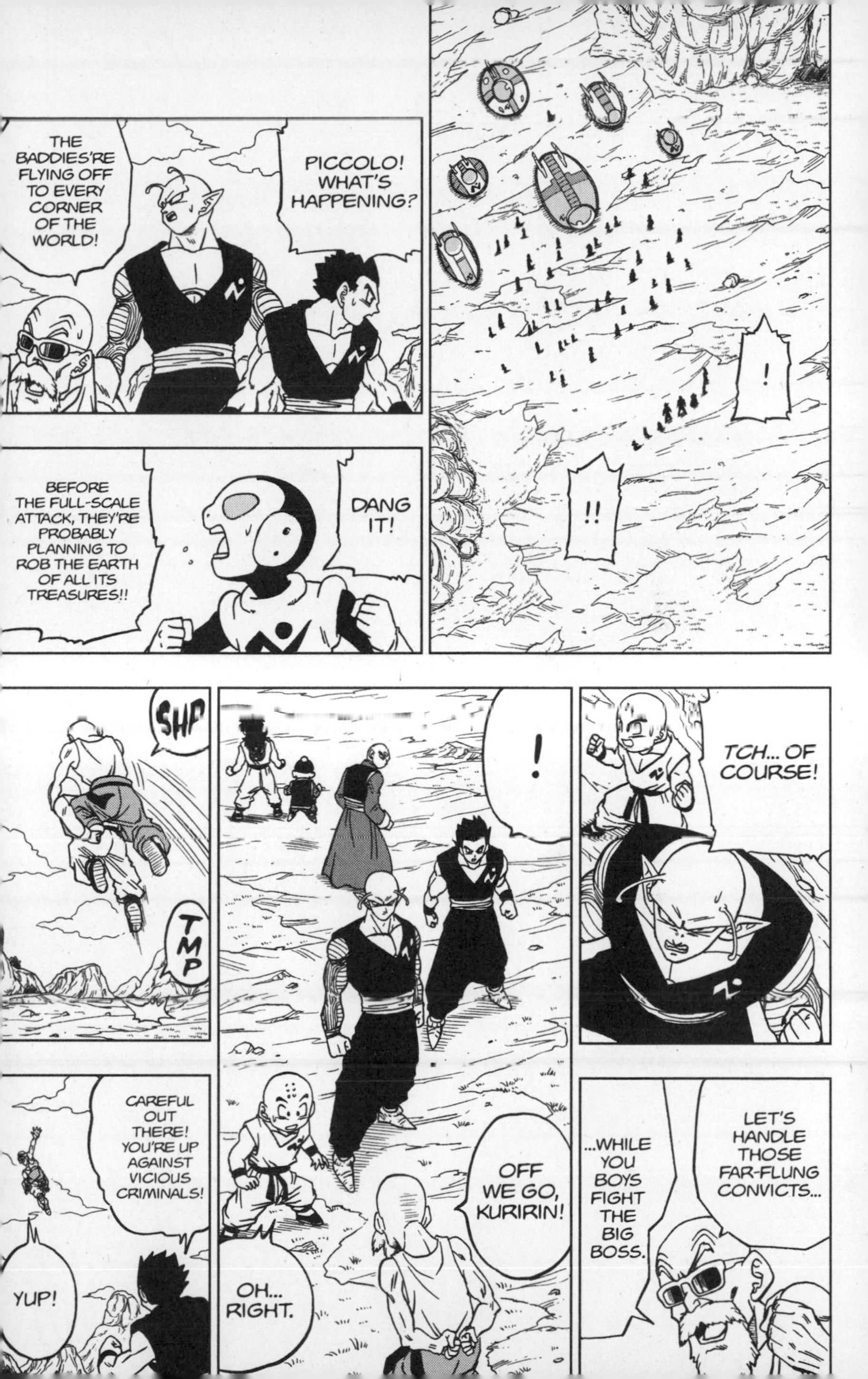
!
!!
PICCOLO! WHAT'S HAPPENING?
THE BADDIES'RE FLYING OFF TO EVERY CORNER OF THE WORLD!
DANG IT!
BEFORE THE FULL-SCALE ATTACK, THEY'RE PROBABLY PLANNING TO ROB THE EARTH OF ALL ITS TREASURES!!
TCH... OF COURSE!
LET'S HANDLE THOSE FAR-FLUNG CONVICTS...
...WHILE YOU BOYS FIGHT THE BIG BOSS.
!
OFF WE GO, KURIRIN!
OH... RIGHT.
SHP
TMP
CAREFUL OUT THERE! YOU'RE UP AGAINST VICIOUS CRIMINALS!
YUP!

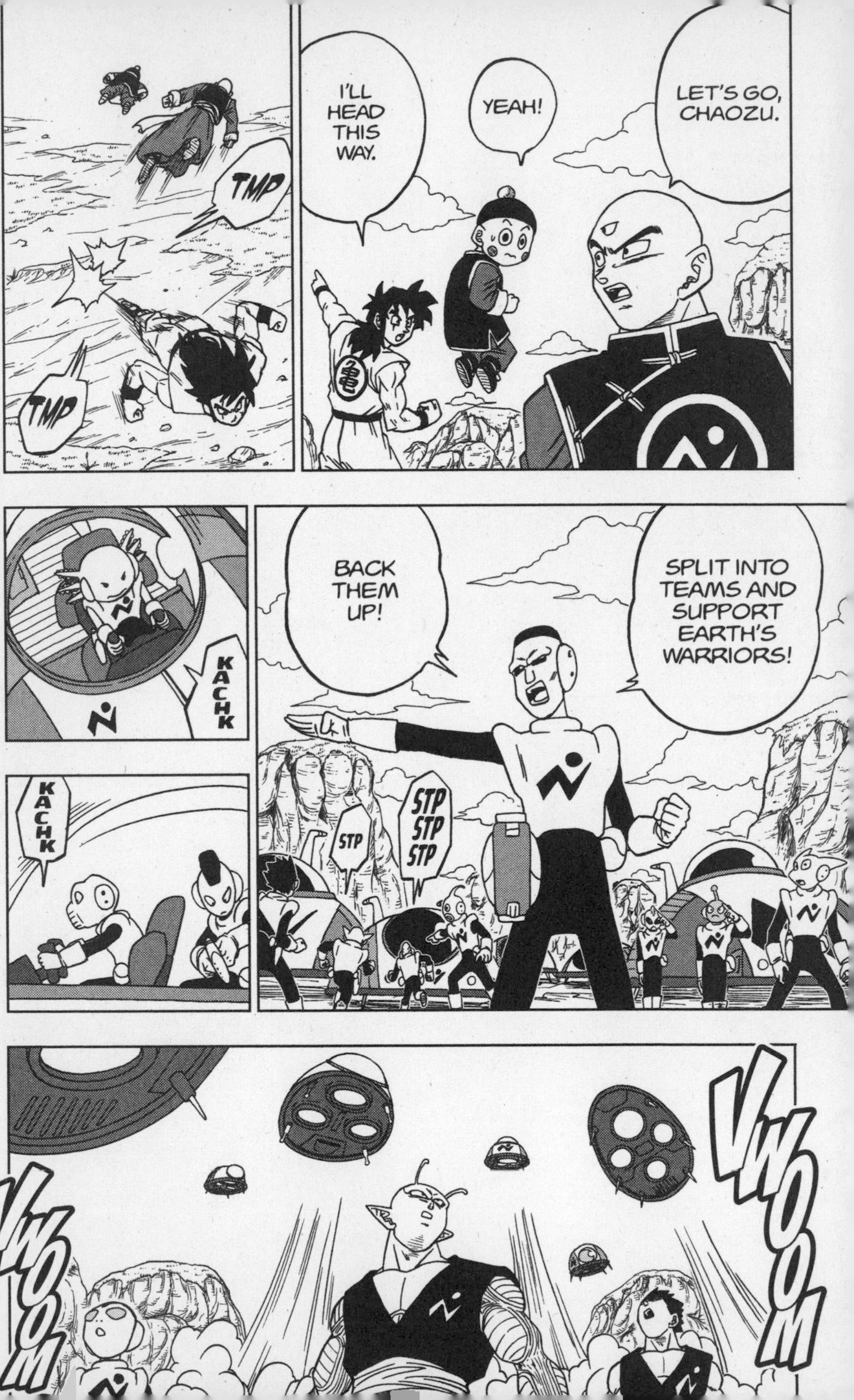
LET'S GO, CHAOZU.
YEAH!
I'LL HEAD THIS WAY.
TMP
TMP
SPLIT INTO TEAMS AND SUPPORT EARTH'S WARRIORS!
BACK THEM UP!
STP STP STP
STP
KACHK
KACHK
VWOOOM
VWOOOM

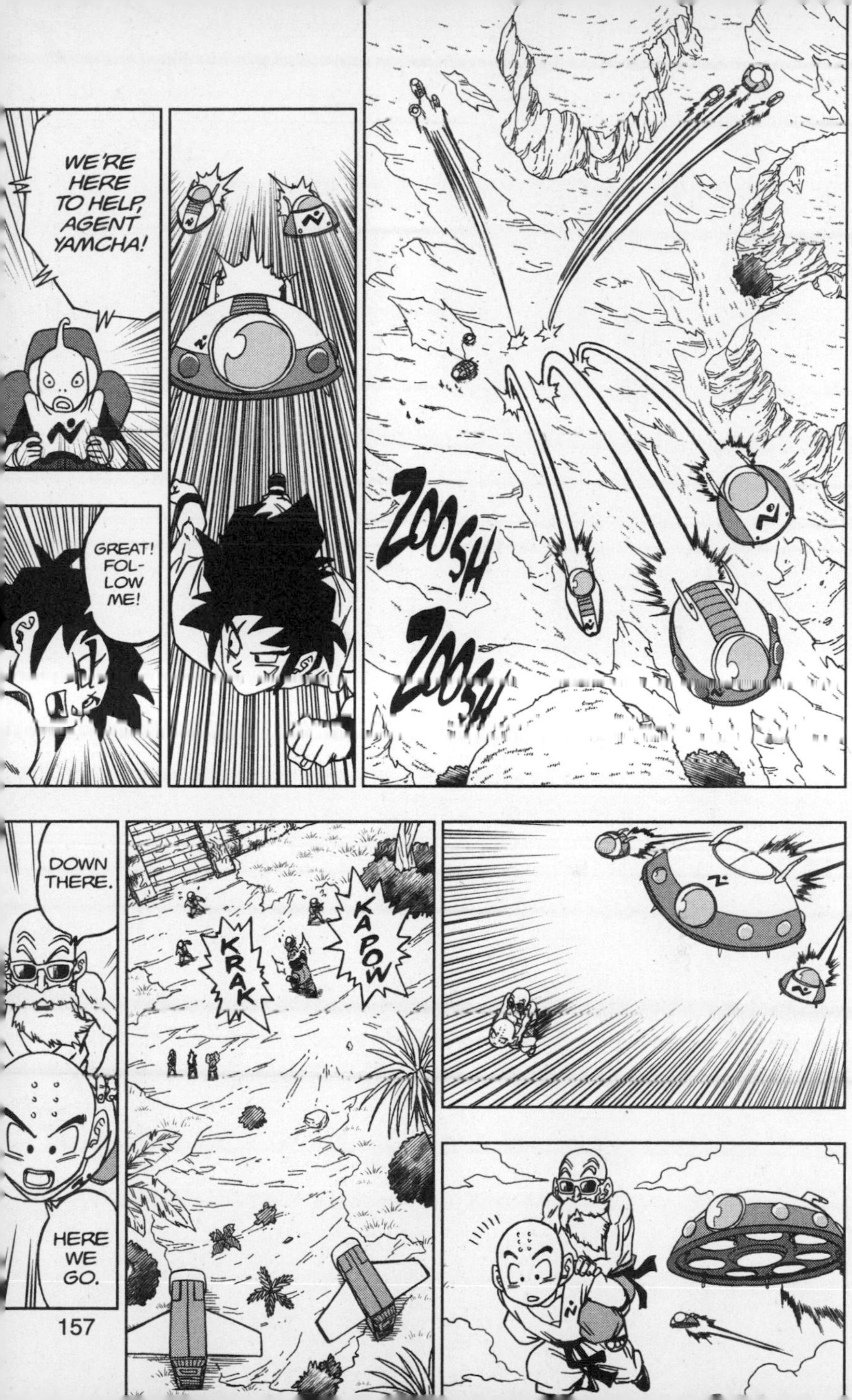
ZOOSH
ZOOSH
WE'RE HERE TO HELP, AGENT YAMCHA!
GREAT! FOL-LOW ME!
KAPOW
KRAK
DOWN THERE.
HERE WE GO.

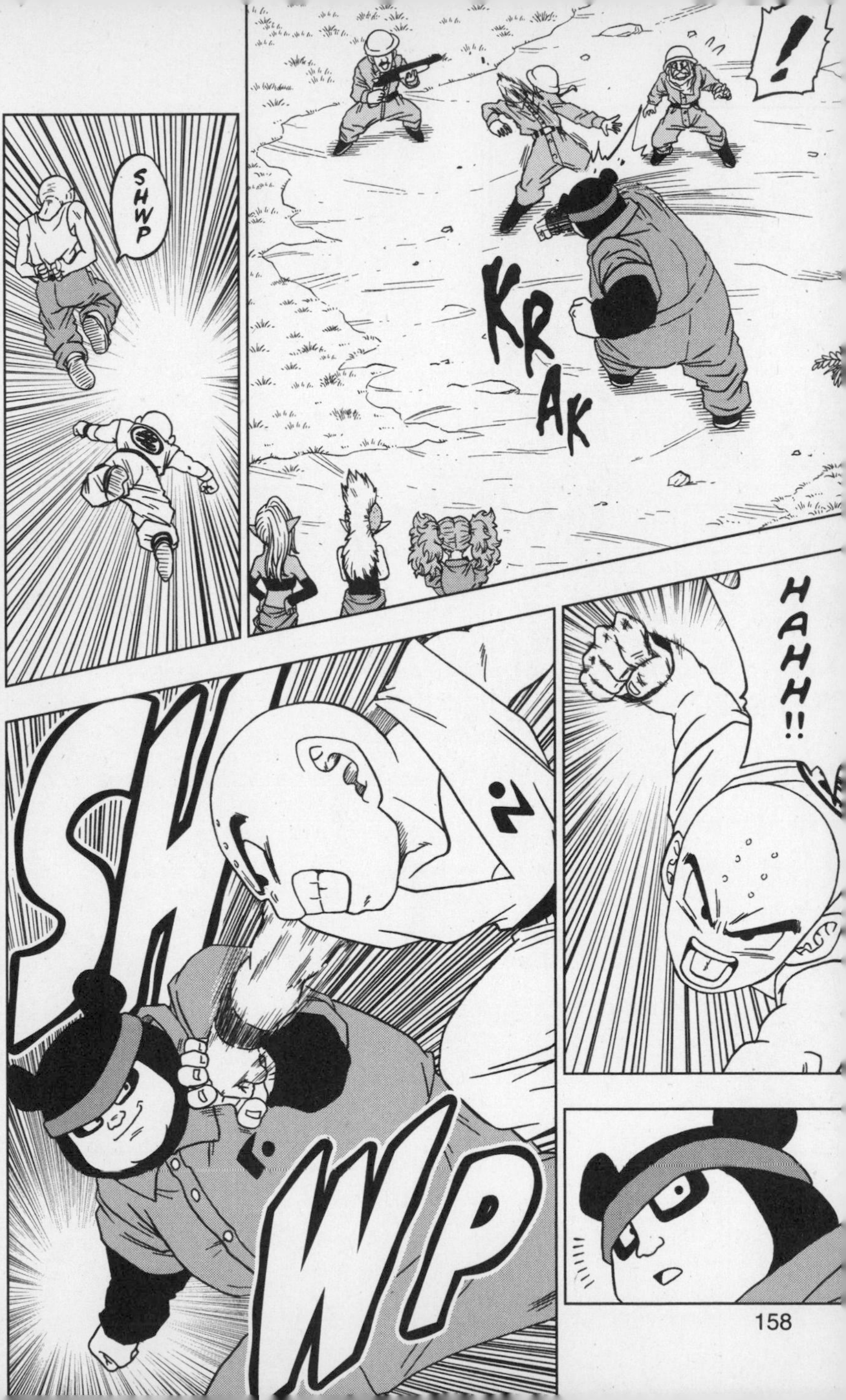
!
KRAK
SHWP
HAHHH!!
SHWP

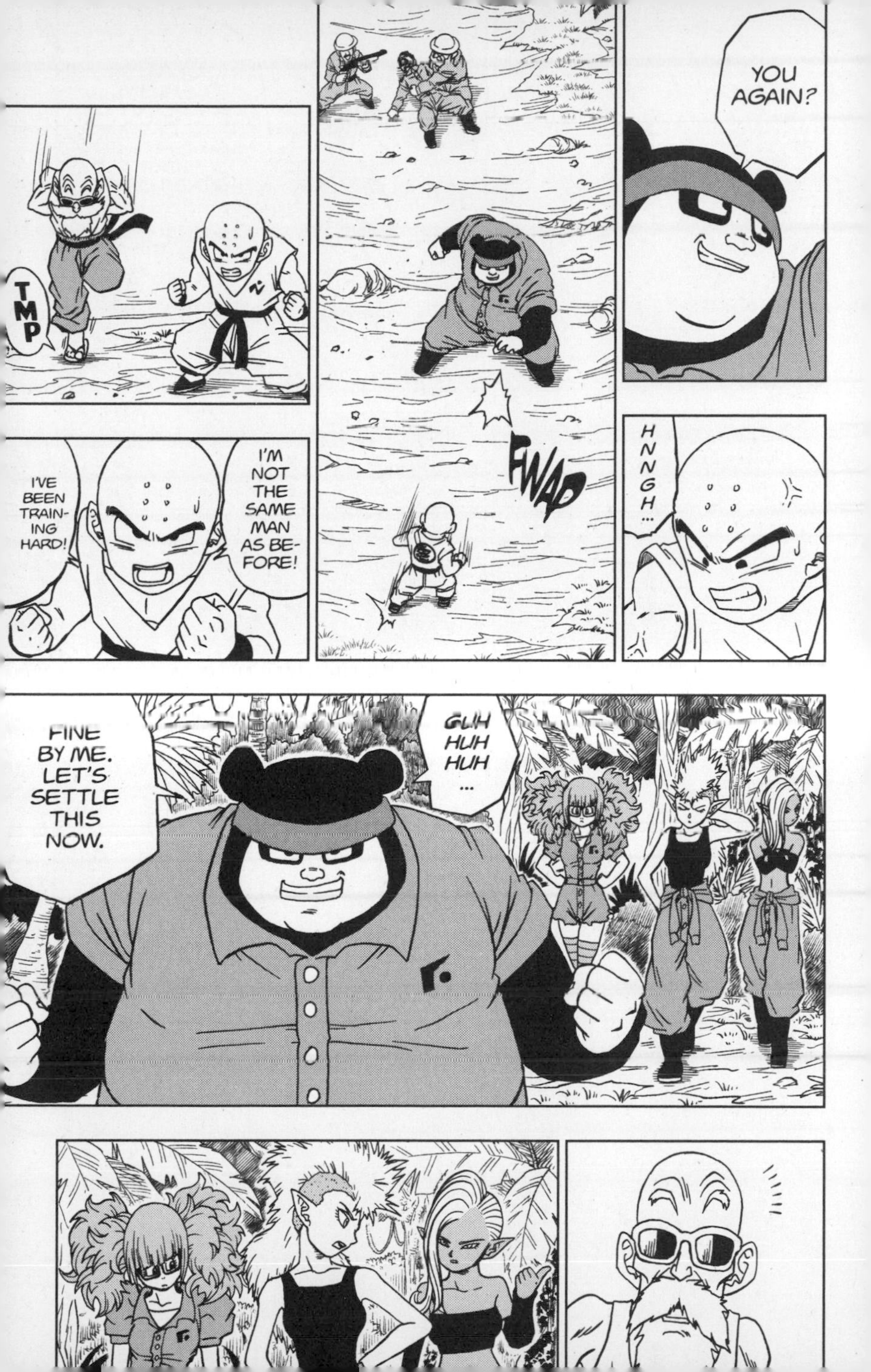
YOU AGAIN?
HNNGH...
FWAP
TMP
I'M NOT THE SAME MAN AS BE-FORE!
I'VE BEEN TRAIN-ING HARD!
GUH HUH HUH ...
FINE BY ME. LET'S SETTLE THIS NOW.

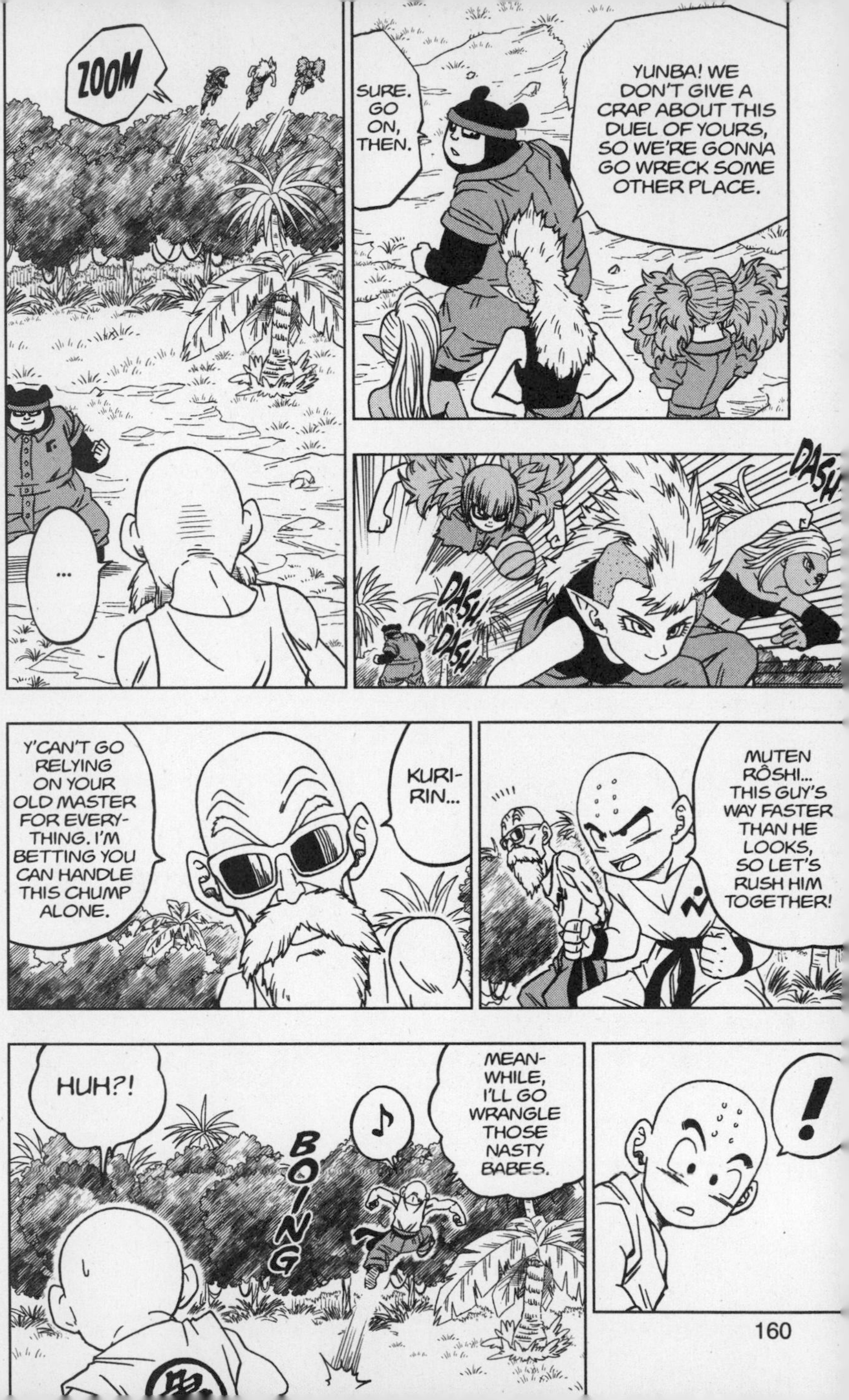
YUNBA! WE DON'T GIVE A CRAP ABOUT THIS DUEL OF YOURS, SO WE'RE GONNA GO WRECK SOME OTHER PLACE.
SURE. GO ON, THEN.
DASH
DASH DASH
ZOOM
...
MUTEN RÔSHI... THIS GUY'S WAY FASTER THAN HE LOOKS, SO LET'S RUSH HIM TOGETHER!
KURI-RIN...
Y'CAN'T GO RELYING ON YOUR OLD MASTER FOR EVERY-THING. I'M BETTING YOU CAN HANDLE THIS CHUMP ALONE.
!
MEAN-WHILE, I'LL GO WRANGLE THOSE NASTY BABES.
♪
BOING
HUH?!

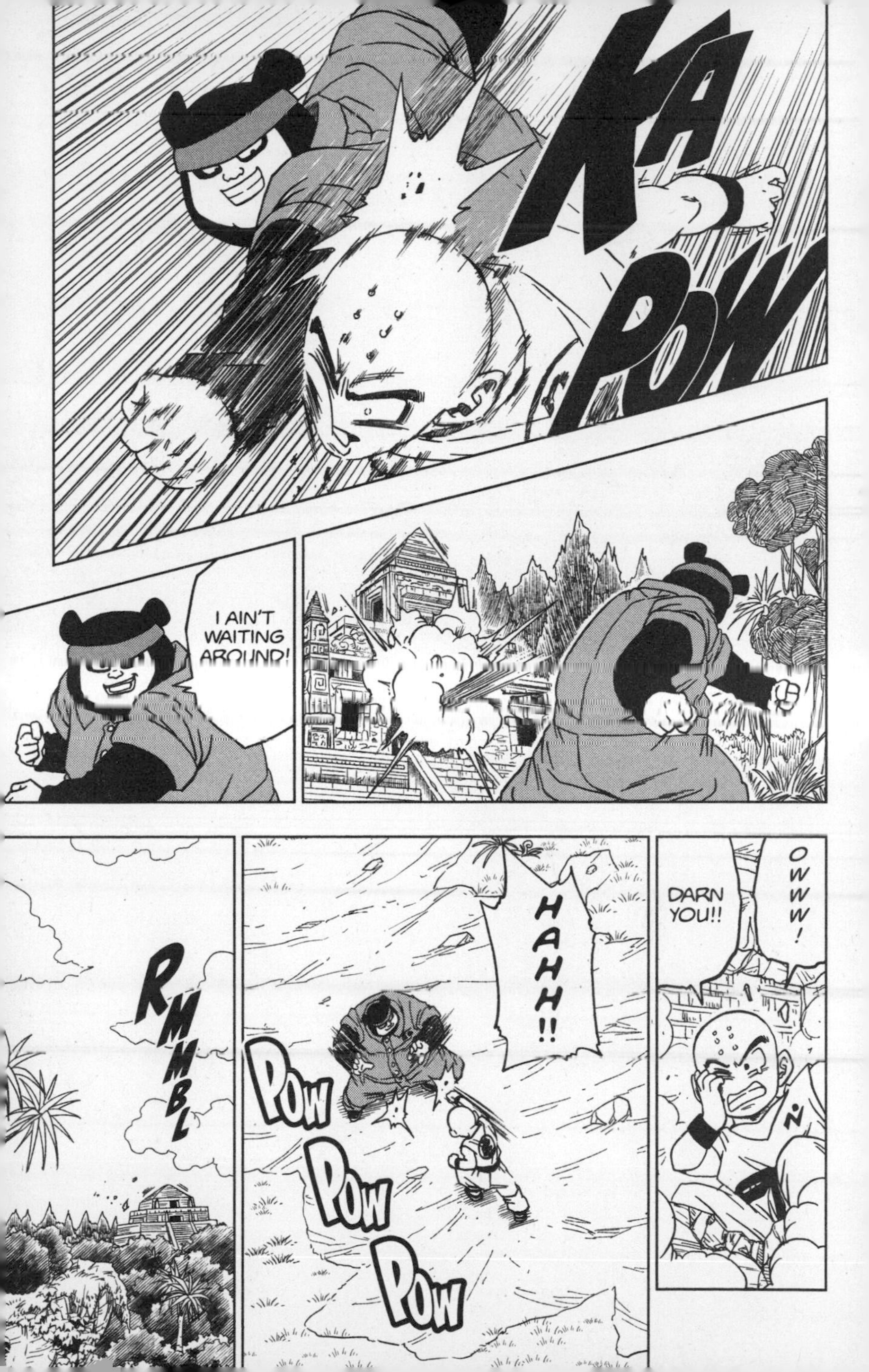
KA
POW
I AIN'T WAITING AROUND!
OWWW!
DARN YOU!!
HAHHH!!
POW
POW
POW
RMMBL

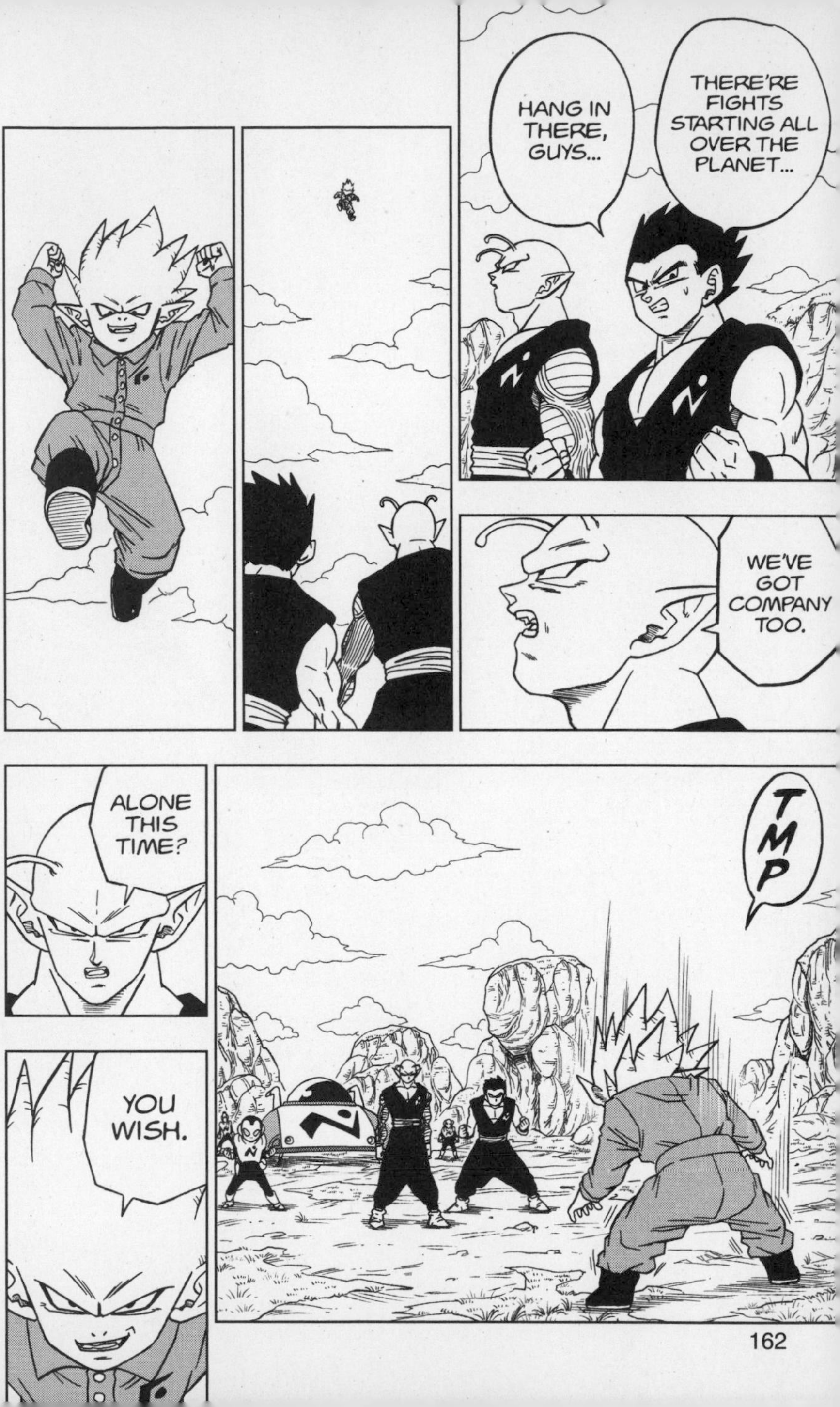
THERE'RE FIGHTS STARTING ALL OVER THE PLANET...
HANG IN THERE, GUYS...
WE'VE GOT COMPANY TOO.
TMP
ALONE THIS TIME?
YOU WISH.

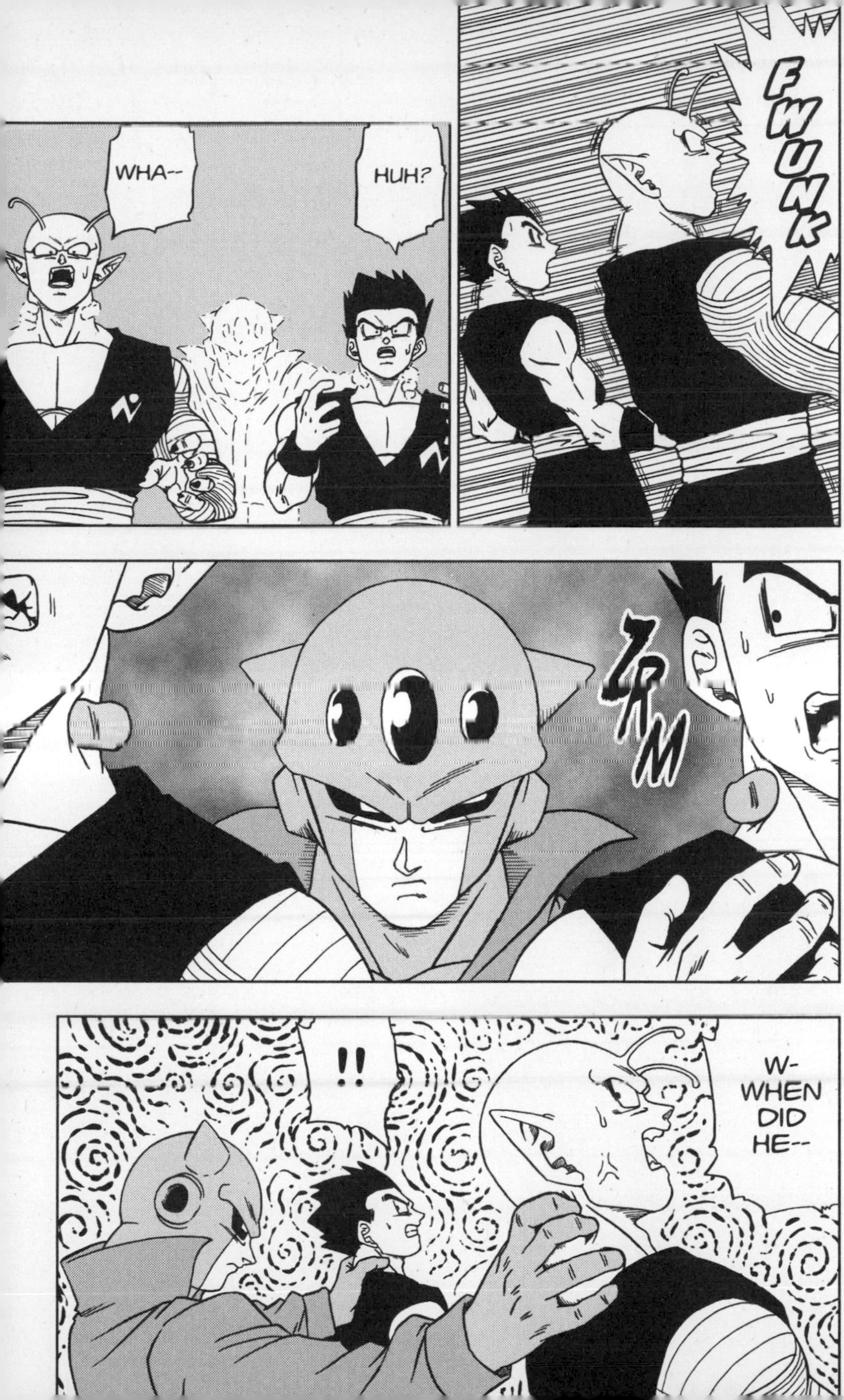
FWUNK
HUH?
WHA--
ZRM
W- WHEN DID HE--
!!

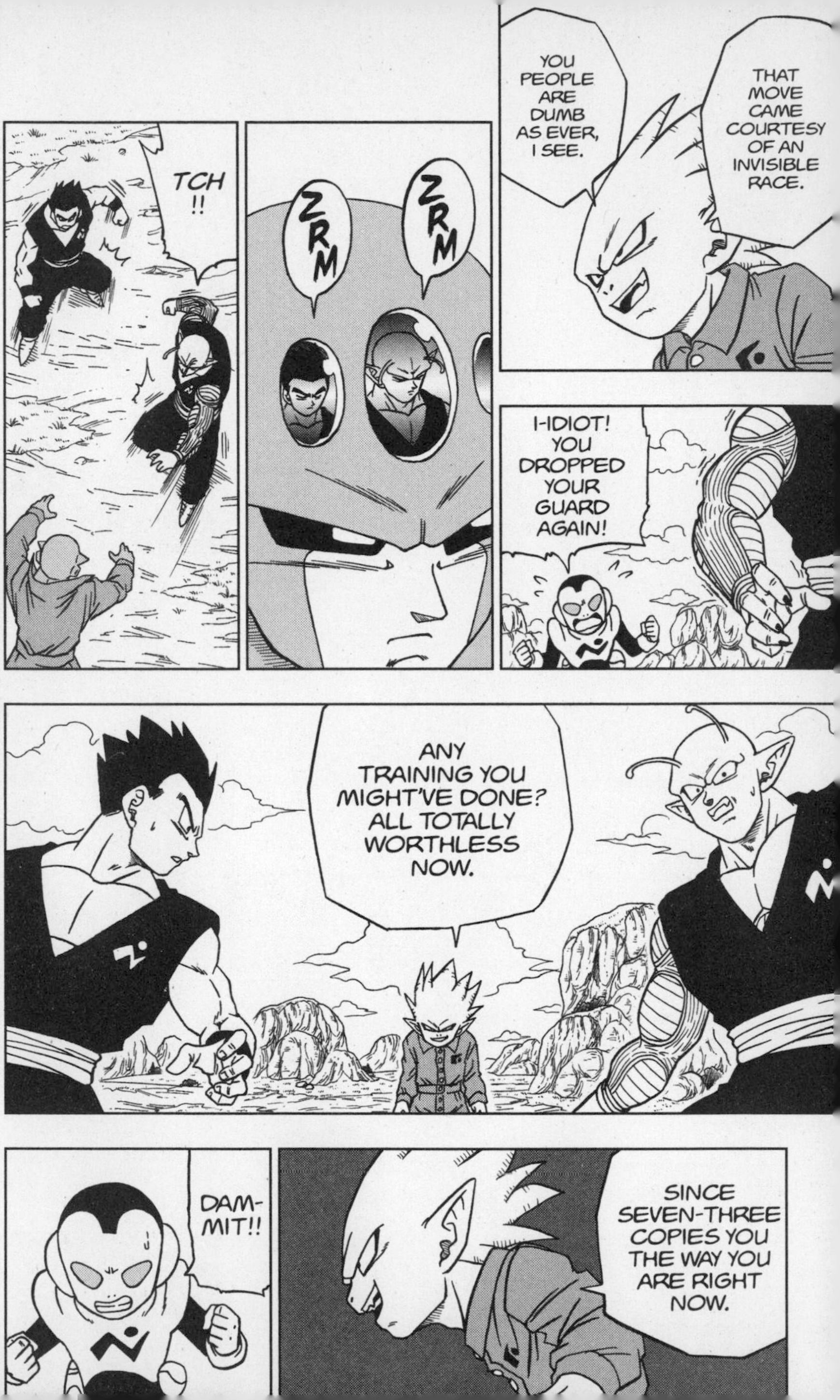

THAT MOVE CAME COURTESY OF AN INVISIBLE RACE.
YOU PEOPLE ARE DUMB AS EVER, I SEE.
I-IDIOT! YOU DROPPED YOUR GUARD AGAIN!
ZRM
ZRM
TCH !!
ANY TRAINING YOU MIGHT'VE DONE? ALL TOTALLY WORTHLESS NOW.
SINCE SEVEN-THREE COPIES YOU THE WAY YOU ARE RIGHT NOW.
DAM-MIT!!

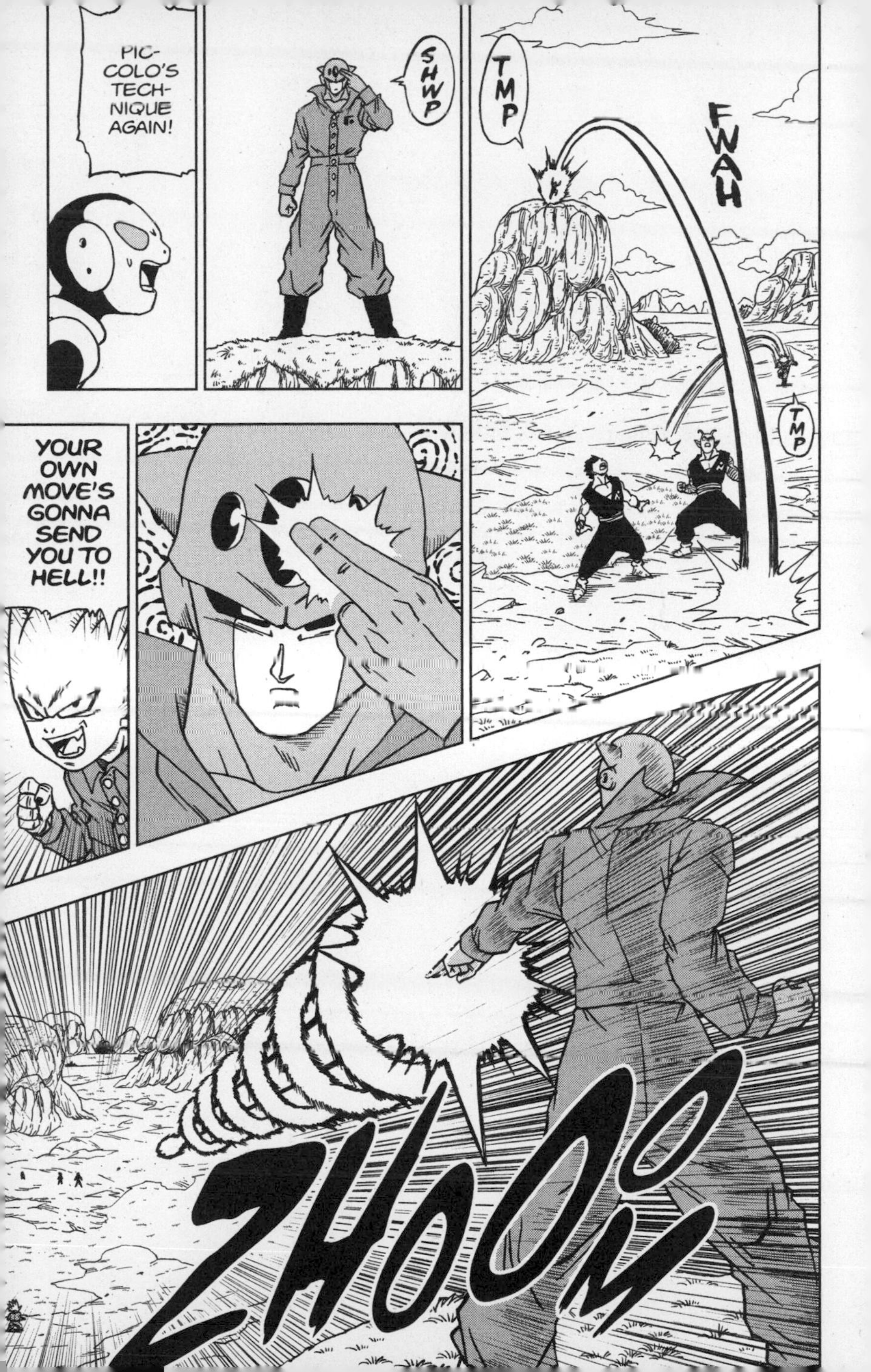
TMP
FWAH
TMP
SHWP
PIC-COLO'S TECH-NIQUE AGAIN!
YOUR OWN MOVE'S GONNA SEND YOU TO HELL!!
ZHOOOM

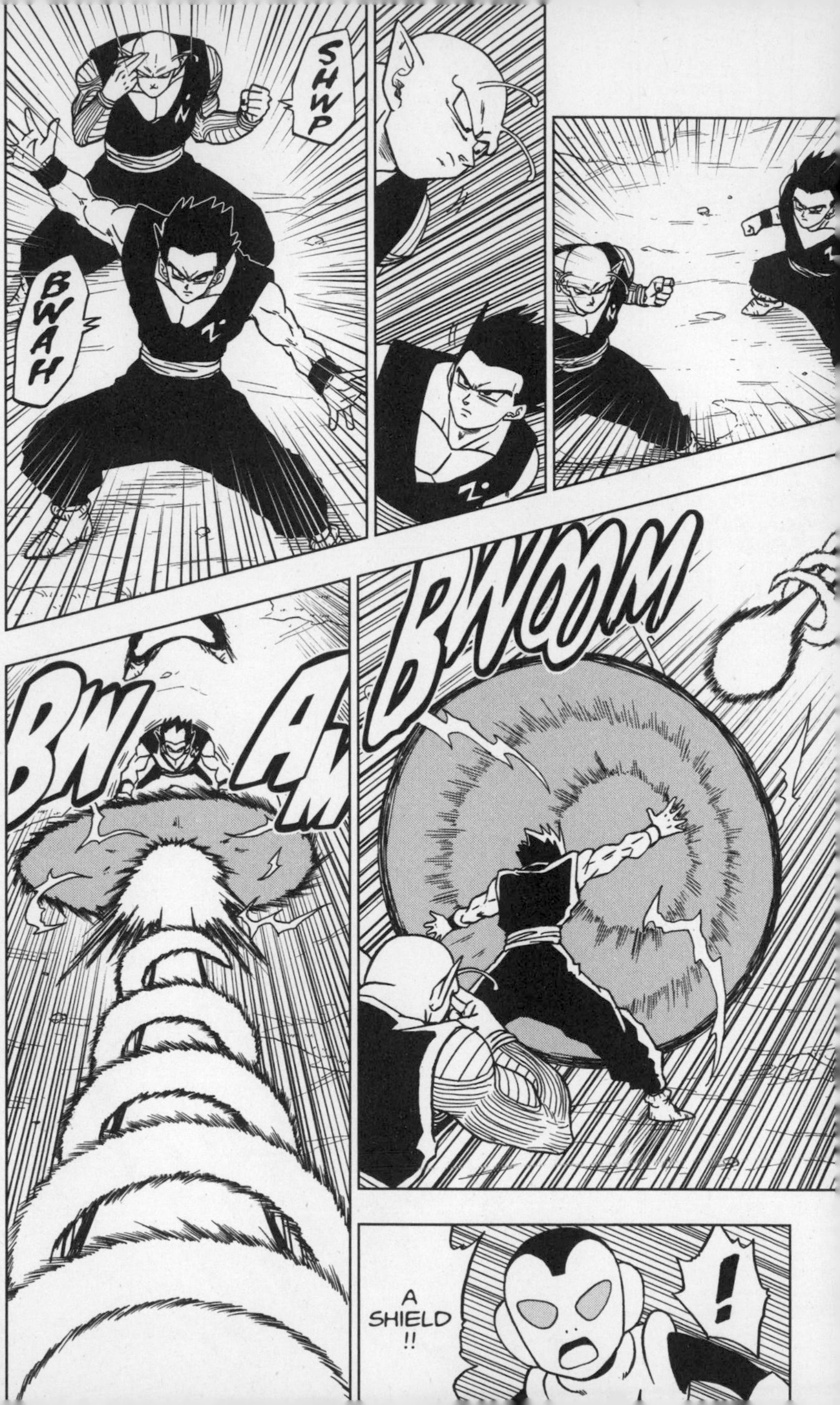
SHWP
BWAH
BWOOM
BWAM
!
A SHIELD !!

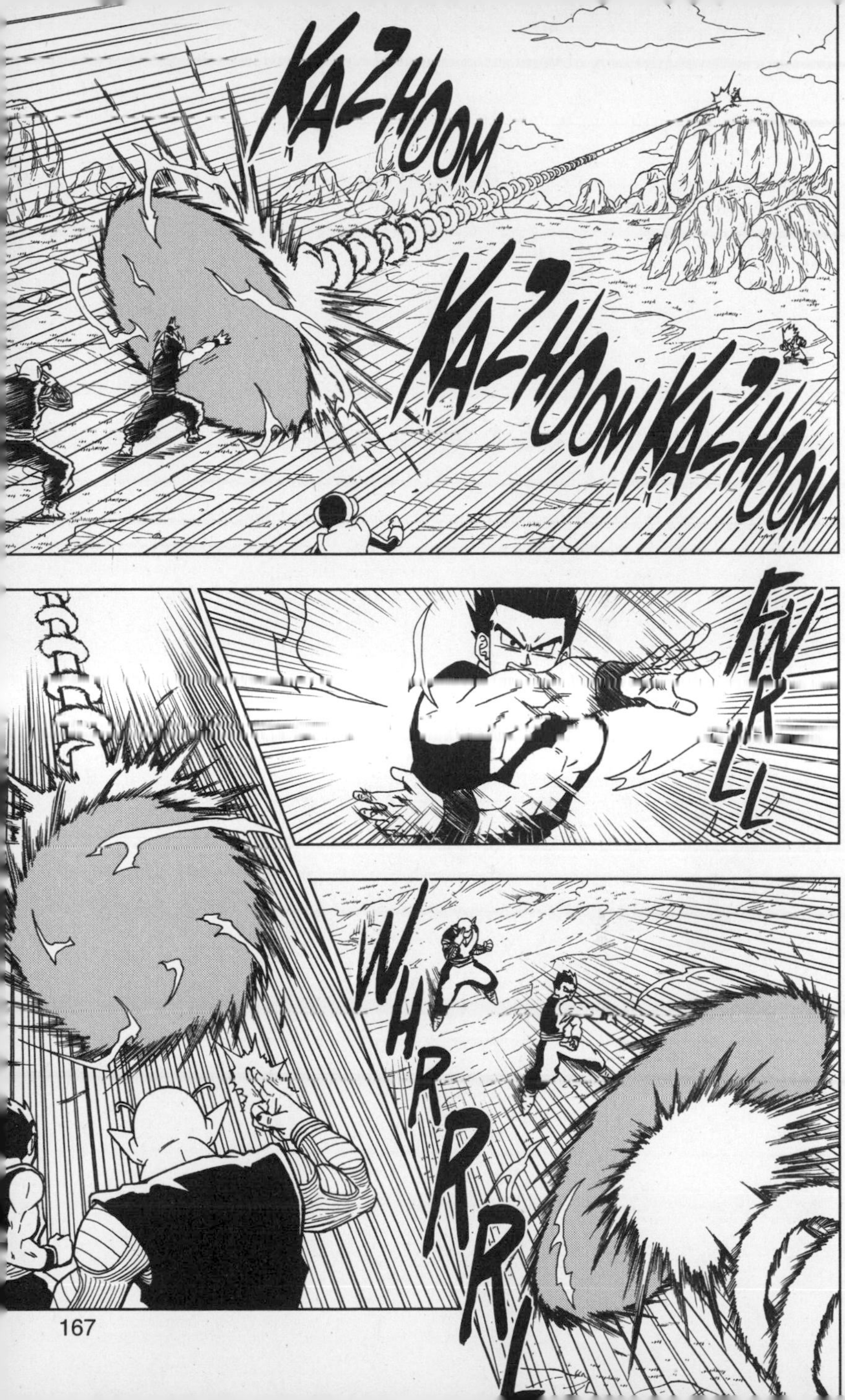
KAZHOOM
KAZHOOM
KAZHOOM
FWRLL
WHRRRRL

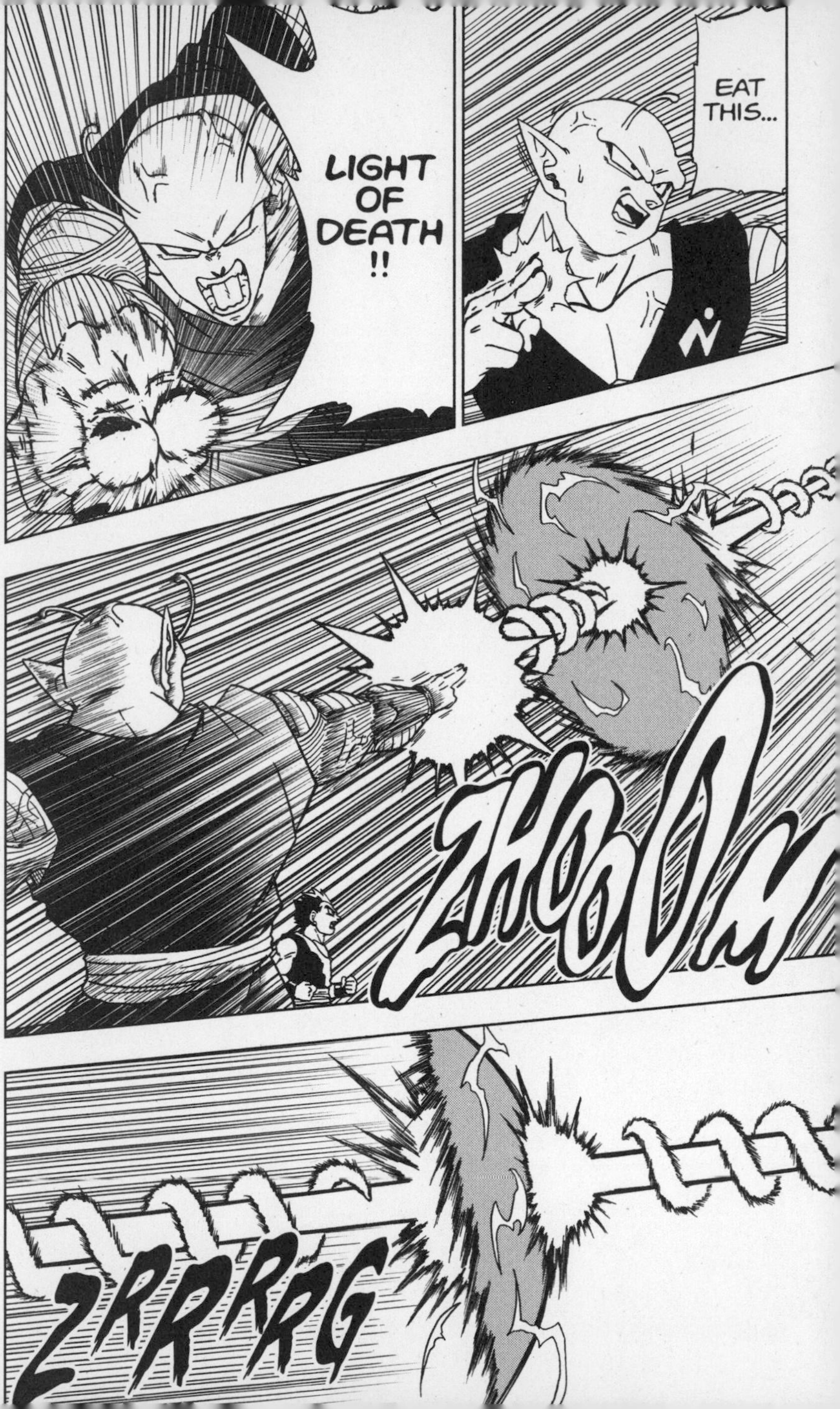
EAT THIS...
LIGHT OF DEATH !!
ZHOOOM
ZRRRRG

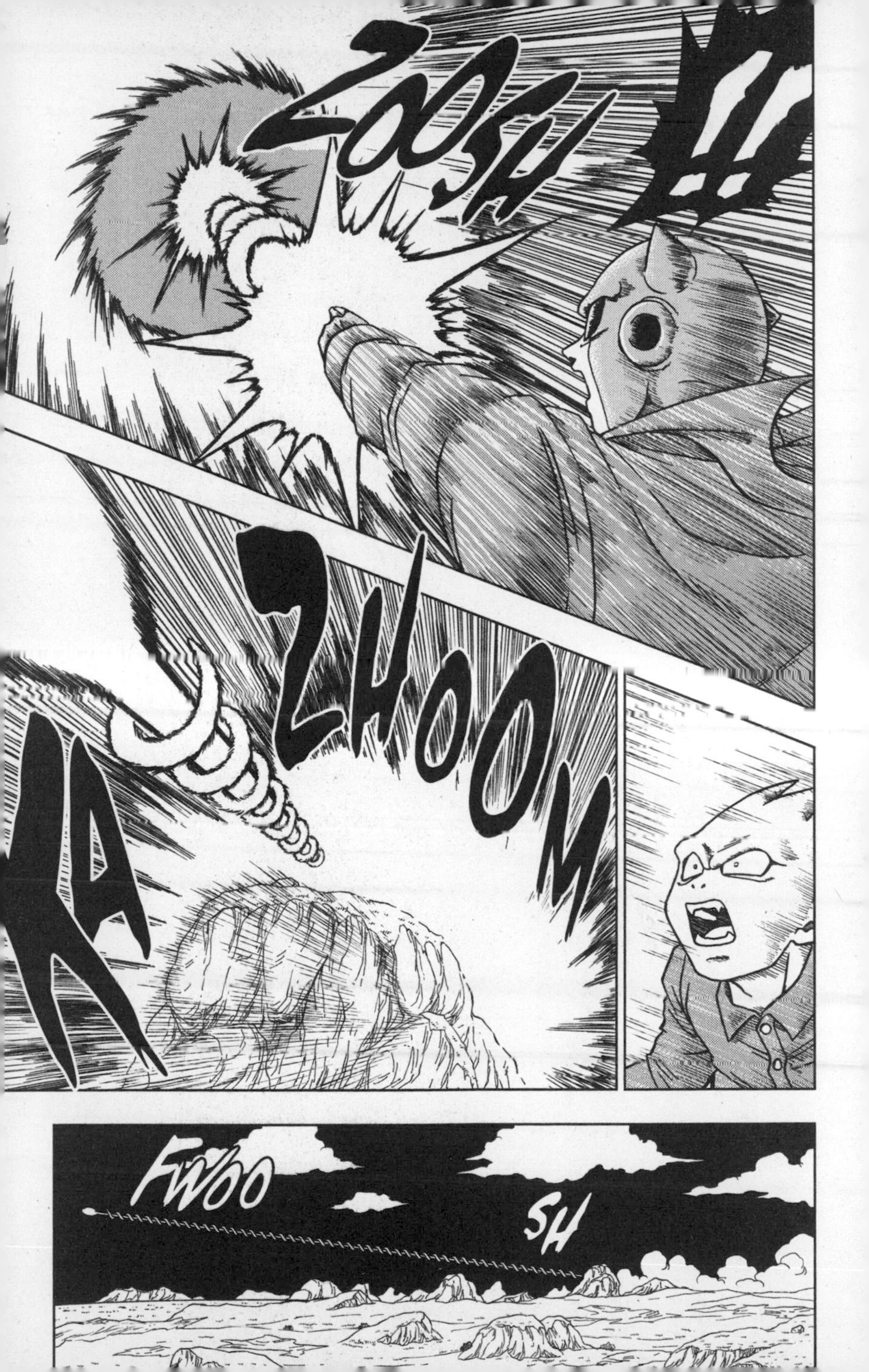
ZOOSH!!
KA
ZHOOM
FWOO
SH

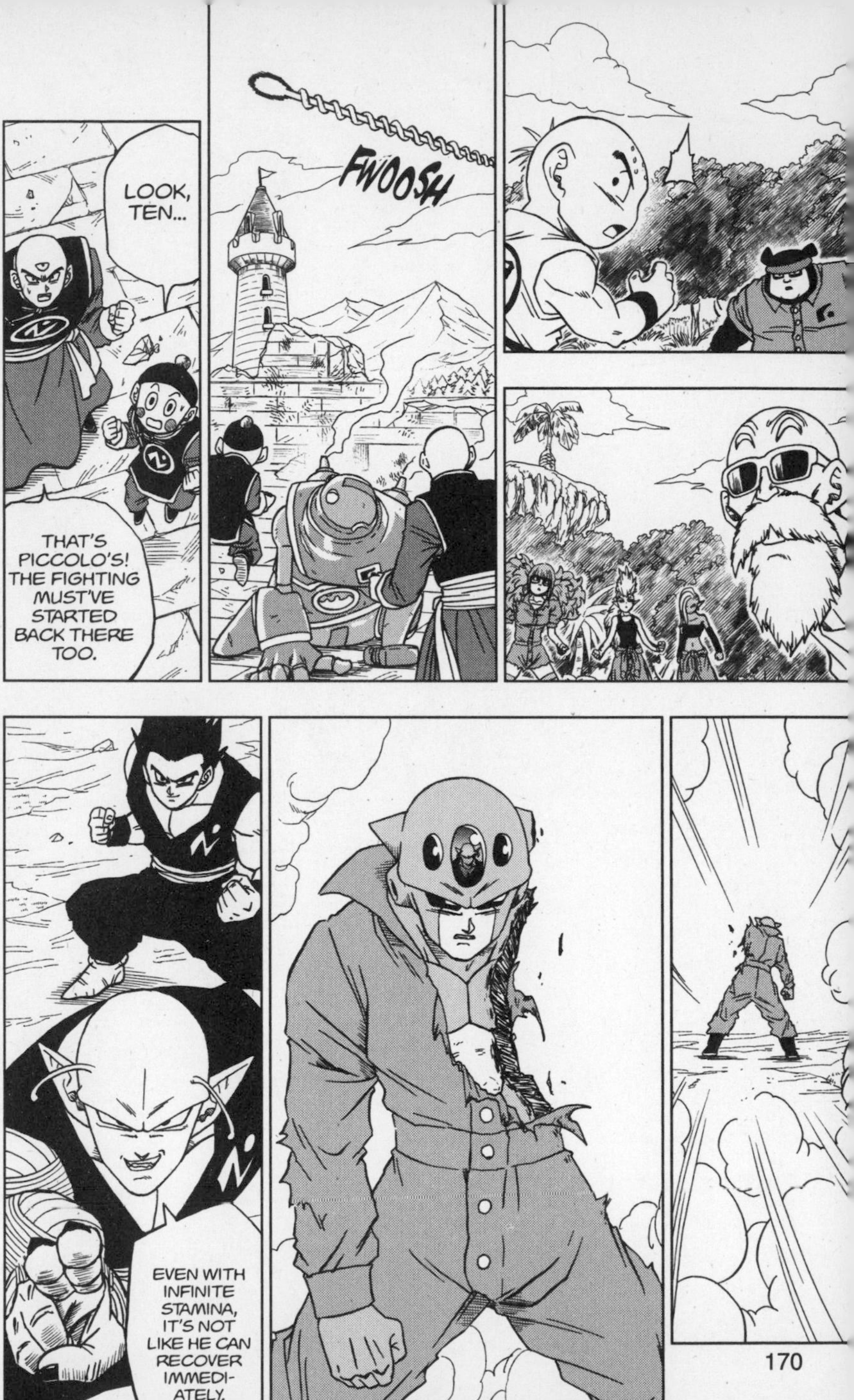
FWOOSH
LOOK, TEN...
THAT'S PICCOLO'S! THE FIGHTING MUST'VE STARTED BACK THERE TOO.
EVEN WITH INFINITE STAMINA, IT'S NOT LIKE HE CAN RECOVER IMMEDI-ATELY.

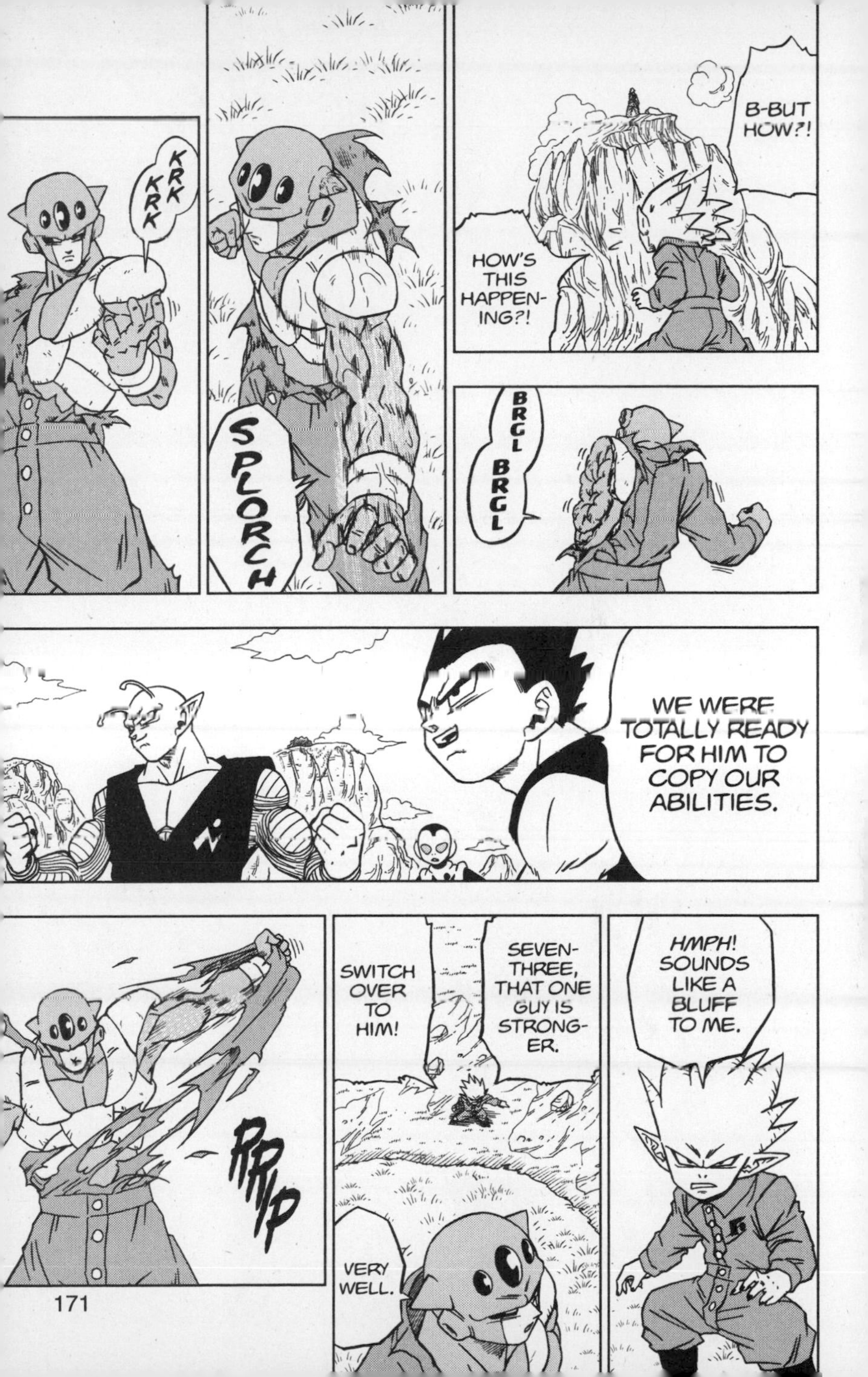
B-BUT HOW?!
HOW'S THIS HAPPEN-ING?!
BRGL BRGL
SPLORCH
KRK KRK
WE WERE TOTALLY READY FOR HIM TO COPY OUR ABILITIES.
HMPH! SOUNDS LIKE A BLUFF TO ME.
SEVEN-THREE, THAT ONE GUY IS STRONG-ER.
SWITCH OVER TO HIM!
VERY WELL.
RRIP

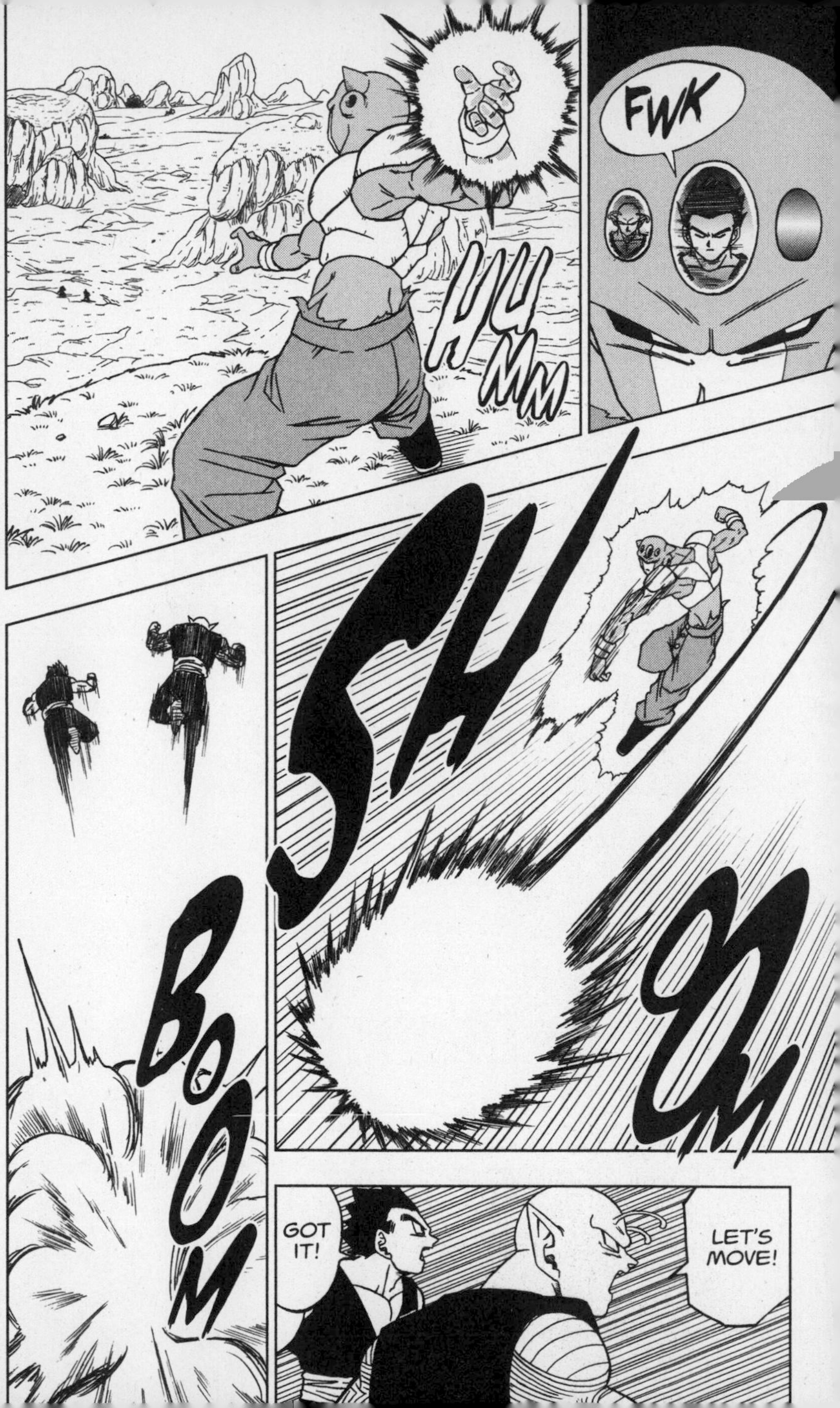
FWK
HUMMM
SHOOM
LET'S MOVE!
GOT IT!
BOOM

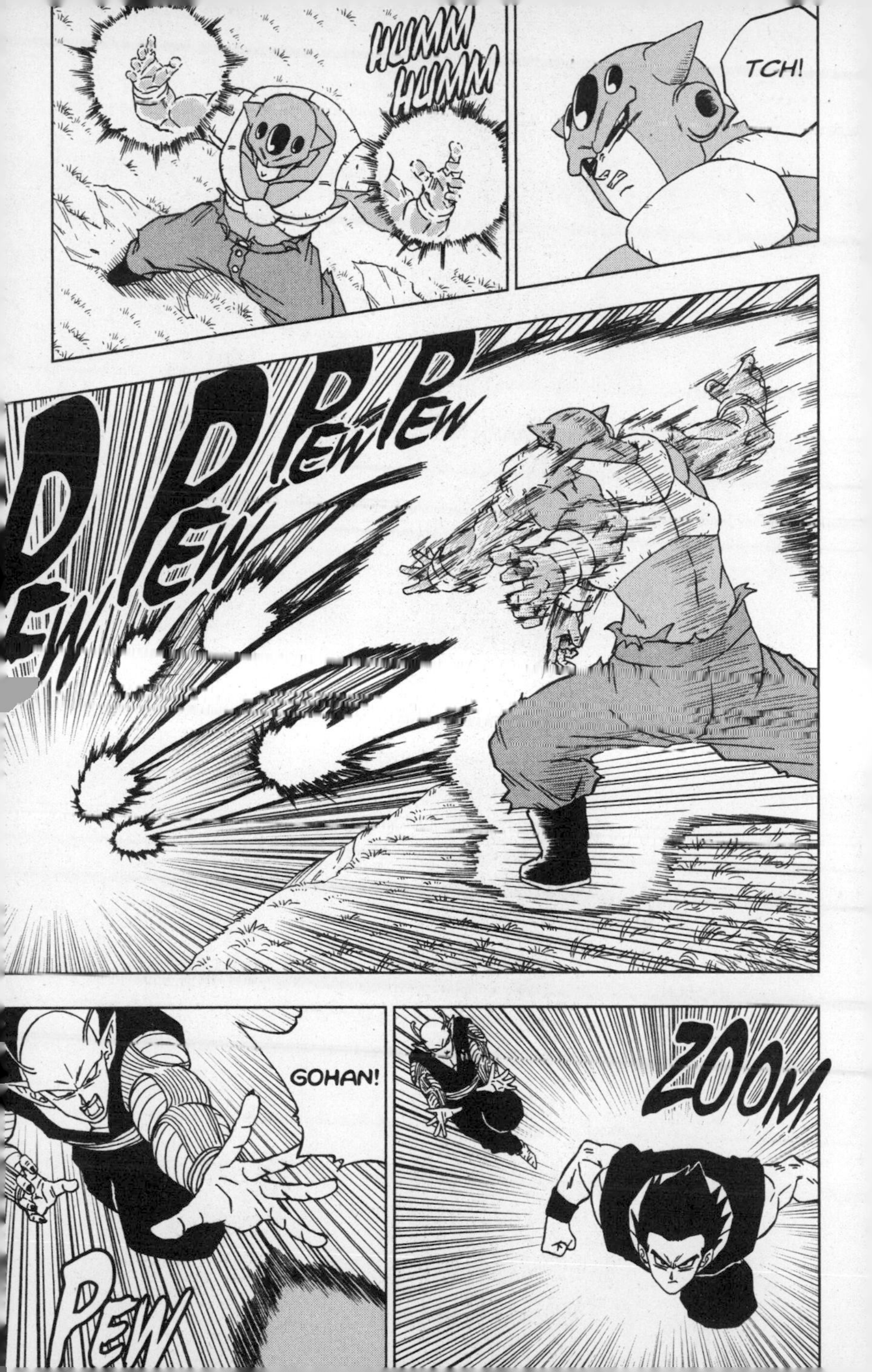
TCH!
HUMM HUMM
PEW PEW PEW PEW
ZOOM
GOHAN!
PEW

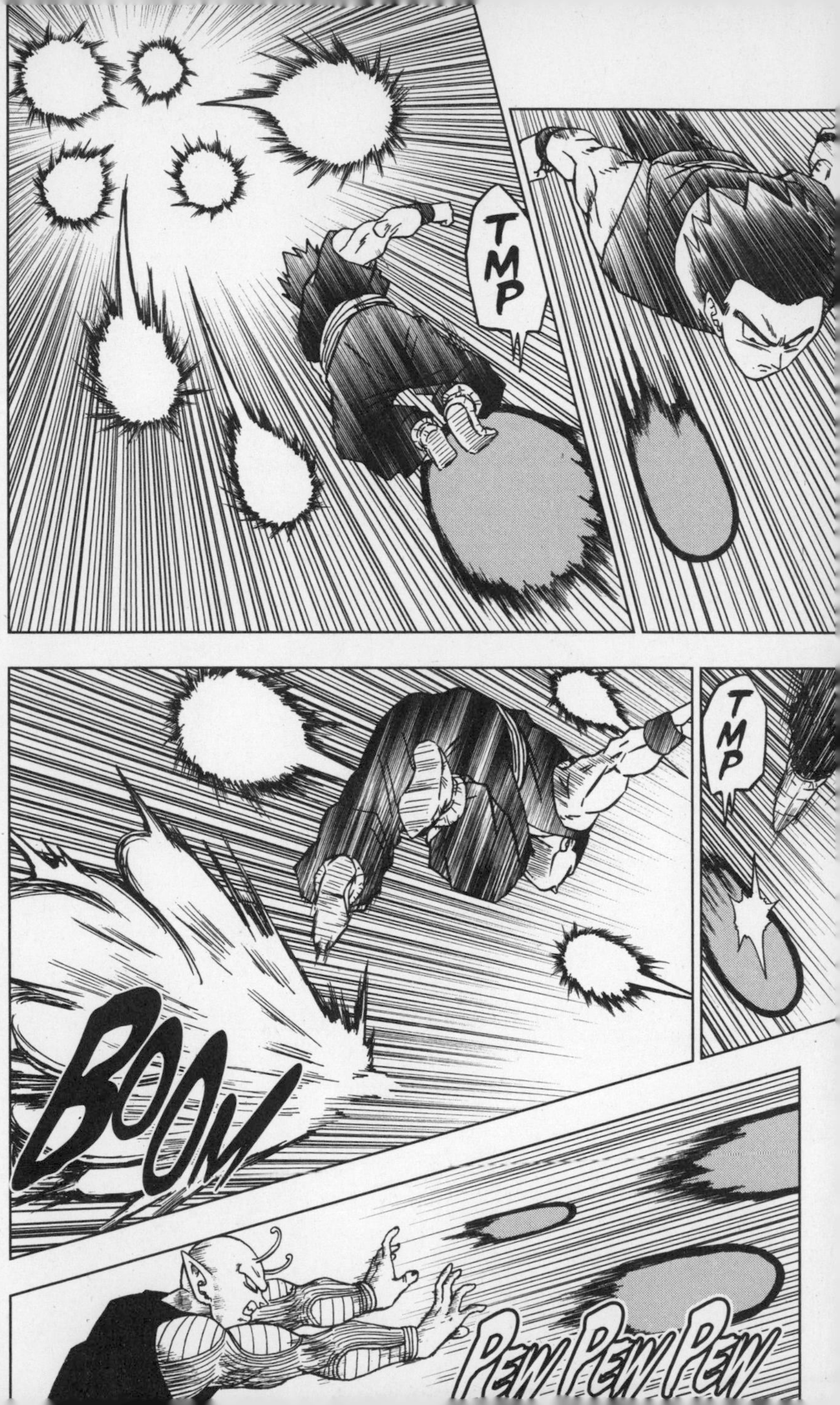
TMP
TMP
BOOM
PEW PEW PEW

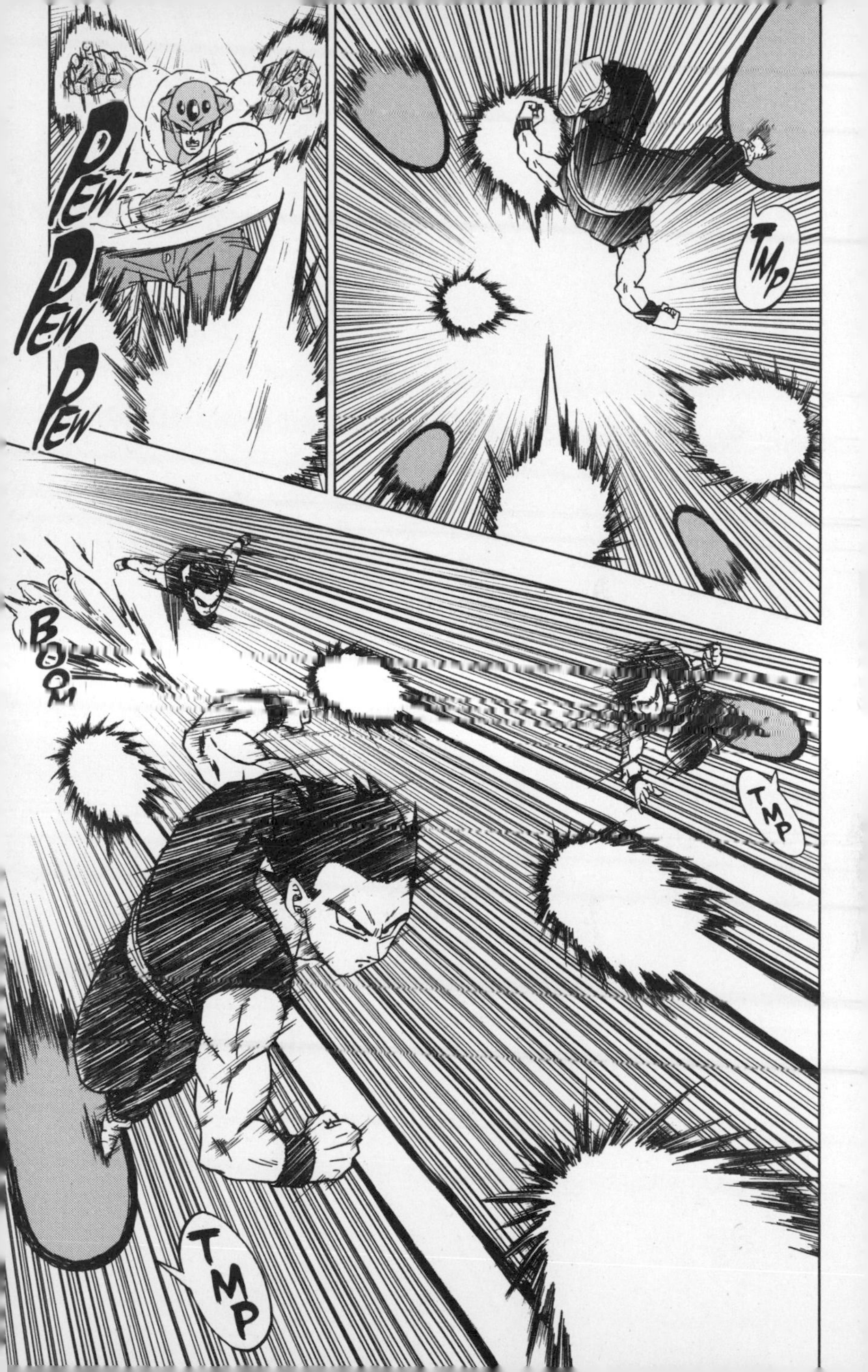
TMP
PEW PEW PEW PEW
TMP
BOOM
TMP

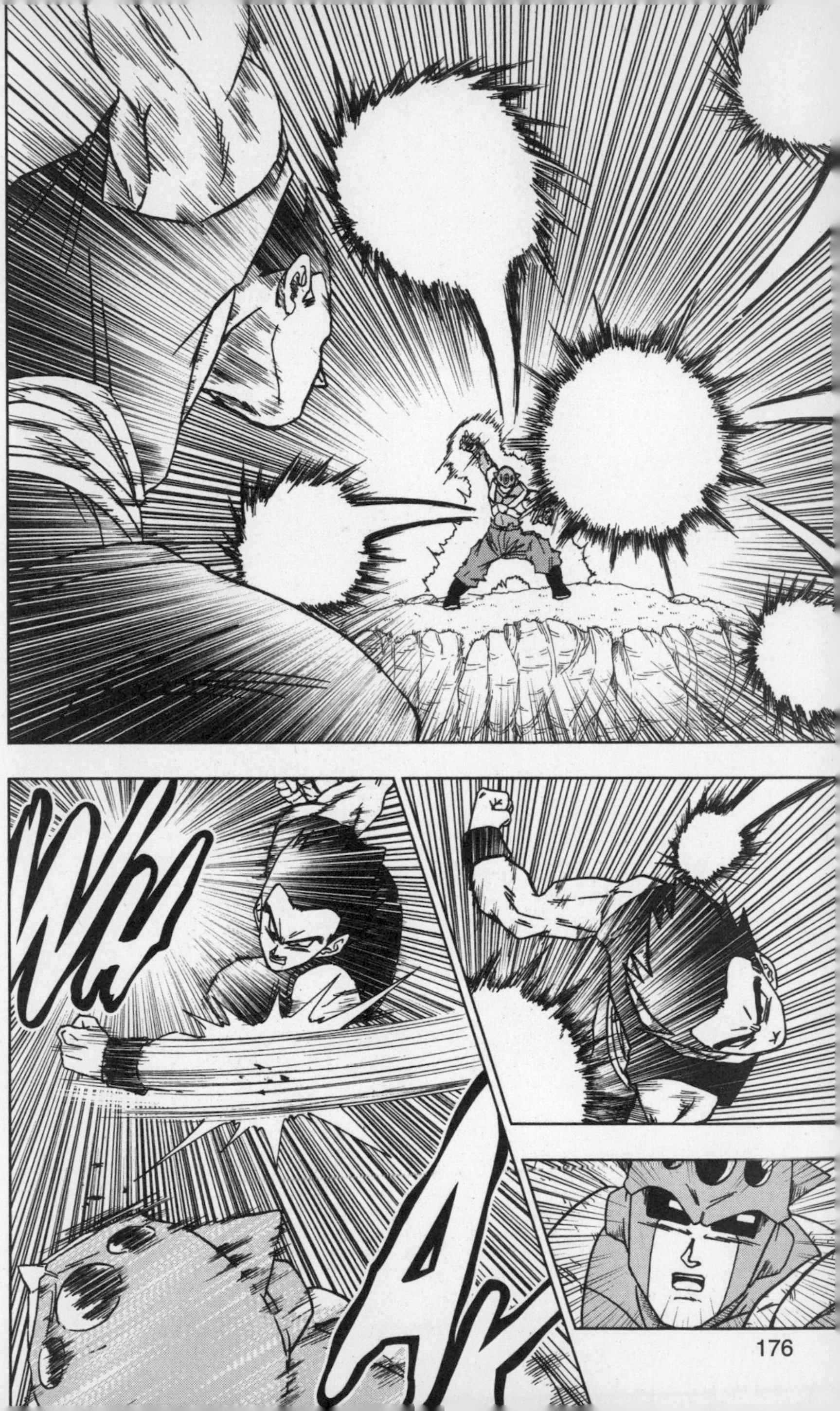
WHAAH

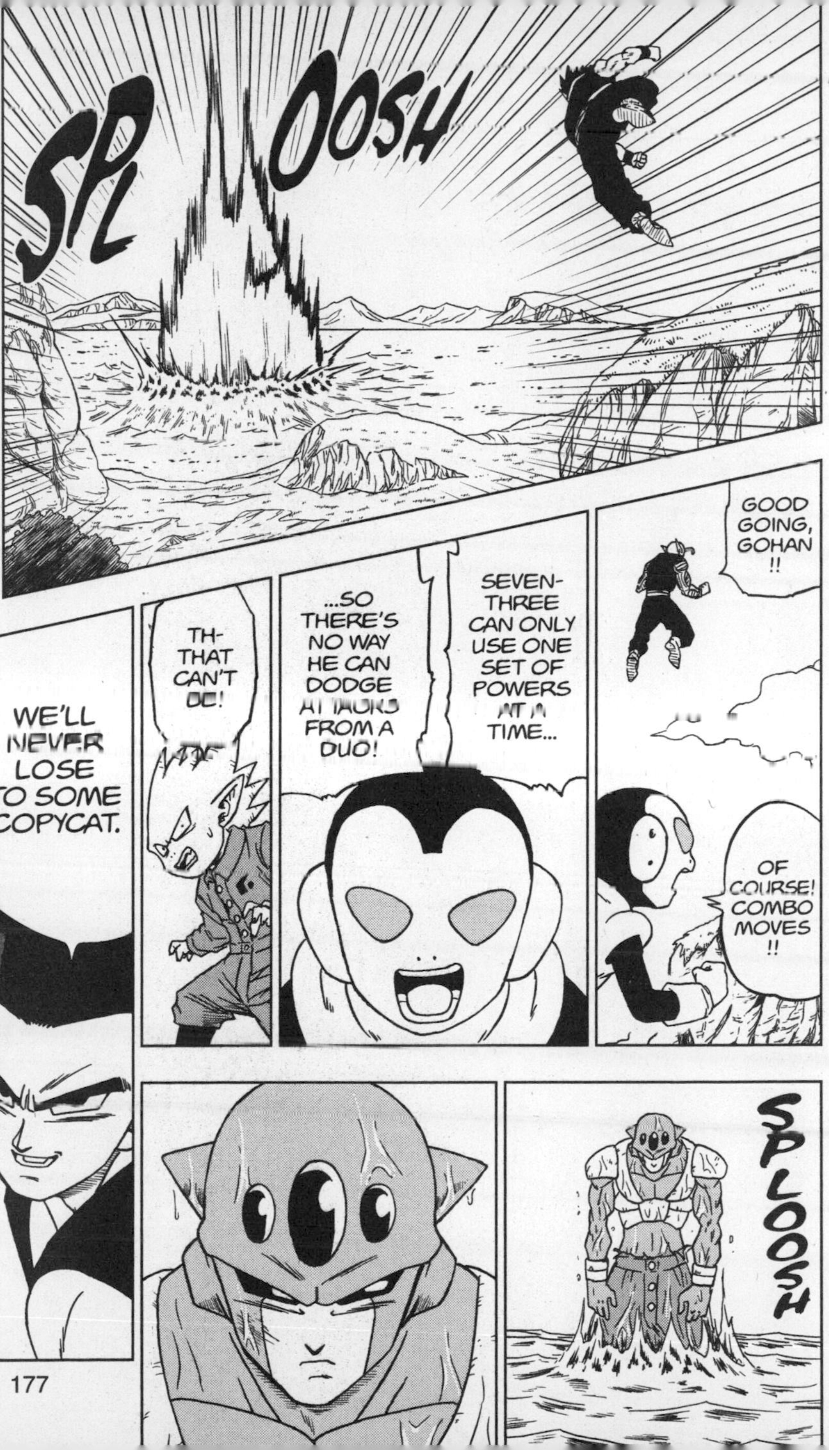
SPLOOSH
GOOD GOING, GOHAN!!
OF COURSE! COMBO MOVES!!
SEVEN-THREE CAN ONLY USE ONE SET OF POWERS AT A TIME...
...SO THERE'S NO WAY HE CAN DODGE ATTACKS FROM A DUO!
TH-THAT CAN'T BE!
SPLOOSH
WE'LL NEVER LOSE TO SOME COPYCAT.

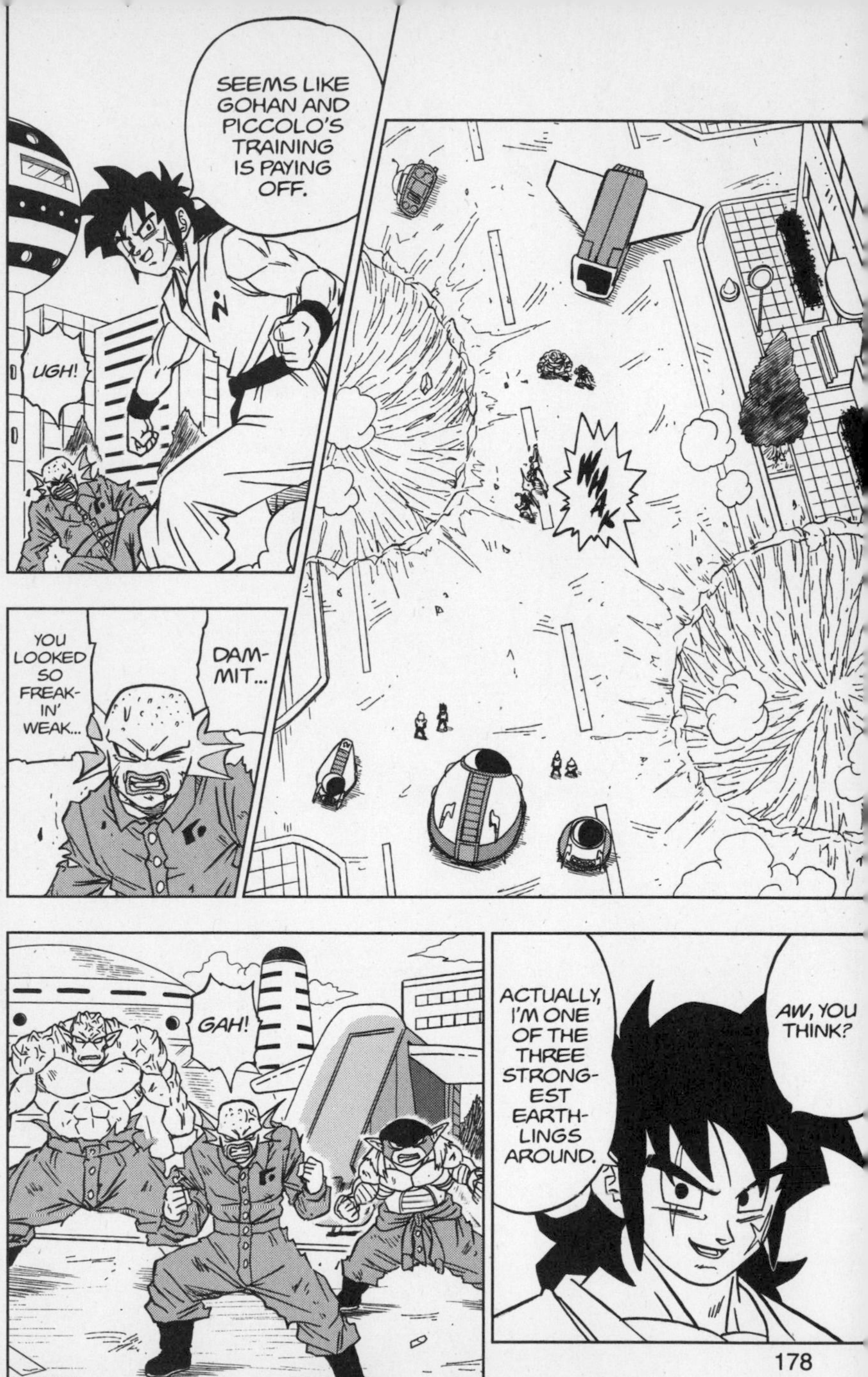
WHAK
SEEMS LIKE GOHAN AND PICCOLO'S TRAINING IS PAYING OFF.
UGH!
DAM-MIT...
YOU LOOKED SO FREAK-IN' WEAK...
AW, YOU THINK?
ACTUALLY, I'M ONE OF THE THREE STRONG-EST EARTH-LINGS AROUND.
GAH!

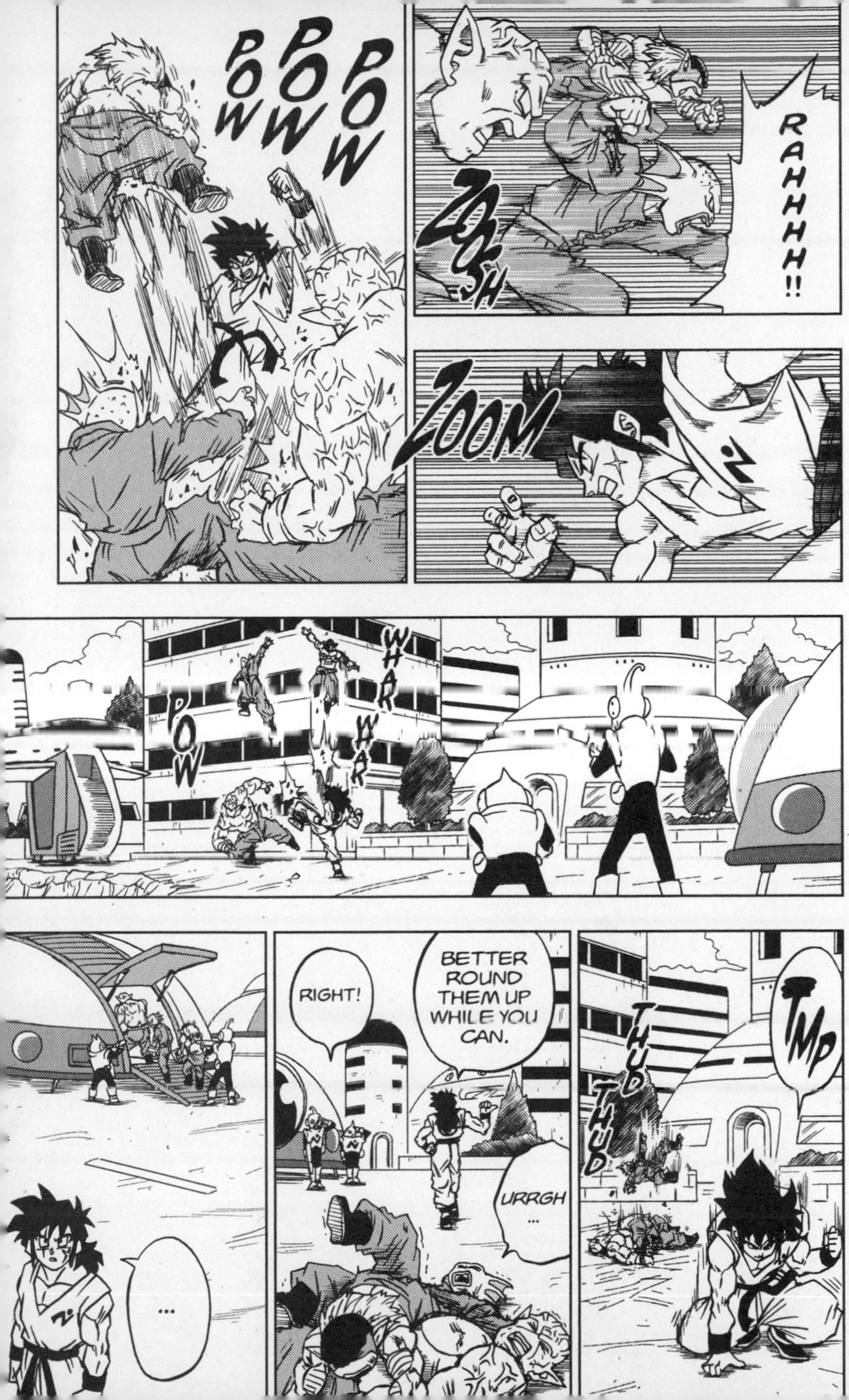
RAHHHH!!
ZOOSH
ZOOM
POW POW POW
WHAR WHAR
POW
TMP
THUD THUD
BETTER ROUND THEM UP WHILE YOU CAN.
RIGHT!
URRGH ...
...

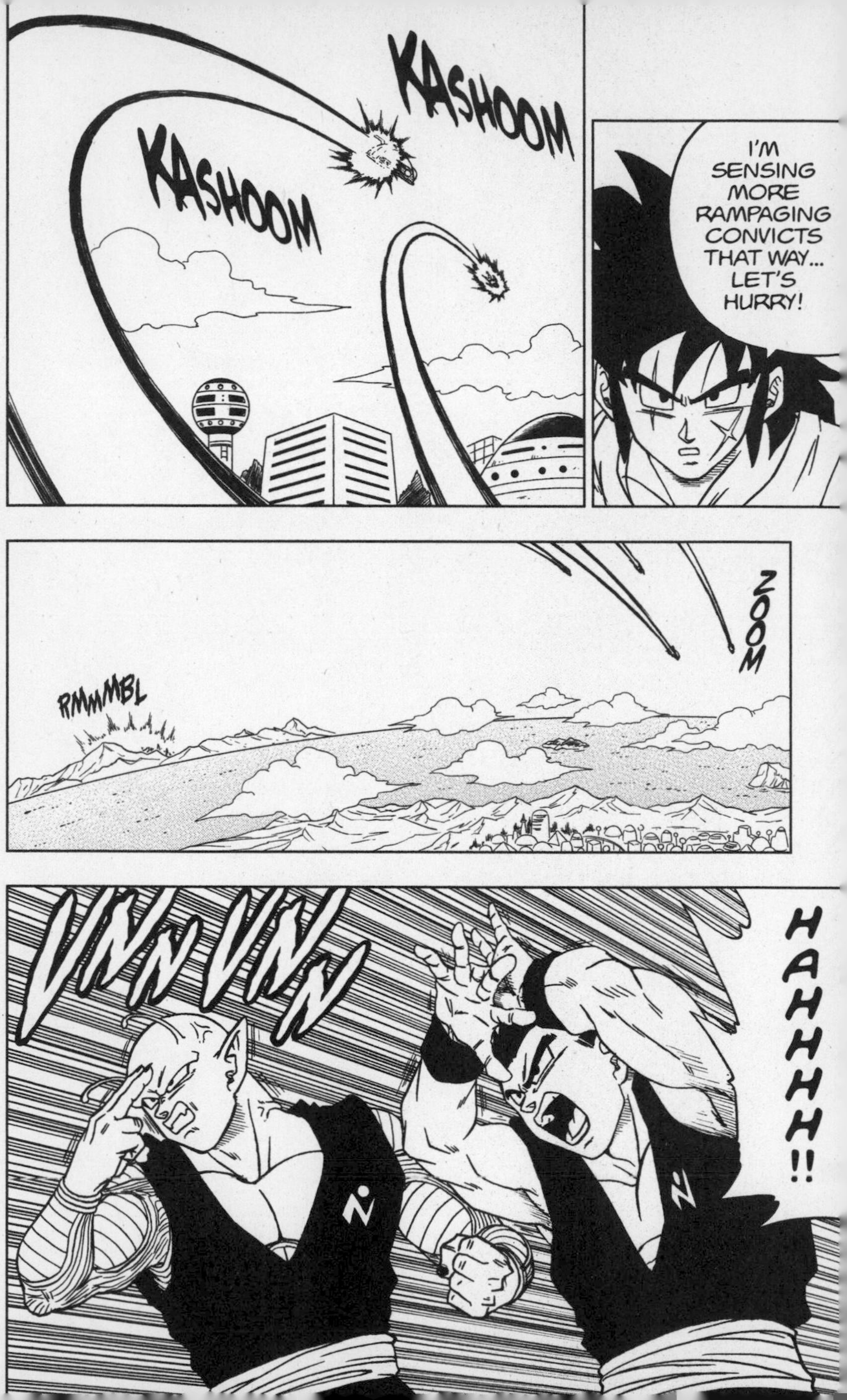
I'M SENSING MORE RAMPAGING CONVICTS THAT WAY... LET'S HURRY!
KASHOOM
KASHOOM
ZOOM
RMMMBL
HAHHHHH!!
VN VN VN VN

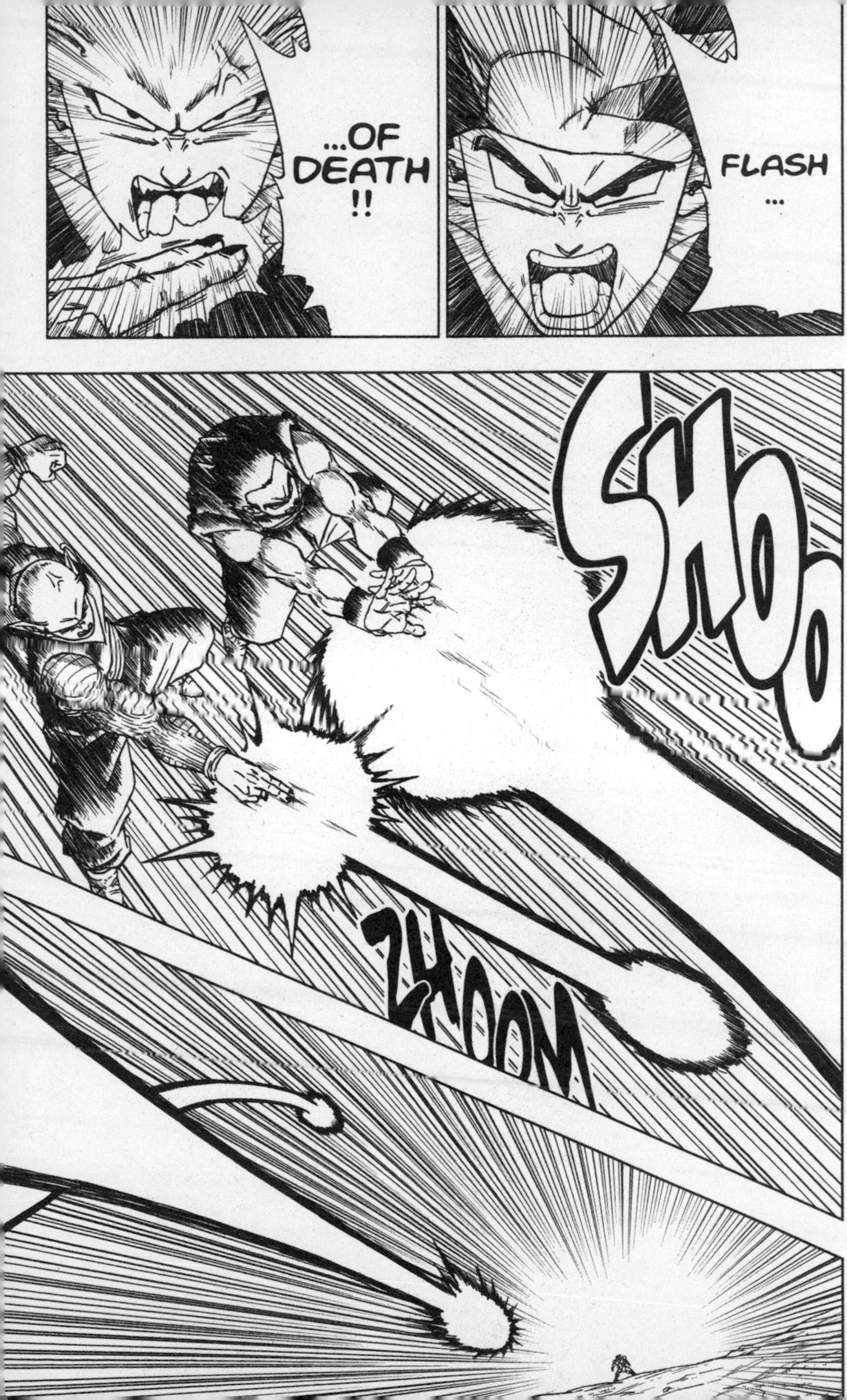
FLASH ...
...OF DEATH !!
SHOOO
ZHOOM

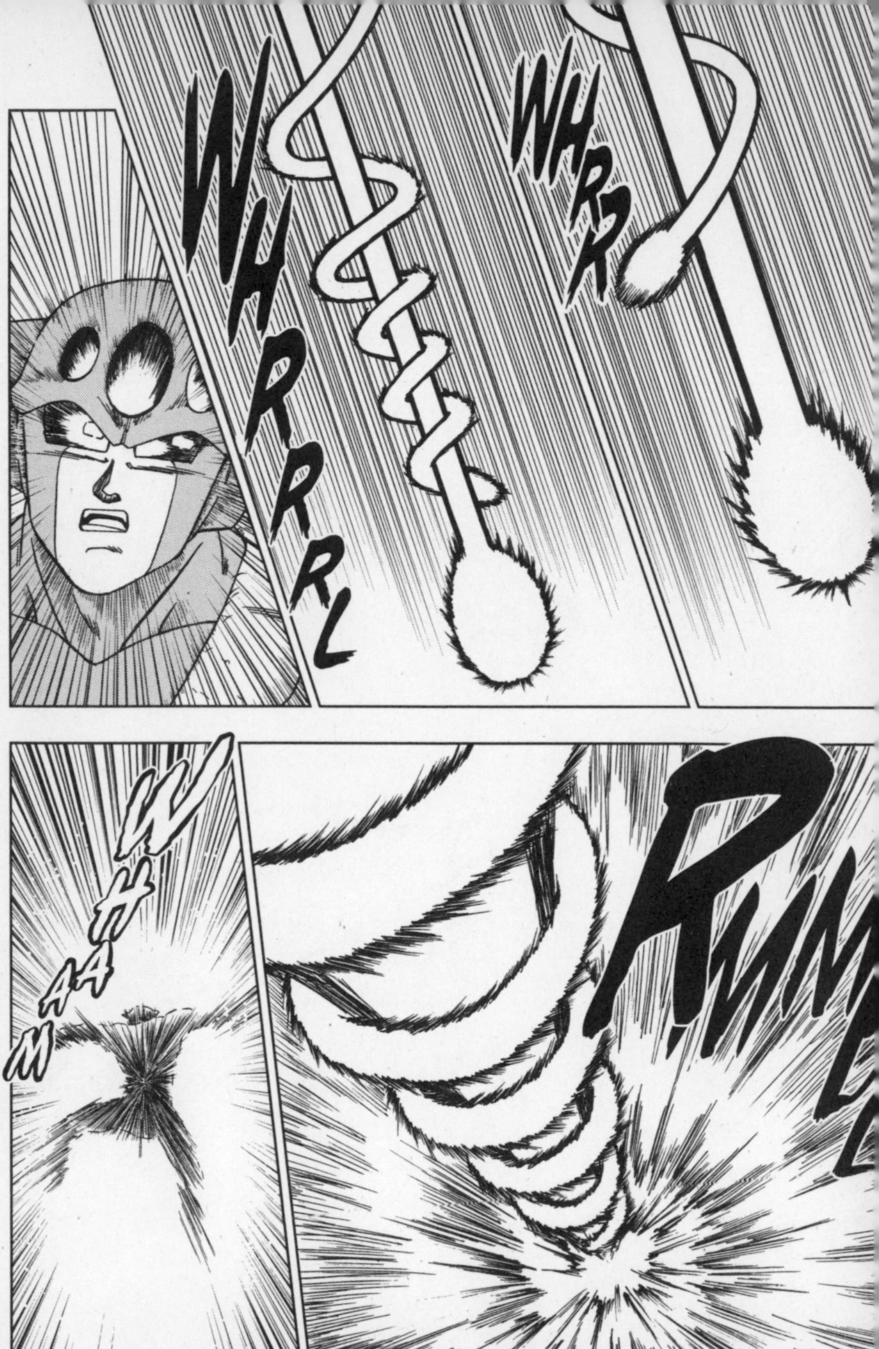
WHRRR
WHRRRRRL
RUMBL
WHAAM

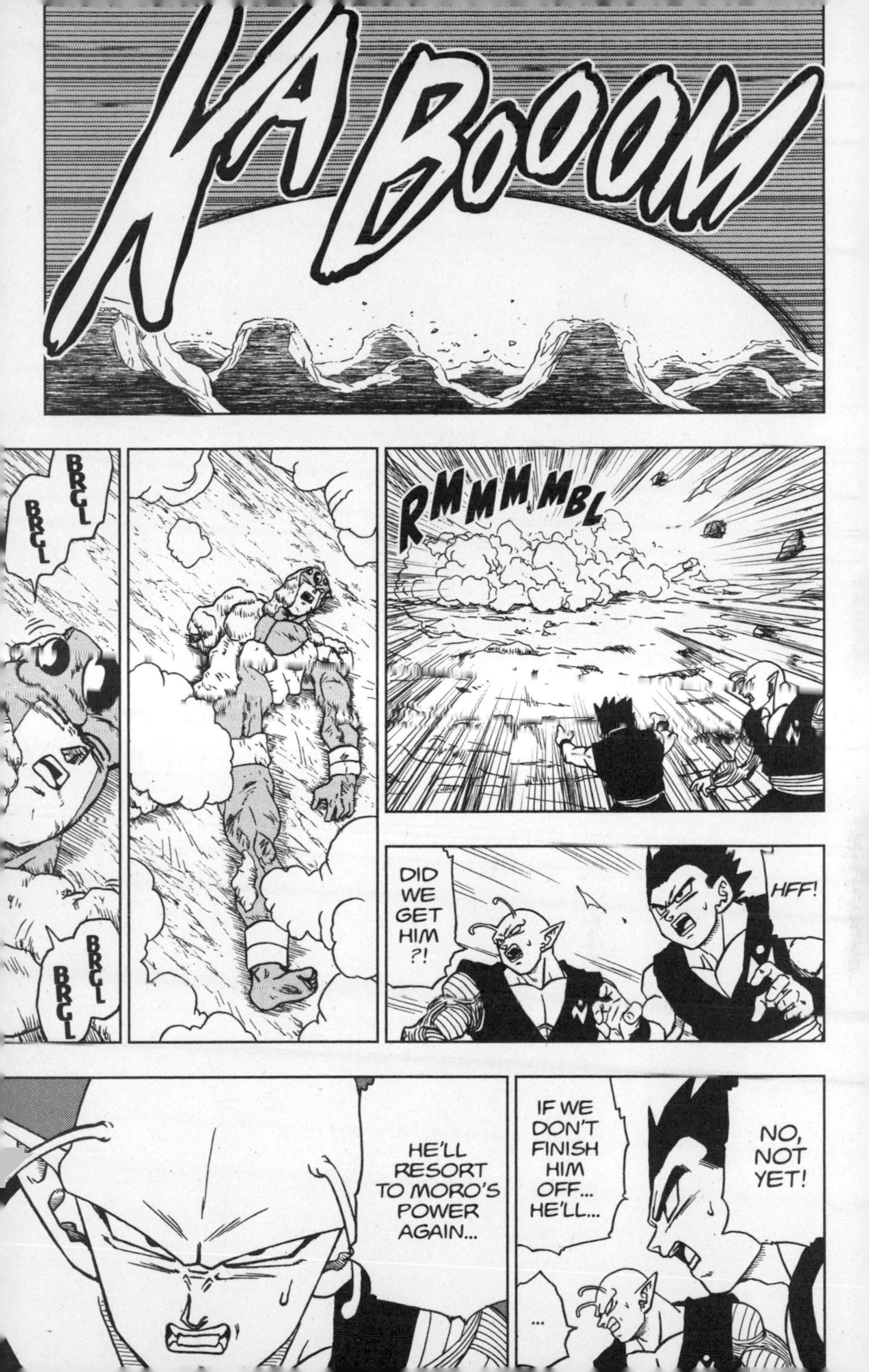
KA BOOOM
RMMMMBL
HFF!
DID WE GET HIM?!
BRGL BRGL
BRGL BRGL
NO, NOT YET!
IF WE DON'T FINISH HIM OFF... HE'LL...
...
HE'LL RESORT TO MORO'S POWER AGAIN...

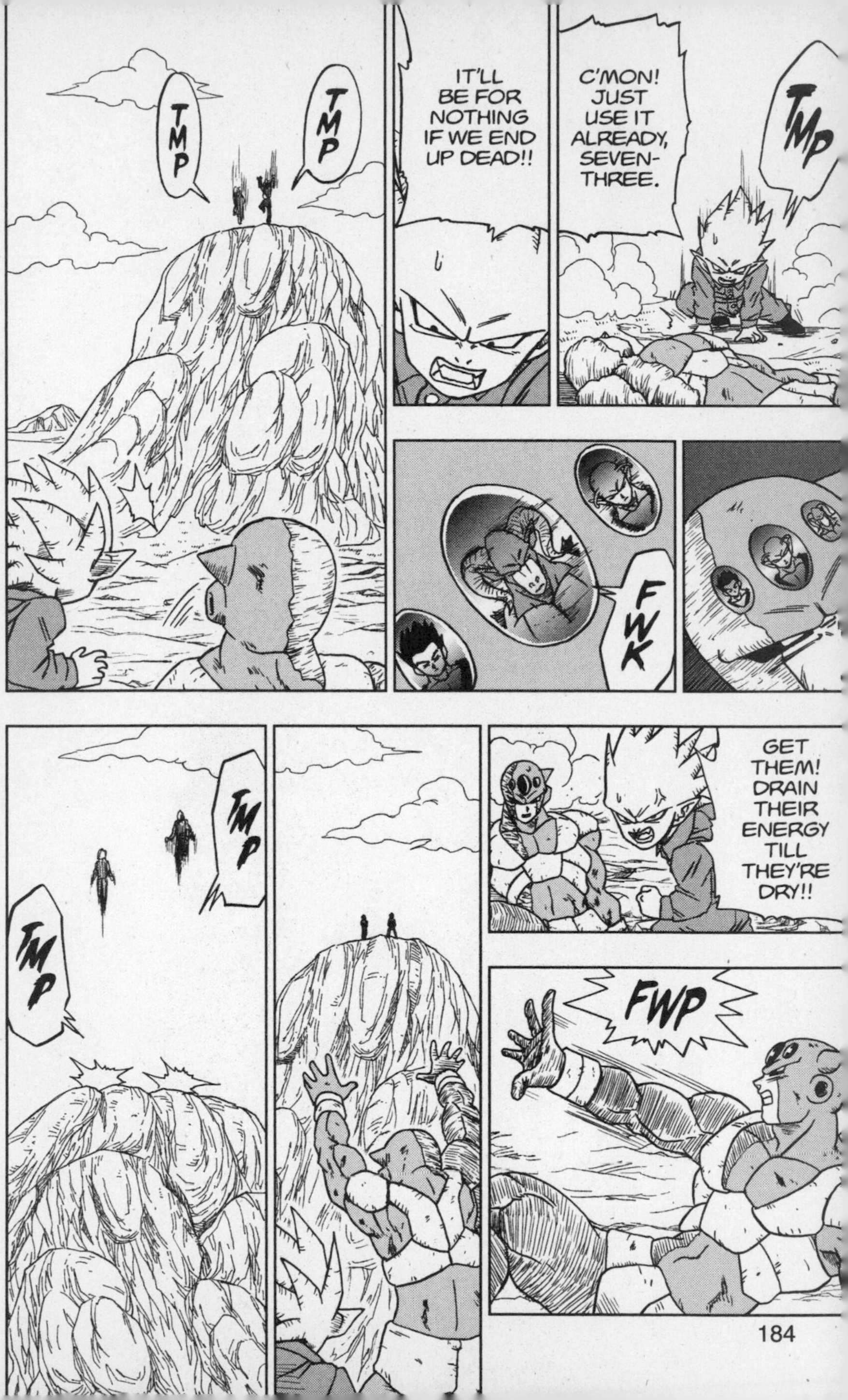
TMP
C'MON! JUST USE IT ALREADY, SEVEN-THREE.
IT'LL BE FOR NOTHING IF WE END UP DEAD!!
FWK
TMP
TMP
GET THEM! DRAIN THEIR ENERGY TILL THEY'RE DRY!!
FWP
TMP
TMP

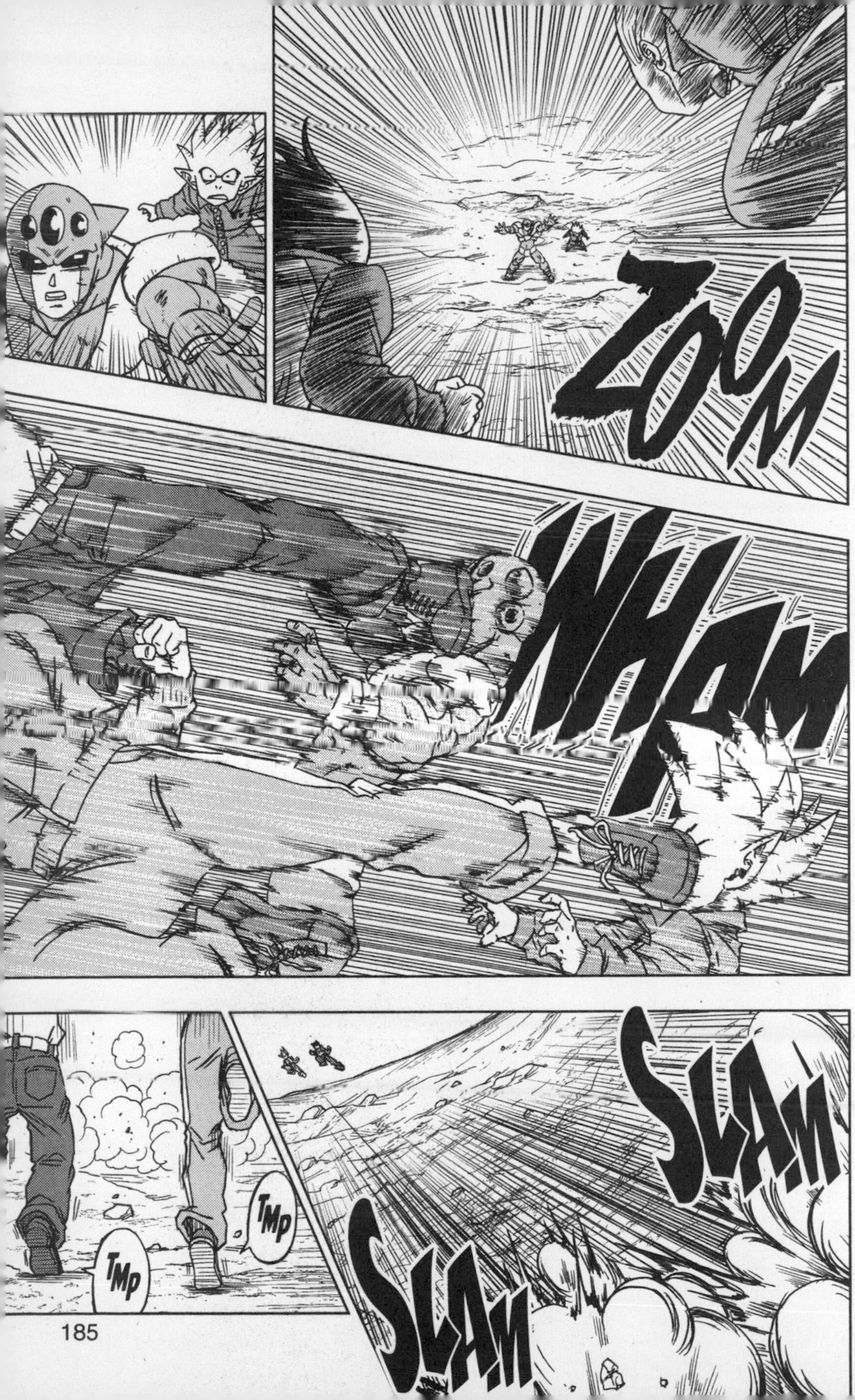
ZOOM
WHAM
SLAM
SLAM
TMP
TMP

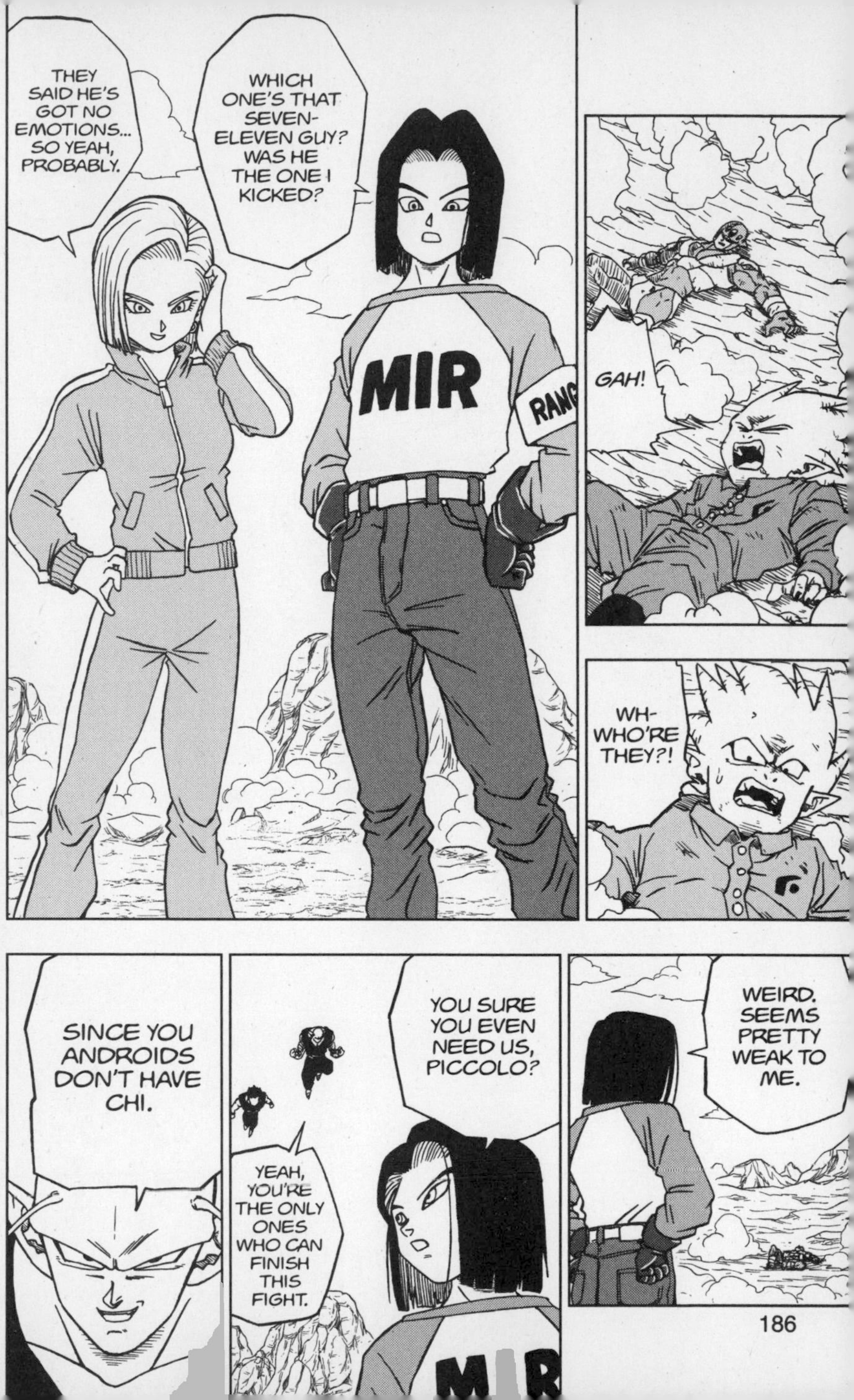

GAH!
WH- WHO'RE THEY?!
MIR
RANG
WHICH ONE'S THAT SEVEN-ELEVEN GUY? WAS HE THE ONE I KICKED?
THEY SAID HE'S GOT NO EMOTIONS... SO YEAH, PROBABLY.
WEIRD. SEEMS PRETTY WEAK TO ME.
YOU SURE YOU EVEN NEED US, PICCOLO?
YEAH, YOU'RE THE ONLY ONES WHO CAN FINISH THIS FIGHT.
SINCE YOU ANDROIDS DON'T HAVE CHI.

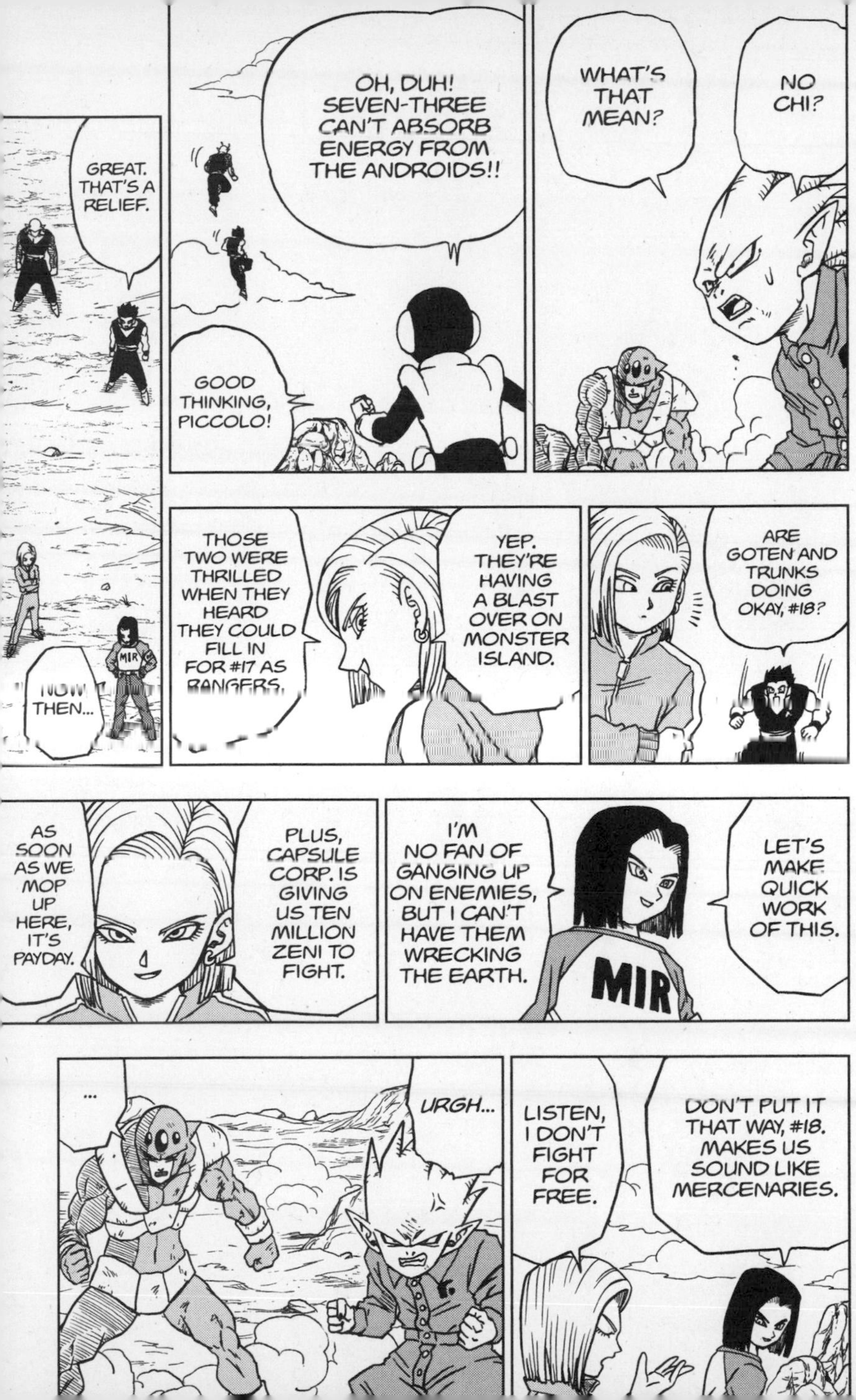
NO CHI?
WHAT'S THAT MEAN?
OH, DUH! SEVEN-THREE CAN'T ABSORB ENERGY FROM THE ANDROIDS!!
GOOD THINKING, PICCOLO!
ARE GOTEN AND TRUNKS DOING OKAY, #18?
YEP. THEY'RE HAVING A BLAST OVER ON MONSTER ISLAND.
THOSE TWO WERE THRILLED WHEN THEY HEARD THEY COULD FILL IN FOR #17 AS RANGERS.
GREAT. THAT'S A RELIEF.
NOW THEN...
LET'S MAKE QUICK WORK OF THIS.
I'M NO FAN OF GANGING UP ON ENEMIES, BUT I CAN'T HAVE THEM WRECKING THE EARTH.
MIR
PLUS, CAPSULE CORP. IS GIVING US TEN MILLION ZENI TO FIGHT.
AS SOON AS WE MOP UP HERE, IT'S PAYDAY.
DON'T PUT IT THAT WAY, #18. MAKES US SOUND LIKE MERCENARIES.
LISTEN, I DON'T FIGHT FOR FREE.
URGH...
...

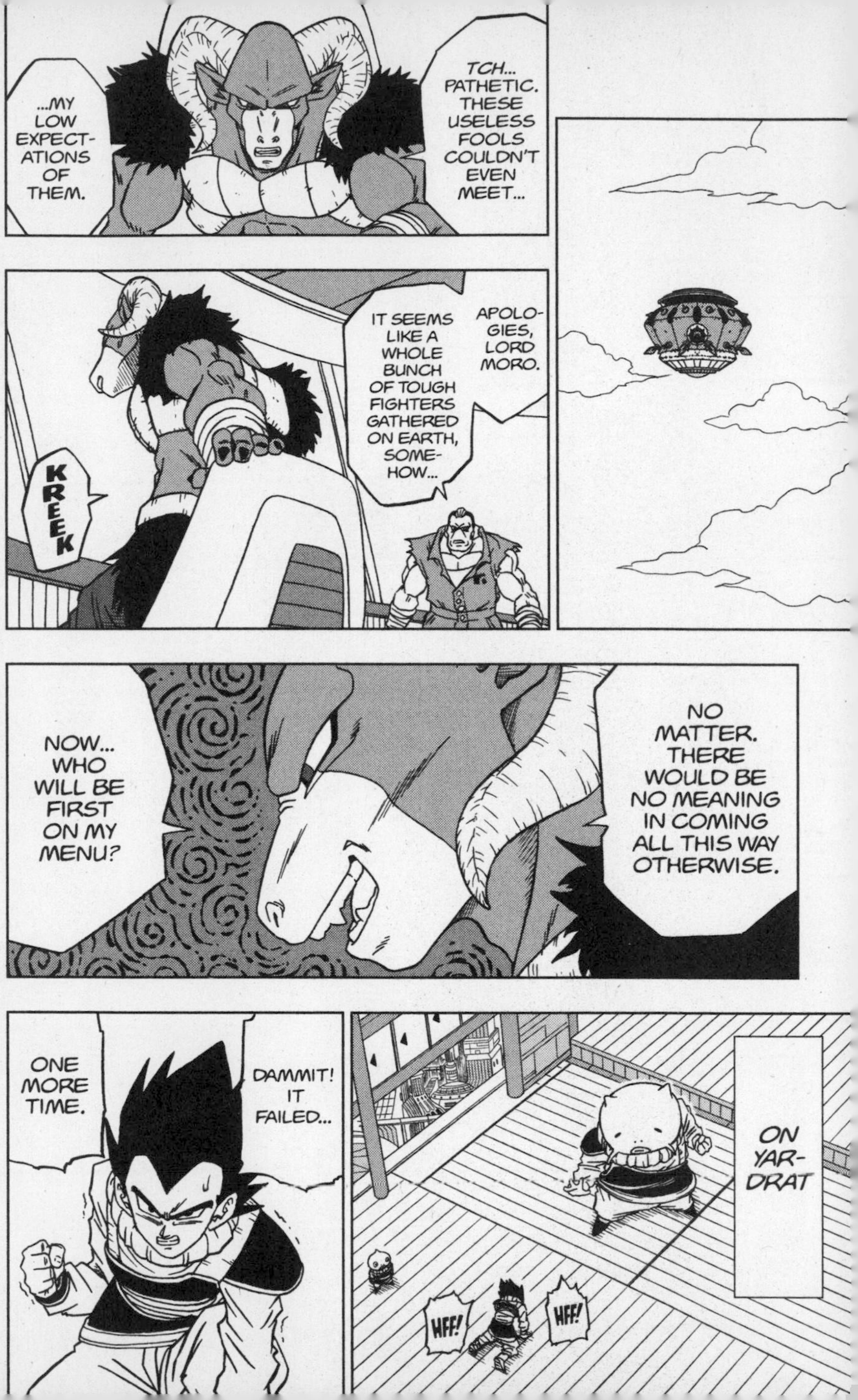
TCH... PATHETIC. THESE USELESS FOOLS COULDN'T EVEN MEET...
...MY LOW EXPECT-ATIONS OF THEM.
APOLO-GIES, LORD MORO.
IT SEEMS LIKE A WHOLE BUNCH OF TOUGH FIGHTERS GATHERED ON EARTH, SOME-HOW...
KREEK
NO MATTER. THERE WOULD BE NO MEANING IN COMING ALL THIS WAY OTHERWISE.
NOW... WHO WILL BE FIRST ON MY MENU?
ON YAR-DRAT
HFF!
HFF!
DAMMIT! IT FAILED...
ONE MORE TIME.

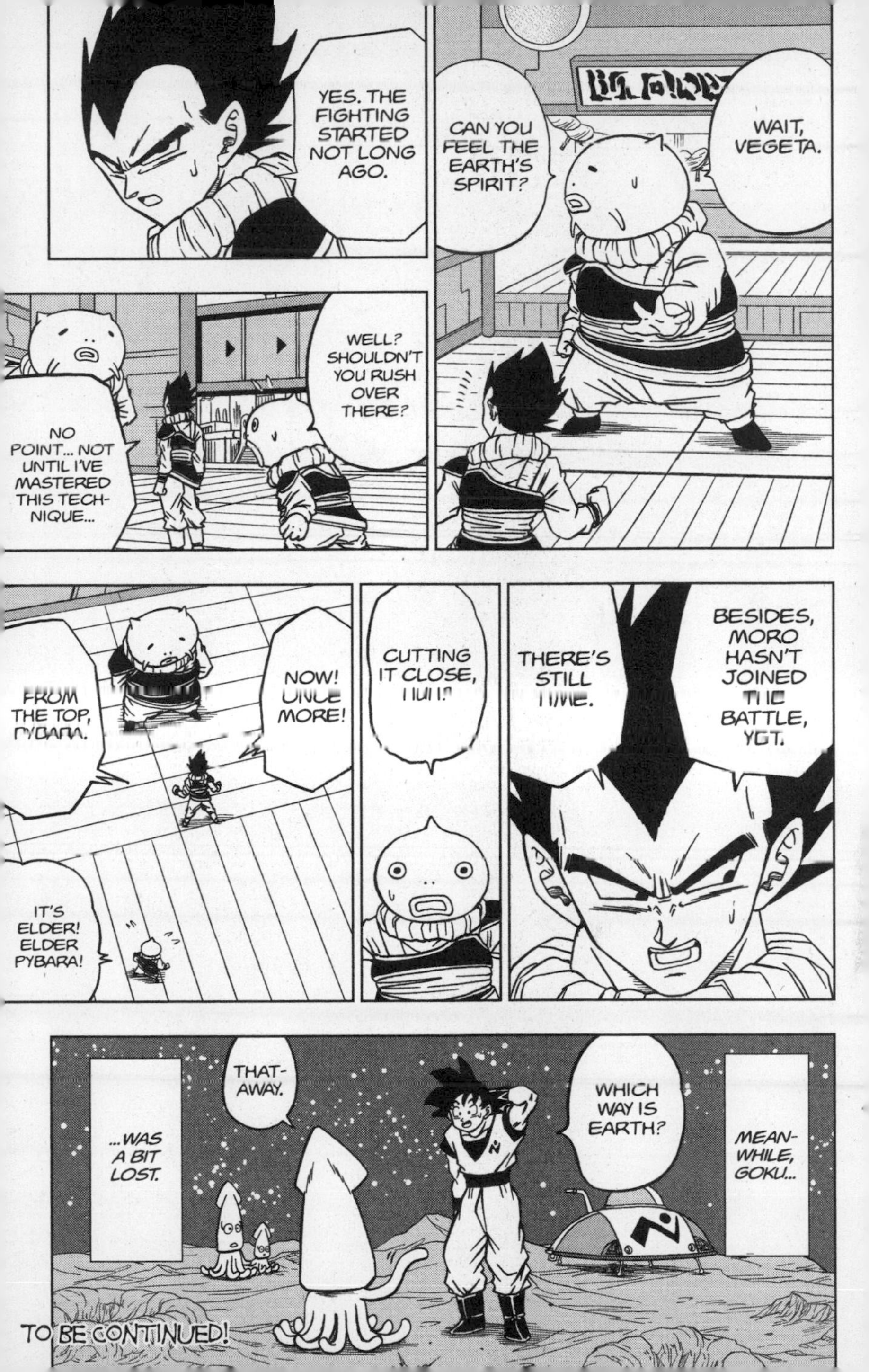
WAIT, VEGETA.
CAN YOU FEEL THE EARTH'S SPIRIT?
YES. THE FIGHTING STARTED NOT LONG AGO.
WELL? SHOULDN'T YOU RUSH OVER THERE?
NO POINT... NOT UNTIL I'VE MASTERED THIS TECHNIQUE...
BESIDES, MORO HASN'T JOINED THE BATTLE, YET.
THERE'S STILL TIME.
CUTTING IT CLOSE, HUH?
NOW! ONCE MORE!
FROM THE TOP, PYBARA.
IT'S ELDER! ELDER PYBARA!
MEANWHILE, GOKU...
WHICH WAY IS EARTH?
THAT-AWAY.
...WAS A BIT LOST.
TO BE CONTINUED!

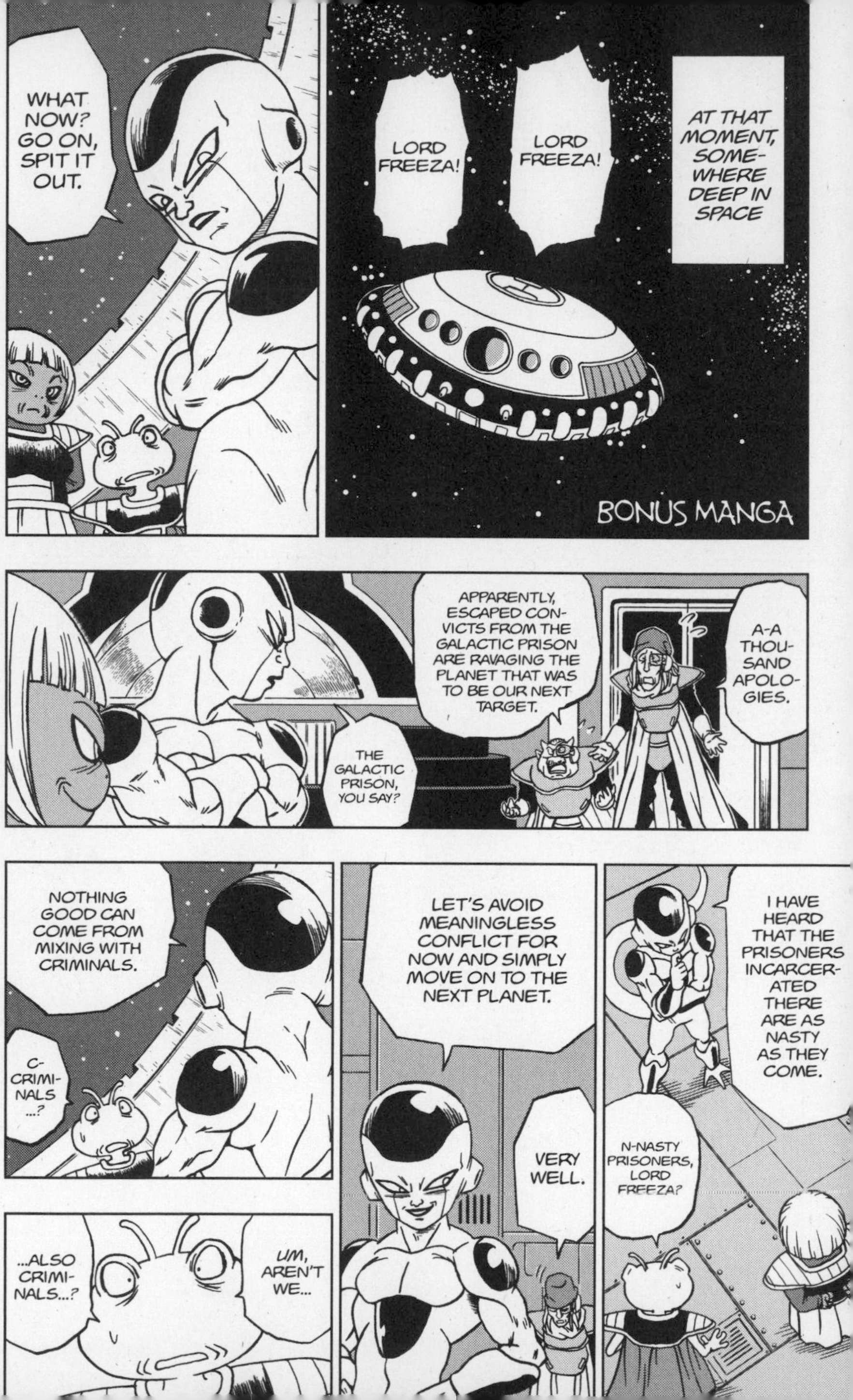
AT THAT MOMENT, SOMEWHERE DEEP IN SPACE
LORD FREEZA!
LORD FREEZA!
BONUS MANGA
WHAT NOW? GO ON, SPIT IT OUT.
A-A THOUSAND APOLOGIES.
APPARENTLY, ESCAPED CONVICTS FROM THE GALACTIC PRISON ARE RAVAGING THE PLANET THAT WAS TO BE OUR NEXT TARGET.
THE GALACTIC PRISON, YOU SAY?
I HAVE HEARD THAT THE PRISONERS INCARCERATED THERE ARE AS NASTY AS THEY COME.
N-NASTY PRISONERS, LORD FREEZA?
LET'S AVOID MEANINGLESS CONFLICT FOR NOW AND SIMPLY MOVE ON TO THE NEXT PLANET.
VERY WELL.
NOTHING GOOD CAN COME FROM MIXING WITH CRIMINALS.
C-CRIMINALS...?
UM, AREN'T WE...
...ALSO CRIMINALS...?

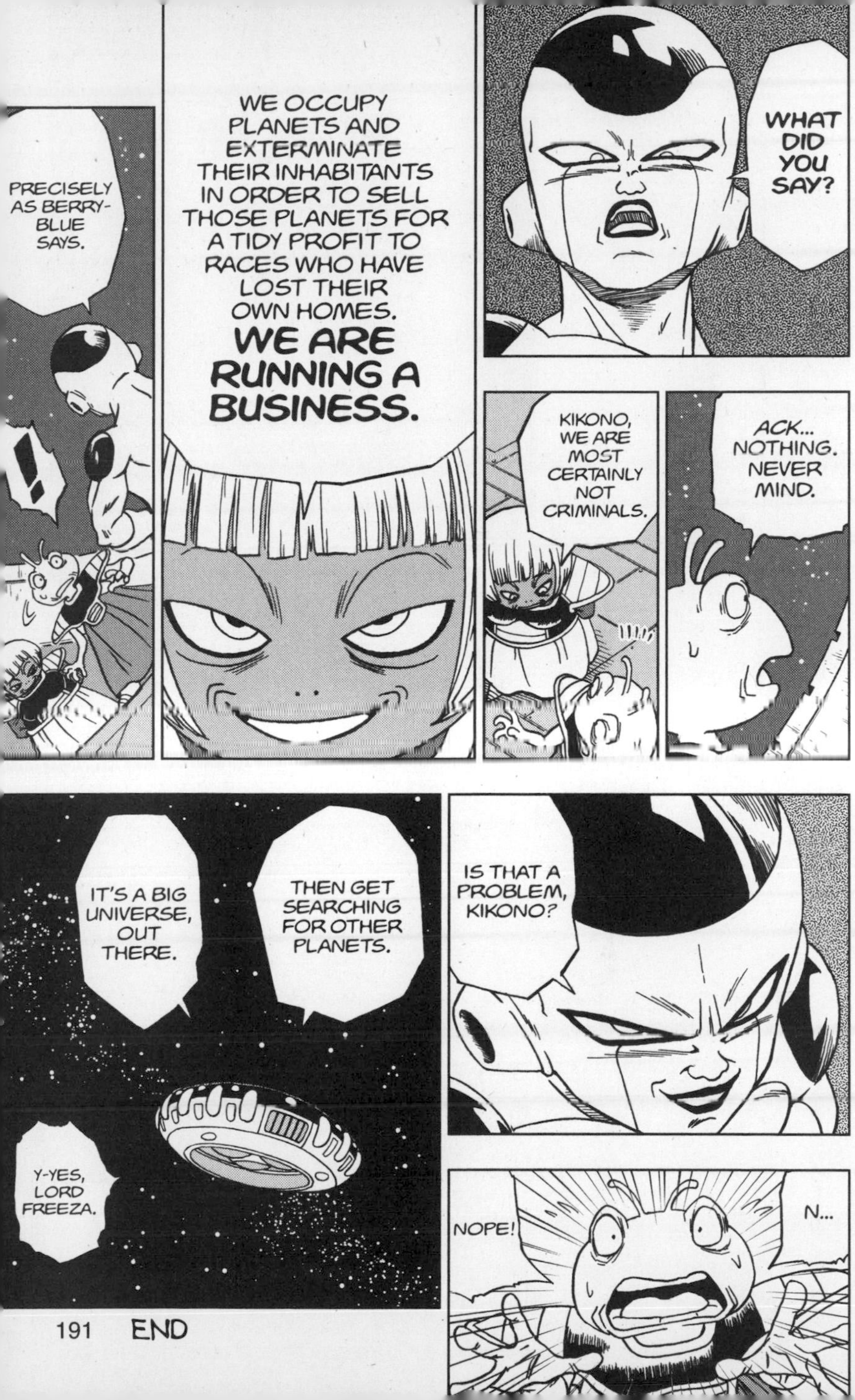
WHAT DID YOU SAY?
ACK... NOTHING. NEVER MIND.
KIKONO, WE ARE MOST CERTAINLY NOT CRIMINALS.
WE OCCUPY PLANETS AND EXTERMINATE THEIR INHABITANTS IN ORDER TO SELL THOSE PLANETS FOR A TIDY PROFIT TO RACES WHO HAVE LOST THEIR OWN HOMES. **WE ARE RUNNING A BUSINESS.**
PRECISELY AS BERRY-BLUE SAYS.
IS THAT A PROBLEM, KIKONO?
N...
NOPE!
THEN GET SEARCHING FOR OTHER PLANETS.
IT'S A BIG UNIVERSE, OUT THERE.
Y-YES, LORD FREEZA.
END

YOU'RE READING THE WRONG WAY!

Dragon Ball Super reads from right to left, starting in the upper-right corner. Japanese is read from right to left, meaning that action, sound effects, and word-balloon order are completely reversed from English order.